An Introduction to
Philosophy

Stephen Welch

Copyright © 2024 Stephen Welch

ISBN: 978-1-917129-43-5

All rights reserved, including the right to reproduce this book, or portions thereof in any form. No part of this text may be reproduced, transmitted, downloaded, decompiled, reverse engineered, or stored, in any form or introduced into any information storage and retrieval system, in any form or by any means, whether electronic or mechanical without the express written permission of the author.

Cover Design: Scott Gaunt

For: -

My Grandchildren

I've watched them grow, explore, and learn about the world in which they find themselves. As they get older, I hope they can also learn to love exploring the world of ideas.

About the Author

Stephen Welch was born in Bedford, England in 1952. He studied Maths at Southampton University, switched to a medical career in Scotland for a number of years, and then turned to computing as a Systems and Business Analyst.

He has had a lifelong interest in both science and philosophy and, since retirement, he led the philosophy group at the Shepway and District University of the Third Age for five years.

His previous book was a popular science one entitled **Stardust, Our Cosmic Origins**, which examined the latest scientific finding concerning our origins from the big bang through to the current day.

Praise for Stardust

"The author's knowledge of the subject is extensive and his enthusiasm is infectious ... Most of all, there is an unfailing sense of wonder; this drives the scientific quest and occasionally spills over into poetry."

Anne Padley MA
Philosophy Lecturer (University of Kent)

"The book discusses in the widest terms who we are and how we got here, using scientific evidence but keeping the presentation non-technical."

Dr Jack Pike AECS
Aeronautical Scientist

"Stardust is a brilliant overview of who we are and how we came to be here."

Ashton West
Chief Executive of the M.I.B.

"The unexamined life is not worth living".

Socrates

Reportedly spoken by Socrates at his trial. He believed that philosophy (the love of wisdom) was man's most important pursuit. He exemplifies, more than anyone else in history, the pursuit of wisdom through thinking, questioning, and logical argument.

Contents

1. Introduction ... ix

Part one – The Main Elements of Philosophy ... 1

2. The Scope of Philosophy ... 3
3. Epistemology ... 6
4. Arguments ... 18
5. Difficulties in Rational Thinking ... 24
6. Tools for Rational Thinking ... 30
7. Basic Ideas in Philosophy ... 40

Part two – Western Philosophy ... 47

8. A Chronological List of Western Philosophers ... 48
9. The Early Greeks ... 50
10. Socrates ... 56
11. Plato ... 60
12. Aristotle ... 67
13. Epicurus ... 76
14. Plotinus ... 82
15. St. Augustine ... 89
16. St. Thomas Aquinas ... 97
17. Francis Bacon ... 105
18. Thomas Hobbes ... 112
19. René Descartes ... 119
20. John Locke ... 127
21. Benedictus Spinoza ... 135
22. Gottfried Wilhelm Leibniz ... 143
23. George Berkeley ... 151
24. David Hume ... 159
25. Thomas Reid ... 166
26. Jean Jacques Rousseau ... 169
27. Immanuel Kant ... 177
28. Jeremy Bentham ... 185
29. G.W.F. Hegel ... 192
30. Arthur Schopenhauer ... 200
31. John Stuart Mill ... 207
32. Soren Kierkegaard ... 215
33. Karl Marx ... 223
34. William James ... 231

35. Friedrich Nietzsche	239
36. Edmund Husserl	247
37. John Dewey	255
38. Bertrand Russell	262
39. Ludwig Wittgenstein	271
40. Martin Heidegger	278
41. Jean-Paul Sartre	286
42. M. Merleau-Ponty	293
43. A.J. Ayer	301
44. Daniel C. Dennett	309
45. Other Ideas in Recent Western Philosophy	319

Part three – Eastern Philosophy — 327

46. Introduction to Eastern Philosophers	329
47. Taoism	335
48. Confucianism	339
49. Buddhism	344

Part four – Philosophy Informed by Science — 351

50. Introduction to Philosophy Informed by Science	353
51. Religion	356
52. The Philosophy of Science	360
53. Philosophy of Mind	375
54. Perception	383
55. Concepts and Understanding	388
56. Language and Meaning	396
57. Free Will	408
58. Ethics and Morality	421
59. Politics	441
60. The Meaning of Life	460

Acknowledgements	468
Bibliography	469
Index	474

1

Introduction

The reason we teach the history of philosophy is that it "is in large measure the history of very smart people making very tempting mistakes, and if you don't know the history, you are doomed to making the same mistakes all over again".

Daniel C. Dennett

What is Philosophy?

The word "philosophy" comes from an Ancient Greek phrase meaning "love of wisdom".

Here are a few definitions: -

1. Philosophy is the study of general and fundamental problems, such as those connected with reality, existence, knowledge, values, reason, mind, and language. And it is distinguished from other ways of addressing such problems by its critical, generally systematic approach, and its reliance on rational argument.

2. Philosophy is thinking about thinking.

3. It is an activity of asking questions, challenging assumptions, re-examining traditionally held views, unpacking the meaning of words, weighing up the value of evidence, and examining the logic of arguments.

4. It is also the large body of knowledge and cumulative wisdom of past (and present) thinkers.

An Introduction to Philosophy

Note here that a number of definitions have just been given above. The word 'philosophy', like all other words, can be used in different ways, and people will mean different things when they use it. Often, of course, the meaning becomes apparent by the context in which it is being used.

One big difference in usage, however, is between a colloquial use and an academic one. For instance, someone might declare that their "philosophy of life is to treat people kindly". This is a worthy aspiration, and people will understand what the speaker means when they say it, but it is not the more rigorous usage implied by the four definitions presented above.

Another person might be tempted to turn to philosophy as a means of searching for the best way to live their life, and someone else may well be looking for some kind of spiritual enlightenment. All well and good, but again that is not really in line with the usage implied above.

In the more academic sense of the word, philosophy is a search for the best understanding we can have about the world in which we find ourselves. It also analyses the methods used to reach that understanding, and it considers the degree of confidence to place on any understanding reached. In this sense, philosophy is not a search for solace; it is a purely disinterested search for understanding, wherever that leads. That is not to say it places no value on life, or on how to live it, once methods are agreed, and reality addressed as far as it can be, philosophy does cover the fields of ethics, morality, and systems of government, but here too it tries to be both rigorous and rational in its approach.

This book, then, is an introduction to philosophy in the more academic sense. Having said that, the hope is to be as clear as possible in the presentation of what is often regarded as a complicated subject. Thinking can be difficult; it is easy to be misled, or to reason incorrectly. Reading what past philosophers have said on a subject, and then reading the critiques other people have written in response, is a good basis for understanding philosophy. But more than that, with the addition of a list of tools available to philosophy and a summary of logical fallacies to avoid, the book also aims to provide clarity to thinking logically about philosophy.

The book is split into four parts. In part one the main ideas and concepts of philosophy are discussed, along with a description of some of the tools and terminology philosophers use. Part two is a chronological introduction to Western philosophy, looking at the main Western philosophers and their ideas, stretching from ancient Greece to the present day. Part three looks at some of the Eastern philosophies, and then part four presents an overview of current philosophy, which includes philosophy informed by science.

Introduction

Philosophy, like all academic disciplines, has its own language and its own terms. These can be a little off-putting to start with, but it is worth becoming familiar with them because once any given term is mastered then the idea behind it is more easily understood and remembered. So, to that end, here is a list of some of the main terms used together with a short description of their meaning.

Philosophical Terms

American Pragmatism: – A view that rejected the dualistic epistemology and metaphysics of previous philosophy in favour of a naturalistic approach that viewed knowledge as arising from an active adaptation of the human organism to its environment.

Analytical Philosophy: – Using ideas from logic and mathematics to try and build logical, unambiguous sentences from smaller 'atomic like' facts, combined together with logical connectives such as 'and' and 'or'.

A posteriori: – Reasoning from effects to causes [Latin – 'from what comes after'].

A priori: – Reasoning from causes to effects, from general to particular [Latin – 'from what is before']. Also – Existing in the mind independently from sensory experience.

Axiom: – A statement or proposition which is regarded as being established, accepted, or self-evidently true, and on which other logical structures are built.

Empiricism: – Relying on observation and experiment.

Epistemology: – The study of the methods and grounds of knowledge.

Existentialism: – A loose term roughly covering a view of life from the perspective of the 'existing individual'.

Idealism: – This is not the usage meaning the pursuit of an ideal. It is a metaphysical theory about the nature of reality, arguing that what is real is confined to (or at least related to) the contents of our own mind.

Intentionality: – The relationship between mental acts and the external world is that our conscious thoughts are always **'about'** something. You are never merely conscious, you are always conscious of something: a book, a tree, or a headache, for example, (termed 'intentional objects').

Metaphysics: – Concerned with explaining the fundamental nature of being and the world that encompasses it. Traditionally, metaphysics attempts to answer two basic questions in the broadest possible terms: - What is ultimately there? And what is it like? This branch of philosophy examines the nature of reality, including the relationship between mind and matter, substance and attribute, fact and value.

Ontology: – The nature of being.

Phenomenology: – The investigation of how consciousness works by studying the objects of conscious awareness, (i.e. the 'intentional objects' as described above under Intentionality).

Premise: – A previous statement or proposition from which another is inferred or follows as a conclusion.

Rationalism: – Relying on reason, intuition, and introspection, in contrast to relying on the senses. This can be extreme, saying all knowledge comes from within (like Idealism above), or more moderate,

Introduction

saying that just some knowledge comes to us other than through the senses.

Syllogism: – Aristotle logic – (Here is one example but there are other variations).
  All men are mortal (major premise)
  Socrates is a man (minor premise)
  Therefore, Socrates is mortal (conclusion – based on the premises).

Teleological: – Developments are due to the purpose that is served by them – the study of final causes.

Don't be daunted by these terms. When later in the book any of them are used, it is probably worth-while referring back to this list for a quick reminder of the meaning. The above is by no means an exhaustive list, almost all philosophers invent their own terms, but included here are many of the main terms used throughout philosophy.

Different Philosophies

Many different philosophies are covered here, one important difference being that between Eastern and Western philosophies. This book's main focus is on Western philosophy; a flavour of Eastern philosophies is provided as a contrast, but it is in no way comprehensive. The Western philosophers are presented chronologically because later philosophers often built upon and further developed the ideas from the earlier ones.

Having noted that there are many different philosophies in the world, that does not mean that anything can be regarded as philosophy whenever someone wants to call it thus; philosophy is not merely an opinion. For a system of ideas to be called philosophy it should be logically consistent, and it should fit with the known facts. Just because philosophy is difficult to prove to be correct does not mean that any idea is acceptable. Philosophy needs to be justified.

A related misconception is that truth is relative. This is just wrong; something can't be true for one person and at the same time be not true for someone else. It might be difficult to know in a particular given case whether a statement about that case is true or false, but it must be one or the other. The real difficulty of philosophy is often in ascertaining the facts, sometimes they are not discovered until much later, but sometimes it can be completely impossible to determine them.

Some people also claim right and wrong to be culturally relative, but is this just another version of claiming truth to be relative? Kant talks about our moral duty to do the right thing, he calls it the 'Categorical Imperative', and Bentham says that "the greatest happiness of the greatest number is the foundation of morals and legislation", but Hume says morality is subjectivity and that you can't derive 'ought to be' from 'what is'. Can right and wrong be relative? One would probably not want to defend the holocaust after learning the facts, but in the absence of facts we do need some sort of guide or structure for our moral behaviour. This question will be explored throughout parts two, three and four of this book.

Of course, people can have their own opinions, but just having your own opinion does not make it right. If you want to convince other people about it, you have to do so by rational argument based on agreed facts and sound reasoning. Philosophy also entails intellectual honesty, it is necessary to present any opposing arguments to your ideas in their most rigorous form before arguing against them, and it is also necessary to admit when you are wrong. [For more on arguments see chapter 4.]

One final point of introduction: - Philosophy is an exercise of the mind, people will have different ideas about things, but it is not something to go to war about! Other people should be respected even if their ideas are wrong, the good philosopher convinces by rational argument.

Part One

The Main Elements of Philosophy

This section of the book provides an introduction to the scope of philosophy, the main ideas involved, and an outline of how people go about doing philosophy.

2

The Scope of Philosophy

There are more things in heaven and earth, Horatio,
Than are dreamt of in your philosophy.

Shakespeare (Hamlet)

What does Philosophy cover, what is its scope?

Philosophy is a very wide-ranging subject, including as it does the nature of reality, ethics, morality, mathematics, logic, political systems, scepticism, the nature of knowledge and even things like the meaning of meaning.

There are several ways to sub-divide the subject to make it more manageable, and different people might sub-divide it differently. Here, however, is one of the main ways to organise the subject into logical categories. Philosophy is about trying to get the best answers we can to the questions we have about the world. Such questions could be grouped under the following headings: -

Metaphysics

- What is the nature of the world?
- What does it mean to exist?
- How do we explain things that change?
- What is the nature of consciousness?
- What is matter?
- What is time?
- What is the Mind and how does it work?
- Do we have free will?
- Is the world deterministic?

Epistemology (the theory of knowledge)

- What is the nature of knowledge?
- How do we give credence to what we think we know?

An Introduction to Philosophy

- What is the nature of perception?
- What is the difference between Reason and Faith?
- How do we form concepts?
- What is the role of Logic and Mathematics in knowledge?
- How do objective and subjective views feed into knowledge?
- What is the relationship of language with knowledge?
- What is the role of science in knowledge?

Ethics

- How should we act?
- How should we make choices?
- What is required in order to say that one choice is better than another?
- Do the ends justify the means?
- What do we mean by the terms good and evil?
- What values and virtues should we aspire to?
- What moral principles should we adopt?

Politics

- How should people interact with each other?
- What should be the nature and limits of government?
- How should we create and think about the law?
- What is a social contract?
- What is the legitimacy of self-defence?
- When is the use of force justified?
- How should we deal with fraud?
- How should society deal with: - Fairness, Privilege, and Property?

Aesthetics

- What is the nature of art?
- What is the need for art?
- What is beauty and where does our sense of beauty come from?
- What is form and where does our sense of form come from?
- Is art (in all its forms: visual, written, and auditory) useful?

This is just one way to sub-divide the scope of philosophy, but when we do this there are still obvious connections and overlaps between these divisions. It can be very difficult to discuss one area without bringing in ideas, definitions, and arguments from other areas. That makes it hard to know where to start in philosophy; what do we take for granted, how can we be sure that those things we think we know are actually correct?

It is that last question about how to give credence to our understanding of things that should be the starting point – **epistemology** (the theory of knowledge). Once we understand what we mean when we say we know something, then we can begin to construct our philosophical theories based on more solid ground. So, the next chapter is devoted to epistemology.

As noted, philosophy is about asking questions, but attempting to answer all (or even any) of the above list of questions is an ambitious task. The aim of this book is not to provide all the answers; indeed, many questions are still at the asking stage. The book's more modest aims are: to introduce the subject and scope of philosophy; to present as clearly as possible what previous philosophers have said on these topics; and to conclude with an overview of the current, modern position of philosophy.

3

Epistemology

Though experience be our only guide in reasoning concerning matters of fact; it must be acknowledged, that this guide is not altogether infallible, but in some cases is apt to lead us into errors. ... A wise man, therefore, proportions his belief to the evidence.

David Hume

The Theory of knowledge

- How do we know that those things that we think we know, are actually correct?
- In other words: how do we give credence to our understanding of the world?

Epistemology (the theory of knowledge) is the basis of all philosophy because if we don't understand what constitutes knowledge, we can't reliably draw any conclusions about anything. Therefore, before diving into any particular philosophical theory, we should start by trying to get a good understanding of the following: -

a) What do we mean when we claim something to be true?
b) What are the limitations of our own thinking?
c) How should we think about our own perceptions of the world?

The Definition of the word Knowledge

The early Greek philosopher Socrates tried to obtain clarity of knowledge by asking people to define things. For instance, he wanted to know what justice was, so he went to the courthouse and asked judges and lawyers what justice was. But despite repeated questioning all he could get were

Epistemology

examples of justice, not a definition of it. Questioning and scepticism are an important part of philosophy, but in the case of Socrates it backfired on him. Those in power got fed up with him and had him tried in court on a trumped-up charge of corrupting the youth of the city. He was found guilty and sentenced to death by being made to drink a cup of the poison hemlock.

A number of other early philosophers tried to 'systemise' their knowledge of the world into an overarching logical format, some fairly successfully, given the understanding of their time, for example both Plato and Aristotle.

Before Plato, it was thought that you could be considered to know something if you had a true belief about that thing. However, Plato realised that it was possible to have a true belief without understanding why it was true. Therefore, he said, it is only possible to label a true belief as knowledge if it is justified in some way. So, the definition of knowledge then became having a 'justified true belief'. There is still a slight problem with this definition however, because you might have a belief, that is actually true, and that you think is justified, but the justification you used was flawed in some way. This was pointed out by philosopher Edmund Gettier in a short paper entitled "Is Justified True Belief Knowledge?" published in 1963.

Gettier proved his point by providing a number of counter examples in which individuals have a justified true belief, but they don't have knowledge. Here is one example (as presented by David K. Johnson in his 'Great Courses' philosophy lectures) ...

A man is driving through a corner of a county called Barn County, and he sees a barn in a field. He now has a belief that he has seen a barn, and it is justified because he saw it himself. What he doesn't know is that the county is called Barn County because many of the farmers there build facades of barns facing the road. However, there is actually one, and only one, real barn in Barn County and it just happens that this was the barn the man saw. So, the man does have a 'justified true belief', but it can't be considered knowledge because if he had known why the area was called Barn County, he would not have had that belief in the first place.

Gettier's paper was an important constraint on the definition of the concept of knowledge, but it should not be taken as saying that knowledge is impossible. What it does do is confirm that a degree of scepticism is often a good approach to things. Note in the above example, the man could have stopped his car, got out, and walked round the barn; that would have increased his belief that he had seen a barn because his justification would have been greater. It would still not be 100% (maybe it looks like a barn but is really used as a house) but the more evidence that can be collected about a proposition, the higher the certainty can be ascribed to it being true.

Logic and Knowledge

Aristotle's main contribution to the theory of knowledge was to do with logic, indeed he is often referred to as the father of logic. It was he that originally defined an area of logic called Syllogisms. There are several different versions or categories of these, but the overall intention is that, given one or more initial premise, something else (a conclusion) necessarily follows. The famous example being: -

    All men are mortal (major premise)
    Socrates is a man (minor premise)
    Therefore, Socrates is mortal (conclusion).

This will be considered in more detail in the next chapter on philosophical arguments.

Systems of Knowledge

It was probably the great French mathematician and philosopher, Rene Descartes, who was the first to try to start the enterprise from first principles, and his famous statement 'I think, therefore I am' was an excellent beginning. This is self-evidently true, if there is thought something must be doing the thinking, (although it leaves open any exact definition of what 'I' is).

Unfortunately, however, despite making such a good start, Descartes didn't entirely work from first principles as he aspired to. He made a couple of initial assumptions about the world which he introduced into his work without providing any proof: firstly, he took for granted that God exists; and secondly, he assumed the duality of mind and matter (understandable, because it does feel that there is a 'separate' 'I' inside us looking out on the world through the windows of our eyes). [Please note that this does not mean that these two assumptions were wrong (or indeed right), just that, if you are trying to work things out from first principles, you really can't make any assumptions!]

We then come to British Empiricism. [Empiricism is knowledge which relies on observation and experiment]. Both Locke and Berkeley made good attempts at an empirical understanding of the world, but it was not until the Scottish philosopher David Hume came along that Descartes' errors were first really identified and addressed. Hume (1711 -1776) was writing in the period called The Enlightenment, or The Age of Reason, which stretched from the 1650s through to the 1780s, and Edinburgh (where Hume lived) was a great cultural centre at that time.

There is a lovely quote from the philosopher Bertrand Russell to the effect that "Hume took the empiricism of Locke and Berkeley and produced a scepticism that no-one could deny, but no-one could accept". Scepticism is the key however, as Socrates well knew. If you really want to give any credence to your understanding of the world, everything should be doubted and everything questioned - de omnibus disputandum.

Hume's first major work was called "A Treatise of Human Nature", written when he was just 28. But the following introduction is based on his revised and clarified work, called "An Enquiry concerning Human Understanding", which was written nine years later.

What Hume says about our knowledge of the world is that we can divide it into two basic categories, Deductive knowledge, and Inductive knowledge.

Deductive knowledge comprises things that we can give 100% credibility to. Examples would be: - the statement 'all bachelors are unmarried'; and from Euclidian geometry, for instance, 'the square of the hypotenuse of a right-angled triangle is equal to the sum of the squares of the other two sides'. Also, falling into this category would be Aristotle syllogisms.

Deductive knowledge then is mostly about logic and mathematics, things you can know with certainty. These are things that we can be as confident about as is possible.

Inductive knowledge, on the other hand, is everything else that we think we know. This does not mean that inductive knowledge is wrong of course, just that we have to take it with a pinch of salt. Indeed, what we actually do is assign probabilities to it based on our experience of the world; we can be very sure about some things (but not 100%) and less sure about others. As we know, however, people can be fooled (e.g. by an illusion), or just mistaken (by picking up the wrong end of the stick for instance). Therefore, keeping an open mind and adopting a sceptical, questioning approach to things, is probably best until the evidence for something mounts to the point it becomes compelling. But even then, we should be prepared to revise our thinking in the light of further evidence.

The way Hume presents this is as follows. If you saw one billiard ball knocking into another one, and then saw the other one roll away, you would not be surprised; it is what you would expect to occur. But why do you expect this? Only, says Hume, because you have seen it happen many times before (if not on the billiard table, then from other examples of balls, or any colliding things). If, however, says Hume, a newborn baby witnessed this, it would not have any expectations.

In other words, our understanding of how the world works comes about purely from being exposed to many examples. It is an 'inductive' process; we all build mental models of the world, and we use these to form predictions. Take those billiard balls, what if someone had glued the second one to the table without our knowledge, we would be very surprised when it didn't move, but it is a possibility (however remote). Or what if the person striking the first ball had put spin on it, the two balls would react differently than if there was no spin. We would then update our mental model to cater for spin, improving our model each time we observed it. Our brains are past masters at this, recognising patterns, building models, and making predictions, mostly processed (note this) at a subconscious level.

The important point here is that most of the time the two balls will react as expected. But not all the time, you never know when there might be a factor that we have not considered. So, in reality, you can only attribute a probability of less than 100% to our expectation of the outcome of an event. Of course, exactly the same reasoning applies to everything we observe in the world. All we can do is apply a percentage probability to our understanding of anything that happens or anything that we think might occur. Some probabilities will be close to 100, others we may well have much less confidence in (until we obtain more examples).

All our inductive knowledge and understanding of the world is based only on experience, and all we can do is attribute probabilities to things, based initially on scepticism until we obtain more data that can give us more confidence. When we then share our experiences with others and find that they have similar experiences, then we start to get some objectivity into our understanding. And it is here that science is born: - repeatable experiments and measurements being performed and shared and tested with others. This gives us our scientific laws of nature; they are still models, but ones we credit as being very accurate.

Take the law of gravity for instance. We all know that if we drop something it will fall to earth, but it took Newton to formalise the equations, and then Einstein to improve them by taking relativity and space-time into account. Even now, however, we have not yet updated our model to include quantum mechanics. Having said that, the current model of gravity we do have can be considered to be of the order of 99.9999% correct or better, and as noted, we all know from common sense (i.e. experience!) that dropped things fall.

Hume then goes on to extend these ideas by saying that extraordinary claims need to be backed up with extraordinary evidence for us to believe

Epistemology

them (i.e. to give them a high probability of being correct), and he uses this to argue against reported miracles. Here is an example of this using another popular British game, that of darts.

If a man said to you 'I was playing darts yesterday and I won one of the games by finishing with a bull's-eye', well then you would probably believe him, perhaps even more so if you knew him well, and, in your experience of him, you had always found him truthful.

If instead he said 'I was in the pub yesterday and for a bet I got the others to blindfold me, give me a dart and turn me towards the board. I then threw the dart and it just landed straight in the bull's-eye; it was brilliant!' Well, I think you would probably give that less credence than the previous example, but you might still perhaps just give him the benefit of the doubt, in the absence of any other evidence either way. If, however, another of your friends said 'yes, I was there and I saw it. It was amazing!' Then your estimation of the truth of the claim would increase, although still maybe with reservations, (are they playing a joke on you perhaps?)

But what if the man said 'I was outside the pub yesterday, about 100 meters down the road, and I took a dart and threw it as hard as I could towards the pub. The wind was quite strong from behind me and carried the dart all the way to the pub, and just then a sideways gust blew it in through an open window, and it landed right in the bull's-eye of the dartboard on the other side of the room.' Here I think your credibility would be stretched to breaking!

If another friend, or even several other friends, said they were there and it really happened, I don't think you would believe it. And even if they showed you a video of it you probably wouldn't believe it because it doesn't fit with your understanding of the world based on your experience, also, as we know, videos can be fixed. You would ask yourself what the most likely explanation is. Is it true, or are they trying to fool you, or have they themselves been fooled, perhaps by a magic trick of some kind? Both these explanations are far more probable than the claim being true.

This is Hume's point; extraordinary claims require extraordinary evidence. And in the case of the miracles reported in the bible, he says that we don't have any extraordinary evidence, all we have is written evidence of the type 'I was there, and I saw it'. And even those accounts have been transcribed and translated many times since the supposed miracle. Many other explanations (e.g. miss-translations, mass hallucinations, tricks, fiction taken as fact or even deliberate misrepresentation for some reason) are, according to Hume, much more likely.

Some people have claimed that Hume was saying if we can't be certain of things then anything could happen, and we shouldn't be surprised at it.

Also, that there is no such thing as cause and effect. This is to completely misunderstand him. He was actually arguing in favour of common sense, but a common sense matched with a healthy dose of scepticism. His writings, in the early to mid 1700's, put philosophy, science, probability and the theory of knowledge on its initial very sound footings.

We all have beliefs about the world, and these are based on experience and on things we have learned from others that make sense to our world view. We can't help it; evolution by natural selection designed us that way. And most of the time it works well. We can believe in something, for instance, when we have evidence for it (e.g. that the world is round and not flat, or that the Earth goes round the Sun and not the Sun round the Earth). We have to have beliefs, because, as Hume pointed out, this is Inductive Knowledge, so by definition we can't be 100% certain about things.

Religion, on the other hand, tries to introduce a new category of knowledge called Revealed Knowledge. Now presumably that feels quite convincing to the person receiving the revelation, but thereafter it has to rely on word of mouth and written accounts. To help convince people of this type of knowledge, religion uses a concept called 'faith'. This is very different from belief based on evidence and experience. Faith is the belief in something without evidence (indeed often in the face of existing evidence). A better answer, in the absence of evidence, is to admit that we don't yet know, although of course we might well attribute a probability (high or low) depending on our experience of the world.

Many people use the words 'belief' and 'faith' as if they are interchangeable, but that is not the case. You can legitimately believe in something if you have evidence for it e.g. that evolution is true (the evidence for evolution is overwhelming) but, as noted above, faith is belief without evidence.

So, returning to the original questions - How do we know, that those things that we think we know, are actually correct? And how do we give credence to our understanding of the world? Hume's analysis is as appropriate today as when he first proposed it. Everything should be doubted, and the honest approach to the unknown is to admit that we don't know but continue by saying let's work on it together.

More on Inductive Knowledge

- Aristotle compared inductive arguments to scientific reasoning – reasoning about causes.
- This is often reasoning from the particular to the universal.

Epistemology

- With deductive logic, the premises are intended to guarantee the conclusion, but not so with inductive logic. Here they are merely intended to provide good support.
- This does not mean inductive logic is inferior. Firstly, it is much easier to show a conclusion is likely true than to prove it is 100% true. Secondly, inductive arguments can generate such a high probability of their conclusion being true that the fact that it is not 100% is irrelevant.
- All science is based on induction.

Types of Inductive Logic

There are three kinds of inductive logic: - Enumerative induction; Argument from analogy; and Abduction (or inference to best explanation). Here is a list of the main components of each.

1. **Enumerative Induction**

    - This kind of argument is used for things like opinion polls. We draw conclusions about a whole population from a representative sample.
        - This assumes several things, one being that the future will resemble the past (e.g. that people will believe tomorrow what they believed yesterday). This is a fairly safe assumption, so, if done correctly, polls can be fairly reliable.
    - With Enumerative Induction it is important to check for errors. For example: -
        - Was the sample big enough?
        - Has the statistical margin of error been reported?
        - Was the sample random? (I.e. did the poll either select or ignore any subgroups?)
        - Were there leading questions in the poll?
    - The same logic is used when a doctor takes a blood sample and assumes that the small sample is representative of your entire bloodstream.

2. **Argument from Analogy**

    - Here we take two or more objects, note their similarities, and conclude that they must have an additional similarity.

- Although the conclusion is not guaranteed, this method can establish a strong likelihood.
- This type of argument is often used in the legal world, with previous cases used as precedents. It's also used in medical research with mice being used as a good model for humans.
- Again, this assumes that the future will resemble the past.

3. **Abductive Reasoning**

- Abductive Reasoning is '**an inference to the best explanation**', and it is crucial to all scientific reasoning.
- This was the method Sherlock Holmes used to solve crimes (it is often claimed he used 'deduction' but it was actually 'induction by abduction').
- Also, in the medical field, induction by abduction is the basis of every diagnosis.
- Thomas Huxley said, "Science is simply common sense at its best." E.g. if you came downstairs and the window was open and the silver gone, you would conclude you had been robbed, you wouldn't think that a ghost was responsible.
- Sometimes, however, abduction actually goes against common sense, e.g. if you took some experimental medicine and later felt better you might think that the medicine worked, but that is only one data point (remember correlation doesn't imply causation). What is needed is a large, properly controlled, trial.
- In fact, science was developed as a method of guarding against instinctive reasoning errors because our senses and memory often lead us astray.
- With sight we can fall for optical illusions, and we suffer from expectation bias.
- We impose patterns on limited data like seeing a face on a piece of toast.
- With memory we often remember evidence that confirms our beliefs and forget what doesn't. Also, some things are just more memorable than others.
- Memory is not like a video; we usually just remember the basics and discard the details. When we recall this later, we often confabulate the details. Then a later recall is of the previous recall, not the original memory.
- Science is designed to guard against the many ways our instincts lead us astray.

Epistemology

- When we feel better after taking medicine was it the result of the pill or was it the placebo effect?
- Science uses controlled 'blind' studies to tell the difference. A large group of subjects is split in two, half get the real medicine and half get a sugar pill. Both groups of subjects are told they are getting the real medicine.
- To be even better, the study will be 'double blind'. Here the people giving the pills don't know which subject gets which pill (so they can't influence the result), also the people analysing the results don't know (so their expectations don't influence what they find).
- Science is not done by one person working alone, conclusions are derived from the work of an entire community – a community that is aware of the kinds of errors that we are prone to, and that takes specific and careful steps to guard against such errors.

Five Criteria of Abduction

- If abduction is choosing which hypothesis is the best explanation of a phenomenon in question, how should we go about that selection?
- Here the philosophers Theodore Schick and Lewis Vaughn articulate a very straightforward method based on five criteria.
- Their five criteria used to help abduction selection are: **testability**, **fruitfulness**, **scope**, **simplicity** and **conservatism**.
- When figuring out the best explanation, two (or more) hypotheses are compared based on these five criteria, and whichever one fits best overall is accepted as the best explanation.
    - **Testability**. Can it be tested? Any hypothesis should be used to make predictions that can be tested for, otherwise it explains nothing.
    - **Fruitfulness**. When a hypothesis is fruitful, it gets those predictions right.
    - **Scope**. The more a hypothesis explains, and the more it unifies our knowledge, the more reason we have to think it true.
    - **Simplicity**. This does not mean the hypothesis is easy to understand. It means that the hypothesis does not

- invoke more assumptions, entities, or forces than necessary.
   - **Conservatism**. When something is conservative, it simply coheres with what we already know; it doesn't contradict already established knowledge.

Epistemology – A Summary

- Knowledge is a 'justified true belief' but taken with a pinch of salt.
- You can believe in something if you have evidence for it, but faith is belief without evidence.
- Knowledge becomes objective when experiences are shared and compared with others.
- All science is based on inductive knowledge, with repeatable experiments together with sharing data and checking each other's analysis of that data.

Methods for Acquiring Knowledge	
Deduction	**Induction**
<ul><li>100% Correct</li><li>Restricted to Maths & Logic</li></ul>	<ul><li>Less than 100% correct but can get very close to it.</li><li>This is how our brains work: building concepts relating to our understanding of the world though our experience of the world.</li><li>It is also the basis of science when applied rigorously.</li><li>There are three kinds of inductive logic:<ul><li>Enumerative induction</li><li>Argument from analogy</li><li>Abduction (or inference to best explanation).</li></ul></li></ul>

Epistemology

The next few chapters will consider how philosophers go about building their theories.

4

Arguments

It would be argument for a week, laughter for a month, and a good jest for ever.

Shakespeare (Henry IV, Part 1)

What do Philosophers do?

Here is a list of many of the things they do: -

- Ask questions.
- Challenge assumptions.
- Re-examine traditionally held views.
- Unpack the meaning of words.
- Weigh up the value of evidence.
- Examine logical arguments.
- Search for truth.
- etc.

But what is the main thing they do?

Philosophers create arguments!

Oh no they don't... Oh yes they do...

No, not the John Cleese type of argument from Monty Python where people just contradict each other. And not angry or belligerent arguments either.

Philosophers use the term 'argument' in a very precise and narrow sense. For them, an argument is the most basic complete unit of reasoning, an atom of reason if you like. An 'argument' is an inference from one or more starting points to an end point. The starting points are called 'premises' and the end point is called a 'conclusion'.

Arguments

Note that arguments are not explanations. A philosophical argument attempts to demonstrate *that* something is true, while an explanation attempts to show *how* that something is true.

An argument is a **Set of Sentences** designed to move you on from where you are by claiming one sentence is true based on preceding ones.

Here is an example argument: -

> It's Jim's philosophy group meeting today.
> Jim always gets up early on philosophy group meeting days.
> Therefore, Jim will get up early today.

The above three statements comprise an argument, the first two statements are premises and the third is a conclusion based on the premises.

Note that arguments cannot be true or false! They can only be good or bad. It's the Assertions (or Premises) that are true or false.

> It's Jim's philosophy group meeting today.
> Jim always gets up early on philosophy group meeting days.
> Therefore, Jim will get up early today.

For this argument, let's say the first premise is true, however, the second premise may not be true, it might be the case that in the past Jim has always got up early on philosophy group meeting days, but there is the possibility, however slight, that he won't today.

Here it is important to make a distinction between something philosophers call **'Validity'** and **'Soundness'**: - This is the point that an argument might be 'valid' (i.e. the conclusion logically follows from the premises) but it might not be 'sound', presumably because one or more of the premises were invalid.

> [Politician joke: - Two politicians are debating on stage, the first one says, "you're lying", and the second one replies, "Yes I am... but hear me out".]

In the philosophy group example above, the argument is actually 'valid' – the conclusion does follow logically from the premises, but the argument is not really 'sound' because the second premise can't be considered to be true.

An argument is only sound if **both**: -

a) All the premises are true, and
b) The conclusion follows logically from the premises.

Having said that, however, most of philosophy is concerned with (b) i.e. does the conclusion follow from the premises?

Complex arguments can then be built up with the conclusions of earlier arguments becoming the premises for later ones. This is how philosophers build up whole systems of their philosophy.

Refutation of an argument

You can refute an argument in three ways: -

1. You can show the conclusion does not follow logically from the premises, or
2. You can show that one or more premise is wrong, or
3. You can prove the conclusion wrong even if you can't find the flaw in the argument.

One of the main thing philosophers do is to look for flaws in their own and in other people's arguments. This is a bit like how science works, people sharing their analysis with each other and checking their own and other people's analysis. Indeed, if you go to the philosophy section of any library, you will find that books by philosophers about their own ideas are vastly outnumbered by books from other philosophers commenting on and critiquing previous philosophy systems.

This is actually a good state of affairs, because the best way to learn about something is to read round the subject as widely as possible; read what the original proposer says, read what different critics say, and then read critics of the critics etc.

Arguments

Types of Arguments

There are two main types of argument, causal arguments, and rational arguments, and both involve conclusions based on premises: -

Causal	Rational
If the fire alarm goes off at night, David will jump out of bed.	Bedford is north of London. Edinburgh is north of Bedford. Therefore, Edinburgh is north of London.

(Note by the way: in the first example there is an implied sentence 'a fire alarm means...')

Symbolic Logic

Philosophers sometimes put their arguments into a kind of mathematical shorthand. This can get quite complicated, but here is a simple introduction. It uses letters to represent statements and then joining words (or sometimes symbols) such as 'and', 'or', 'not', and 'if'.

So, an argument such as: -

>If the fire alarm goes off when David is in bed, then David will jump out of bed.
>The fire alarm did go off when David was in bed.
>Therefore, David did jump out of bed.

In Symbolic Logic this could be written as: -

>If A then J
>A
>Therefore J

Or even shorter: - $(A \rightarrow J, A \therefore J)$.

As you can imagine, these can build up into quite off-putting pages of analysis, but most philosophers do stick to using ordinary words, albeit with their inherent ambiguity of meaning, and the philosopher's own definitions (which, hopefully, the philosopher makes clear).

Facts and Beliefs

Firstly, note that facts are not, in themselves, true or false. They are just facts! It is statements about facts that are either true or false e.g. "It is raining", or "the world is flat'.

Facts are things that make statements (or premises) true or false. So, we say that facts are the truth-makers of the world. The difficulty comes, of course, in ascertaining the facts (note, however, the fact of a matter does actually exist, even if you don't know what it is, it is still there). As discussed in chapter 3 on epistemology, science can only use induction to ascertain facts, so we can't be 100% certain about them, but science can produce such high percentage probabilities in many instances that we do attribute the word fact to those cases.

Beliefs, on the other hand, are either true or false. If I believed the world was flat, my belief would be a false belief. Often, however, beliefs can't be proven one way or the other, but they are still either true or false. In these cases, one naturally adopts an assessment of probability based on previous experience, but with the caveat that more evidence might settle the matter.

Language as a tool

Much of the time philosophy is concerned with language, so language itself is one of the main tools of philosophy. Indeed, some philosophers see their whole task as linguistic. In this, it is important to distinguish between 'first order' language and 'second order' language.

For example: -

First order:	'A caused B'.
Second order:	'What does it mean to say that A caused B?'
First order:	'Is it right to do this?'
Second order:	'What does it mean to say that something is "right"?'

Such analysis is an important part of philosophy, all philosophers have is language and they need to be as clear as possible in their thinking. This is not easy, the philosophers Bertrand Russell and Ludwig Wittgenstein both tried to make language as logical and unambiguous as possible, but neither really succeeded. Indeed, Wittgenstein later changed his ideas on language and considered it to be like a game of words. For more on this see the chapter on language in part four of this book.

Analysing the Question

When debating any particular question, there is a natural inclination to jump straight in with the answer. In philosophy that should be avoided. The first thing to establish is what does the question mean, if people think it means different things, they will not all be discussing the same thing.

Take the question "**Do we have Free Will?**" This is a widely debated question, but the first task should be to analyse the question, i.e. as framed, what exactly is the question asking?

- What is meant by "we"? Could we substitute the word "I", what difference would that make? This (for instance, among many other things) might raise the thought: - does the question imply just the conscious part of ourselves?
- What does the question mean by "free"? Choosing to obey the law? Being coerced? Etc...
- Does the wording imply free all the time? What about when asleep, or intoxicated? What about doing something automatic (like walking), or doing something on impulse?
- Etc. etc...

In any philosophical debate it is important that all involved first understand the question, otherwise they will be making different assumptions and talking at cross purposes.

Thinking logically is not easy. The next chapter will look at the many ways that thinking can be led astray.

5

Difficulties in Rational Thinking

No more be grieved at that which thou hast done:
Roses have thorns, the silver fountains mud,
Clouds and eclipses stain both moon and sun,
And loathsome canker lives in sweetest bud;
All men make faults, and even I in this,

Shakespeare (from sonnet 35)

Rational Thinking is not easy.

Humans possess two different types of thinking: the quick intuitive kind; and the slower more rational kind. Our Intuitions are patterns that we have learnt via experience of the world as we grew from babyhood onwards (the brain is a pattern recognition device *par excellence*). These intuitions are shortcuts to thinking, enabling us to make snap decisions when the need arises, without having to spend time logically thinking through all the pros and cons of an action. This is obviously an excellent survival ability; don't think, just run at the slightest hint of danger, if it was a false alarm it doesn't matter, you've lost nothing.

When there is time, however, the other gift from evolution is our ability to think rationally, to weigh up the evidence and make logical decisions, to plan our actions. Even here our intuitions are a good starting point, but with the time to think about it we can look to see if we have missed anything or misunderstood something. This is especially effective when working together with others.

Sounds easy, and it is a very powerful ability, but it is also easy to go wrong, and to go wrong without knowing it. Philosophy itself is not a life-or-death matter, but some things we use our rational thinking for are life and death, or at least do have consequences for society, so it is important to be aware of the possible pitfalls to our thinking. And when it does come to philosophy, it would be good if we can trust our reason.

Our rational thinking is prone to two different types of errors. Firstly, there are the errors connected to how the mind works, and secondly, there

Difficulties in Rational Thinking

is a whole list of logical fallacies that it is very easy to fall for without knowing it.

Errors Connected with How the Mind Works

1. **Confirmation Bias**: - When listening to others, or reading an article, we give more weight to arguments and ideas that we already agree with, and we have a great tendency to dismiss out of hand (without looking properly at the evidence being presented) things we don't agree with. This confirms our existing beliefs and blinds us to any evidence to the contrary. The mind works like this because it looks for patterns, so when something is said that we already agree with, it strengthens our existing ideas. Also, we want to be accepted by the group we are in, so there is a big incentive to agree with the group's views.

2. **The Reliability of Memory**: - We instinctively believe that our memories are reliable, indeed we have to rely on them to live. And in court for instance, the testimony of an eyewitness is given great weight as being very reliable evidence.

    But time and again studies have shown how unreliable our memories are. When you remember something it's not like watching a film, it's more like a series of impressions, any of which may have been wrong at the time (it's easy to suffer an illusion). But it gets worse, because when you remember that thing a second time, you are often remembering not the incident itself but the first remembering of it, and so on.

    This is how the mind works, the memories of our ideas and concepts are designed to be updateable, that's how we learn, it's part of the pattern recognition process of building a concept. Each time you learn a little bit more about a concept it slightly changes how you think about it and how it links to other concepts you have.

3. **Correlation and Causation**: - As stated, the mind constantly looks for patterns, and if one thing occurs soon after another thing, the mind will often jump to assuming a link between the two, but correlation by itself is not causation. For instance, some people thought that the MMR vaccine caused autism: it doesn't, it just happens that autism usually first appears in infants at around the same time they are due their immunisation injections. It took quite a while, however, to prove the vaccine did not cause

An Introduction to Philosophy

autism, only careful scientific analysis of the data was able to provide to answer.

Errors due to Logical Fallacies

What are Fallacies? Fallacies are arguments that are bad, that is, they are either invalid or unsound, (or indeed both, see the previous chapter for these definitions). In short, they are arguments that contain one or more flaws of some kind.

A '**formal fallacy**' is where the logic is wrong, i.e. the conclusion does not follow from the premises.

An '**informal fallacy**' is where one or more of the premises are wrong (even though the logic of the argument might be correct).

To find informal fallacies all the premises of the argument in question should be fact-checked. But finding formal (or logical) fallacies can be very difficult. They are like tricks or illusions that make arguments look stronger than they actually are, and they often play on people's emotions. If used in rhetoric (by a politician say, either deliberately, or just unknowingly) they can seemingly make a weak argument strong.

The fact that an argument includes a logical fallacy does not, in itself, mean that the conclusion is wrong, only that the conclusion can't rely on that part of the argument, that logical fallacy should be left out and the argument should stand or fall on its own merits.

There are many such logical fallacies to look out for, either in everyday life or in philosophy. Listed below are some of the more common ones.

Logical Fallacy List

- **The Slippery Slope**: - This asserts that if we allow A to happen it will open the floodgates all the way to allowing Z to happen. This is not a valid argument about allowing A. The argument for A should stand on its own merits, and if someone later wants to argue for B or C etc. those arguments too should only stand on their own merits.

Difficulties in Rational Thinking

- **The Strawman**: - This is where someone arguing against argument A, first creates a caricature of the A argument, and then argues against the caricature because that is easier. When depicting an opponent's argument, it is incumbent on you to address the opponent's argument in its strongest form.

- **Begging the Question**: - This is a circular argument in which the conclusion is included in one of the premises i.e. the person using it is assuming the truth of the thing they are trying to prove.

- **The Appeal to Nature**: - This uses the argument that because something is 'natural' it must be good or valid. It can be a very appealing argument, witness the rise of alternative medicine and beauty products containing natural products. By itself, however, it is not an argument; there are many harmful things in nature, and even more things that are neither harmful nor helpful.

- **The Middle Ground**: - This is where someone claims that because there is an argument for something and an argument against it, then the truth must be somewhere in the middle. For example, one person says climate change is caused by man, and another says it is not, then a third person might say that perhaps just a bit of the change is caused by man.

- **Ad Hominem:** - Attacking your opponent's character instead of addressing any flaws in the arguments they are using.

- **No True Scotsman**: - An appeal to purity as a way of dismissing valid criticisms. For example, Hamish says that all Scotsmen put a knife in their sock when they wear a kilt. You point out that Duncan over there in a kilt does not have a knife in his sock and he is Scottish. Hamish responds that Duncan can't be a **true** Scotsman because no **true** Scotsman would wear a kilt without having a knife in his sock.

- **Appeal to Ignorance**: -A person says that if you can't prove I am wrong then I must be right. It is often impossible to completely prove something wrong, but that in itself does not make it right, it is up to the person claiming something to be the one to prove it.

- **Mystery Therefore Magic**: - This is a version of the appeal to ignorance fallacy. It says that if you don't have a natural explanation for something then it is ok to invoke a supernatural explanation.
  (One has to be very careful that, when trying to find an answer to a question, one does not replace the unknown with the unknowable, or with an answer that introduces a host of unsupported ideas.)

- **False Dichotomy**: -This is where you are presented with two choices as if these were the only possibilities, when actually other options do exist. Also called the Black or White fallacy.

- **Appeal to Emotion**: - Trying to create an emotional response in the listeners in the absence of any good arguments for the proposition.

- **Appeal to Authority**: - Using the opinion of an authority figure or institution in place of actual arguments.

- **Bandwagon**: - Claiming that something must be true because so many people do believe it to be true.

- **Special Pleading**: - When a claim is shown to be false, the claimant moves the goalposts to allow for exceptions. For example, if a psychic can't reproduce their results in a laboratory, they might claim that it is because there were too many negative thoughts around at the time.

- **Cherry Picking**: - This is where someone presents only that information about a subject that backs his argument and ignores facts that don't fit.

- **Anecdotal**: - Here someone uses an isolated example from personal experience in place of a valid argument. It is often used to counter statistics, as in "I know someone who is ninety-six and he has smoked all his life".

- **Ambiguity**: - This is where someone uses double meanings (not necessarily deliberately) which confuse the logic of the argument.

- **The Gambler's Fallacy**: - Arguing that because there has been a long run of, say, heads in a coin toss, the next toss is more likely to be tails.

These next two fallacies are where people think they are making a valid deductive argument, but the logic is invalid. Take time to see what is wrong in each case.

- **Affirming the Consequent**: -
    - If P is true, then Q is true.
    - Q is true.
    - Therefore, P is true.

- **Denying the Antecedent**: -
    - If P is true, then Q is true.
    - P is not true.
    - Therefore, Q is not true.

The above seems quite a long list, but it just includes the more obvious fallacies, there are plenty of others. Thinking logically and rationally is not easy, arguments (both your own and other people's) need to be inspected carefully to find such errors, which is why philosophy should be a collaborative process, in the same way science is.

The next chapter will look at some of the tools philosophers use to help them think rationally.

6

Tools for Rational Thinking

> *Man is a tool-using Animal. Nowhere do you find him without tools; without tools he is nothing, with tools he is all.*
>
> **Thomas Carlyle**

What are Philosophy Tools?

As Carlyle said, man is a tool user. A carpenter uses tools, a surgeon uses tools, a labourer uses tools, even an office worker uses tools: - pen, paper, computer etc. But, apart from the office equipment, what tools could a philosopher use? Well, these tools are conceptual ones, they are used to evaluate, analyse and create philosophical theories. Indeed, we have already met a number of them.

Tools already described.

We have met **Arguments**, **premises**, and **conclusions**, which are used to build up philosophical theories. We touched on **language** itself as a tool with the difference between first order and second order questions. We also looked in more detail about the following tools: -

Deduction: - This is a rigorous form of reasoning such that if the premises are true then the conclusion is true, e.g. It is Monday today, Steve always wears a tie on Mondays, therefore Steve will wear a tie today. It is mainly concerned with maths and logic.

Induction: - This involves reasoning from a limited number of observations, and inferences from past regularities to future ones, e.g. the sun came up every day before, therefore it will come up again tomorrow. Note this often involves generalisations and probability.

Also, the three sub-divisions of Induction: **Enumerative Induction**; **Argument from Analogy**; and **Abduction**. Along with the five criteria for comparing two or more abduction hypothesis: **Testability**; **Fruitfulness**; **Scope**; **Simplicity**; and **Conservatism**.

Validity and Soundness: - This is the point that an argument might be valid (i.e. the conclusion follows from the premises) but it might not be sound, presumably because one or more of the premises were invalid.

Consistency: - If someone said, "murder is wrong" but, later said: "that particular murder was ok", then they are being inconsistent.

Fallacies: - This is to do with poor reasoning, which is sometimes quite hard to detect. The most common fallacies were listed in the previous chapter.

Refutation: - You can refute an argument in three ways: you can show the conclusion does not follow from the premises; you can show that one or more premise is wrong; or you can prove the conclusion wrong even if you can't find the flaw in the argument.

More Philosophy Tools

There are many tools that philosophers use; indeed, whole books have been devoted to describing them. Below, however, a few of the more common ones are listed and explained.

Axioms: -

Remember that obtaining a true conclusion in an argument requires: - a) that the argument is valid (i.e. the conclusion follows from the premises), and b) that the premises are true. The more difficult of these is assessing whether or not the premises are true.

Here, the concept of an axiom becomes useful as a philosophical tool. An axiom is a special kind of premise in a specific kind of rational system. These stand as initial claims that need no justification – at least from within the system being investigated.

The first person to formalize this was Euclid with his system of geometry as described in his book The Elements. His axioms are the basis from which, through various stages of deductive reasoning, his whole theoretical geometrical system is derived.

Ideally, an axiom is a statement which no rational person could possibly object to. Although this initially seems a powerful tool, its use is

An Introduction to Philosophy

fairly limited. If, for example your axiom was 'all bachelors are unmarried', this may well be true but it's not going to get you very far, indeed it's a bit circular. Alternatively, if your axiom was that 'the shortest distance between two points is a straight line', this will be very useful within Euclidean geometry, but not for much else.

Definitions: -

"Define your terms" someone might say when partaking in a philosophical argument.

Definitions are important because without them it is very easy to argue at cross purposes. Remember the idea (from chapter 4) of analysing a question before jumping in with an answer, in order to ensure everybody is talking about the same thing. Meanings can be slippery things.

It is important to lay out your definitions as clearly as possible, and perhaps even modify them during the discussion, with the agreement of the person you are arguing with, so that you can both be talking about the same thing.

It's not easy to define something accurately and completely, sometimes it becomes too narrow and sometimes too broad. It is also a good rule of thumb to correspond as closely as possible to the way in which the term is ordinarily used. Philosophers do have a tendency to stretch meanings too far, or even to invent their own definition of a word.

Many philosophical questions often come down to searches for adequate definitions, e.g. what is knowledge? What is beauty? etc.

Note here we are dealing with the ambiguities, and limitations, of language. Any given word or phrase can only be defined in terms of other words. Also, different people may use the same word in different ways. Pinning down meaning is difficult, but that said, it is important to try if you want to argue about the same thing and not argue at cross purposes.

Category Mistakes: -

This tool was first fully described by British philosopher Gilbert Ryle (1900 – 1976) in his classic book The Concept of Mind (1949). He was a representative of the generation of British ordinary language philosophers who shared Wittgenstein's approach to philosophical problems. He was also heavily influenced by the German phenomenologist Edmund Husserl (1859 – 1938). Chapter one of his book is the first (and probably the last) word about the nature of category mistakes.

It is perhaps easier to describe a category mistake using an example. One that Ryle gives is of a foreign tourist who is taken round all the colleges, libraries, and other buildings of Oxford University, and then he asks, 'But where is the university?' His mistake was in thinking that the university was a building whereas it is really an institution that buildings belong to.

Ryle showed that it is a category mistake that causes much of the confusion about the nature of mind. He said that the mistake made by Descartes, and others, was to think of the mind as if it were an object, like a brain is an object, or a tree is an object. Descartes then said this mind object was obviously not material in the way that brains, or trees are, therefore it that it had to be a non-physical kind of object of some sort. This, says Ryle, was a category mistake. Mind is not an object; rather it is a process, i.e. the brain working in real time, and this can be understood without bringing in any ghostly, non-physical, substance. He coined the, now well known, term 'the ghost in the machine' to describe Descartes' mind-body dualism.

The tool 'category mistake' is very powerful for philosophical analysis, but it is not enough to just make the claim that someone has made a category mistake. To prove your claim, you must show how the categorization is wrong.

Intuition Pumps: -

These are stories or scenarios that are designed to help us think about a given issue. Note that they don't have to be true (or even possible); they are just structured to enable us to think more clearly about an idea. These are also very like thought experiments, which are often used in science.

The philosopher Daniel Dennett recommends something he calls "turning the knobs" with intuition pumps. This is where you have a story of some kind which gives you an intuition about something, but you then change elements of the story slightly to see if that changes your intuition.

For example: - in a prison, every night after the prisoners are asleep, a whimsical jailer unlocks all the cell doors and the doors to the outside, and then in the morning he locks them again. Question: - what is your intuition, are the prisoners free at night?

Now turn the knobs, does it change our intuition? What if the prisoners were drugged while the doors were open? What if the doors were opened by accident? What if the jailer did it because he was worried about fire? What if the prison was the size of Australia? Alternatively, what if a diabolical host locked the doors of his houseguests only when they were asleep?

One of the points of this story is to do with the difficulty of making good decisions about things if you don't have all the relevant information.

An Introduction to Philosophy

Not all intuition pumps are good at presenting the idea they were invented for. Richard Dawkins' use of the 'selfish gene' was excellent at presenting a new view of evolution from a genetic perspective, but many people took the wrong message from this. They thought he was saying that humans are basically selfish and that this was due to our genes, which is not at all what he was saying. Indeed, later he said that he could have easily called his book 'the co-operating gene'.

Occam's Razor: -

This idea (also known as the law of parsimony) is attributed to the English Franciscan friar William of Ockham (c. 1287–1347), a scholastic philosopher and theologian. The basic idea is that the simplest explanation is most likely the right one, or put another way, entities should not be multiplied without necessity. It is often used as an 'abductive heuristic' in the development of theoretical models rather than as a rigorous arbiter between candidate models.

The Intentional Stance: -

This is an assumption that the behaviour of an entity (be it person, animal, artefact, whatever) is the result of deliberation, or choice, by a rational agent. This stance allows us to usefully predict that behaviour without spending time working out how that entity produced that behaviour.

This differs from the 'Physical Stance' where you just assume an inanimate object will follow the laws of nature e.g. a dropped stone falls. Or the 'Design Stance' in which you assume that something manmade for a purpose will act in line with that purpose e.g. a lift.

Memes: -

This is a term, invented by the biologist Richard Dawkins, meaning 'a unit of culture'. This could be an idea, a belief, a fashion in clothing or behaviour, or a method of making something e.g. a better stone axe. The point here is that the meme (pronounced meem) can be passed from one person to another, it resides in brains. Memes can be true or false, as in 'the sun will come up tomorrow' or 'the moon is made of cheese'.

Dawkins invented the term to be similar to a biological gene. Genes and memes are similar in that both can evolve and be subjected to natural selection. Some memes are good at getting themselves copied, especially so when a group of memes support each other (as in a political theory, or a religion). Using the term meme gives a good insight into how ideas and culture develop and spread around the world. Memetics is not an exact science (partly because it is difficult to define the term) but it is a useful way of viewing things.

Dennett says that two main insights flow from this tool. Firstly, we usually think good design either comes from evolution or from genius, but with memes we see that good design can also emerge through the 'natural selection' of ideas, a survival of the fittest. Secondly, however, although mostly beneficial, we pay a price for their success. The fitness of a meme does not necessarily coincide with what is good for us; they could be described as parasites of the mind (think of conspiracy theories, or vaccine scares).

The Laws of Thought: -

These are three axioms (which stretch back to the ancient Greeks) that all arguments must meet: -

1. The law of identity – Everything is identical to itself.
2. The law of non-contradiction – No proposition can be both true and false.
3. The law of an excluded middle – Every proposition is either true or false.

Laws 2 and 3 are fairly obvious requirements, but law 1 might seem somewhat unnecessary. When using logic, however, it is important that you are clear what is being said. It can be thought of like this: - If A equals B in all aspects and B contains nothing more than A, then A is B, we are talking about the same thing.

Bertrand Russell, in an essay called *On Denoting*, put it this way: -

> "*If a is identical with b, whatever is true of the one is true of the other, and either may be substituted for the other without altering the truth or falsehood of that proposition. Now George IV wished to know whether Scott was the author of Waverley; and in fact Scott was the author of Waverley. Hence we may substitute "Scott" for "the author of Waverley" and thereby prove that George IV wished to know whether Scott was Scott.*"

Tools for Binary Category Distinctions

It is common in philosophy to categorise arguments into one of two opposing types. For instance, we have already met the distinction between Deductive arguments and Inductive ones. Such a categorisation helps us to think about and analyse the argument involved. There are quite a number of such binary categories, but listed below are a few of the more common ones, some of which we will meet again when we look at individual philosophers. (Note: - some of these terms were defined in the introduction, but here they are put together as binary categories.)

A priori / A posterior: -

This is to do with where we think knowledge comes from (it's a bit like the deduction / induction distinction). So, for instance, the fact that the internal angles of a triangle add up to 180 degrees is inherent in the axioms of geometry and hence is a priori knowledge (i.e. existing without the need for sensory experience). Most of our knowledge, however, relies on reasoning from effects to causes based on our experience of the world, and hence is a posterior.

This binary distinction is somewhat controversial with different philosophers claiming different things and introducing new terms like 'synthetic a priori', and some even saying there is no such thing as a priori knowledge. We will see this later when looking at individual philosophers.

Empiricist / Idealist (or Rationalist): -

Empiricist philosophers, like Locke and Hume, base their philosophy on observation and experimentation. Idealists (sometimes known as rationalists), like Descartes and Kant, base their philosophy on reason, introspection, and intuition, saying that we can't directly know the external world, all we can rely on is the mind. There are many versions of both positions, and the dividing line can be somewhat variable (as we will see), but the distinction is still a useful one as a kind of extreme position against which to compare a philosopher's ideas.

Objective / Subjective: -

The subjective experience or understanding is how an individual person perceives the world, what it feels like to them, and what concepts they have about the world. When people share their subjective experience and ideas about the world with other people, if most people agree on what the

Tools for Rational Thinking

world is like, then this becomes an objective view. Note that the word subjective is often used in a pejorative sense, as in 'that's just your subjective opinion', thus implying it's a wrong opinion. But it is not necessarily wrong, it's just not how the majority see it, think of religion for example.

Syntax / Semantics: -

Much of philosophy is to do with the analysis of language; either a philosopher's own use of language, as in "how can I be as clear and logical as possible?" or when analysing another philosopher's language "what does he mean by that?" Indeed, what do we mean when we use the word 'mean'?

When a sentence is analysed, we look at two things, its grammar (syntax) and its meaning (semantics). It is easy to be misled by a sentence that is grammatically correct but has no real meaning. But likewise, it is also easy to dismiss a sentence that has poor grammar but does mean something.

Absolute / Relative: -

This binary distinction is fraught with political ideologies. In science the distinction is well defined, things are measured and described with reference to other things. So, for instance, because the speed of light is absolute, measurements of space and time vary depending on the observer's position and velocity.

In the area of morality and politics, however, things are not so straight forward. For more on this please refer back to the discussion on different philosophies at the end of chapter 1 of this book.

How something is measured is by comparing it to some set of defined standards. Now it is perfectly possible for more than one set of standards to exist at the same time, but great care needs to be taken in a) defining the standards in the first place to ensure they are valid and logically consistent, and b) identifying exactly which set of standards is being used.

Necessary / Sufficient: -

This distinction is often used when trying to define something, some things might be considered necessary for the definition, but by themselves they would not be enough. So, for instance, to be able to vote in a U.K. general election it is a necessary condition that you must be eighteen or over on the polling day. But this is not sufficient; there are several other conditions that also need to be met, such as being on the electoral register, or not being legally excluded from voting for some specified reason.

Analytic / Synthetic: -

This is another distinction about the use and structure of language. Take the sentence 'cats are mammals'. The subject of the sentence is 'cats' and the predicate (the thing being affirmed of the subject) is the word 'mammals'. In his book *Critique of Pure Reason*, Immanuel Kant introduced the distinction Analytic / Synthetic to deal with the case where the predicate in a sentence is necessarily implied by the subject or is a new piece of information.

In the sentence above the idea of mammal is already contained in the concept 'cat' and stating that would be considered an 'analytic' judgement. But if the sentence was 'some cats are black', then the predicate 'black' is not contained in the subject, so stating that would be considered a 'synthetic' judgment.

When using simple sentences this distinction might appear fairly straightforward, but things can get more involved with more complex examples. Some philosophers, however, claim that this distinction is impossible to apply because the metaphor 'contain' cannot be adequately defined, see for example the 1951 paper entitled *Two Dogmas of Empiricism* by Willard Quine.

Types / Tokens: -

This is to do with the identity of things. For instance, a pack of pencils purchased new from a shop contains a number of 'identical' pencils. Using the word 'identical' in this way we are saying that each pencil has the same attributes as the others in the pack, the same length, width, colour, material etc. They are of the same 'type'. Any individual pencil is known as a 'token' of that 'type'.

Once again this might seem straightforward, but it is important to be clear, when saying one thing is identical to another, which meaning is intended. A famous version of this is Plato's idea of 'forms', which we will come to in the chapter on Plato, although he does seem to introduce a slightly more mystical element to the distinction.

Acquaintance / Description: -

This distinction is most often associated with Bertrand Russell, and we will explore it in more depth in the later chapter on Russell. But in short it is to do with the acquisition of knowledge. Some things we know about

Tools for Rational Thinking

through more direct acquaintance via things like the senses, memory, and introspection. Other things that we come to know about are via the combining of things that we already know from our more directly acquired knowledge.

In Summary on Tools

The above list of tools is not, by any means, complete, it is just the ones that are more often used, and ones we will meet in more detail later in this book. It might seem odd to talk of tools in relation to writing and thinking, but this is an important aspect to philosophy. The need to think clearly and logically about a subject, both initially when writing about it, or when later criticising an existing piece of writing, is vital. And any tool that aids your analysis in this respect is welcome.

7

Basic Ideas in Philosophy

> *In history, we are concerned with what has been and what is; in philosophy, however, we are concerned not with what belongs exclusively to the past or to the future, but with that which is, both now and eternally – in short, with reason.*
>
> **G.W.F. Hegel** (German idealist philosopher)

Review so far

After laying out the scope of philosophy, we started this book with epistemology (the theory of knowledge) because that is the ground on which philosophy is built. We looked at defining what constitutes knowledge, and then at the methods of attaining it. Our working definition was that knowledge is 'justified true beliefs' (i.e. beliefs that have evidence of some kind to back them up) but with the caveat that we should always apply a degree of scepticism, in case more evidence arises that means we have to modify, or even abandon, a particular belief.

Knowledge was split into deductive knowledge (mainly maths and logic) and Inductive knowledge (everything else). Deductive is 100% certain, Inductive is always less than 100% but can get very close to it. There are a number of ways of attaining inductive knowledge, but the main way is via abduction (inference to best explanation).

We then looked at how philosophers go about their business with a chapter on creating logical philosophical arguments. This was followed up with a chapter on the difficulties of rational thinking, including a list of the pitfalls and fallacies that need to be avoided. Lastly, we looked at some of the many tools philosophers use in their analysis.

Before moving on to a chronological review of the main western philosophers and their ideas, and having equipped ourselves with some definitions and tools, together with an awareness of the limitations and pitfalls of the discipline, we will spend a short time considering some of the basic problems that philosophy addresses.

Basic Ideas in Philosophy

These problems can be grouped around six basic questions: -

- What is knowledge? (Epistemology – already discussed in chapter 3)
- What is the nature of reality? (Metaphysics)
- What do we mean by 'meaning'? (Language)
- How should we treat others? (Ethics)
- How should we organise society? (Politics)
- What is the meaning of life? (Philosophical)

The idea of this section is not to provide answers to these questions, but just to outline the issues that philosophers spend their time thinking about. The intention here is to provide some familiarity with the scope of these questions prior to tackling how individual philosophers have addressed them. Below we take each of these questions in turn: -

What is the Nature of Reality?

This is perhaps the most basic question of all, if we don't know what's real then other questions don't make much sense. Is what we perceive via our senses a true picture of reality, and if not, then how close is it, and what are we missing?

The word perceive in the above sentence is a key one. When using the words 'see', 'hear', 'touch' etc. we naturally assume a direct knowledge to the world; but is that understanding correct; is what we see through our eyes a true picture of reality? When we replace 'see' with 'perceive' it brings in the idea that we are not looking out on the world through the windows of our eyes, but that there is, at least some, mental pre-processing involved in our perception.

If two people are looking at the same thing, do they perceive it the same? The angle they are looking from will be slightly different, and the lighting will be slightly different, but their understanding of it might also depend on their memories. Have they seen it before, are they familiar with it, have they seen other examples of the same type? Even if they both use the same words to describe it, does that mean they perceive it the same? And anyway, how could we tell? They might both use the word red to describe it but how can we know they perceive the colour red the same way?

Here we meet one of the main dividing lines in philosophy, it is one we have already described in the previous chapter, but the above few paragraphs bring it into greater perspective. It is the Empiricist versus Idealist (or Rationalist) division. Empiricists claim that we can get to know the reality of the world through the use of observation and measurement, but the idealists or rationalists claim that we can never know reality directly, and the only thing we can know is what we find in the mind, i.e. our pre-processed perceptions.

The exact position of the dividing line, however, is as variable as the number of philosophers on each side of it. Each philosopher has their own take on the matter, with extreme examples at each end but many softer positions towards the centre. As we look at individual philosophers in the next part of this book, we will see not only examples on both sides, but also how the debate has evolved over time.

Another aspect of this debate is the question 'is there such a thing as matter, and if so, what is it?' The idea that it is made of atoms goes back to the ancient Greeks with the thought experiment that if you kept dividing something, an apple say, you would get down to a smallest bit of that particular thing which could not be divided further. More recently of course, science has taken over that question, and found that even atoms are mostly empty space.

In fact, many aspects of what was originally thought of as philosophy have since been hived off into separate disciplines (such as science, biology, medicine, psychology, etc.) and as we discovered more about the world, those fields became more specialised. Having said that however, philosophy is still needed even here; it is needed when we try to understand the implications of the findings from those disciplines, and how those findings fit together in our understanding of the world.

What do we Mean by 'Meaning'?

The next main issue philosophy has to address is how to accurately describe, record and share any ideas and findings we might have. In maths this is straight forward; we can define our axioms and our logic operations, and then write down our equations for all to see. But in language this is not so easy, language is ambiguous and imprecise. Definitions of words and ideas are inexact, and they can only be defined in terms of other words and ideas. Many would say, however, that this is also one of the strengths of language: it is versatile (temporary definitions can be supplied in situ); extendable (with the possibility of adding multiple explanations); and poetic (it can approach ideas obliquely).

Several philosophers have tried to create a more workable algebra of language, such that a statement in it can be proved in a way similar to maths. We will meet such attempts in the next part of this book, but as a spoiler, they never really succeeded.

All we have with which to express our ideas is language, but despite its shortcomings, it is overall very effective, and often it is context that helps clarify meaning for us. In part four of this book, we have a chapter just on language, and prior to that, a chapter on where concepts come from and what their relationship is to meaning. A number of philosophers have tried to address this, as we shall see, most notably Plato with his idea of 'forms', Russell with his treatment of 'universals', and with a more modern take, Daniel Dennett using ideas from the science of how the brain works.

How Should we Treat Others?

This question is concerned with ethics and morality. It is often the case that these two words are used in general conversation as if they were interchangeable, however, although similar, they are different concepts: -

- Morality is to do with understanding the difference between right and wrong; it is more of an overriding guiding principle, often concerned with goodness or badness of character.
- Ethics, on the other hand, is to do with having specific sets of rules to help us implement our morality when we relate to other people.

Many of the philosophical questions outlined in this chapter are interconnected and overlap with each other. So (as Socrates knew well with his statement "the unexamined life is not worth living") before asking how to treat others, we should try to understand ourselves, then we can consider what kind of life is right for beings like us. We can suffer, and we can experience pleasure, but would it be right to just aim for a hedonistic life for ourselves knowing that others are the same as us and can suffer too?

What values should we have, indeed what values do we already have and where do they come from? Are they just our prejudices, perhaps a reflection of the culture we live in? What do we mean when we call something a virtue? We look up to people who we believe live a virtuous life but is virtue something that can be taught? These are some of the questions that Socrates was interested in.

Religion is also strongly involved in questions of conduct, with many religions proscribing strict rules for the treatment of others (think of the Ten Commandments for example). We will look at some religious philosophers, like St Augustine and St Thomas Aquinas, and some Eastern philosophies where philosophy and religion are more closely intertwined. There is also a short chapter just on religion in part four of this book.

Most philosophers we will meet struggled with these questions, and for many the answer was not just about treating others individually, but how to organise society in such a way as to be fair to as many people as possible. Jeremy Bentham and John Stuart Mill, for instance, developed the theory of utilitarianism, also known as the "greatest-happiness principle". It holds that one must always act so as to produce the greatest aggregate happiness among all sentient beings.

And as we move nearer to the current day, science becomes more involved. We get questions about 'nature and nurture', about our biology, and about how much our character is influenced by our genetic predisposition.

How Should we Organise Society?

As noted above, this question is closely related to how we should treat others. In this case it is how we should organise society in order that we can best implement the care of everybody, including ourselves, and here we meet the concepts of fairness and justice. Having said that, do we know what we mean when we use those terms? Socrates wanted to know what justice was and so he went to the courts and asked the judges and lawyers. Despite all his questioning however (which of course really annoyed people) he could not find anyone to give him a definition of justice, all he could get were examples of it in practice.

Most philosophers have proposed theories on the best form of government, as we shall see in the part two of this book. The idea of government by democracy started in ancient Greece, although neither Plato nor Aristotle were real supporters of it, they considered it weak in times of crisis. Greek democracy at that time was very different from what we consider democracy to be today. Then it was limited to individual 'city states' rather than whole nations (which didn't really exist at that time), also, it was limited in that women and slaves could not vote.

Having said that, we do not have full democracy today, we have 'representative democracy'. In a full democracy, every eligible person would vote on every issue, which might be a good way to run a club, but not a nation. People are too busy earning their living to spend time learning about the systems of government and the details of every issue to be discussed and decided on. Instead, we vote for individuals to represent us in government, it is their profession so they can spend the time on it, and if they don't do a good job they can be voted out.

The attraction of a strong government is obvious, it has been said that the best form of government is a benevolent dictatorship, but how do we guard against exploitation and corruption? These are issues we will meet in part two, the idea of a 'social contract' between citizens, the idea of checks and balances in government, the idea of separation of powers and of limited terms of office. It is not easy to design a system of government; most systems just evolve, and indeed are still evolving. It was Churchill who said 'democracy is the worst form of government, apart from all the others'!

What is the meaning of life?

This sounds like the big one, and it's probably the question most people think of when they think of philosophy. It's essential to take these questions in order however. Remember in chapter 4 there was a section on the importance of analysing a question before jumping in with an answer, that way people can be more certain that they are using the same definitions and assumptions before discussing any topic in question.

That is why this question is last in the list. It would be very difficult to attempt an answer before first agreeing what we take to be real about the world, and second understanding language, its limits and the nature of meaning in language. Also, it would be valuable to think about how we should treat others, and organise society, as a prelude to answering a personal question about what is important to us.

As we look at different philosophers and philosophies in the remaining parts of this book, we will see that each has a view on this question; and that's important, because if you want to understand something, the best approach is always to read widely around the subject to obtain as many different perspectives as possible. Therefore, we will return to this question at the end of the book when perhaps we will be in a better position to attempt an answer.

Summary

As stated earlier, the intention of this chapter was not to answer any of the above questions, it was just to set the scene for part two of this book in which we look at some of our most important western philosophers and their ideas. Having outlined these main questions, the hope is that the reader will be more familiar with what these philosophers are trying to do as they build their theories.

The ordering of part two is chronological, so not only will we see how these philosophers have addressed the issues outlined above, but we will also see how our ideas on these issues have evolved through time.

Part Two

Western Philosophy

This section comprises a chronological review of the main western philosophers, stretching from the early Greeks right up to the present day. Apart from chapter 9 on the early Greeks and chapter 45 on Recent Western Philosophy, each individual philosopher has been given: - an introduction; a background outline of their life and times; a discussion of their philosophy; and some notes on their legacy.

While there are, of course, many western philosophers, the selection made here is of those who have been deemed to have presented something new to the world, as opposed to just criticising, compiling, and re-ordering the ideas of previous philosophers.

This part of the book can be taken as just a reference section if required. But, for those interested, time should be taken to read through it in chronological order as this should bring out both the development of western thought through time, and any links and influences between the different philosophers.

Lastly, a note on sources: - many books and internet sources were consulted in the compilation of this section (for a full list please refer to the bibliography) but one authority in particular could not be ignored, that of Bertrand Russell. Therefore, imbedded throughout this chronological history are a number of valuable quotes and observations from his writings.

8

A Chronological List of Western Philosophers

Name	Dates	Broad Classification	Page
Early Greeks	5th & 4th c. B.C.	Ancient Philosophers	50
Socrates	d. 399 B.C.	Ancient Philosopher	56
Plato	428 - 347 B.C.	Ancient Philosopher	60
Aristotle	384 - 322 B.C.	Ancient Philosopher	67
Epicurus	341 - 270 B.C.	Ancient Philosopher	76
Plotinus	205 - 270	Neo-Platonist	82
St. Augustine	354 - 430	Medieval Philosopher	89
St. Thomas Aquinas	1225 - 1274	Medieval Philosopher	97
Francis Bacon	1561 - 1626	British Empiricist	105
Thomas Hobbes	1588 - 1679	British Empiricist	112
René Descartes	1596 - 1650	Rationalist	119
John Locke	1632 - 1704	British Empiricist	127
Benedictus Spinoza	1632 - 1677	Rationalist	135
Gottfried Wilhelm Leibniz	1646 - 1716	Rationalist	143
George Berkeley	1685 - 1753	British Empiricist	151
David Hume	1711 - 1776	British Empiricist	159
Thomas Reid *	1710 - 1796	British Empiricist	166
Jean Jacques Rousseau	1712 - 1778	Romantic	169
Immanuel Kant	1724 - 1804	German Idealist	177
Jeremy Bentham	1748 - 1832	British Empiricist	185
G.W.F. Hegel	1770 - 1831	German Idealist	192
Arthur Schopenhauer	1788 - 1860	German Idealist	200
John Stuart Mill	1806 - 1873	British Empiricist	207
Soren Kierkegaard	1813 - 1855	German Idealist	215
Karl Marx	1818 - 1883	Political Philosopher	223

A Chronological List of Western Philosophers

William James	1842 - 1910	American Pragmatist	231
Friedrich Nietzsche	1844 - 1900	Romantic	239
Edmund Husserl	1859 -1938	Phenomenologist	247
John Dewey	1859 - 1952	American Pragmatist	255
Bertrand Russell	1872 - 1970	Analytical Philosopher	262
Ludwig Wittgenstein	1889 - 1951	Analytical Philosopher	271
Martin Heidegger	1889 - 1976	Phenomenologist	278
Jean-Paul Sartre	1905 - 1980	Existentialist	286
M. Merleau-Ponty	1908 - 1961	Existentialist	293
A.J. Ayer	1910 - 1989	Analytical Philosopher	301
Daniel C. Dennett	1942 -	Current Scientific Philosopher	309

* Although Reid was born a year earlier than Hume it is usual to put Hume first chronologically because Hume wrote much earlier, and a lot of Reid's work was in response to Hume.

9

The Early Greeks

Introduction

There had been civilisations prior to the Greeks, for instance the Egyptians, the Babylonians, the Mycenaeans, the Ionians, and the Cretans among others, not to mention what was happening in China, India, and South America. And writing was invented over 4,000 years ago. But it was not until the Greek civilisation that philosophy came into its own as a structured, critical, inquiry into the nature of knowledge itself, together with its sub-disciplines of maths, logic, science, biology, ethics, law, and governance.

There have been numerous suggestions as to how this flourishing came about: was it the leisure time provided by the use of slaves; was it the fact that there was no official state religion to lay down a single way of thinking (many religions and beliefs existed side by side in Greece); was it perhaps the structure of the language that lent itself to the logical analysis of ideas; or was it the cultural art of rhetoric that had developed around that time? Maybe it was a combination of these elements in some way. Still, however, such a sudden flowering of abstract thought seems unlikely. Perhaps we should remember Sir Isaac Newton saying 'if I have seen further, it is because I have stood on the shoulders of giants'. Ancient Greece was a melting pot of peoples and ideas, and a centre of trade and commerce for the known world at that time.

Whatever the cause, philosophy as a discipline (as opposed to just folk wisdom) started here. Over those few centuries B.C. Greek philosophers produced many volumes of written text on maths and philosophy, much of which has been lost to us; only a small amount survived in the original. However, some of the missing texts have since been rediscovered because they had been copied into Arabic by Arab scholars, and these have been found and translated back again.

There are several, so called, pre-Socratic philosophers, including Heraclitus, Parmenides, Empedocles, Anaxagoras, and Protagoras; too many to include in this short chapter. Three of them, however, will be discussed individually here as having contributed something original to philosophy: Pythagoras, Leucippus, and Democritus (these last two are usually considered together under the title 'The Atomists').

Pythagoras

Pythagoras (circa. 570 B.C. – 495 B.C.) was born on the Greek island of Samos. Knowledge of his life is clouded by legend. The German scholar Walter Burket says *"There is not a single detail in the life of Pythagoras that stands uncontradicted. But it is possible, from a more or less critical selection of the data, to construct a plausible account."* His political and religious teachings, however, were well known at the time and influenced the philosophies of both Plato and Aristotle.

Around 530 B.C., he travelled to Croton, a Greek city in southern Italy, where he founded a school in which initiates were sworn to secrecy and lived a communal, ascetic lifestyle. This lifestyle entailed a number of dietary prohibitions, traditionally said to have included vegetarianism, although modern scholars doubt that he ever advocated for complete vegetarianism. Here he started a religion based round the idea of the transmigration of souls, together with his strict dietary proscriptions.

He is best known these days for his logic and mathematics, most schoolchildren will learn his famous theorem that the square of the hypotenuse of a right-angled triangle is equal the sum of the squares of the other two sides. He was also credited with many other mathematical and scientific discoveries, including Pythagorean tuning, the five regular solids, the Theory of Proportions, the sphericity of the Earth, and the identity of the morning and evening stars as the planet Venus. It was said that he was the first man to call himself a philosopher (meaning "lover of wisdom").

His mathematics, however, was more than just an academic exercise; it was a crucial part of his religious beliefs. Aristotle says that the Pythagoreans used mathematics for solely mystical reasons, devoid of practical application. The number one (the monad) represented the origin of all things and the number two (the dyad) represented matter. The number three was an "ideal number" because it had a beginning, middle, and end and was the smallest number of points that could be used to define a plane triangle, which they revered as a symbol of the god Apollo, and so on. Ten was regarded as the "perfect number".

In some accounts, Pythagoras and his followers saw that the world was described by numbers, and that therefore, the creative force behind existence must also be based on the divinity of number in its abstract, transcendental nature. Other scholars debate whether these numerological teachings were developed by Pythagoras himself or by the later Pythagorean philosopher Philolaus of Croton. There is no doubt, however, that these arithmetic discoveries did contribute significantly to the beginnings of mathematics.

His legacy is far reaching. As well as mathematics, his ideas have been used in astronomy, architecture, music and art, and his ideas on the immortality of the soul and its transmigration into other bodies after the death of the current body, hugely influenced Plato and thereafter other early Christians. Isaac Newton firmly believed in the Pythagorean teaching of the mathematical harmony and order of the universe, and though Newton was notorious for rarely giving others credit for their discoveries, he attributed the discovery of the Law of Universal Gravitation to Pythagoras.

Out of his theories on mathematics arose the idea of geometry as a separate field within mathematics. This was taken up and expanded on by the Greek mathematician Euclid, writing around the year 300 B.C., and known as the *"father of geometry"*. He produced a book called **Elements**, which Bertram Russell has described as "one of the greatest books ever written". In it Euclid constructs a whole concise theory of geometry by starting with basic axioms (such as a straight line is the shortest distance between two points) and combining them into more and more complex results, all logically derived from his initial axioms.

This book by Euclid became incredibly influential in philosophy. If you can build logical mathematical systems from basic axioms, then why not philosophical systems too, all you have to do is to state your axioms and build from there. Many tried, and even if they didn't succeed, at least people could see what things were being taken as starting points, and what logical reasoning was being employed. Philosophy started to become logical rather than just opinions and beliefs.

The Atomists

The first of the Greek **Atomists** were Leucippus and Democritus. Leucippus was the older, born in the 5th century B.C. and living around 440 B.C. Democritus, however, is the more definite figure, flourishing about 20 years later. This was from a time just prior to Plato and Aristotle, but Democritus was a contemporary of Socrates. It can be quite difficult to separate the work of Leucippus and Democritus and so they are usually considered together.

Aristotle knew the ideas of Democritus well, but it is not clear whether Plato did because he never mentions him. There is one third party report, however, that Plato hated Democritus so much that he wanted all his books burnt!

One of the things that Leucippus and Democritus were responding to were the ideas of the earlier philosopher Parmenides who argued that there was no such thing as either change or motion. He claimed this for

The Early Greeks

two reasons. Firstly, from a naming point of view, if someone, or something, has a name then it always exists. Secondly Parmenides claimed that there was no such thing as a void: since we can talk about the void, it can't be 'nothing', and hence space can't, therefore, be empty. Also, if there is no space between things then one thing can't move because the next thing can't move out of the way, hence motion is an illusion. [Note that one (more modern) way to agree with this is to argue along the lines that all moments in time always exist.]

Leucippus and Democritus took a more common-sense approach. They argued that if you use a knife to cut an apple, for instance, the knife does not cut the particles that constitute the apple, instead it goes through the spaces between the particles. Therefore, there is such a thing as the emptiness of space. The interesting distinction here is between void and space. Parmenides argued that there can be no such thing as a void, but this is treating the void as a thing. If instead you talk about 'space' as a 'place' it becomes a different type of phenomena, and then matter can reside, and move around, within space. The discussion of what exactly constitutes both matter and space (and indeed time) became elemental to both philosophy and science for two thousand years, and continues to be fundamental to our quest to understand reality to our present-day world of Einstein, quantum mechanics and the Large Hadron Collider.

Leucippus and Democritus believed that everything is made of atoms; that those atoms are physically indestructible; that there is empty space between the atoms; and that atoms are always in motion. There are an infinite number of atoms and they come in different sizes and shapes. They also differ in terms of heat, for instance spherical atoms, which compose fire, are the hottest. There was some disagreement on how they moved, some thought they were always falling, with the heavier ones overtaking the lighter ones and colliding like billiard balls, while others believed the motion of atoms was random.

Democritus said that there was neither up nor down in the infinite void and compared the movement of atoms in the soul to that of motes in a sunbeam. Collisions of atoms gradually built-up larger bodies of material. Some rejected these ideas on the basis that it relied on chance, but Democritus specifically denied that anything can happen by chance. They were both strict determinists, believing everything happens in accordance with natural laws. All things, for them, had a cause, but having said that, however, they don't seem to have had anything to say about a creator or a first cause.

Also (unlike Socrates, Plato, and Aristotle) they wanted to explain the world without using the concept of a 'final cause'. Russell explains this as follows: - Why does a baker bake bread? Answer, because people will be hungry. When we ask "why?" we can either be asking about the purpose it serves, or about the earlier circumstances that caused the event. The first question is a teleological one (i.e. to do with its final cause) but the second is a mechanistic one. Russell says that mechanistic questions lead to scientific knowledge, but teleological ones do not. The Atomists asked mechanistic questions, while their successors, until the Renaissance, were more interested in teleological ones, which thus led science up a blind alley for many years.

It is interesting to note that in terms of causes, neither a mechanistic nor a teleological explanation can say anything about a first cause or creator, because both look at what happens 'in' the world rather than at reality as a whole.

With regards to the theory of atoms, it might be thought that it was by good luck that the atomists hit on a hypothesis for which, two thousand years later, some evidence would be found, but this is perhaps a little harsh. If the problem of what constitutes matter is thought about logically one might well come to the conclusion that if you keep cutting something in half you get a smaller version of the same thing, but that it would be impossible to keep cutting something in half for ever, and therefore you must get to a point where you have the smallest possible element of that substance.

Democritus expanded on this by saying that: - Each atom was impenetrable, and indivisible because it contained no void. Atoms are internally unchanging but when they hit each other they sometimes combine when they have shapes which can interlock. Life developed out of primeval slime. There is some fire everywhere in a living body, but mostly in the brain or in the breast. Thought is a kind of motion, and both perception and thought are processes. He also thought that some attributes of an object, such as warmth, taste and colour are not really in the object but are due to our sense organs, whereas other qualities such as weight, density and hardness are really in the object. This is very modern thinking for that time.

Democritus reasoned that the solidness of the material corresponded to the shape of the atoms involved. Thus, iron atoms are solid and strong with hooks that lock them into a solid; water atoms are smooth and slippery; salt atoms, because of their taste, are sharp and pointed; and air atoms are light and whirling, pervading all other materials.

The knowledge of truth, according to Democritus, is difficult, since perception through the senses is subjective, and different impressions are obtained by different individuals. Therefore, just by using our sense-impressions, we cannot judge the truth. We can only interpret our sense data through the intellect to enable us to grasp at the truth through inductive reasoning (again very modern).

He can be considered a real materialist because, even though he talked about the soul, it was for him something made of atoms. Also, he said that thought was a physical process, and that there was no purpose in the universe, just mechanical laws. He disbelieved in popular religion and considered cheerfulness to be the goal in life. (One can see how Plato might have hated his ideas!) He disapproved of sex because it overwhelmed consciousness by pleasure, and he didn't want children because their education would interfere with his pursuit of philosophy!

He also wrote on ethics, politics, mathematics, geometry, anthropology, biology, and cosmology, although much of that is lost to us and is only known through citations. Russell calls him the last of the Greek philosophers with "an adventurous delight in the world". What's amiss in even the best philosophy after Democritus, he goes on to say, is an undue emphasis on man as compared to the universe, and despite the genius of Plato and Aristotle, it was not until the Renaissance that philosophy regained its vigour and independence.

10

Socrates

Introduction

Socrates (circa. 470 B.C. – 399 B.C.) did not write anything of his own, and that makes the study of him a little difficult because all the sources are secondary. Much has been written about him however, and so, through comparing sources, we can get a good fairly good idea of his life, his philosophy, and of his famous demise.

Most of the sources are from his pupils, especially Xenophon and Plato; having said that, it is difficult with Plato to separate the fact from the fiction. Plato's early work, particularly his book called the '**Apology**' is thought to be the most accurate, and covers the trial and death of Socrates, but in his later works he uses Socrates as a fictional character in dialogues, arguing and questioning other characters to uncover philosophical truths.

This questioning is the hallmark of the Socratic approach to philosophy; indeed, it is known as the Socratic Method (see below). He is also famous for the circumstances surrounding his death – that of being made to drink from a cup containing the poison hemlock.

Background

Socrates was born in Alopeke, near Athens. His father was Sophroniscus, a sculptor, or stonemason and his mother was a midwife. It seems likely that Socrates himself trained as a stonemason. He also spent some time as a soldier, taking part in the Peloponnesian War, a conflict which stretched intermittently over a period spanning 431 to 404 B.C. and which led to the defeat of Athens by Sparta and its allies. As Athens began to recover from this, many of its citizens turned away from democracy thinking it was a weak form of government, and Socrates appears to have agreed with this view.

He married when in his 50's to Xanthippe who bore him three sons, although Aristotle claims two of the sons were from another woman, presumably an earlier wife.

According to Plato, Chaerephon (a friend of Socrates) asked the Oracle at Delphi if anyone was wiser than Socrates; the Oracle responded that no one was wiser. Socrates did not believe this because he thought that he didn't know very much, so he decided to test this by questioning men considered wise by the people of Athens – statesmen, poets, and artisans. He found, however, that although these men considered themselves wise, they couldn't answer his questions, and so they weren't wise after all. Socrates, therefore, was wiser because he already knew that he didn't know anything.

This made the prominent Athenians he publicly questioned look foolish, which turned them against him and led to accusations of wrongdoing, and he was arrested and put on trial for 'corrupting the youth of Athens' among other charges. He was found guilty and was sentenced to death by being made to drink from a cup containing the poison hemlock.

Philosophy

Socrates' method of teaching was through dialectic discussion in which a series of questions is asked not only to draw individual answers, but also to encourage fundamental insight into the issues at hand. For instance, he would ask "If I wanted a shoe mended, who should I go to?" And a pupil would probably say "A shoemaker." Socrates would then continue with a carpenter, a coppersmith, and others. Then he would ask something like "so who should mend the ship of state?"

It seems fairly certain that Socrates was more interested in ethical matters than scientific ones, indeed Plato quotes him as saying "I have nothing to do with physical speculation." He is wise in the sense that he knows that he knows nothing, however he doesn't think knowledge is unobtainable; on the contrary, he thinks that the search for knowledge is of the utmost importance.

It is worth noting that ethics for Socrates was not the good versus evil of Christian morality, with its commands and prohibitions; it seems that there was no idea of evil in the Greek way of thinking. Socrates believed that if you knew the true nature of things then you could not help being good.

The Socratic Method is a way to examine a subject by repeated questioning about it. For example, Socrates wanted to know what justice was, so he went to the courts and asked lawyers and judges, but all he could get was examples of justice, nobody could give him a definition. The same problem occurred when he asked people what virtue was. This method is good, however, for the elimination of bad hypothesis, and for identifying people's underlying beliefs and the extent of their knowledge.

He believed the best way for people to live was to focus on the pursuit of virtue rather than the pursuit, for instance, of material wealth. He also was not a great fan of democracy, because the leaders that he put questions to did not seem to him to be very wise. He came to the conclusion that the philosopher was the type of person best suited to govern others.

His famous maxim – "The unexamined life is not worth living" – shows that he was interested in knowledge, and that, before looking at the relationship between the citizen and the state, we need to know what 'we' are. He understood that the problem of knowledge, the problem of conduct and the problem of governance are all interconnected.

He was finally arrested and put on trial at the age of 71, the main charge being that of 'corrupting the youth of Athens'. When found guilty he was given the choice under Athenian law to propose some lesser penalty than death, and then the judges had to choose between the death penalty demanded by the prosecution and the lesser one suggested by the prisoner. Obviously, it would be advantageous for the prisoner to suggest a fairly harsh lesser penalty in order to sway the judges to forgo the death sentence. Socrates, however, angered the judges by proposing that he receive a wage paid by the government and free dinners for the rest of his life. He knew the consequences, but he didn't want to make concessions that would seem to acknowledge his guilt.

He didn't seem to fear his death. He says that death is either a dreamless sleep (which is plainly good) or the soul migrates to another world, where he hopes he would be able to converse with and question the great names of the past. There seems no doubt that in life he claimed to be guided by an oracle of some sort, also that he believed in some form of immortality (but that was probably the norm for that era). He never doubted, however, that the world was rational. He was put to death by being made to drink the poison hemlock, and in death he has thus achieved his own immortality by attaining the status of a martyr for philosophy.

Socrates could have chosen exile, or even escaped with the help of friends. He chose, however, to drink the hemlock because he had devoted his life to the search for truth and the rule of law, and if the law found him guilty then it was only right to obey the law.

Legacy

Bertrand Russell makes a slight criticism of the Socratic method by saying that a question such as 'what is justice?' is eminently suitable for this style of dialogue because we can examine the way we use words like 'just' and 'unjust'. But, he says, when our enquiry is concluded, we have only made a linguistic discovery, not an ethical one. This is perhaps a little harsh. Yes, words are mental models, human constructions which are only defined by more words, and as Socrates demonstrated exact definitions of ideas are not easily attainable, but meaning can also be conveyed by context as well as by definition. And anyway, as Russell really knew, it is the process of sceptical questioning that is the important activity.

Interestingly, although he wasn't that enamoured with physical speculation himself, the Socratic Method of questioning has actually become the bedrock of our modern scientific method, whereby hypotheses are examined, and better ones are found, by the elimination of those that lead to contradictions.

Socrates exerted a strong influence on philosophers both in later antiquity and in the modern era. Depictions of Socrates in art, literature and popular culture have made him one of the most widely known figures in the Western philosophical tradition.

To this day, different versions of the Socratic Method are still used in classrooms and law schools: discourse to expose underlying issues in both subject and the speaker. And the Socratic Method has often been considered as a defining element of American legal education.

11

Plato

Introduction

Plato (428 B.C. – 347 B.C.) is one of the two giants of ancient philosophy (the other being Aristotle). There is no real way to concisely summarise Plato's work in just a few pages, his output is huge, he wrote at least 25 major works, some of which were subdivided into smaller works called books. His famous work **The Republic** for instance is divided into 10 separate books. Many of his works are written in the form of dialogues, usually involving the character of Socrates taking part in question-and-answer sessions. His legacy is massive; it spreads down through the years influencing philosophical and religious thought for centuries after his death.

It can be quite difficult to read his works through by themselves, trying to follow the long, protracted arguments involved. As with many philosophers, it is probably easier to approach Plato via a combination of his own works together with commentary from other people, the more different perspectives the better.

The approach taken here is to split his work into a few separate sub-headings, and summarise the main ideas in each, concentrating on those areas that are perhaps most interesting. It should be noted, however, that the sub-headings chosen do not correspond to individual works or books by Plato, the ideas involved are spread throughout his works.

Before starting, however, here is a general observation, one that harps back to chapter 3 on epistemology (the theory of knowledge). As stated before, there are two main schools of thought in philosophy: -

- **Empiricism** – all knowledge starts with the senses.
- **Rationalism** – all knowledge starts with the mind.

We saw from chapter 3 that Hume is the embodiment of the **empiricist** position, and Descartes (with his "I think therefore I am" statement) is an example of the **rationalist** approach. Plato is firmly in the **rationalist** camp, (although those definitions were not in use at that time).

Background

There is some dispute as to the exact year of Plato's birth, but most historians use 428 B.C. as the date. He was born into an aristocratic family during the time of the Peloponnesian war, and was a young man when Athens was defeated by the Peloponnesian league which was led by Sparta.

Plato was a bright child and was given a good education by his wealthy parents. As a youth he became a pupil of Socrates, who he loved and respected. The fact that Socrates was put to death by a democracy, taken together with his own aristocratic birth, and the defeat of democratic Athens by Sparta (a monarchy); combined to give Plato his strong dislike for democracy.

He spent some time travelling in Sicily, Italy, and North Africa, returning to Athens when he was about forty. Then, in 387 B.C. he founded his Academy on an area of land not far from Athens; this was the first institution of higher learning in the Western world.

In later life, Plato became entangled with the politics of the city of Syracuse. Plato initially visited Syracuse while it was under the rule of Dionysius, but the tyrant himself turned against Plato. Plato almost faced death, but instead was sold into slavery. Anniceris, a Cyrenaic philosopher, subsequently bought Plato's freedom and sent him home. There are different reports of his eventual death, but it seems probable that he just died in his sleep around the age of 81.

In his philosophy, his influences were the previous philosophers Pythagoras, Parmenides, Heraclitus, and Socrates. From Pythagoras he derived his respect for mathematics; his mystical beliefs in the immortality of the soul; and his otherworldliness outlook. Heraclitus taught that all things are continuously changing, or becoming, as in a river with ever changing waters, but Parmenides argued that all change is an illusion. These ideas about change and permanence, or becoming and being, influenced Plato in formulating his theory of Forms (see below). And from Socrates he derived his deep interest with ethical problems.

Philosophy

Plato's Politics

In his main work, **The Republic**, Plato lays out his concept of utopia. It must be said that his ideas in this area are somewhat on the Conservative side (that's Conservative with a capital C). This is understandable, perhaps, when you remember he was born into an aristocracy, he was used to the idea of owning slaves, and he was a young man when Athens was defeated, which he attributed to it being weakly ruled as a democracy. [Politics at that time was concerned with the city state model, which is very different from today's world of large countries and international economics. Note also that democracy then only included male citizens; women and slaves had no vote.]

Plato proposes that societies should have a tripartite class structure, one which, he says, corresponds to the appetite/spirit/reason structure of the individual soul. The appetite, spirit and reason are then analogous to the three castes of society: -

- **Productive** (The Workers) — the labourers, carpenters, plumbers, masons, merchants, farmers, ranchers, etc. These correspond to the "appetite" part of the soul.
- **Protective** (The Warriors or Guardians) — those who are adventurous, strong, and brave, in the armed forces. These correspond to the "spirit" part of the soul.
- **Governing** (The Rulers or Philosopher Kings) — those who are intelligent, rational, self-controlled, in love with wisdom, well suited to make decisions for the community. These correspond to the "reason" part of the soul and are very few.

He sees this as mostly hereditary but does concede that any child showing potential could be moved up to the next level, or in the opposite direction if necessary. There was a lot of Spartan influence in these ideas, where children were trained hard for their role from an early age. The main problem Plato envisaged was how to make sure the warrior-guardians would carry out the intentions of the philosopher-rulers, and so he spends a lot of time detailing educational and religious proposals to ensure the structure of his utopia.

Much of The Republic is concerned with defining the idea of 'justice'. And Plato's conclusion is that it consists of everybody doing his own job, without interfering with the other classes. Our modern idea of justice is more to do with equality, but the ancient Greek idea was more concerned with property rights in law. It may be the case that an exact translation of their idea is not possible because we don't have separate words that fit their different nuances.

Plato's Cosmology

This is set forth in the work called **Timaeus** which, it should be noted, is the only one of Plato's dialogues that was known in the West in the Middle Ages, and hence was extremely influential to the philosophical and religious thinking at that time. Unfortunately, however, according to Russell, it contains more ideas that are simply silly than are to be found in his other writings. As philosophy this work is unimportant, he says, it only becomes interesting due to its historical influence.

The work is a rather rambling collection of much of the popular Greek thinking from that time. The world must have been created by God, but this differs from the Christian creation in that God did this by bringing order to pre-existing disordered material. The world is made of four elements: fire, air, water, and earth. Time came into existence when God made the sun, and he made one soul for each star. If a man lives well, he goes to death to live happily in his star, but if he lives badly, he will, in the next life, be a woman, and if she persists in evil doing she will become a brute.

We don't have time here to consider this more fully, but here is Bertrand Russell's summary: -

> 'Death is the separation of the soul and the body. Here we see Plato's dualism: between reality and appearance, ideas and sensible objects, reason and perception, soul and body. These pairs are connected: the first in each pair is superior to the second, both in reality and goodness. An ascetic morality was the natural consequence of this dualism, the philosopher should not care for eating any more than is necessary or for money etc, he should try to get away from the body and turn to the soul. The body is a hindrance to the acquisition of knowledge; sight and hearing are inaccurate witnesses; true existence is revealed in thought'.

For instance, Plato says that we perceive *through* the eyes and ears, rather than with them. Russell goes on to strongly criticise this **rationalist** approach, he is firmly in the **empirical** camp, along with Hume.

Plato's Theory of Forms or Ideas

This is one of the most interesting parts of Plato, and it rests on the distinction he sees between reality and appearance. He builds here upon the teachings of Parmenides, but he then adds a religious tone to reality stemming from Pythagoras, which Russell says, produced "a very powerful synthesis that influenced most of the great philosophers, down to and including Hegel".

Plato introduces these ideas in **The Republic**, but they also appear throughout his other works. He makes a distinction between a man who loves beautiful things and another man who loves the concept of beauty. Particular things can be both beautiful and not beautiful, and hence combine contradictory characters, therefore, he says, particular things are not real. The reason he gives for this is that opinions about the world come through our senses, but knowledge (e.g. the concept of beauty) comes from a different realm, which, he holds, is eternal.

This is known as his theory of 'forms', which is partly logical and partly metaphysical. Take the word cat, for example. This is obviously something different from any specific cat, it must, therefore, refer to some sort of universal cattiness, something eternal that has no position in time or space. That much is a logical and linguistic point, and we could have a good discussion about that aspect of Plato's theory.

The metaphysical element comes in, however, when Plato claims that 'cat' means a certain ideal cat, '*the* cat', which was created by God and is unique. Particular cats partake of the nature of this ideal (or universal) cat, but only more or less imperfectly, thus the ideal cat is real and particular cats are only *apparent*. Of course, the same applies to everything in the world, including people.

Plato then, to make this idea clearer, gives us his (now famous) simile of the cave. You have to imagine that there are some prisoners in a cave, and that they are only able to look at the wall of the cave in front of them. On the wall they see shadows cast by a fire behind them. These are shadows of objects situated behind the prisoners, i.e. between them and the fire; there are also shadows of themselves on the wall. Plato says that they will inevitably regard all these shadows as real and will have no knowledge of the actual objects from which they are due.

This is intended to show that if we see a cat, for instance, in the street, what we are actually seeing is not real, it is only a shadow of the ideal or universal cat. Knowledge, for Plato, is being aware of this ideal cat, and this can be obtained only through introspection and understanding gained via the light of the internal soul, a bit like a prisoner brought out of the cave into the sunlight. [Referring back to chapter 3 on epistemology (the theory of knowledge), even though Plato considered knowledge to be 'justified true belief', he also believed the soul knows things intuitively.]

To us, although there are problems with the metaphysical elements of these arguments, there is no getting away from the fact that we all use universals: – words like 'man', 'cat' and 'chair', and relational words like 'similar' and 'before'. These obviously have meaning even though they are not individual particular objects. Russell comments that this was a very important advance in philosophy because Plato's theory of 'forms' was the first real work to emphasize the problem of universals, a problem which, in various forms, has persisted to the present day.

Plato revisited his ideas in a later work called **Parmenides**, where he seems to acknowledge some of the logical inconsistencies of his theory. But although discussing it through, no definite conclusion is reached, and his theory of ideas is definitely not abandoned.

Legacy

Plato's contribution to metaphysics, logic, language, mathematics, ethics, and politics has been just as great. He really was the father of philosophy, and unfortunately, there isn't space to do him full justice in this short introduction.

Regarding Plato's 'forms', the historian Peter Watson notes that, the Platonic idea that there is a different realm, a superior realm, a more real realm, in existence somewhere, has resonated down the years, and influenced much in the way of both Christian and spiritualist thinking in Western culture since then.

As we will see, the metaphysical side of Plato's work was picked up by the philosopher Plotinus, and then this in turn was expanded upon by both St. Augustine and St. Thomas Aquinas when they began to define the early tenets of Christian thinking.

Also note that the use of the Socratic method of questioning and dialogue is great when discussing something logically but is not as much use in scientific discovery where one wants to establish new facts. In this respect, both Socrates and Plato tended to limit themselves.

Platonism (sometimes distinguished from Plato's particular view by the lowercase) refers to the view that there are many abstract objects. Still to this day, Platonists take number and the truths of mathematics as the best support in favour of this view. Most mathematicians think, like Platonists, that numbers and the truths of mathematics are perceived by reason rather than the senses yet exist independently of minds and people, that is to say, they are discovered rather than invented.

The Stanford Encyclopaedia of Philosophy says that Plato "was not the first thinker or writer to whom the word "philosopher" should be applied. But he was so self-conscious about how philosophy should be conceived, and what its scope and ambitions properly are, and he so transformed the intellectual currents with which he grappled, that the subject of philosophy, as it is often conceived—a rigorous and systematic examination of ethical, political, metaphysical, and epistemological issues, armed with a distinctive method—can be called his invention. Few other authors in the history of Western philosophy approximate him in depth and range."

12

Aristotle

Introduction

Aristotle (384 B.C. – 322 B.C.) was, according to Russell, the last of the great Greek philosophers, and that 'it would be two thousand years before the world produced another philosopher who could be regarded as his equal'.

It was Aristotle's habit to teach philosophy while walking about in the Lyceum in Athens, and we get our word **peripatetic** from here, which derives from the Greek word for walking up and down. You might be familiar with the term a 'peripatetic teacher', i.e. one who travels between different schools or colleges rather than being based in one location.

In general, Aristotle immersed himself in empirical studies and shifted from Platonism to empiricism, believing that concepts and knowledge were ultimately based on perception. He was a great classifier of knowledge, ordering things into categories and subcategories. He compiled a huge amount of observational data, especially in the field of biology, indeed he could really be considered the first real scientist because he identified and documented about 500 different species of birds, mammals, and fishes. His views on physical science went on to profoundly shape medieval scholarship, and their influence extended into the Renaissance period. Indeed, they were not really replaced systematically until the age of the Enlightenment.

Much of Aristotle's work was lost to the West after the fall of the Roman Empire. What we now have we owe to the safe keeping of Arab philosophers, but it is thought that only about a third of his original output has survived.

Background

Little is known about his life. He was born in the city of Stagira in Northern Greece. His father, Nicomachus (a physician to the king of Macedonia), died when Aristotle was a child, and he was brought up by a guardian.

He came to Athens at the age of 18, and there became a pupil of Plato, remaining in the Academy for nearly twenty years until Plato's death. A few years later he became tutor to Alexander who was then thirteen, and continued in that position until Alexander was appointed regent at the age of sixteen. Russell makes light of this however, believing that there is little evidence they had much influence on each other.

From 335 B.C. to 323 B.C. (when Alexander died) Aristotle lived in Athens, and it was in this period that he founded his school, called the Lyceum, and wrote most of his books. At the death of Alexander, the Athenians rebelled and turned on his friends, including Aristotle. Unlike Socrates, he fled to avoid punishment, but then died in the next year. When asked why he left Athens he replied, "so that this city will not sin against philosophy a second time".

Those works of his that have survived are in treatise form and were not, for the most part, intended for widespread publication; they are generally thought to be lecture aids for his students.

Philosophy

Aristotle's Politics

His ideas in this area are, like Plato, largely governed by the city state model, the dominant political structure at that time. However, where Plato was more dogmatic, with his utopia ruled by philosopher/kings, Aristotle was more academic, laying out, discussing, and categorising several different possible forms of government.

He said three types of government were possible: – a **Royalty**, an **Aristocracy,** or a **Constitutional Government**. A government is good when it aims at the good of the whole community and through discussing these three types, he thinks that Royalty is better than Aristocracy and Aristocracy better than a Constitutional Government. However, when government becomes bad, Royalty turns into Tyranny, Aristocracy turns into Oligarchy and a Constitutional Government turns into a Democracy. Tyranny is then worse than Oligarchy and Oligarchy worse than Democracy. In this way Aristotle arrives at a qualified defence of democracy. He also defends democracy with the thought that you get more wise thoughts from 100 people than from one, and any flaws will be identified and cancelled out.

Again, it should be remembered that the Greek idea of democracy from that time is different from our current concept. Rather than elections being held, citizens would be chosen for office by lot, and citizen, of course, did not include women or slaves. Also, as Russell says, 'the aim of the state was to produce cultured gentlemen – men who combine the aristocratic mentality with love of learning and the arts.'

Aristotle's work on politics also contains a number of general observations, such as the statement that "Law is reason without passion", and the idea that things have two uses, a proper one and an improper one. A shoe for instance may be worn, which is proper, but it may also be sold, which is improper. In this way, trade in general is looked down upon, and lending money is even worse.

He also has a few, to our way of thinking, odd notions, but these were probably the norms for that culture at that time. For instance, people should not marry too young, because if they do so the children will be weak and female, and the wives will become wanton. The right age for marriage is thirty-seven for men and eighteen for women!

Physics and Metaphysics

Aristotle thought that everything was made from five substances: Earth, Water, Air and Fire (like Plato) but he introduces as a fifth element called Aether, which, he says, is a divine substance that makes up the heavenly spheres and heavenly bodies (i.e. stars and planets).

He makes a distinction between **form** and **matter**, but his **form** is not the 'ideal' form of Plato, residing in some other realm. It is that which makes a thing a separate thing, e.g. for a marble statue, marble is its matter, but its shape is its form. One of his examples is: - if you take some wax and give it a particular shape using a mould or stamp; there is no shape without the wax, but at the same time the shape is not the same thing as the wax that forms it. By analogy, in the case of a man, it is his soul that makes the body one thing with its own unity of purpose. In this doctrine, bare matter is conceived as a potentiality of form, and all change leaves the thing in question as having more form than before. God is pure form or pure actuality, and everything is in development towards something better that it was before.

Aristotle disagreed with Plato on the idea of universals; he says that universals reside within the thing being referred to. Whereas Plato says that there is an ideal cat and that specific cats are just an imitation or shadow of this ideal cat, Aristotle says that the notion of 'cattiness' is a property, or attribute of, the specific cat in question, as would be, for instance, its whiteness. Russell, while acknowledging the difficulties of Plato's concept of ideals, says that Aristotle's 'common sense' approach does not really address the problem with universals like 'cat' and 'white', or relational words like 'similar' and 'before'. For Russell this was still a problem, but one that was tied up with the way we perceive the world and with our use of language.

Aristotle also introduces a new attribute of things, and that is their **essence**, which is "what they are by their very nature" (i.e. those properties that can't be lost without changing or destroying the thing). He uses the analogy of the eye saying that the eye is not the same thing as 'seeing', but you can't see without an eye, and if the eye cannot see then it is not an eye, therefore the essence of the eye is 'seeing'. Russell, however, finds this a rather 'muddled-headed notion', mainly because it can't seem to be precisely defined.

Another famous conception of his is that of causality: he identifies four different types of cause, any of which could be simultaneously active within a given event.

- **Material cause** – describes the material out of which something is composed. Thus, the material cause of a table is wood.

- **Formal cause** – is the arrangement of matter in a thing. Its form, pattern, and essence; also, the idea existing in the first place (as in an idea in the mind of the sculptor for instance).

- **Efficient cause** – is "the primary source", or that agent or agency, or particular state of affairs that brings about the change, e.g. take two dominoes, the first falling over makes the second fall over. [Note that today, this is usually the only idea of 'cause' we still use.]

- **Final cause** – is its purpose, or the reason why a thing exists. The final cause or '**teleos**' is the purpose or function that something is supposed to serve. [This covers modern ideas of motivating causes, such as volition, need, desire or ethics.]

Although not that religious, he identifies God as the unmoved mover in the sense of the final cause of all activity. God exists as pure thought, happiness, and complete self-fulfilment, so while the sensible world is imperfect, all things are moved to action by love of God and in the direction of greater form.

Aristotle makes a further distinction between the mind and the soul. He holds that the mind is higher than the soul and less bound to the body. The mind is the part of us that understands mathematics and philosophy, and hence is timeless, it has (he says) no relation to the body or the senses. The soul (which as noted is more to do with his concept of form) has three parts, vegetative (which is found in everything, including plants), appetitive (which exists in all animals) and rational (which consists of contemplation and the movement towards complete happiness, although that is not fully attainable in man). The immortality of the mind is not a personal immortality of separate men but a share of God's immortality, so, in as far as men are rational, they partake in the divine.

Ethics

Aristotle's approach to ethics is an example of what today is called Virtue Ethics, the aim of which is to figure out how to achieve living a good life, because once you have become a good person, good actions will follow. For this, one needs three things: virtue, practical wisdom, and eudaimonia. Eudaimonia is often translated as happiness but that is inadequate, it is more to do with fulfilling one's unique function, and for humans this involves using reason (which is something unique to us). Hence doing philosophy is an important part of achieving a good life.

This is a somewhat different approach to ethics than usual. Instead of attempting to become the right kind of person by working out what actions to perform, you aim to become a good person first and then good actions will follow.

Aristotle considered ethics to be a practical rather than theoretical study, i.e. one aimed at becoming good and doing good, rather than knowing for its own sake. He wrote several treatises on ethics, three of which survive today, including his famous ***Nicomachean Ethics***. In this he describes three types of a happy life: a life dedicated to vulgar pleasure; a life dedicated to fame and honour; and a life dedicated to contemplation.

He taught that virtue has to do with the proper function of a thing. An eye is only a good eye in so much as it can see, because the proper function of an eye is sight. Aristotle reasoned that humans must have a function specific to humans, and that this function must be an activity of the soul in accordance with reason. The optimum activity of the soul is happiness or wellbeing, and to have the potential of ever being happy in this way necessarily requires a good character. This requires a first stage of developing good habits, instilled by teachers and experience, leading to a later stage in which one consciously chooses to do the best things. When the best people come to live life this way their practical wisdom and their intellect can develop towards the highest possible human virtue, and they can become a philosopher.

He identified four cardinal virtues that men should cultivate: -

1. **Prudence** – also known as practical wisdom.
2. **Temperance** – or self-control, simply meaning moderation.
3. **Courage** – moderation or observance of the mean with respect to feelings of fear and confidence.
4. **Justice** – recognizing what is good for the community.

One of his famous ethical doctrines is that of the 'golden mean'. Every virtue is a mean between two extremes, each of which is a vice, e.g. pride between vanity and humility, or wit between buffoonery and boorishness. Russell comments, however, that not all virtues seem to fit this pattern, for instance it is hard to see how truthfulness can be accommodated into this analysis.

Aristotle linked his ethics to his whole understanding of human life and saw man as both a thinking animal and a political animal. His ethics, therefore, becomes a study of rational choice in action and thus has a social as well as an individual aspect, unlike Plato's ethics, for instance, which have a mystical or religious element.

Russell asks the question: - "Can we regard as morally satisfactory a community which, by its essential constitution, confines the best things to a few, and requires the majority to be content with the second best?" He then continues with: -

> "Plato and Aristotle say yes, and Nietzsche agrees with them. Stoics, Christians, and democrats say no. But there are great differences in their ways of saying no. Stoics and early Christians consider that external circumstances cannot prevent a man from being virtuous; there is therefore no need to seek a just social system, since social injustice affects only unimportant matters. The democrat, on the contrary, holds that, at least as far as politics are concerned, the most important goods are power and property; he cannot, therefore, accept a social system which is unjust in these respects."

Aristotle takes the view that virtues are a means to an end, i.e. human happiness. Christians, however, hold that, while the consequences of virtuous actions are in general good, they are not as good as the virtuous actions themselves, which should be valued on their own account, and not on account of their effects.

Russell also makes one other, somewhat damning, comment on Aristotle's ethical writings. He says that: -

> "There is an emotional poverty there, which is not found in earlier philosophers, something unduly smug and comfortable. Everything that makes men feel a passionate interest in each other seems to be forgotten. He leaves out the whole sphere of human experience with which religion is concerned."

Although perhaps mainly relevant to the culture of his time, Aristotle's ethical writings (despite Russell's concerns) went on to become a major influence on medieval European and early Islamic cultures, and his *Nicomachean Ethics* is still considered to be relevant to philosophers today.

Logic

This was the field in which Aristotle's influence was probably the greatest; he made huge advances over all his predecessors (including Plato) and his supremacy survived through the Middle Ages right up to the start of the modern era. His major contribution was a section of logic called **syllogisms**, an area we touched on in chapter 3 (on the theory of knowledge) and chapter 4 (on philosophical arguments). A syllogism is an argument consisting of three parts, a major premise, a minor premise, and a conclusion. For example: -

All men are mortal (major premise)
Socrates is a man (minor premise)
Therefore: Socrates is mortal (conclusion).

There are several different types of syllogism, and mathematicians give them different names to identify them. There is not space to go into detail of the differences here, but just give you a couple more examples, the first is more general than specific, and the second deals with negatives: -

All men are mortal (major premise)
All Greeks are men (minor premise)
Therefore: all Greeks are mortal (conclusion)

No fish are rational (major premise)
All sharks are fish (minor premise)
Therefore: no sharks are rational (conclusion)

Aristotle documented some of these different types, although he missed quite an important logical distinction in that he thought using the name 'Socrates' was the same as using the group name 'Greeks'. One is an individual item but the other is a set of items, and a set may contain many, one or even zero elements, making the logic somewhat more involved. He was very aware that syllogisms were deductive logic, and that there was another branch of logic to do with induction (again mentioned in chapter 3 on knowledge). Also, he wrote quite a lot on how to trust the premises in the first place. Having said that, Russell still says he relies a little too much on syllogisms.

His other main contribution to logic was that of **Categories**. He identifies ten ways in which you can categorise things: substance, quantity, quality, relation, place, time, position, state, action, and affection. This was an important advance in structuring knowledge about the world, and again was very influential to later thinkers. [When we come to look at Kant, for instance he talks about some errors in philosophy as being 'category errors'.] Russell, however, is less convinced. Why ten he asks, what is the origin of these categories and what is the definition of a category in the first place?

Aristotle's Poetics

Aristotle also wrote a lot about poetry and literature. His *Poetics* has been a central document in the study of aesthetics and literature for centuries, proving especially influential during the Renaissance. The *Poetics* is Aristotle's attempt to explain the basic problems of art. He both defines art and offers criteria for determining the quality of a given artwork. He is less interested in the abstract "existence" of art than he is in looking at specific artworks by specific playwrights. Art, he says, is both good and useful, no matter how philosophers like Plato try to dismiss it.

The *Poetics* seeks to address: - different kinds of poetry; the structure of a good poem; and the division of a poem into its component parts. Aristotle defines poetry as a 'medium of imitation' that seeks to represent or duplicate life through character, emotion, or action. His definition of poetry is very broad, including epic poetry, tragedy, comedy, dithyrambic poetry, and even some kinds of music.

According to Aristotle, tragedy came from the efforts of poets to present men as 'nobler,' or 'better' than they are in real life. Comedy, on the other hand, shows a 'lower type' of person, and reveals humans to be worse than they are on average. Epic poetry, however, imitates 'noble' men like tragedy, but only has one type of meter - unlike tragedy, which can have several.

He then tackles the question of whether the epic or tragic form is 'higher.' Most critics of his time argued that tragedy was for an inferior audience that required the gesture of performers, while epic poetry was for a 'cultivated audience' which could understand a narrative form through their own imaginations. But Aristotle notes that epic poetry can be marred by overdone gesticulation in the same way as a tragedy; moreover, tragedy, like poetry, can produce its effect without action. He says that tragedy is superior to epic because it has all the epic elements as well as spectacle and music.

Legacy

The above has only scratched the surface of the breadth and depth of Aristotle's thinking. Other writings of his, not mentioned, include works on, among other things, geology, motion, optics, medicine, psychology, memory, sleep, and dreams. He is undoubtedly one of the greatest philosophers in the Western tradition.

It was from his teachings that the West inherited its intellectual lexicon, as well as its methods of inquiry. As a result, his philosophy has exerted a unique influence on almost every form of knowledge in the West, and it continues to be a subject of contemporary philosophical discussion today.

A few years before Aristotle, Hypocrites (a pupil of Pythagoras, and known as the father of medicine) brought a new vision of disease as being body based and biological rather than punishment from the gods. He called his method empirical, and Aristotle advanced this view as well. This was immensely influential to later thinkers and lead to a more scientific outlook about the world in general.

For Aristotle, knowledge is something acquired via the senses, placing him firmly in the empiricist camp, as opposed to Plato, a rationalist, who thought knowledge starts with the mind. The differences between these two approaches (as we will see) are argued over down the ages even to the present day.

In terms of ethics, the Stanford Encyclopaedia of Philosophy notes that Aristotle's influence is seen in the resurgence of virtue ethics which began in the last half of the twentieth century. Also, a quick search of the Stanford Encyclopaedia turns up more Aristotle references than any other philosopher or philosophical movement. Only Plato comes close.

13

Epicurus

Introduction

Epicurus (341 B.C. – 270 B.C.) was the founder of the school of philosophy called Epicureanism. He taught that the purpose of philosophy was to attain the happy, tranquil life, characterized by peace, freedom from fear and the absence of pain. He and his small community of followers and friends lived a simple, self-sufficient life. He suffered all his life from bad health, but he learnt to endure it with fortitude.

Background

Epicurus was born on the Greek island of Samos to Athenian parents. He grew up during the final years of the Greek Classical Period, Plato having died seven years before Epicurus was born. As a boy, he studied philosophy for four years under the Platonist teacher Pamphilus. Then, at the age of eighteen, he went to Athens for his two-year term of military service.

After that he re-joined his family (who were now living in Turkey) and there he studied under Nausiphanes, who followed the teachings of Democritus. Epicurus never seemed to have much respect for his teachers, but his mature philosophy owes more to Democritus than any other philosopher. He returned to Athens in 306 B.C. where he remained until his death, and there he founded *The Garden*, a school named for the garden he owned that served as the school's meeting place.

His school was the first of the ancient Greek philosophical schools to admit women as a rule rather than an exception, and it is recorded that an inscription on the gate to The Garden read: "Stranger, here you will do well to tarry; here our highest good is pleasure". Epicurus emphasized friendship as an important ingredient of happiness, and the school resembled in many ways a community of friends living together. However, he also instituted a hierarchical system of levels among his followers and had them swear an oath not to change any of his teachings.

Epicurus wrote over 300 works, but the only original writings of his that remain are just a few letters, some fragments, and a statement of "Principal Doctrines". The main source we have that describes his philosophy comes from a long, six volume poem called *De Rerum Natura* (On the Nature of Things) written some 200 years later by the Roman poet Lucretius. This looks to be accurate because wherever it can be compared to the actual fragments it always agrees completely. Indeed, we are actually very lucky to still have this poem, because Atomism was viciously persecuted as heresy throughout the early Christian era, and only one copy of this manuscript survived the flames.

It is reported that he died a slow and painful death in 270 B.C. at the age of seventy-two from a stone blockage of his urinary tract. Despite being in immense pain, however, Epicurus is said to have remained cheerful and to have continued to teach until the very end.

Philosophy

Epicurus's epistemology bears an unacknowledged debt to the later writings of Aristotle who rejected the Platonic rationalism and instead relied on nature and empirical evidence for knowledge about the universe. Also, during Epicurus's formative years, Greek knowledge about the rest of the world was rapidly expanding and Epicurus's philosophy was consequently more universal in its outlook than those of his predecessors.

Epicurus was a key figure in the development of science and scientific methodology because of his insistence that nothing should be believed, except that which was tested through direct observation and logical deduction. Like Democritus, he was an atomist, believing that the fundamental elements of the world were indivisible, small bits of matter moving through empty space.

He was a materialist but not a determinist, i.e. he believed everything (even the soul) was made of matter in the form of atoms, but he did not believe (as Democritus did) that the atoms are at all times controlled by natural laws. He thought that atoms falling in empty space sometimes swerved slightly from the direct downward path and so would come into contact with other atoms. What made them swerve was, according to Epicurus, something along the lines of free will rather than natural laws. The soul is material and composed of particles (rather like breath and heat) and soul atoms are distributed throughout the body. At death, soul atoms are dispersed and survive, but are no longer capable of sensation because they are no longer connected with the body.

As for the gods, Epicurus believes in their existence since he cannot otherwise account for the widespread existence of the idea of gods. But he thinks that they do not interfere with human affairs, they just want the good life themselves. Storms, earthquakes, and the like are entirely of natural origin, and any form of religion, worship, divination, or belief in fate is purely superstitious, therefore there is no ground to fear that we will incur the anger of the gods. In one of his letters, he writes: -

> "It is not the man who denies the gods worshipped by the multitude, who is impious, but he who affirms of the gods what the multitude believes about them."

Lucretius, who lived from 99 BC to 55 BC, was a contemporary of Julius Caesar. He was a passionate but troubled man who suffered bouts of temporary insanity (brought on, it is said, by the pains of love) and committed suicide at the age of 44. Russell comments that he feels towards Epicurus as towards a saviour and applies a language of religious intensity to the man whom he regards as the destroyer of religion.

Here are some extracts from his long poem ***On the Nature of Things***: -

> When prostrate upon earth lay human life
> Visibly trampled down and foully crushed
> Beneath Religion's cruelty...
> ...
> ... first did a man of Greece
> Dare lift up his mortal eyes against her;
> The first was he to stand up and defy her.
> ...
> ... he passed onwards, voyaging far
> Beyond the flaming ramparts of the world,
> Ranging in mind and spirit far and wide
> Throughout the unmeasured universe; and thence
> A conqueror he returns to us, bringing back
> Knowledge both of what can and what cannot
> ...
> Therefore now has Religion been cast down
> Beneath men's feet, and trampled on in turn.

Epicurean Paradox

The "Epicurean paradox" is a version of the problem of evil. It is a three-part argument that says 'if God is omnipotent, and God is good, why then does Evil exists? Or it is more commonly seen as this quote: -

> Is God willing to prevent evil, but not able?
> Then he is not omnipotent.
> Is he able, but not willing?
> Then he is malevolent.
> Is he both able and willing?
> Then whence cometh evil?
> Is he neither able nor willing?
> Then why call him God?

Although this argument has traditionally been attributed to Epicurus, it may not have been written by him. There are several different versions and other Greek authors could well have written it, having said that, however, it does seem to fit with his viewpoint against superstition and religion.

Pleasure as the absence of suffering

For Epicurus, the purpose of philosophy was to help people attain a happy, tranquil life characterized by ataraxia (peace and freedom from fear) and aponia (the absence of pain).

Although he wrote a fair amount about how the world works, his main interest was in how to live the good life. His philosophy is based on the theory that all good and bad derive from the sensations of what he defined as pleasure and pain: What is good is what is pleasurable, and what is bad is what is painful. His ideas of pleasure and pain were ultimately, for Epicurus, the basis for the moral distinction between good and evil. If pain is chosen over pleasure in some cases, it is only because it leads to a greater pleasure.

He has sometimes been misunderstood in that he was thought to advocate the pursuit of pleasure at all costs. Actually, his teachings were more about striving for an absence of pain and suffering, both physical and mental, and for a state of tranquillity that was free of the fear of death and the retribution of the gods. He argued that when we do not suffer pain, we are no longer in need of pleasure. Indeed, he explicitly warned against overindulgence because it often leads to pain.

As mentioned, Epicurus also valued friendship very highly, he held that: -

> "Friendship cannot be divorced from pleasure, and for that reason must be cultivated, because without it neither can we live in safety and without fear, nor even pleasantly".

He also believed (contrary to Aristotle) that death was not to be feared. When a man dies, he does not feel the pain of death because he no longer is and therefore feels nothing. He famously said, "death is nothing to us." By this he means that, when we exist, death is not; and when death exists, we are not. All sensation and consciousness ends with death and therefore in death there is neither pleasure nor pain. The fear of death arises from the belief that in death, there is awareness.

From this doctrine arose the Epicurean epitaph: "I was not; I was; I am not; I do not care", which is inscribed on the gravestones of his followers and seen on many ancient gravestones of the Roman Empire. This quotation is, apparently, often used today at humanist funerals.

As an ethical guideline, Epicurus emphasized minimizing harm and maximizing happiness of both oneself and others: -

> "It is impossible to live a pleasant life without living wisely and well and justly, and it is impossible to live wisely and well and justly without living pleasantly".

The word "Justly" in the above quote meaning: 'to prevent a person from harming others or being harmed by another'. For him justice is an agreement neither to harm nor be harmed and we need to have such a contract in order to enjoy fully the benefits of living together in a well-ordered society. Laws and punishments, he says, are needed to keep misguided fools in line who would otherwise break the contract. But the wise person sees the usefulness of justice, and because of his limited desires, he has no need to engage in conduct prohibited by the laws in any case.

(Note: - this is an early version of the idea of 'the social contract' which we will meet later in both Thomas Hobbs and John Locke.)

Legacy

Epicureanism rapidly spread beyond the Greek mainland and across the Mediterranean world. But although he had many followers, his philosophy was also strongly rejected by others, and he was sometimes portrayed as an ignorant buffoon.

In terms of his legacy, Russell writes that his philosophy survived in diminishing form for around six hundred years. Then, as people went through a period of being increasingly oppressed, they wanted something stronger from their philosophy or religion. Philosophers took refuge in

Neo-Platonism, and the uneducated turned, in increasing numbers, to Christianity, which in its early form placed all good "in the life beyond the grave" – the exact opposite of the ideas of Epicurus!

As mentioned above, very little of his work survived the purges of the Middle Ages and only one copy of Lucretius' poem 'On the Nature of Things' survived. We are fortunate to still have these because, since then, Epicurus's ideas have gone on to inspire great thinkers like John Lock, David Hume, Jeremy Bentham, and Thomas Paine among others, especially so after Lucretius' poem was translated into English.

Thomas Jefferson (1743–1826), one of the Founding Fathers of the United States, declared in 1819, "I too am an Epicurean. I consider the genuine (not imputed) doctrines of Epicurus as containing everything rational in moral philosophy which Greece and Rome have left us."

Karl Marx, as a young man, was influenced by him, as was The British poet Alfred, Lord Tennyson. And Lucretius was one of Shelley's favourite authors.

14

Plotinus

Introduction

Plotinus (205 – 270) is widely considered the father of **Neo-Platonism**. Writing some six hundred years after Plato he was well versed in the philosophy of both Plato and Aristotle, to which he added several of his own ideas and interpretations, creating the philosophy that has since become known as Neo-Platonism. He is not as original as either Plato or Aristotle, and his philosophy is not as wide ranging in terms of subjects covered, but what he did achieve was to provide a more systematic structure to those parts of Platonism concerned with cosmology and metaphysics.

It is difficult, however, to reduce Neo-Platonism to a concise set of ideas that all Neo-Platonist philosophers hold in common. While they generally share some basic assumptions about the nature of reality, there are also considerable differences in their views and approaches.

Neo-Platonism is often considered as a bridge from Greek philosophy to modern Christianity. Although at the time Plotinus rejected early Christianity as being superstitious, later Christian thinkers drew heavily on his work.

Background

We have little direct knowledge of the life of Plotinus; much of our biographical information about him comes from the preface to Porphyry's edition of Plotinus' *Enneads*. Although Plotinus lived through difficult and dangerous times for the Roman Empire, he made no reference to this in his works, he turned aside from the misery of the world to contemplate the eternal world of goodness and beauty. Russell calls him the last of the great philosophers of antiquity, he also (rather engagingly) describes him as a 'melancholy optimist'. Originally from Alexandria, he moved to Rome at the age of forty, and there he began to teach. Apparently, he then wrote nothing until the age of forty-nine, but thereafter he wrote extensively.

His works were edited and arranged by Porphyry, who was, a student of Plotinus, a fellow teacher, a friend, and critic of him. Russell comments that Porphyry was more Pythagorean than Plotinus was and that this: -

> "Caused the Neo-Platonist school to become more super-naturalist than it would have been if it had followed Plotinus more faithfully".

Porphyry took the series of 54 carefully reasoned philosophical essays that Plotinus composed over a fourteen-year period later in his life, and edited and arranged them into a book with six divisions of nine essays each, called the *Enneads* (the nines). Porphyry notes that the Enneads, before being compiled and arranged by himself, were merely the enormous collection of notes and essays which Plotinus used in his lectures and debates.

It is reported the final words of Plotinus were: "Try to raise the divine in yourselves to the divine in the all."

Philosophy

Russell says that Plotinus "has, in many respects, clarified Plato's teaching... His arguments against materialism are good, and his whole conception of the relation of the soul and body are clearer than that of Plato or Aristotle."

Having said that, the *Enneads* only deal with a subsection of Plato, covering: - the theory of ideas; the mystical doctrines; and discussions of love. The political interests, the definitions of different virtues, the interest in mathematics, and above all the playfulness of Plato, are wholly absent.

His revision of Plato takes on board many of the criticisms that Aristotle made. And he reshapes Plato's basic teachings into a new, more rational, and logical metaphysical system.

He agrees with the main tenants of Plato's philosophy, namely: -

1. The non-materiality of the highest form of reality.

2. The belief that there must be a higher level of reality than visible and sensible things.

3. A preference for intellectual intuition over empirical forms of knowing.

An Introduction to Philosophy

4. A belief in some form of immortality.

5. A belief that the universe is essentially good.

Where he differs from Plato is that he is less of a dualist in his thinking, he wants to assert a real identity between the natural and the supernatural, both in man and throughout all of nature.

The Metaphysics of Neo-Platonism

In his metaphysics Plotinus sets out a vision of the logical structure of all being. He identifies a trinity structure to existence: - The One, the Spirit and the Soul. These are not equal, the One is supreme, the Spirit comes next and the Soul last.

The One is the ultimate being, the Supreme. It is: - supernatural, self-caused, absolute free and absolute good. It transcends all things and all we can say of it is that 'it is'. Although sometimes spoken of as the Good we are also told that it precedes both the Good and the Beautiful. It would be a mistake to speak of God as 'the All' because God transcends the All and is present in all things. Since it is absolutely good it extends its goodness and its power into all lower stages of itself (i.e. the Spirit and the Soul) without any loss of its own essence.

We then come to the Spirit, which is the second level of existence. There is some confusion, however, as to which English word to use for this that best matches its translation. Plotinus uses the word '*nous*', and the standard dictionary translation for this is 'mind', however that doesn't have the correct connotations, particularly when the word is used in religious philosophy. If, for instance we were to say that Plotinus put mind above soul that would give completely the wrong impression. One translator uses the phrase 'Intellectual-Principle', but as Russell says, that is awkward, and it doesn't suggest an object suitable for religious veneration.

Most translators use 'Spirit', which is perhaps the best word available, but this leaves out the intellectual element important to Greek philosophy. Mathematics and the world of ideas have, for Pythagoras, Plato and Plotinus, something of the divine about them, and this is implicit in their use of the word 'nous'. Therefore, while continuing with the word 'Spirit', it should be remembered that an intellectual connotation is also implied which is usually absent from our own, current use of the word 'Spirit'.

The One then becomes the many by projecting itself as the nous or Spirit. In its self-quest it has vision, and this seeing is 'nous'. Plato gave the analogy of God as the sun, the light-giver. By pursuing this analogy in Neo-Platonist terms, Spirit may be considered as the light by which the One sees itself. It is possible for us to know the divine mind if we let go of self-will, forget the body, and forget its desires and impulses; what is then left is an image of the Divine Intellect. In the *Enneads* he writes: -

> "We stand towards the Supreme when we hold *nous* pure;
> we know the Divine Mind within, that which gives Being
> and all else of that order."

Thus (comments Russell) when we are 'divinely inspired' we see not only nous but also the One, but we cannot reason or express the vision in words; this comes later. We know we have had a vision when the Soul has taken light. This light is from the Supreme, and is the Supreme; thus, the Soul remains unlit without that vision, but lit, it possesses what it sought. And this is the true end for the Soul, to take that light and to see the Supreme.

Apparently, the experience of 'ecstasy' (or standing outside one's own body) happened frequently to Plotinus, and he became quite poetic about it. Again, from the *Enneads*: -

> "Many times it happened: Lifted out of the body into
> myself; becoming external to all other things and self-
> encentred; beholding a marvellous beauty; then, more
> than ever, assured of community with the loftiest order."

The mention of Soul, a few paragraphs above, brings us to the third and lowest member of Plotinus' trinity. The Soul, although inferior to the Spirit, is the author of all living things; it made the sun and the moon and stars, and the whole visible world. It is an offspring of the Divine Intellect; or a further extension or projection of the One, via the Spirit, into a lower stage of itself. All things in nature, namely all life-forms and all corporeal beings, including man, are Souls, and, as such, they are both in a state of becoming and dependent upon *nous* for the fixed orders of their being.

The Soul has two aspects; one part is the inner soul, which is intent on *nous*, the other faces externally and is concerned with Nature and the world of the senses. Plotinus regards this second aspect as 'the lowest sphere', it emanates from the Soul when it forgets to look upwards towards the Spirit. This doesn't imply a Gnostic view (that the world is evil), he says that the physical world is beautiful and is the abode of blessed spirits, it only implies that it is less good than the intellectual world. Indeed, in a discussion of the Gnostic view (i.e. that the cosmos and its Creator are evil) he admits that some part of that doctrine, such as the hatred of matter, may be due to Plato, but other parts, which do not come from Plato, are untrue.

Russell says that Plotinus' objections to Gnosticism are of two sorts. On the one hand he says that Soul, when it creates the material world, does so from memory of the divine and not because it is fallen; the world of sense, Plotinus thinks, is as good as a sensible world can be. He feels strongly the beauty of things perceived by the senses. The other reason for rejecting Gnosticism is their belief that sun, moon and stars were created by evil spirits (only the soul of man, they held, has any goodness). Plotinus, however, thinks that the heavenly bodies are bodies of God-like beings, immeasurably superior to man. Again, Russell comments that: -

> "There is in the mysticism of Plotinus nothing morose or hostile to beauty. But he is the last religious teacher, for many centuries, of whom this can be said. Beauty, and all the pleasures associated with it, came to be thought to be of the Devil; pagans, as well as Christians, came to glorify ugliness and dirt."

Plotinus says that matter is created by the soul and has no independent reality. When the time is right it descends into the body suitable for it. When the soul leaves the body, if it has been sinful, it must enter another body, for justice requires that it should be punished. If you have murdered your mother, you will, in the next life, be a woman, and be murdered by your son. Sin must be punished, but the punishment happens naturally.

On immortality, Plotinus says that the body is clearly not immortal, but the soul grows towards eternal life, to become one with the *nous*, and as it does this it will slowly forget the memories of our personal life. Aristotle, remember, considered the soul to be the 'form' of the body, but Plotinus rejects this on the grounds that the intellectual act would be impossible if the soul was just the 'form'. For him, the soul is neither matter (as the Stoics and the Atomists thought) nor form; it is Essence, and Essence is eternal. This is implicit in Plato's argument – that the soul is immortal because ideas are eternal; but it is only with Plotinus that this view becomes explicit.

The Soul enters the body through something like appetite. It has the desire of elaborating order on the model of what it has seen in the *nous*. When it lives in the world of pure essence, it is not separated from other souls, but as soon as it becomes joined to a body, it has the task of governing what is lower than itself, so, except for a few moments of enlightenment, it is chained to the body. He holds that 'the body obscures the truth'.

Plotinus

Russell says: -

> "This doctrine, like Plato's, has difficulty in avoiding the view that the creation was a mistake. The soul at its best is content with *nous*, the world of essence; if it were always at its best, it would not create, but only contemplate. It seems that the act of creation is to be excused on the ground that the created world, in its main lines, is the best that is logically possible; but this is a copy of the eternal world, and as such has the beauty that is possible to a copy."

Because the world is a copy, it inevitably has imperfections, and Plotinus (like the Christians) had to account for sin. He says that sin is a consequence of free will, which he upholds against both the determinists and the astrologers. Porphyry tells of a rival philosopher who tried to put evil spells on Plotinus, but the spells rebounded on the rival because Plotinus was so holy and wise. Indeed, although his followers were more superstitious, Plotinus himself was as least superstitious as was possible in that age.

Neo-Platonist believed human perfection and happiness were attainable in this world, without awaiting an afterlife. Perfection and happiness— seen as synonymous— could be achieved through philosophical contemplation. They did not believe in an independent existence of evil. They compared it to darkness, which does not exist in itself but only as the absence of light. So, too, evil is simply the absence of good. Both Plotinus and Porphyry rejected the new religion of Christianity from that time, mainly because of its personalistic brand of supernaturalism and its doctrine of salvation by grace through faith. But their rejection did not prevent later Christian philosophers from importing large elements of Neo-Platonism into their own philosophy.

Legacy

Plotinus is, according to Russell, the end as regards the Greeks, and the beginning as regards Christendom. The work of transmitting what could survive of his philosophy was performed by the Christian philosophers of the last age of Rome. During the centuries which followed the barbarian invasion, western civilisation came near to total destruction, theology was the sole surviving mental activity, and it preserved (though sometimes deeply buried) doctrines which embodied much of the work of the Greek intellect. This made possible the rise in scholastic philosophy, and later, with the Renaissance, it provided the stimulus for the renewed study of Plato and others.

Russell comments, however, that the philosophy of Plotinus also contained a defect; that of encouraging men to look within rather than to look without. When we look within, we see *nous*, which is divine, when we look without, we see the imperfections of the sensible world. This subjectivism brought an end to scientific curiosity, and only virtue was thought important. Plato's idea of virtue included all mental activity, but in later centuries it became seen as only involving the virtuous will. Christianity, in its ethical doctrines, was not free from this defect.

Porphyry, his student, and his successor at the academy, deserves most of the credit for the survival of Neo-Platonism, especially Porphyry's own version of it, and, as noted, his rejection of Christianity didn't stop many later Christian philosophers from adopting large sections of it into their own philosophies. It spread widely through Europe, and then on into England in the late 1400s. This paved the way for the emergence, in the seventeenth century, of a group of Christian Neo-Platonist who became known as the 'Cambridge Platonists'.

It spread wider than just Europe however. Some medieval Jewish thinkers also imported elements of Neo-Platonism into their philosophies. Also, one of Porphyry's own students, Lamblichus, returned to his native Syria around 300 A.D., and set up his own school there teaching Plotinus' version of Platonism, thus spreading these ideas to the Arab world, and from there they later became incorporated into Islamic thinking.

Neo-platonic themes also influenced the German idealists, some French philosophers, especially Bergson, and they can be found in British poets (for example Blake, Shelley, and Keats). They also occur in Emerson and the New England Transcendentalists in America.

The attraction of Neo-Platonism seems to be that it emphasises both reason and experience in its philosophy, and sanctions the idea that human experience may go beyond metaphysics on rare occasions, thus providing a holistic way of thinking.

As noted at the start, however, it is difficult to agree a concise set of ideas that all Neo-platonic philosophers share in common. Over the ages, people have taken from it those elements that attracted them, and in doing so they hoped to adopt the authority of Plato. So, although Neo-Platonism helped to keep alive Greek ideas during the medieval period, it also contributed to, as Russell stated, an end to scientific curiosity for many years.

15

St. Augustine

Introduction

St. Augustine (354 – 430) is known as one of the four Doctors of the early Christian church, the others being St. Ambrose and St. Jerome (who were his contemporaries) and Pope Gregory the Great from some 200 years later. Of these, St. Augustine is the most influential, and many of the doctrines of Western Christianity owe much to his perseverance as a philosopher. In the history of philosophy itself he is a secondary figure, partly (it is said) because he didn't have the taste, or leisure, to acquire more than a scrappy knowledge of the 800-year tradition which preceded him. He is interesting, however, for two reasons, firstly his philosophy did have one or two new ways of looking at the world and man's place within it, and secondly because of his great influence on the direction of Christian thinking.

Ambrose, Jerome and Augustine all lived during that brief period between the victory of the Catholic Church in the Roman Empire and the barbarian invasion; Russell says that it would be nearly a thousand years before Christendom produced men who were their equal in learning and culture. At that time the state itself was not very strong and the Emperors were corrupt and self-serving. **Ambrose** (the bishop of Milan) was eminent as a statesman, and, in several conflicts with the Emperor, he had the popular support of the people and achieved some significant victories. His legacy was in defining the relationship of the Church to the State. As a result of his influence, it became established that there were matters in which the State must yield to the Church. **Jerome**, on the other hand, was more of a scholar, and he is mainly notable as the translator who produced the Vulgate (the Latin version of the bible), which remains today the official Catholic version of the bible.

Background

Augustine was born nine years after Jerome and fourteen years after Ambrose. He was a native of Algeria, and his mother was a Christian, but his father was not. At the age of 16 he left home and moved to Carthage, and by nineteen he was a teacher of rhetoric and had become a Manichaean. This was a widely influential Gnostic religion which taught a radical dualism of good and evil that is grounded in eternal and independent cosmic powers of Light and Darkness. For them, the world is regarded as a mixture of good and evil in which 'spirit' represents Light and 'matter' Darkness. Manichaean morality was severely ascetic. Augustine was also, at this time, addicted to astrology, although he rejected it in later life because it taught that the cause of someone's sin was in the sky, whereas he later believed in free will.

As he read more philosophy, he began to doubt the Manichaean religion, and interestingly, many of his doubts came from science. And as he learned more astronomy, he found that the Manichaean explanations for solstices, equinoxes and eclipses made no sense whatsoever. He says: "I was commanded to believe; and yet it corresponded not with the reasoning obtained by calculations, and my own observations." He took his doubts to a Manichaean bishop, reputedly the most learned member of the sect, but Augustine found him "utterly ignorant of liberal sciences".

He decided to go to Rome to teach, and after a year there (still associating with the Manichaeans) he went to Milan where he met Ambrose. He came to love Ambrose for his kindness and gradually he became converted to the Catholic religion, helped by his mother who had joined him there. Also, in Milan, he first came across Latin translations of the Platonists.

At this time, he already had a mistress who had given him a son, but his mother wanted him to get married. He became engaged to a girl of whom his mother would approve and had to give up his mistress, but, before his marriage could take place, his conversion became complete, and he gave up both his profession as a teacher and his bride. Two years later, at the age of 34, he returned to Algeria where he set up a community of disciples and started writing, and then at 37 he became presbyter, and later Bishop, of Hippo, where he remained until he died.

Augustine's written output (nearly all of which survives) is larger than any other ancient author. He wrote on evil, order, language, and learning, but later in life the subject matter became more polemical. Two works are considered to be his masterpieces, **Confessions** and **City of God**, both written while he was at Hippo, and both have a pastoral purpose. *Confessions* is a public meditation on his own slow road to Catholic Christianity, and *City of God* is an attack (which was to have important historical effect) on the pretentions of pagans to possess a valuable, independent culture. At the end of his life, he also catalogued and reviewed 93 of his works in his *Retractationes*.

St. Augustine

Philosophy

Most of the time Augustine does not occupy himself with pure philosophy, and even when he does, he is (like many Christians after him) constrained by the necessity of agreeing with the scriptures. Where he is original is because of the influence of Plato. The best of his philosophy comes in chapter XI of the *Confessions*, however most popular editions of the *Confessions* stop with chapter X, on the grounds that what follows is uninteresting – being philosophy and not biography!

In chapter XI he is concerned with the creation. In Greek thought: matter is pre-existing, and God's role is to bring order to it; substance is thought to be eternal and uncreated, and God is the artificer or architect rather than a Creator; only 'form' is due to the will of God. The Christian view, expounded in Genesis, is that the world was created from nothing. 'If then God created the world from nothing,' Augustine imagines an objector asking, 'why then did he not create it sooner, or even, as soon as possible?'

Here Augustine becomes original. Genesis is explicit and that is enough for him, so he maintains that God did not create the world sooner because time was created when the world was created, so there was no such thing as 'sooner'. God is eternal in the sense of being timeless, in God there is no before and after, but only the eternal present. He is exempt from time; all time is 'present' to Him at once. He did not precede His own creation of time, for that would imply that He was in time, whereas He stands eternally outside the stream of time. "This leads," says Russell, "to a very admirable relativistic theory of time".

"What then is time?" asks Augustine. "If no one asks me, I know; if I wish to explain to him who asks, I know not." He says that only the present is real, the past is memory and the future expectation, and both of these are aspects, or facts, of the 'present'. There are three times, he says: 'a present of things past (which is memory), a present of things present (which is sight), and a present of thing future (which is expectation)'. He realises, however, that he has not really solved things with this theory, and says "My soul yearns to know this most entangled enigma." But the main idea here is that time is subjective, and it is in the human mind. Russell, although he doesn't agree with this, says that it is a very able theory, and deserves to be taken seriously; indeed, it anticipates Kant's subjective theory of time, and is, in some respects, more clearly stated.

Subjectivism was something that had been slowly growing since early Greek thought, and its emotional component was an obsession with sin, which Augustine fully embraced in his *Confessions*. But on an intellectual side, not only did he anticipate Kant's theory of time, but he also seems to have foreshadowed Descartes' 'I think therefore I am'. In one of

Augustine's books he says: - "You who wish to know, do you know you are? I know it. Whence are you? I know not. Do you feel yourself single or multiple? I know not. Do you feel yourself moved? I know not. Do you know that you think? I do." As a philosopher, he was, when he applied himself, very innovative.

The rest of his philosophy, however, is more Platonic in its influences, and this provided a route to his Christianity by rescuing him from Cicero's scepticism and from the materialism and good-evil dualism of the Manichaean sect. He believed that there were three kinds of substance: bodies, mutable in time and space; souls, incorporeal, but mutable in time; and God, incorporeal and immutable. God makes everything, and it is good. Badness arises from the tendency of things to decay. God illuminates truths as the sun illuminates visible things. The senses do not supply knowledge because their objects are mutable.

Confessions

This book has had famous imitators, particularly Rousseau and Tolstoy. St. Augustine was, like Tolstoy, obsessed in his later years by sin, and this made his non-metaphysical philosophy somewhat inhuman. The book is autobiographical and charts his path to Christianity. One of the first incidents he relates is from his childhood. He and a few friends went into a neighbour's garden and stole some pears from a pear tree. He points out that he was not hungry at the time, and that his parents actually had better pears at home. It would not have been so bad if he had been hungry or if he had had no other means of getting pears; but, as it was, it was an act of pure mischief, inspired by the love of wickedness for its own sake. He pleads with God to forgive him: -

> "Behold my heart, O God, behold my heart, which Thou hadst pity upon in the bottom of the abyss. Now, behold, let my heart tell Thee, what it sought there, that I should be gratuitously wicked, having no temptation to that evil deed, but the evil deed itself. It was foul, and I loved it; I loved to perish, I loved mine own fault, not that for the sake of which I committed the fault, but my fault itself I loved. Foul soul, falling from the firmament to expulsion from Thy presence; not seeking aught through the shame, but the shame itself."

He goes on like this for seven chapters, all about some pears plucked from a tree in a boyhood prank. Russell says that sin was very important to the medieval mind because it explains how a beneficent Deity can come to cause men to suffer. It also increased the power of the Church because no

St. Augustine

one can be saved unless he has first been baptized; this ensures that the Church becomes an intermediary between the soul and God.

He tells how he learned Latin from his mother, but he never really learned Greek even though his schoolmasters beat him. You might think from this that he would favour gentle methods of education, but no, even though they failed to make him learn Greek, the schoolmaster's blows cured him from being wayward and departing from God's laws. He says that even infants at the breast are full of sin, i.e. gluttony, jealousy and other horrible vices.

Further chapters detail his adolescent sins when the 'lusts of the flesh' overcame him, and he resigned himself wholly to the madness of it. This was when he left home to go to Carthage, where he acquired a mistress and had a son with her, both of whom he loved. Later, before his conversion, he became more troubled by these things, and he used to pray: "Give me chastity and continence, only not yet."

It was Augustine's writings that helped shape the early Church's doctrine on original sin. He taught that it was the sin of pride and disobedience to God that made Adam and Eve eat the apple. The tree was a symbol of the order of creation, and self-centeredness made them eat from it, thus not respecting God's creation. They would not have fallen into pride, however, if the devil had not sown into their senses "the root of evil". Their nature was wounded by libido which affects human intelligence and free will, as well as affections and desires, including sexual desire.

City of God

In 410 A.D., when Rome was sacked by the Goths, the pagans attributed the disaster to the Emperor turning away from worshiping Jupiter and other ancient gods. Augustine, then bishop of Hippo in back in Algeria, decided that this pagan argument called for an answer, and so he wrote his book called *City of God*. This took him around fifteen years to fully complete because its focus widened to become a complete Christian scheme of history – past, present, and future. It became an immensely influential book throughout the Middle Ages, especially in the struggles of the Church with secular governments, and its broad conception of a contrast between the City of this world and the City of God has remained, to this day, an inspiration to many.

The book starts with a rebuttal to the argument that turning away from the old gods and towards Christianity was the cause of the sack. It points out that even worse things had happened in the past before the advent of Christianity. Also, during the sack, many people sought sanctuary in the churches, and the Goths, being Christians themselves, respected this. On the other hand, in the sack of Troy for instance, Juno's temple offered no protection, and the gods did not stop the city from being destroyed. Indeed, the Romans never spared any temples in conquered cities.

It continues by saying that any Christians who suffered in the sack had no right to complain for a number of reasons. If any wicked Goths prospered, they will suffer hereafter: if all sin was punished on earth there would be no need of the Last Judgment. Also, if any Christians suffered, if they were virtuous, they would, in the loss of temporal things, lose nothing of value, and they would gain in the hereafter. He next considers the question of virgins who were raped during the sack, and says that they had not lost their virginity because chastity is a virtue of the mind. There was one proviso, however, they must not enjoy it, if they do then they are sinful.

Augustine did not consider the old gods to be only stories, he thought that they existed but that they were devils; they liked to have bad stories told about them because they wanted to dominate the people. He says that "Plato, who would not allow poets to dwell in a well-governed city, showed that his own worth was better than those gods that desire to be honoured with stage plays." The book then continues with many chapters devoted to the sinfulness of Roman imperialism, and the wicked things done by Romans in the past.

The City of God is the society of the elect, and knowledge of God is obtained through Christ. There are some things that can be discovered by reason (as shown by the Greek philosophers) but for all religious knowledge we must rely on the scriptures. He maintains that there is no true virtue apart from true religion, any pagans displaying something that looks like a Christian virtue are actually acting falsely and they have been influenced by devils.

There is also (as in the *Confessions*) a long section on Adam and Eve, and original sin. This leads to a detailed discussion of sexual lust, to which we are subject as part of our punishment for Adam's sin. Intercourse within marriage is not sinful provided the intention is to produce children, but it should be conducted without lust. What is shameful about lust is its independence of the will: virtue, it is held, demands complete control of the will over the body.

Augustine taught that Adam, before the fall, had free will, and could have abstained from sin. But when he and Eve ate the apple, corruption entered into them, and descended to all their posterity, none of whom can, of their own power, abstain from sin. Only God's grace enables men to be virtuous. Hence, we must be baptized, and anyone unbaptized (even newborn infants) will go to hell and suffer unending torment. We have no reason to complain about this since we are all wicked. Only a will that was once free can be subjected to sin's corruption, sin impairs free will,

St. Augustine

while grace restores it. It is true that God has foreknowledge of our sins, but we do not sin because of His foreknowledge. Augustine saw free will (or perhaps more exactly free control of the will) as essential to Catholic theology, because otherwise an almighty God would not be justified in punishing ill-doers.

Legacy

What was influential in Augustine was the separation of Church and State, with the clear implication that the State could only be part of the City of God by being submissive towards the Church in all religious matters. This has been the doctrine of the Church ever since, and Augustine supplied the Western Church with the theoretical justification of this policy. Also influential were his writings on free will, which the Catholic Church fully endorsed. His ideas on free will became the focus of such later philosophers as Schopenhauer, Kierkegaard, and Nietzsche.

In connection to his theory of time, the German philosopher Edmund Husserl (who established the school of phenomenology) writes: -

> "The analysis of time-consciousness is an age-old crux of descriptive psychology and theory of knowledge. The first thinker to be deeply sensitive to the immense difficulties to be found here was Augustine, who laboured almost to despair over this problem."

St. Augustine's work, as a whole, however, contains little that is original, drawing as it did heavily from the existing scriptures, and mixing them with some of the ideas from Neo-Platonism. What he achieved was to bring together these elements and relate them to the history of his own time in such a way that the fall of the Western Empire, and subsequent period of confusion, could be assimilated by Christians without any undue trial of faith.

Russell says that: -

> "A great deal of what is most ferocious in the medieval Church is traceable to his gloomy sense of universal guilt."

And that: -

> "It is strange that the last men of intellectual eminence before the dark ages were concerned, not with the saving of

civilization or expelling the barbarians or reforming the abuses of the administration, but with preaching the merit of virginity and the damnation of unbaptized infants. Seeing that these were the preoccupations that the Church handed on to the converted barbarians, it is no wonder that the succeeding age surpassed almost all other fully historical periods in cruelty and superstition."

16

St. Thomas Aquinas

Introduction

St. Thomas Aquinas (1225 – 1274) was born some nine hundred years after St. Augustine. The intervening years, known as the Middle Ages or the dark ages, produced little in the way of original philosophy, and chiefly consisted of a struggle between the church and the state following the fall of Rome. Then, in the twelfth century, a lot of the religious energy was focused on the Crusades. The thirteenth century, however, saw a new flowering of culture and thinking: we get the Gothic cathedrals of France, the romantic literature of Charlemagne, and the beginnings of constitutional government with Magna Carta and the House of Commons. On the other hand, however, this era also saw the start of the Inquisition, different waves of which lasted even into the nineteenth century.

Early in the thirteenth century the Church was in danger of a revolt against it, but it was saved from this largely by the rise of two mendicant orders, the Dominicans, and the Franciscans, which did more for orthodoxy than any of the popes from that period of time, (a mendicant order is one relying on begging or alms). Started with the best of intentions (in respect of scholarship and poverty) by St. Dominic and St. Francis respectively, both orders soon became wealthy, and both were later fairly active in the Inquisition.

One of the main areas of scholarship for the Dominicans was in trying to bring about a reconciliation between the philosophy of Aristotle and the teachings of Christ. It was the Dominican friar and Catholic priest Thomas Aquinas who finally accomplished this task, succeeding about as well as it could possibly be done, and, mainly due to this, he is now regarded as the greatest of the scholastic philosophers. Note that, in all Catholic educational institutions that teach philosophy today, his system has to be taught as the only right one, as decreed in a **rescript** by Pope Leo XIII in 1879, and Pope Benedict XV (who died in 1922) declared: -

> "This (Dominican) Order ... acquired new lustre when
> the Church declared the teaching of Thomas to be her
> own and that Doctor, honoured with the special praises

of the Pontiffs, the master and patron of Catholic schools."

Background

St. Thomas was the son of the Count of Aquino, whose castle was in the kingdom of Naples. At the age of five he was sent to the nearby Abbey of Monte Cassino where his education began. In his teens he progressed to the University of Naples where he stayed for six years, then around the age of 19 or 20 he became a Dominican and went to Cologne to study under Albertus Magnus, who was the leading Aristotelian philosopher at that time. He returned to Italy in 1259 and remained there for the rest of his life, apart from a three-year period in Paris.

He was sent to Paris to resolve a dispute between the Dominicans and the university authorities on the interpretation of Aristotle with respect to the nature of the soul. He did this very successfully by demonstrating that the university was using an Arabian translation of Aristotle rather than a Greek one, and that the university's version was actually contrary to the Catholic faith.

Until this time, knowledge of Aristotle had been obscured by Neo-Platonism ideas, but St. Thomas was provided with new translations straight from the Greek. He became an authority on Aristotle, and he persuaded the Church that Aristotle's system was a much better fit with Christianity than Plato's. His written output is vast, estimated at over eight million words, much of which was in the form of commentaries, especially on the gospels and upon Aristotelian treatises, (a remarkable output really, considering that he died at the young age of 50). His two most important works, however, are ***Summa contra Gentiles*** and ***Summa Theologiae***.

Philosophy

Summa contra Gentiles

The ***Summa contra Gentiles*** was subtitled '*On the truth of the Catholic faith against the Gentiles*', and may well have been written as a handbook for those seeking to convert others, in particular Muslims, to the Catholic faith.

He starts by considering what it means to be wise. A man can be wise in terms of building a house, for instance, because for that particular end he has the knowledge. But all particular goals are subordinate to the task of gaining knowledge of the universe, which he equates with the *truth*. The pursuit of wisdom, via the intellect, is the most perfect and sublime of all pursuits. He says his purpose with this book is to declare the truth of the Catholic faith, but that he has to do so by reason because the gentiles do not accept the authority of the scriptures. He says reason can prove the existence of God and the immortality of the soul, but there are a few things it can't prove, such as the Trinity, the Incarnation, and the Last Judgment. The *Summa contra Gentiles* is therefore divided into four books, the first three of which make no appeal to revelation except to show that it is in accordance with the conclusions reached. The fourth book deals with matters that can't be known apart from revelation.

He says, however, that faith is important too, because the proofs are difficult and can only be understood by the learned, therefore faith is needed for the ignorant, the young and anyone who from practical preoccupations does not have the time for philosophy.

He first considers the ontological argument for God (i.e. imagine the most perfect thing, if that doesn't exist then it would be more perfect if it did exist, therefore the most perfect thing must exist.) This was put forward by St. Anselm (1033 – 1109). But St. Thomas rejects this on the grounds that we are not capable of imagining something so perfect as God's essence.

The existence of God is proved, he says, by the Aristotelian argument of the unmoved mover. Whatever is moved must be moved by something else, and that thing itself must have been moved by something prior to it. Since, however, an endless regress is impossible, we must arrive at something which starts the other movements; this unmoved mover must be God. (This is one of five proofs of God he gives in the **Summa Theologiae** which we will look at below.)

Having proved that God exists, he can then go on to say many things about Him. He is unchanging; He is eternal; He is unmoved; He has no composition, and therefore He is not body because bodies have parts; He is His own essence, since otherwise He would not be simple; He cannot be defined; He is good, and He is intelligent; He understands all things at the same instant... and so on. God is the truth (and this is to be understood literally).

We then come to a question that troubled both Plato and Aristotle: - Can God know particular things, or does he only know universals and general truths? A Christian, since he believes in Providence, must hold that God does know particular things, but there are strong arguments against this. Aquinas lists seven of these arguments but then refutes them by saying that God knows particular things just as an artificer knows the details of the thing he is making. Also, as God stands outside time, he knows all things as if present.

God has free will because He is able to do things, but Aquinas (rather bravely) then lists several things that God can't do. He cannot do things that are in themselves impossible; for example He cannot make a contradiction come true; He cannot make a man into an ass; He cannot be a body or change Himself; He cannot fail; He cannot be weary, or forget, or be angry or sad; He cannot make a man have no soul; He cannot make the angles of a triangle sum to anything other than two right angles; He cannot undo the past; He cannot commit sins; and he cannot make another God or make Himself not exist.

The problem of universals is discussed. Plato, remember, held that they existed in their own right, but Thomas sides with Aristotle; universals do not subsist outside the soul. The intellect, however, in understanding universals, understands things that are outside the soul.

The third book largely concerns itself with ethics. Human happiness does not consist of having carnal pleasures, honour, glory, wealth, worldly power, or goods, and is not seated in the senses. It also does not consist in acts of moral value, because these are means; what it does consist of is the contemplation of God. Even this we are told is not fully possible in this life, it will happen in the hereafter, and not by our own power, but by the divine light. By this vision we become partakers of eternal life, outside of time.

In further ethical discussions he says marriage should be indissoluble, because the father is needed in the education of the children, being both more rational than the mother and stronger when punishment is needed. Incest is forbidden because it complicates family life, and against brother-sister incest he says that if the love of husband and wife were combined with the love of brother and sister, the mutual attraction would be so strong as to cause unduly frequent intercourse!

Aquinas says that, although all these arguments are derived from, and appeal to, reason, he is then able to point to specific texts within the scriptures that are in harmony with them. He is pleased that he has done it this way round, rather than appealing to the authority of the scriptures first. The fourth book is then concerned with the Trinity, the Incarnation, the supremacy of the pope, the sacraments, and the resurrection. It is mainly addressed to theologians rather than philosophers.

One of the last points discussed is a difficulty that people have pointed out with bodies being resurrected at the last judgment. What happens, it is asked, to a man who in his life only ate human flesh, because the body is made of the matter it has consumed. It would seem unfair to his victims if he were resurrected with his original body. St. Thomas gets round this by saying that although he will have the same body at the resurrection it will not be composed of the same actual matter that was in the body when he died.

St. Thomas Aquinas

Summa Theologiae

The *Summa Theologiae,* or Summation of Theology, was actually left unfinished at his death. On 6th December 1273 (four months before his death) he underwent an experience in Mass, and thereafter wrote nothing. His reported explanation was: - 'All that I have written seems to me straw compared to what has now been revealed to me.'

The book was intended as an instructional guide for theology students, including seminarians and the literate laity, and was a compendium of all the main theological teachings of the Catholic Church. The *Summa's* topics follow a cycle: the existence of God; Creation; Man; Man's purpose; Christ; the Sacraments; and back to God. Being mainly a theology work, as opposed to philosophy, we will only touch on those parts which address the subject matter of philosophy, and even then, most of that, including its metaphysics, is pure Aristotle. The main interest, from a philosophical perspective, is his five proofs of the existence of God, known as his five ways.

The five ways:

1. **Motion:** Some things undoubtedly move, though cannot cause their own motion. Since, as Thomas believed, there can be no infinite chain of causes of motion, there must be a First Mover not moved by anything else, and this is what everyone understands by God.

2. **Causation:** As in the case of motion, nothing can cause itself, and an infinite chain of causation is impossible, so there must be a First Cause, called God.

3. **Necessity:** Some things might be unnecessary, but not everything can be unnecessary, because at one time there was nothing and now there is something, hence, some things must have been necessary. Therefore, there must be an ultimate source of this necessity. (This is also known as the **Cosmological Argument**: before any physical things existed there must have been something non-physical that brought them into existence.)

4. **Gradation:** If we can notice a gradation in things in the sense that some things are more hot, good, etc., there must be a superlative that is the truest and noblest thing, and so most fully existing. This then, we call God.

5. **Ordered tendencies of nature:** We find even lifeless things serving a purpose, which must be that of some being outside them, since only living things can have an internal purpose. (This is also known as the **Teleological Argument** or the **Argument from Design**: things that look designed, of which we are an example, must have had a designer.)

The modern response: - (A modern response is provided here instead of in part four of this book in order that the arguments can be directly compared.)

- The third argument is really a reformulation of the second, and the first three arguments all rest on the impossibility of an infinite regression, or in mathematical language on the impossibility of a series having no first term (i.e. these three arguments make an assumption that there must be a beginning without giving a reason for that assumption). Indeed, every mathematician knows that this is not an impossibility; series can go on forever.

- Also, if there is to be a beginning of some kind, arbitrarily calling it God is jumping the gun. Think of the current evidence in cosmology pointing towards a 'big bang' of some sort, physicists don't immediately say 'well God must have caused it', they are more honest by saying 'we don't know, but let's work on it'. Given that the cause of the big bang is currently unknown, you could call it anything you want just to give it a name but calling it God brings a whole lot of other, unjustified, baggage with it.

- There are also other ways to look at arguments of causality. Kant, for instance, argues that causality is one of the ways in which our minds make sense of the world; we impose causality on our experience. And for Hume, all knowledge is based on our observation of the world, but in the case of the world itself you have a unique effect, you cannot get outside the world to see both the world and its cause. (See the chapters on Hume and Kant for more on their ideas in this area.)

- The fourth argument is another version of an infinite series, but more than that, it is just silly. You might as well say things vary in badness, therefore there must exist the worst and baddest thing possible, so this must be God. Or things vary in smelliness,

St. Thomas Aquinas

therefore there must exist the smelliest thing possible, so that must be God, etc...

- The fifth argument has been fully answered by Darwin. We look designed and of course we are designed, we have been designed by evolution through natural selection, which works by itself without the need of a designer, or even a guiding hand of any kind.

Returning to the *Summa Theologiae*, as noted, most of the philosophy and morality in it are from Aristotle but stated in such a way as to agree with the scriptures. One original idea developed by Aquinas, however, was a concept called the 'direction of fit' when talking about truth.

He uses the example of a house. It is primarily the idea of the house in the mind of the architect that is true. If the builder constructs the house differently from the plans, then the builder has made a mistake. It is not that the plan does not fit the house, it is the house that does not fit the plan. On the other hand, if a passerby does not form an accurate idea of the house, then it is his idea that is not true. This distinction enables Aquinas to say that truth is, in different ways, both in the mind and in that to which the mind is directed. Or, if the thing is essentially related to the knowing mind, then truth is primarily in the mind and secondarily in the thing, but if the thing is only accidentally related to the knowing mind, then truth is primarily in the thing and secondarily in the mind. In each case, what is said is determined by the order of dependency; truth is secondarily in that which is dependent.

In view of this, one needs to make a judgement on dependency, and it is here that Aquinas says the intellect is needed. It is a central doctrine of the *Summa Theologiae* that truth is a transcendental term, in short, whatever exists is true, and truth lies in the conformity between a thing and the intellect.

One other point of interest in the *Summa Theologiae* is his view on the morality of war. He uses the authority of Augustine's arguments (that war must not be pre-emptive, but defensive, to restore peace) and he attempts to define the conditions under which a war could be just: -

- First, war must occur for a good and just purpose rather than the pursuit of wealth or power.
- Second, just war must be waged by a properly instituted authority such as the state.
- Third, peace must be a central motive even in the midst of violence.

Finally, it should be mentioned that for centuries there have been recurring claims that Aquinas had the ability to levitate. For example, G. K. Chesterton wrote that, "His experiences included well-attested cases of levitation in ecstasy." Claims of being able to levitate have also been made of other saints, and of holy men from non-Christian religions.

Legacy

Although his philosophy is from Aristotle, Aquinas is original in his adaptation of it to Christian dogma. He was considered a bold innovator in his day, and after his death many of his doctrines were condemned by the universities of Paris and Oxford. Two things about him greatly impressed Russell: firstly, whenever he wishes to refute some doctrine, he states it first, often with great force, and always with fairness; and secondly the sharpness and clarity with which he distinguishes arguments derived from reason and arguments derived from revelation.

Having said that, these merits do not seem enough to justify his immense reputation. The appeal to reason, for instance, is, in a sense, insincere, since the conclusion to be reached is often fixed in advance by the scriptures. If he can find rational arguments to support some parts of the faith, so much the better, but if he can't he need only fall back on revelation. Russell says that "the finding of arguments for a conclusion given in advance is not philosophy, but special pleading."

Despite being widely referred to as an influential philosopher, his legacy is mainly in the area of religion, especially Catholicism. Even where his Virtue Ethics is held up as an alternative to Bentham's utilitarianism or Kant's "sense of duty" (called deontology) this is really straight from Aristotle. [See later chapters re Kant and re Ethics.]

17

Francis Bacon

Introduction

Before looking at Francis Bacon, the first of the more modern empirical philosophers, it might be appropriate to quickly review some of the ideas of the earlier Western philosophers that we have looked at so far. Then we will be better able to position Bacon's philosophy in relation to them.

Socrates' main emphasis was to question everything (via dialectic discussion) to arrive at the truth of things. He was not so interested in scientific questions about the world, but was more concerned with ethical ones, although questioning everything is certainly also a good approach to science. One important legacy of his method is that it focused on the individual, rather than on the state or the dogma of a religion; people could deduce things for themselves instead of being told what to do.

Plato, remember, was a rationalist (believing knowledge starts with the mind) rather than an empiricist (who believes knowledge starts with the senses). Known as the father of philosophy, he wrote extensively on politics, cosmology, logic, mathematics, language, and ethics. But one of the main concepts of his to remember here is his theory of **Forms**. The universal word 'cat' is obviously different from any specific cat, and universals have no position in space or time. So far so good. But Plato took this to an extreme by claiming universals actually exist in some different, superior, and more real realm, and that specific things (or singulars) are imperfect copies, or shadows of their associated universal (be that a cat or a person).

The other great figure in philosophy at that time was Aristotle, and like Plato, he wrote extensively on politics, metaphysics, ethics, maths, and logic. He disagreed with Plato with respect to universals, believing that they reside partly in the properties of the singular things in question and partly in the mind. He also put logic on a very firm footing with his analysis of syllogisms (remember the example: All men are mortal, Socrates is a man, therefore Socrates is mortal). And he was a great cataloguer of things, listing around 500 different species of animals.

Other Greeks and Greek ideas we looked at included the Atomists, the Epicureans, Plotinus, and Neo-Platonism. Then we moved into the dark ages with St. Augustine who tried to fit Neo-Platonism into Catholic thinking and St. Thomas Aquinas who rediscovered Aristotle and tried to fit him into Catholic thinking. Note that: all these philosophers (apart from Aristotle) were rationalist and deductive in nature, believing knowledge starts with the mind (and, in the case of Christianity, those areas where reason can't supply agreement with the scriptures, then revelation suffices).

Francis Bacon (1561 – 1626) changed things. He was the first in a long line of empirical philosophers; a founder of the modern inductive method of reasoning; and a pioneer in the methodology of scientific procedures. For example, see this quote from him: -

> "Men have sought to make a world from their own conception and to draw from their own minds all the material which they employed, but if, instead of doing so, they had consulted experience and observation, they would have the facts and not opinions to reason about, and might have ultimately arrived at the knowledge of the laws which govern the material world."

With Francis Bacon, 1st Viscount St. Albans, we witness the entry of the amateur into philosophy. The old philosophers were servants of the church, but the new men were of the world. Bacon was a lawyer and a statesman, and the next two we will look at are Thomas Hobbes who was a tutor and secretary, and Descartes who was a soldier. Bacon spoke for them all when he said, "I have taken all knowledge to be my province". Russell's opinion was that although his philosophy is wanting in some respects, he is important because he is the initiator of this new, empirical way of understanding the world.

Background

He was born into a prominent and well-educated family and went on to become one of the leading intellectuals in the courts of Elizabeth 1, and then James 1. He studied law and became a member of parliament in 1582. He was knighted in 1603 and subsequently held the posts of Solicitor General, Attorney General, and then Lord Chancellor of England in 1618.

Four years later he fell from grace when accused of taking bribes (even though receiving gifts from plaintiffs was common practice in those days). He admitted this but claimed it never influenced his decisions. On being convicted he was fined, stripped of his titles, banned from public office, and held briefly in the Tower for four days, but the fine was never collected. He spent the remainder of his days studying and writing.

As a young man he had studied the scholastic philosophers while at university in Cambridge (Christian scholars in the Middle Ages, culminating in St Thomas Aquinas), but he was not impressed by them because they spent most of their time pondering Aristotle, and constructing syllogistic arguments. This armchair approach to scientific enquiry was, he thought, completely wrong, and he developed an alternative method based on performing experiments and collecting data, the ultimate aim to establish the fundamental laws governing nature. Significantly, he stressed that scientists should not only prove their hypotheses by experiment, but should also strive to disprove them as well, because there is great value in conclusively ruling something out. He also laid great emphasis on the idea that observation and experiment must precede the formulation of theory.

His death was strangely fitting for someone who taught the necessity for the verification of facts by experiment. He was out riding in a coach with a friend in winter, with snow on the ground, and it suddenly came to him that flesh might be preserved in snow as well as it is in salt. They got down from the coach, purchased a chicken from a nearby house, and stuffed it with snow. A few days later he was dead from pneumonia, but not before eating the chicken.

Philosophy

Bacon was the first person to write a philosophy book directly in English; his ***Advancement in Learning*** was written in the form of a letter to King James. It is divided into two books, the first giving philosophical, civic, and religious arguments for the engaging in the aim of advancing learning, and the second being an analysis of the state of the sciences of his day, detailing what was being done incorrectly, what should be bettered, and in which way they should be advanced. In total the work lists fifty-eight necessary fields of study, from 'a history of monsters' to 'the doctrines of the affections, passions, or perturbations of the mind'.

An enlarged edition of the *Advancement* was translated into Latin and published under the title De ***Dignitate et Augmentis Scientiarum*** (Natural and Experimental History). This became significant in that it inspired the later production of the French ***Encyclopedie***. Knowledge, said Bacon, was not an opinion to be held, but a work to be done. He is also commonly regarded as the originator of the saying "knowledge is power". Other noteworthy works of his were on medicine, and on the law.

He believed in God (which was the norm in those days) but he held that a mixture of philosophy (or science) and religion produces an heretical religion and a superstitious philosophy, and he had a fear that spiritual quests might: 'interfere most mischievously in the discovery of causes'. He thought that science and theology were two separate and incompatible spheres, the laws and conclusions of one being invalid for the other. This marks the beginning of the secularization of scientific thought. He also wrote that "They that deny a God destroy man's nobility; for certainly man is of kin to the beasts in his body; and, if he be not of kin to God by his spirit, he is a base and ignoble creature." Philosophy, however, should depend only on reason, he says, and Russell comments that "How far Bacon's orthodoxy was sincere it is impossible to know."

Bacon was, in scholastic terms, a nominalist (i.e. one who believes that universals are just names), he totally rejects Plato's idea of 'Forms', where universals actually exist in some superior and more real realm. Nothing, for him, exists in nature except individual bodies, exhibiting clear individual effects, according to particular laws. He didn't regard this nominalism as opposed to Christian thought because, as noted, he considered science and theology as two incompatible spheres of inquiry. In fact, Bacon's nominalism is really materialism, even the atomic materialism of Democritus [refer back to chapter 9 on the early Greeks].

Probably his greatest work is his ***Novum Organum*** (or New Method), the title of which was a reference to Aristotle's work on logic. He rejects Aristotle's syllogistic methods as being too confused, because, while no one can doubt that those things which agree with the middle term also agree with each other, there is nevertheless a source of error in that the propositions are constructed of words, and these can be vague and not clearly defined. Hence this method may be useful for some things but not for the 'active branch of the sciences'. He recommends instead using induction as the best method for investigating nature. Even empiricism is not to be fully trusted, because our senses by themselves are not to be trusted, they can both fail us and deceive us.

The conclusions of this new Inductive philosophy must be drawn from a new natural history in which theory follows the careful ascertainment of fact, not vice versa. The Inductive method for him begins with the collection of all known facts, or instances of any problems, of the field to be considered, without any prior judgment. And the laws concerning the field must be derived from the facts, including an examination of any contradictory ones. Observation and experiment must precede the formulation of theory.

He says that traditional metaphysicians are like spiders spinning elaborate webs that float in the air, and all from material produced within their own bodies. The empirics (such as alchemists) are, by contrast, like ants, busily collecting material together but never producing anything from it. Scientists, says Bacon, should be like bees, gathering new material but also digesting and transforming it into honey. The job of scientists is not only to amass data, but to also develop theories that will allow them to understand and explain the data. This will then allow them to predict things which can also be tested for. A suggested law should be tested by being applied in new circumstances, and if it worked, then that would strengthen confidence in it. Some such tests can be especially valuable because they allow us to decide between two theories, each possible as far as previous observations are concerned.

Bacon's Idols

One of the most famous parts of his philosophy is his enumeration (within the ***Novum Organum***) of what he calls idols of the mind. Most religions warn about idols or false gods, and Bacon adopts the term to create a general theory of 'the ideology of the mind', by which he means bad habits of thinking that cause people to fall into error. Bacon warns the student of empirical science not to tackle the complexities of his subject without purging the mind of its idols: the mind is not a blank slate; it is a crooked mirror, on account of the implicit distortions it produces.

Most sources attribute four such categories of idols to him, but Russell gives a fifth category (it may be that the fifth one was noted elsewhere in Bacon's work). Bacon was the first philosopher to clearly identify and list common errors and traps to accurate analysis and thinking, and in doing so, he seems to have anticipated modern psychology.

We all think that we see or understand the world clearly, but psychology studies and logical analysis have now uncovered many ways in which the mind and our thinking can be tricked into error (refer back to chapter 5 on this). It is only the working together, and the checking of each other's work, that gives the empirical approach its power to overcome these false idols of the mind.

Bacon gives his idol categories specific names in order to make them easy to remember: Idols of the tribe; Idols of the cave; Idols of the marketplace; Idols of the theatre and Idols of the schools.

1. **Idols of the tribe:** These are innate tendencies of **human nature** that we all share, including: -

    a. The tendency of our senses to deceive us about what is really there (he recommends the careful use of scientific instruments to correct this).

b. Our inclination to impose more order and structure on nature than is really there.
   c. Our inclination towards wishful thinking, and
   d. Our tendency to jump to conclusions before sufficient careful investigation.

2. **Idols of the cave (sometimes referred to as the den):** Unlike idols of the tribe, these idols vary from person to person, and are the result of our particular cultural background or upbringing. We view phenomena in terms of our pre-existing points of view. We also have an excessive reverence for the opinions of our own particular authorities and experts.

3. **Idols of the marketplace:** These are obstacles to understanding and reasoning that arise from interactions between people, and particularly from language. Bacon warns against the use of vague and obscure jargon. He also thinks the tendency to use language too casually can cause problems in science, and warns against naming things that do not exist. [Note that both Russell and Wittgenstein wrote extensively on the problems with the use of language when doing philosophy, see later chapters.]

4. **Idols of the theatre:** We are attracted to the grandiose and the theatrical, and this can lead us astray. Those theories and dogmas that we are already familiar with entrance us like a play at the theatre. Also, scientists have a tendency to try and explain everything in one grand theory (based, maybe, on only a few observed cases).

5. **Idols of the schools:** This is the thinking that some blind rule (such as the syllogism) can take the place of judgement in investigation.

Legacy

His reputation was immense. Alexander Pope called him "the wisest, brightest, meanest of mankind", Voltaire called him the father of the scientific method, and Thomas Jefferson (the third President of the United States) wrote: -

"Bacon, Locke and Newton. I consider them as the three greatest men that have ever lived, without any exception, and as having laid the foundation of those superstructures which have been raised in the Physical and Moral sciences".

Bacon had attempted to set up a college, specially equipped with laboratories, in which scientists could work together applying his new scientific methods, but unfortunately the necessary royal funding could not be found. Later however, a group of natural philosophers began to meet in the mid-1640s to discuss his ideas, and this eventually led to the foundation of the Royal Society in 1660.

Russell is a little more critical, noting for instance that Bacon rejected the Copernican theory (of the sun at the centre of the solar system) even though it had been backed up by the recent, careful measurements made by Kepler. Another omission seems to be that he makes no mention of William Harvey's discovery of the circulation of the blood, even though Harvey was his medical attendant.

Russell also thought that Bacon's inductive method placed insufficient emphasis on hypotheses, and that it played down deductive reasoning a little too much. However, Russell does credit him with being the founder of the modern inductive method, and a pioneer in the attempt at a logical systematization of scientific procedure.

His legacy is also large in the area of law reform. Although few of his proposals for reform were adopted during his lifetime, Bacon's ideas influenced the drafting of the Napoleonic Code (the French civil code) as well as the law reforms introduced by 19th-century British Prime Minister Sir Robert Peel. The historian William Hepworth Dixon referred to the Napoleonic Code as "the sole embodiment of Bacon's thought", saying that Bacon's legal work "has had more success abroad than it has found at home", and that in France "it has blossomed and come into fruit".

American author Harvey Wheeler attributed to Bacon the creation of three distinguishing features of the modern common law system: -

- Using cases as repositories of evidence about the "unwritten law".
- Determining the relevance of precedents by exclusionary principles of evidence and logic.
- Treating opposing legal briefs as adversarial hypotheses about the application of the "unwritten law" to a new set of facts.

18

Thomas Hobbes

Introduction

Thomas Hobbes (1588 – 1679) was an English philosopher who is considered to be one of the founders of modern political philosophy. He is best known for his 1651 book ***Leviathan***, in which he expounds an influential formulation of **Social Contract** theory.

In addition to political philosophy, Hobbes contributed to a diverse array of other fields, including history, jurisprudence, geometry, the physics of gases, theology, and ethics, as well as philosophy in general.

He, like Francis Bacon, was an empirical philosopher, believing that knowledge is acquired through observation and experimentation.

Background

Hobbes was born in Wiltshire, prematurely (it is said) when his mother heard of the coming invasion of the Spanish Armada. His father, a vicar, abandoned the family, leaving them in the care of a relative, when he was forced to flee to London after being involved in a fight with another clergyman outside his own church. Hobbes did well at school, and around the age of 15 he went to university at Magdalen Hall, Oxford. On leaving university he became companion and tutor to William, the eldest son of Lord Cavendish.

His life from then on was as a tutor or scholar, mainly employed in country houses, and it was through this association that he was able to meet many at the centre of English cultural life at that time, including Francis Bacon and Ben Jonson. In 1610 he accompanied William on a grand tour of Europe, where was exposed to European scientific and critical methods of thinking.

England was going through turbulent times with the building conflict between parliament and Charles 1st, and in 1640 Hobbes's writing on the subject made him a marked man, so he fled to Paris, where he stayed for eleven years. Here he associated with a group of brilliant mathematicians and scientists led by Mersenne (an admirer of Galileo). Through them he was invited to make comments on Descartes' *Meditationes de prima philosophia*. These were forwarded to Descartes in Holland and were printed among the *Objectiones*, with Descartes' reply, when the treatise was published in 1641.

Hobbes became a tutor to Prince Charles of Wales in 1646, but this position, even in a court in exile, was ultimately impossible because his political and philosophical views pleased no one, least of all the clerics. In the end he was forced to make his peace with Cromwell and return to England for greater safety. His friendship with the Stuarts, however, was valuable to him after the Restoration. Even so, because some of his writings were thought to be heretical, for the last years of his life he had to get his work printed abroad. He died on 4 December 1679, aged 91.

Philosophy

His philosophical interests were a product of his mature years. It is recorded, for instance, that he didn't study geometry until he was forty years old, and that happened by accident. He was in a library and came across a copy of Euclid's *Elements* which was lying open on a desk part way through. He looked at the page and then said to himself "this is impossible", so he read the demonstration of it, which referred him back to an earlier proposition. He read that and it referred him back to yet an earlier proposition, and so on until he had been convinced of the truth. This gave him a love of geometry for the rest of his life.

He wrote many books, treatises, and pamphlets concerning mathematics, physics, history and philosophy, but his principal works were the trilogy: - **De Cive** ("On the citizen", 1642) the year the English Civil war began, **De Corpore** ("On the body", 1655), and **De Homine** ("On man", 1658), and his masterpiece, **Leviathan** (1651) two years after the execution of Charles 1st.

Hobbes regarded scholasticism as a collection of absurdities, and felt so certain of his own originality that he claimed there was no civil philosophy before the publication of his **De Cive**. (He dismisses out of hand Plato's *Republic*, Aristotle's *Politics*, Machiavelli's *Prince,* and Dante's *Monarchia* among others!)

He was, like Francis Bacon, a nominalist (i.e. one who denies the real existence of universals like 'red' and 'table'), and a materialist. His nominalism is clearly expressed here: -

> "Of names, some are *proper*, and singular to one thing only, as *Peter, John, this man, this tree*; and some are *common* to many things, *man, horse, tree*; every of which,

though but one name, is nevertheless the name of diverse particular things; in respect of all which together, it is called an *universal*; there being nothing universal but names; for the things named are every one of them individual and singular."

Like other analytical nominalists, he makes a sharp distinction between the realm of reason and that of revelation. The word of God is reviled in three ways, natural reason, revelation, or by the voice of some man via some miracle. But he is at pains to point out that man cannot be sure of revelation or faith, and miracles might be marvellous to one but may not be to another.

He defines philosophy as: - "Knowledge acquired by reasoning, from the manner of the generation of any thing, to the properties". The important part of philosophy for him was what we should now call science. Reasoning is its instrument, but reasoning is also an arithmetic of names, and (as in arithmetic) it is possible to err. So not all science is infallible, and Hobbes' scepticism, therefore, extends to human reason.

He says that there are no conceptions in a man's mind that do not have their origins "in that which we call SENSE". Memory is of sense-impressions and imagination is *decaying* sense, and all the complicated processes of human thought are built up out of multitudes of sense impressions. What distinguishes man from the beasts is the ability to give things names. Yet man is not wholly explained by reasoning power, he has a will, and Hobbes calls this voluntary motion 'endeavour'. Endeavour originates in the vital passions, and can be towards something (appetite) or away from something (aversion). Both of these are types of motion which Hobbes, under the influence of Galileo, thought of as the final reality.

By the time of *Leviathan* and *De Corpore*, Hobbes was convinced that human beings (including their minds) were entirely material. His materialism is clearly shown by this quote: -

> "I can explain all the workings of the mind using only material resources. What need is there to postulate an immaterial mind when this perfectly good, and more minimal, explanation is available?"

Hobbes' Trilogy

These three books are described here only briefly because some of the details are repeated in his **Leviathan** (which we'll come to below), and his other main themes have already been covered in the general section on philosophy above.

De Cive ("On the citizen") is the first of a trilogy of works written by Hobbes dealing with human knowledge. The work comprises three parts: Libertas (liberty), Imperium (dominion), and Religio (religion). In the first part, he describes man's natural condition, dealing with the natural laws; in the second, the necessity of establishing a stable government is indicated; and finally, in the third part, he writes something about religion.

De Corpore ("On the body"), the second book of the trilogy was ten years in the drafting, mainly due to putting it aside for other matters. Although the chosen title would suggest a work of natural philosophy, *it* is largely devoted to foundational matters. It consists of four sections. Part I covers logic and Part II is a repertoire of scientific concepts. Part III is on geometry and mathematics, and adopts ideas from Galileo and Cavalieri. Part IV covers natural phenomena, and includes a discussion of physics.

De Homine ("On man") was the third in the trilogy to be published but was actually written before *De Corpore*. It includes a naturalistic treatment of the origin of human beings, his theory of optics and his ideas on Human Nature. Most of this is covered in his other works and he probably only published it to complete his trilogy.

Leviathan

Leviathan was written during the English Civil War, and, while also covering much of the philosophy noted above, most of the book is to do with political theory. It is mainly concerned with demonstrating the necessity of a strong central authority, to avoid the evil of discord and civil war. He begins with an analysis of Human Nature in which he says men are driven by their passions. Each man has the natural right to seek his own preservation, but the struggle for self-preservation, in a natural state in which all men are free and equal, can only result in constant war:

> "To this war of every man, against every man, this is also consequent; that nothing can be unjust. The notions of right and wrong, justice and injustice, have no place. Where there is no common power, there is no law: where no law, no justice."

Here he coins two phrases that have ever since been associated with him: firstly, the life of man is 'solitary, poor, nasty, brutish and short'; and secondly, the 'war of all against all'.

> "In such condition, there is no place for industry; because the fruit thereof is uncertain: and consequently no culture of the earth; no navigation, nor use of the commodities that may be imported by sea; no commodious building; no instruments of moving, and removing, such things as require much force; no knowledge of the face of the earth; no account of time; no arts; no letters; no society; and which is worst of all, continual fear, and danger of violent death."

He says that the only way to resolve this is for every man to come to an agreement with every other man an abrogation of certain rights: -

> "as if every man should say to every man: *I authorise and give up my right of governing myself, to this man, or this assembly of men, on condition, that thou give up thy right to him, and authorise all his actions in like manner.* This done, the multitude so united in one person, is called a COMMONWEALTH."

Once formed, the sovereign power cannot be taken away from the sovereign (be that an individual monarch, or a parliamentary body), and no citizen can object or take action against the sovereign. Note that the agreement, or covenant as he calls it, is not between citizens and the ruling power, it is a covenant made by the citizens with each other to obey the government chosen by the majority. And this has become known as the Social Contract.

Hobbes preferred the sovereign to be a monarch. He would accept a parliament alone, but he didn't like the idea of a power sharing arrangement between a monarch and a parliament. The English Civil War occurred, he said, because the power was divided between the King, the Lords, and the Commons. He does, however, admit one limitation to the duty of submission to sovereigns. The right of self-preservation he regards as absolute, subjects have the right of self-defence, even against monarchs. And on this ground he holds that a man has the right to refuse to fight when called upon by the government to do so. Russell wryly comments that 'this is a right which no modern government concedes.'

Hobbes and Religion

Hobbes saw that one of the causes of the Civil War was the difficulty men have in obeying, at the same time, both God and man. Faith in God and civil obedience are both necessary to salvation. "Our Saviour Christ hath not given us new laws," he says, "but council to observe those we are subjected to; that is to say, the laws of nature, and the laws of our several sovereigns." Also, to avoid future conflicts and ambiguities, he takes the protestant view that the king should be the head of the church.

He hated the Church of Rome, and thought that many of the clergy sought temporal power under spiritual guise. His approach to religion was essentially sceptical, no man can infallibly know the word of God, or know that another man has had a true revelation. So, exempting Christianity (more by courtesy or caution than conviction) he decides that religion is anthropomorphic; it is a projection of man's fears.

> "Fear of things invisible is the natural seed of that which
> every one in himself calleth religion."

After the Restoration, the young king Charles II, Hobbes' former pupil, remembered him and called him to the court to grant him a pension of £100. The king was also important in protecting Hobbes when, in 1666, the House of Commons introduced a bill against atheism and profaneness.

The only consequence that came of the bill was that Hobbes could never thereafter publish anything in England on subjects relating to human conduct. For some time, Hobbes was not even allowed to respond, whatever his enemies tried. Despite this, his reputation abroad was formidable, and noble or learned foreigners who came to England never forgot to pay their respects to the old philosopher.

Legacy

His legacy is immense in many areas. There is the materialist view of man as compounded of motions in no way different from those of physical bodies. The utilitarianism of Bentham has its roots in Hobbes' view of society as an artefact and man as being moved by the pleasure/pain principle. The empirical school of philosophy has its first thesis on the origin and contents of the mind in sense-experience. And, not least, many important developments in political theory stem from his writings.

Russell says that the merits of Hobbes appear most clearly when he is contrasted with earlier political theorists. He is completely free from superstition, he is clear and logical, and his ethics, right or wrong, are completely intelligible. Also, the reason Hobbes gives for supporting the state, namely that it is the only alternative to anarchy, is a valid one.

There are a number of criticisms, however, to his political theories. Firstly, there is no actual agreement that citizens have signed up to. Secondly, once established, the sovereign power continues for ever,

Hobbes gives no way of keeping the power in check, and, although established by the people for the protection of the people, no thought is given to anything like a regular renewal of the contract. Another omission is that the covenant only covers one state, he gives no thought to relations between states. With the absence of an international government, we are still in a state of nature which is that of a war of all against all.

19

Descartes

Introduction

René Descartes (1596 – 1650) was a French philosopher, mathematician, and scientist who spent most of his life in the Dutch Republic. He has been called the father of modern philosophy, and much subsequent Western philosophy is a response to his writings.

He is seen as being responsible for the increased attention given to epistemology (the theory of knowledge) in the 17th century. He also laid the foundation for continental rationalism (the view that regards reason as the chief source and test of knowledge), which was later supported by Spinoza, Leibniz, and Kant, and opposed by the empiricist school of thought consisting of Hobbes, Locke, Berkeley, and Hume.

As a mathematician he is famous for his new system of co-ordinate geometry, now named after him as Cartesian Geometry.

Background

He was born in La Haye en Touraine in central France, now renamed Descartes. His mother died when he was one and so he was mainly brought up by his grandmother. He was educated at a Jesuit college in La Fleche where he was introduced to mathematics and physics, including Galileo's work. He was, however, particularly dissatisfied with the philosophy teaching he received there, which was mainly the scholastic philosophy that mixed Aristotle with Catholic religious doctrines.

It was during his time here that, due to ill health, he developed the habit of staying in bed late into the morning. He later claimed that this assisted his mind in its natural inclination to meditation, and he preserved the habit for the rest of his life. After La Fleche he went to the University of Poitiers for two years, earning a *Baccalaureate* in law, in accordance with his father's wishes that he should become a lawyer. When his father died, however, he sold the estate and invested the money, giving him an income of six or seven thousand francs a year. Thereafter he said: -

An Introduction to Philosophy

> "I entirely abandoned the study of letters. Resolving to seek no knowledge other than that of which could be found in myself or else in the great book of the world."

In 1618 he joined the Dutch army as a gentleman soldier in its war of independence from Spain, and in the Netherlands, he met the Dutch mathematician and scholar Isaac Beeckman, under whom he studied the latest in mathematics and science. In 1619 he transferred to the army of the Duke of Bavaria, and, during one very cold winter spell, he had to take solitary refuge in a small 'stove heated room' where he meditated and experienced his famous dreams, which he took as revelations. He claimed that his philosophy was half finished when he emerged.

He never saw any fighting as a soldier, and gave it up in 1621, spending a few years in Italy and then settling in Paris. In 1628 he had another year as a soldier, then, in 1629, he moved to Holland where he stayed for the next twenty years. Russell says: -

> 'It was impossible to exaggerate the importance of Holland in the seventeenth century, as the one country where there was freedom of speculation. Hobbes had to have his books printed there; Locke took refuge there during the five worst years of reaction in England before 1688; Bayle (of the Dictionary) found it necessary to live there; and Spinoza would hardly have been allowed to do his work in any other country."

Even in Holland he had a few problems, some people claimed his views led to atheism, but the Prince of Orange intervened on his behalf. There is some claim that Descartes' Catholicism was expediency, but Russell thinks he was a sincere Catholic and merely wanted to persuade the Church to be less hostile to modern science than it showed itself in the case of Galileo.

In 1649 he entered into a correspondence with Queen Christine of Sweden, and this led to a request for his presence at court, she even sent a warship to fetch him! It turned out she wanted lessons from him, but she only had time to spare for him at five in the morning. Early rising was not his thing, also, the cold of the Scandinavian winter was not good for a man of delicate health. He fell ill and died in February 1650.

His Works

Descartes

Descartes' interests were very wide ranging, and for him philosophy was a thinking system that embodied all knowledge. He expressed it in this way: -

> "Thus, all Philosophy is like a tree, of which Metaphysics is the root, Physics the trunk, and all the other sciences the branches that grow out of this trunk".

The list of his works include: -

- *Musicae Compendium* - a treatise on music theory and the aesthetics of music.
- *Regulae ad directionem ingenii* (*Rules for the Direction of the Mind*).
- *La recherche de la vérité par la lumière naturelle* (*The Search for Truth)* - an unfinished dialogue.
- *Le Monde* (*The World*) and *L'Homme* (*Man*) - Descartes' first systematic presentation of his natural philosophy.
- *Discours de la méthode* (*Discourse on the Method*).
- *La Géométrie* (*Geometry*) - Descartes' major work in mathematics.
- *Meditationes de prima philosophia* (*Meditations on First Philosophy*) – his main philosophical work.
- *Principia philosophiae* (*Principles of Philosophy*) – a Latin textbook intended by Descartes to replace the Aristotelian textbooks then used in universities.
- *La description du corps humaine* (*The Description of the Human Body*).
- *Les passions de l'âme* (*Passions of the Soul*).
- Along with many other writings on topics as diverse as optics, the foetus, and conversations he had with notable people of his day.

Mathematics

As a mathematician his work was of huge significance, indeed a whole branch of mathematics is named after him: that of Cartesian Geometry. He literally invented the system of co-ordinate geometry; he used the analytic method (which supposes a problem solved, and then examines the consequences of that supposition); and he applied algebra to geometry. He did have some predecessors in this field, but what was original to him was the use of co-ordinates, i.e. the determination of the position of a point on a plane by its distance from two fixed lines.

Although he didn't discover the full power of this method, he did enough to make further progress easy.

He pioneered the standard notation that uses superscripts to show the powers of exponents, and his treatment of independent variables was very modern. He also discovered an early form of the law of conservation of mechanical momentum (a measure of the motion of an object) and envisioned it as pertaining to motion in a straight line, as opposed to perfect circular motion, which Galileo had conceived.

Philosophy

Descartes is usually considered the founder of modern philosophy, and he is really the first major philosopher to take into account the new ideas and discoveries occurring in physics and astronomy from that time. While he does retain a fair amount of the previous scholastic traditions, he does not accept the foundations for that, laid down by his predecessors; his main ambition is to construct a complete philosophical edifice from first principles.

> "I observed with regard to philosophy that despite being cultivated for many centuries by the best minds, it contained no point which was not disputed and hence doubtful."

No-one since Aristotle had attempted such a comprehensive and systematic approach to all knowledge, and Russell says: -

> "There is a freshness about his work that is not found in any eminent previous philosopher since Plato. All the intermediate philosophers were teachers, with the professional superiority belonging to that avocation. Descartes writes, not as a teacher, but as a discoverer and explorer, anxious to communicate what he has found."

From a philosophy standpoint, his two most important works are the ***Discourse on Method*** (1637) and ***Meditations on First Philosophy*** (1642), and because they largely overlap it is usual to consider them together.

In these books he begins by explaining his method of doubt (often now called 'Cartesian doubt'). In order to have a firm basis for his philosophy, he resolves to make himself doubt everything he can manage to. He begins with his senses. Can I doubt, he says, that I am sitting here by the fire? Yes I can, he answers, because I have dreamt I was here when in fact I was in bed. Also, madmen sometimes have hallucinations, so it is possible that I may too.

He continues by saying that arithmetic and geometry are less easy to doubt, but it is still possible that God could deliberately cause me to make mistakes. It might be wrong to attribute such unkindness to God, but there might be an evil demon, both cunning and powerful, which would mislead me. Indeed, if there were such a demon, it may be that all things I see are only illusions.

And then concludes with the insight that: - there remains, however, something that I cannot doubt: no demon, however cunning, could deceive me if I did not exist. I may have no body, that might be an illusion, but thought is different. And, in a now famous passage, he writes: -

> "While I wanted to think everything false, it must necessarily be that I who thought was something; and remarking that this is truth, *I think, therefore I am* [cogito ergo sum], was so solid and so certain that all the most extravagant suppositions of the sceptics were incapable of upsetting it, I judged that I could receive it without scruple as the first principle of the philosophy that I sought."

Having now secured a firm foundation, he then sets to work to rebuild the edifice of knowledge. Why, he asks, is thinking so evident? He concludes that it is because it is clear and distinct. So, he adopts, as a general rule, the principle: – All things that we conceive very clearly and very distinctly are true. He does admit, however, it is sometimes difficult knowing these things.

In terms of knowledge of bodies (i.e. physical things) he gives the example of a piece of wax from a honeycomb. Certain things are apparent to our senses: its taste, its smell, its colour, its size and shape, and it is hard and cold. But if you place it near a fire then its qualities change, although it is still called wax. Therefore, what appeared to the senses was not the wax itself. He says that the perception of the wax "is not a vision or touch or imagination, but an inspection of the mind." We do not 'see' the wax, any more than we 'see' men in the street when we see hats and coats.

> "I understand by the sole power of judgment, which resides in my mind, what I thought I saw with my eyes."

An Introduction to Philosophy

For him, knowledge of external things must be by the mind, not by the senses. He says that ideas (which include sense-perceptions) come in three sorts: those that are innate; those that are foreign and come from without; and those that are invented by the mind. The ideas that are foreign we naturally suppose to be outside objects, but here we can still doubt. Take the sun, for instance, there are two ideas of it, that as it appears to our senses, and that which astronomers tell us. They cannot both be true, and reason shows that the one from direct experience is less like the real sun than that which astronomers tell us.

These arguments, however, for the existence of real external objects, have not disproved the original sceptical arguments which threw doubt on everything except thinking. His answer to this problem is achieved by first proving the existence of God. Once he has proved God's existence then the rest is easy. Since God is good, He will not act like a demon to deceive us. Therefore, the physical world really does exist. Moreover, he has given us the faculty of correcting errors, which is what we use when we employ the principle that what is clear and distinct is true.

His proofs of God, however, are not very original; they come in the main from previous scholastic philosophy. Firstly, he uses the ontological argument, which (you remember) defines God as "that than which nothing greater can be conceived", and then says that if God was just an idea, then an even greater being would be one that really exists. Therefore God, being the greatest, must really exist. Descartes actually published several variations of this argument. He also used the so called 'trademark' argument for God's existence, which is similar to the ontological argument: -

> "Since I am a thinking thing, and have in me an idea of God, whatever finally the cause may be to which my nature is attributed, it must necessarily be admitted that the cause must equally be a thinking thing, and possess within it the idea of all the perfections that I attribute to the divine nature."

Descartes' Dualism

Descartes allows three different types of substance: God, mind, and matter. Matter is something which is 'extended' (i.e. it occupies space) and it occupies different dimensions than mind. Hobbes, in his correspondence with Descartes, insisted that thinking was a physical thing, saying: -

> "We cannot think of leaping apart from that which leaps, of knowing apart from a knower, or of thinking without a thinker. And hence it seems to follow that that which thinks is something corporeal".

Descartes, however, maintains that thoughts are non-physical things, hence his idea of the dualism of mind and matter. He says that the body works like a machine, that it has material properties. The mind (or soul), on the other hand, is nonmaterial and does not follow the laws of nature. He argued that the mind interacts with the body at the pineal gland. This form of dualism or duality proposes that the mind controls the body, but that the body can also influence the otherwise rational mind, such as when people act out of passion. Most of the previous accounts of the relationship between mind and body had been unidirectional.

Legacy

His 'I think, therefore I am' makes mind more certain than matter, and my mind (for me) more certain than the minds of others. This put a tendency for subjectivism into all philosophy later derived from Descartes, including both Continental idealism and British empiricism. Russell says that: –

> "Modern philosophy has very largely accepted the formulation of its problems from Descartes, while not accepting his solution."

Descartes' philosophy also gave formulation to the growing idea that each person is a reasoning adult (as opposed to a child obedient to God) during a time when the western world was in the process of shifting from the Christian medieval period into the Enlightenment era.

It is often said of Descartes that he inaugurated modern philosophy by making questions about the validation of knowledge the first questions to be dealt with in the subject. However, although he tried very hard to approach philosophy from first principles, he never quite succeeded. He accepted, without fully questioning them, a number of previous scholastic ideas to do with God, the soul, and mind-body dualism.

Indeed his 'Cartesian Dualism' set the agenda for philosophical discussion of the mind–body problem for many years after his death. While a number of philosophers (especially Hume) rejected this dualism, the best analysis of why it is an error was formulated by Oxford philosopher Gilbert Ryle who, in his 1949 book ***The Concept of Mind***, demonstrated that the idea of dualism is a category error, and one that many people still fall for today (see chapter 53 Philosophy of Mind).

Descartes actually had the most influence of anyone on the young Newton, and this is arguably one of his most important contributions. Newton continued Descartes' work on cubic equations, and this provided the basis for the calculus developed later by both Newton and Leibniz.

20

John Locke

Introduction

John Locke (1632 – 1704) is the foremost English philosopher in the early period of post Cartesian philosophy. He is notable as being the founder of not one but two, hugely influential, philosophical systems. In politics he virtually defined Liberalism, laying out the rights of the individual, the role of the state and a structure for government. And in epistemology (the theory of knowledge) he inaugurated the philosophy of British Empiricism (i.e. the theory that all knowledge of the world is ultimately derived from, and grounded in, sense experience).

Background

Locke lived through troubled, but also intellectually stimulating, times. He was a young boy when the Protestant character of England was being assailed by Charles 1st, and men were leaving in their thousands for the free communities of America. The English Civil War broke out when he was ten, and his father, a country lawyer, joined the war, leading a regiment of volunteers on the Parliament side. He went to Westminster School at 12 and was still there as a 16-year-old when, in 1649, Charles 1st was executed in nearby Whitehall; indeed, Locke may even have witnessed the event.

He went to Oxford at the age of 19, but didn't care much for the academic atmosphere there; it was still at that time the home of the scholastic school of philosophy. He received, however, a university appointment, and lectured in Greek, rhetoric, and philosophy, and here he turned with pleasure to studying and teaching the radical philosophy of Descartes. He couldn't make a career of this in the university however, and so he turned to medicine, later taking up the post of physician in the household of Lord Ashley, 1st Earl of Shaftesbury, and tutor to his grandson.

Locke played a great part in the advancement of science, becoming a member of the newly formed Royal Society, along with his friends, the chemist Robert Boyle, and society president Isaac Newton. Here he was

An Introduction to Philosophy

greatly influenced by the scientific philosophy of Francis Bacon, whose ideas the Royal Society was founded around. He was also good friends with the poet and playwright John Dryden.

England continued to be a troubled and dangerous place; the Restoration of the monarchy in 1660 saw Charles II taking the throne; the plague struck in 1665 and the fire of London 1666. Then, in 1683, a plot was uncovered to assassinate Charles II and his brother James. The Earl of Shaftesbury was implicated, and he and Locke had to flee to the Netherlands for safety. James II came to the throne on Charles' death in 1685 but his Catholic ideas were not well accepted. This resulted in the 'Glorious Revolution' (also termed the Bloodless Revolution) when William of Orange invaded, and James II fled to France, without a shot being fired. Locke returned to England in style on the royal yacht with William III's wife and co-monarch Mary II, eldest daughter of James II.

Locke began his greatest work, the *Essay Concerning Human Understanding* while in the Netherlands; it was finished in 1687 and published in 1690, after his return to England. His *Two Treatises on Government* was also published in 1690.

His other work was as follows: -

- *First Letter on Toleration,* published in 1689.
- Two further letters on *Toleration,* published in 1690 and 1692, and
- His book on *Education,* published in 1693.

Although his life was long, all his influential writings were confined to the few years from 1687 to 1693 (i.e. between the ages of 55 and 61).

Philosophy

Political Philosophy

Locke was entirely familiar with the writings of Thomas Hobbes who, having died when Locke was 38, lived through some of the same political upheavals. Hobbes, remember, wanted security and strong government for the protection of citizens. He saw the state of nature as a 'war of all against all' and had called for a 'social contract' of each citizen with every other citizen, to give up their rights to a sovereign (either a king or a parliament) as long as the other citizens did likewise. And having once given up the rights then the sovereign could never again be challenged.

Locke also wanted stability and saw the need for a social contract of some form, because he agreed with Hobbes that in a state of nature man is a free being with rights of his own. He differed from Hobbes, however, in the degree of power a government should have; he became the apostle of law, liberty and constitutionalism, in opposition to political excesses on every side.

> "If man in the state of nature be so free, as has been said; if he be absolute lord of his own person and possessions, equal to the greatest, and subject to no body, why will he part with his freedom? why will he give up this empire, and subject himself to the dominion and control of any other power? To which it is obvious to answer, that though in the state of nature he hath such a right, yet the enjoyment of it is very uncertain, and constantly exposed to the invasion of others: for all being kings as much as he, every man his equal, and the greater part no strict observers of equity and justice, the enjoyment of the property he has in this state is very unsafe, very unsecure. This makes him willing to quit a condition, which, however free, is full of fears and continual dangers: and it is not without reason, that he seeks out, and is willing to join in society with others, who are already united, or have a mind to unite, for the mutual preservation of their lives, liberties and estates, which I call by the general name, property."

This justification of the social contract is strikingly close to Hobbes, but Locke insists that the sovereign power created needs to be one which can be checked by the common people. If they gave the sovereign absolute power, then they would "put themselves into a worse condition than the state of Nature". Locke insists, therefore, that all supreme power must itself govern "by declared and received laws, and not by extemporary dictates and undetermined resolutions". Sovereignty must reside with the people, and they alone can change its form, or appoint new governors.

The Civil War that led Charles I to the scaffold had led to a worse tyranny. The Restoration of the monarchy, intended to be a revival of popular liberties and parliamentary rule, produced in its turn another tyranny. The outstanding need was for a code of laws establishing the rights of the citizens, and the power of kings and parliaments, so that irresponsible power could be held in check. Locke, the lover of toleration and liberty, became the spokesman for that political philosophy. And when the English Parliament, after the abdication of James II, asked William of Orange and Princess Mary to share the throne between them, they read to them (in the Banqueting Hall in Whitehall, from where Charles I had stepped to his death), a Declaration of Rights, inspired by John Locke, which later became the Bill of Rights and ended as 'An Act declaring the Rights and Liberties of the Subject, and settling the Succession of the Crown'. Russell comments: -

> Locke is the most fortunate of all philosophers. He completed his work in theoretical philosophy just at the moment when the government of his country fell into the hands of men who shared his political opinions.

Locke formalised his ideas in his ***Two Treatises on Government***. The first treatise laid out arguments against any form of hereditary government. To us today this seems self-evident, but at the time it was considered somewhat revolutionary. The point here is a separation of economic power from political power. These days we think it natural that we should be able to leave our property and wealth to our children (i.e. we accept the hereditary principle as regards economic power) but we reject it when it comes to political power. In the past these two aspects of power were virtually identical.

In the second treatise Locke sets out what he conceives to be the true origin of government, and it is here (as noted above) that he bases the need for government and a social contract around the need for the protection of lives and property of the citizens of the state. Russell notes that "Property is very important in Locke's political philosophy, and is, according to him, the chief reason for the institution of government." Locke adds, however, that a "supreme power cannot take from any man any part of his property without his own consent." The question of taxes might be supposed to raise difficulties here, but Locke perceives none; the expense of government must be borne by the citizens, but with their consent (i.e. with that of the majority).

Locke notes that men retain a number of rights under his proposed form of government. For instance, if a thief is stealing my property and threatening me, then I may defend myself even to the point of killing him, but if the thief gets away, I must renounce private vengeance and resort to the law. Likewise, if I see a man making a murderous assault on my brother, I have the right to kill him if I can't save my brother in any other way, but if the man succeeded in killing my brother, then I lose the right to kill him, that right is taken over by the state.

Checks and Balances

The theory of checks and balances in government is one of the main ideas in Locke's writings; he saw it was important that the different areas of government can limit each other's powers. The two areas of government he considered were the executive and the legislative, which in his day were the king and parliament. In our day, in the U.K., the executive has come to mean the Prime Minister, the Cabinet, Government Departments and Civil Service, and the legislative is the two houses of parliament (which themselves keep a check on each other).

Also added these days is the separation of the judicial functions from the executive and the legislative. Russell notes that it is surprising that Locke says nothing of the judiciary, even though it was one of the burning questions of his day. The most noteworthy example of the separation of powers today is the United States where the Constitution lays out a strict three-way separation of powers between: the President (the executive); Congress (the legislative) and the Supreme Court (the judiciary), and specifies the powers and limits of each.

Locke's Theory of Knowledge

Locke's ***Essay Concerning Human Understanding*** is his main philosophical work. Although it took him around twenty years in total to complete, he was able to spend much more time on it during his period in exile in the Netherlands, and it was published on his return to England when he was fifty-seven. He says that the essay arose from philosophical discussions he had with friends, during which they could not come to any conclusions on things, therefore, he said, "before we set ourselves upon enquiries of that nature, it was necessary to examine our own abilities, and see what objects our understanding were, or were not, fitted to deal with."

He started, by trying to understand how ideas come to be present in the mind. If there are innate ideas in the mind, placed there by gift at the mind's birth, then the whole process would become complicated by the presence of imponderable elements. Locke, however, could find no evidence that ideas arise from any other source but experience. He writes:

> "Let us suppose the mind to be, as we say, white paper void of all characters, without any ideas. How comes it to be furnished? Whence comes it by that vast store which the busy and boundless fancy of man has painted on it with an almost endless variety? Whence has it all the *materials* of reason and knowledge? To this I answer, in one word, from EXPERIENCE. In that all our knowledge is founded; and from that it ultimately derives itself. Our observation, employed either about external sensible objects, or about the internal operations of our minds perceived and reflected on by

ourselves, is that which supplies our understandings with all the materials of thinking."

Experience he saw as including both sensation and reflection, reflection being what the mind gets by the notice it takes of its own operations. Complex ideas, he says, are built from combinations of simple ones, and in his analysis of simple and complex ideas he makes a distinction between the primary and secondary qualities of objects (as did Galileo before him and accepted by Newton).

He uses the example of fire, which from a distance feels warm but if you touch it you feel pain. He says the idea of warmth is in the fire itself, but the pain is not in the fire. Primary qualities are in objects themselves, these being solidity, extension, number, figure, and motion, and are said to be *real* qualities. Secondary qualities are simply ideas produced in the mind by the operation of our senses, and which we attribute to the objects in question, colour being a conspicuous example, along with smell, taste and sound; without the eye there would be no colour, without the ear no sound, and so on.

Universals

Having demonstrated that ideas and knowledge are based on experience, he then tackles the problem of universals. Plato, remember, held that ideas like 'cat' were not just abstractions but were real, ideal objects of which individual cats were just imperfect copies, like shadows. Locke, however, says they are abstractions created by the mind based on multiple examples: -

> "Thus the same colour being observed to-day in chalk or snow, which the mind yesterday received from milk, it considers that appearance alone, makes it representative of all that kind; and having given it the name *whiteness*, it by that sound signifies the same quality wheresoever to be imagined or met with."

He also gave the example of triangularity which, he said, could not be any particular triangle but: -

> "It must be neither oblique, nor rectangular, neither equilateral, equicrural, nor scalenon; but all and none of these at once. In effect, it is something imperfect, that cannot exist; an idea wherein some parts of several different and inconsistent ideas are put together."

He says that everything in the world is an individual thing and could be given its own proper name, each cat, each tree, and each blade of grass. But that would make talking about things difficult, so general terms were used to aid communication, and this is something the mind does naturally by comparing things and seeing differences and commonalities.

Reason

In his chapter on reason, he argues that reason is not just syllogistic reasoning: - "God has not been so sparing to men to make them barely two-legged creatures, and left it to Aristotle to make them rational." Reason, as Locke uses the term, consists of two parts: first an enquiry as to what things we know with certainty; and second, an investigation of propositions which it is wise to accept in practice, although they have only probability and not certainty in their favour. He says: -

> "The grounds of probability are two: conformity with our own experience, or the testimony of others' experience."

Locke's empiricism, therefore, is very much grounded in common sense.

Religion

Locke is religious, and he accepts as valid Descartes' arguments as to the existence of God. But he also says that our complex idea of God comes from a combination of simpler ideas based on experience, i.e. we have ideas of existence, duration, knowledge, power, pleasure and happiness, and if we enlarge each of these, and add our idea of infinity, then we get our complex idea of God. How his empiricism squares with his belief in God is not entirely clear however, and since he also argued that no God-inspired man could communicate anything by revelation which could not be arrived at by sensation and reflection, it seems his scepticism applies here too.

His political writings are full of references to God, but he also states that no believer in God should be penalized on account of his religious opinions.

Legacy

Locke's influence, from his time right up to the present day, has been huge. Although he was to some extent the right man in the right place at the right time, the job he did of putting these ideas on paper and formatting them into the two logical systems of political theory and empirical philosophy was an immense achievement.

In epistemology (the theory of knowledge), from Locke's time onwards you were either a follower of Descartes' rationalism, such as Spinoza, Leibniz, Kant, Hegel, and others, or you followed Locke's empiricism, such as Berkeley and Hume, and indeed most scientists from Newton onwards.

But it is in politics that it could be claimed that his influence has been even greater. Voltaire spread Locke's ideas widely in France, and Locke's writings on the rights of man lent inspiration to the French Revolution. Thomas Paine took up his ideas and produced his own pamphlets on these rights which contributed to the American Revolution and the Declaration of Independence from England. Also (as noted previously) the **American Constitution** is based around Locke's ideas of separation of powers and checks and balances.

Thomas Jefferson, influenced by Locke, and the main author of the Declaration of Independence, was also in Paris (as the American minister to France) during the French Revolution and helped Lafayette draft the **Declaration of the Rights of Man and of the Citizen**. It was also Jefferson who urged James Madison to create the **Bill of Rights** (i.e. the collective name for the first ten amendments to the American Constitution). These guarantee a number of personal freedoms and add limits to the government's power in a number of areas.

21

Bento Spinoza

Introduction

Bento Spinoza (1632 – 1677) was a Dutch philosopher of Portuguese origin. One of the early thinkers of the Enlightenment and modern biblical criticism, including modern conceptions of the self and the universe, he came to be considered one of the great rationalists of 17th-century philosophy. Inspired by the groundbreaking ideas of René Descartes, Spinoza became a leading philosophical figure of the Dutch Golden Age. He was, according to Russell: -

> "The noblest and most lovable of the great philosophers, intellectually, some others have surpassed him, but ethically he is supreme".

Background

He was born in Amsterdam and lived all his short life in the Netherlands. His parents were immigrant Sephardic Jews who had fled from persecution in Europe. Initially from Spain, the Sephardic Jews suffered greatly from the Inquisition. In 1492 they left Spain in large numbers, around 100,000 crossing the border into Portugal, where until then they had been treated more peacefully. Portugal found it difficult to cope, however, and passed laws taxing them to the hilt, and later requiring them to convert to Christianity. Thus was started a tradition of Marranos, people forced to convert to Christianity but still living secretly as Jews.

However, the persecution of the Jewish community increased again (the inquisition coming later to Portugal than Spain) so Spinoza's parents, along with many others, emigrated to the more tolerant Netherlands, where his father became a respected and prosperous merchant in the Amsterdam Jewish community there. His mother died when he was six, but he had the support of a strong Jewish community. He excelled at school, becoming a brilliant student of Judaism and an authority on the Talmud (the central text of Rabbinic Judaism).

An Introduction to Philosophy

At 18 he enrolled in the school of Frans Van den Enden, with the stated purpose of learning Latin. Van den Enden was a lapsed Catholic, a free thinker and a polymath, and here Spinoza learned philosophy, politics, music, and the arts. He became quite outspoken about these new ideas and the Jewish community was not pleased with him, indeed a murder attempt by a fellow Jew almost put an end to their embarrassment, although there was no real evidence the synagogue was involved. He was only saved from the knife by the large cloak he was wearing, which he kept thereafter as a memento.

His father died when he was 22, and Spinoza, together with his brother, took over running the family business. Things came to a head two years later, however, when he would not renounce the heterodox opinions he had been heard to voice, and after an unsuccessful attempt to buy his silence, he was finally cursed and excommunicated from the Jewish community. Born Bento Spinoza, and know in the community as Baruch Spinoza, he later became known as Benedictus Spinoza, and spent his mature years as a philosopher living in The Hague near Rotterdam.

There, he lived simply, and supported himself by grinding lenses for use in telescopes, microscopes, and other newly invented instruments. He became good at this and many people wanted his lenses. Unfortunately, however, the inhalation of the glass dust from his lens grinding led to his death from lung disease at the early age of 45.

His main work is the *Ethics*, and this was published posthumously by his friends. During his lifetime, however, he published two other books, the *Tractatus Theologico-Politicus* and the *Principles of Descartes' Philosophy* (which is a summary of Descartes' philosophy written for a student of Spinoza). Also published posthumously was the unfinished *Tractatus Politicus*.

Philosophy

Politics and Religion

The *Tractatus Theologico-Politicus* is a combination of biblical criticism and political theory. In it he endeavours to show that the Scriptures can be interpreted to be compatible with a liberal theology. Some of his Christian friends may have hoped that Spinoza would lead to a mass conversion of Jews to Christianity, instead however, he conceived Jesus as at most the last of the great Jewish prophets. Although the book was published anonymously it soon became known that it was Spinoza's work, and he acquired both international fame and notoriety from it.

Bento Spinoza

Its main aim was to recommend full freedom of thought and religious practice, subject to behavioural conformity with the laws of the land. He sees the moral message of the bible as the most important aspect of it; any science and metaphysics within it is limited by the knowledge of the time and should just be regarded as imaginative stories for teaching ethics to the multitude.

His political theory owes a good deal to Hobbes, he uses the idea of a 'social contract' but derives a more liberal and democratic lesson from it. He holds that in a state of nature there is no right or wrong because wrong consists in disobeying the law. He says that the sovereign can do no wrong and agrees with Hobbes that the Church should be entirely subordinate to the State. He is opposed to all rebellion, even against a bad government, and points to the troubles of England as proof of the harm that comes from the forcible resistance to authority. He disagrees with Hobbes, however, over the idea of people sacrificing all their rights to the sovereign, in particular he holds that freedom of opinion is important.

> "Let every man think what he wants and say what he thinks."

At the heart of his metaphysics is the idea of the unity of everything. He argues that if God is infinite then the world cannot be separate from him; there can be nothing that is not God. If there was, then God would not be great, he would have limits, but as God is boundless then everything is God. Descartes, remember, held that there were three substances: God, mind, and matter, but for Spinoza they are really all the same thing. Descartes had the problem that if mind and matter were two different types of thing then he had to find a way for them to interact, which he said occurred in the pineal gland, however the actual interaction remained a mystery. Spinoza's solution is simply to abandon the Cartesian dualism; mind and body are simply two aspects of a single substance.

> "By substance I understand what is in itself and is conceived through itself, that is, that whose concept does not require the concept of another thing, from which it is formed."

His religious views were certainly unorthodox. His God is not a creator God. Nor is he a personal God, with a special affection for human beings. Also, he does not accept the traditional view that we have immortal souls; if mind and body are a single substance then there is not anything personal that survives death. Yet Spinoza did regard himself religious. He is usually described as a pantheist – someone who believes that God is identical with everything there is.

Spinoza is firmly in the camp of the European Rationalists (like Descartes and Leibniz) who believe knowledge of the world (such as the existence of God) can be deduced rationally. As opposed to the British Empiricists (like Locke and Hume) who think that all non-trivial knowledge of the world is ultimately derived from, and grounded in, sense experience. Spinoza was also a thoroughgoing determinist who held that absolutely everything that happens occurs through the operation of necessity.

The *Ethics*

Spinoza's great work is his posthumously published *Ethics*. It is not, however, just about ethics, it develops an entire theory concerning the nature of reality. One of its most striking features is that the structure of the book is like that of a geometrical proof, indeed the full title of the book is *Ethics Demonstrated in a Geometrical Manner*. It seems he was very impressed by Euclid's geometry and the *Ethics* is laid out with definitions, axioms, and theorems. Everything after the axioms is intended to be rigorously demonstrated by deductive argument based on those axioms, and he even ends each 'proof' with the letters Q.E.D.

The work is split into five parts: -

1. Concerning God
2. On the Nature and Origin of the Mind
3. Concerning the Origin and Nature of the Emotions
4. Of Human Bondage, or the Strength of the Emotions
5. Of the Power of the Intellect, or of Human Freedom

Each part opens with a set of definitions and axioms and is followed by a series of theorems proved upon the basis of what precedes them.

We have already met some of the argument concerning God. He starts by defining his idea of a substance (quoted above), and then defines what he means by an attribute of a substance as a kind of perceived essence of it. He defines God as being absolutely infinite. Then he proves that there can be no two substances of the same nature or attribute. Next, he uses the ontological argument to prove the existence of God (i.e. imagine the most perfect thing, if it does not exist then there is something more perfect that does exist). He then says that, given these definitions and axioms, there can't be two substances that are perfect and infinite, therefore God is everything there is.

His definitions, axioms and proofs are, of course, much longer and more involved than we have room for here, and (it must be said) somewhat more difficult to read. Here is an example of one of the shorter proofs, in this case of the statement that "Love towards God must hold the chief place in the mind": -

> "For this love is associated with all the modifications of the body (V, 14) and is fostered by them all (V, 15); therefore (V, 11) it must hold the chief place in the mind, Q.E.D."

Where the proposition referred to respectively state as follows: -

- **V, 14** – "The mind can bring it about, that all modifications or images of things may be referred to the idea of God".

- **V, 15** – "He who clearly and distinctly understands himself and his emotions loves God, and so much more in proportion as he understands himself and his emotions".

- **V, 11** – "In proportion as a mental image is referred to more objects, so is it more frequent, or more often vivid, and occupies the mind more."

Russell gives the following easier interpretation of the proof: -

> Every increase in the understanding of what happens to us consists in referring events to the idea of God, since, in truth, everything is part of God. This understanding of everything as part of God *is* love of God. When *all* objects are referred to God, the idea of God will fully occupy the mind.

This is, therefore, not an instruction to love God, but an account of what will inevitably happen when we acquire understanding. Here he is like Socrates, in saying that when you understand something perfectly then you will act correctly and wisely.

An Introduction to Philosophy

Russell notes that his outlook is intended to liberate man from the tyranny of fear, as when Spinoza says:

> "A free man thinks of nothing less than of death;
> and his wisdom is a meditation not of death, but
> of life."

To God, who understands everything, there is no evil; what seems like sin to us does not exist when viewed as part of the whole. For Spinoza, this is bound up with a complete rejection of free will and a dismissal of chance in the physical world. He also regards time as unreal, and therefore all emotions which have to do with a future or past event are contrary to reason. Pleasure in itself is good, but hope, fear and regret are bad.

> "He who repents of an action is doubly
> wretched or infirm."

Whatever happens, according to Spinoza, is part of the eternal timeless world as God sees it; to Him, the date is irrelevant. Only ignorance, he says, makes us think we can alter the future; what will be, will be, the future is as fixed as the past. Understanding that all things are necessary helps the mind acquire power over the emotions: -

> "He who clearly and distinctly understands
> himself and his emotions, loves God, and so
> much the more as the more he understands
> himself and his emotions."

For Spinoza, knowledge has three main grades, these being, in order of adequacy: (1) knowledge by hearsay and vague experience; (2) knowledge by general reasoning; and (3) knowledge by intuitive rational insight. The first type yields emotion and activity of an essentially enslaved sort, but human liberation consists in movement through the second type to the third type of knowledge. Only at that level do we cease to be the victims of our emotions, progressing to an intellectual love of God.

Spinoza's philosophy has much in common with Stoicism since both philosophies sought to fulfil a therapeutic role by instructing people how to attain happiness. However, Spinoza differed sharply from the Stoics in one important respect: he utterly rejected their contention that reason could defeat emotion. On the contrary, he contended, an emotion can only be displaced or overcome by a stronger emotion. For him, the crucial distinction was between active and passive emotions, active ones being those that are rationally understood and passive ones those that are not. He also held that knowledge of the true causes of a passive emotion can transform it to an active emotion, thus anticipating one of the key ideas of Sigmund Freud's psychoanalysis.

Although he believed in God, he was certainly against all forms of religion which he regarded as superstitious and life-denying, and which view the present life as mere preparation for a life to come. Rather, he thought, our primary aim should be joyous living in the here and now.

He is arguably the only really great 'modern' Western philosopher who develops what can properly be called a personal philosophy of life.

He ends the *Ethics* with these words: -

> "Whereas the wise man, in so far as he is regarded as such, is scarcely at all disturbed in spirit, but, being conscious of himself, and of God, and of things, by a certain eternal necessity, never ceases to be, but always possesses true acquiescence of his spirit. If the way which I have pointed out as leading to this result seems exceedingly hard, it may nevertheless be discovered. Needs must it be hard, since it is so seldom found. How would it be possible, if salvation were ready to our hand, and could without great labour be found, that it should be by almost all men neglected? But all things excellent are as difficult as they are rare."

Legacy

It is easy to understand why the mainstream religions didn't like him. His rejection of the concept of a personal God led many to brand him an atheist, and his books were also later put on the Catholic Church's *Index of Forbidden Books*.

The attraction of Spinoza's philosophy to the late 18th-century Europeans was that it provided an alternative to materialism, atheism, and deism. Three of Spinoza's ideas strongly appealed to them:

- The unity of all that exists;
- The regularity of all that happens;
- The identity of spirit and nature.

Spinoza's "God or Nature" provided a living, natural God, in contrast to the Newtonian mechanical "First Cause" or the dead mechanism of the French "Man Machine". Coleridge and Shelley saw in Spinoza's philosophy a religion of nature, and Spinoza inspired the poet Shelley to write his essay "The Necessity of Atheism".

Spinoza's pantheism was praised by many, but was considered by others to be alarming, and dangerously inimical. Karl Marx liked Spinoza's account of the universe, interpreting it as materialistic. On the other hand, many people pointed to similarities between Spinoza's philosophy and Eastern philosophical traditions, especially the Vedanta tradition of India.

As a last word on this we can turn to Wittgenstein who alludes to a Spinozian understanding of eternity and an interpretation of the religious concept of eternal life, stating that: –

> "If by eternity is understood not eternal temporal duration, but timelessness, then he lives eternally who lives in the present."

22

Leibniz

Introduction

Gottfried Wilhelm Leibniz (1646 – 1716) is one of the great German philosophers of modern times, and perhaps the last of the purely rationalist school of philosophers (i.e. those that hold that reason is the chief source and test of human knowledge). He was also a brilliant mathematician, an avid student of languages, and an all-round polymath.

The amount, variety, and disorder, of Leibniz's writings are a predictable result of a situation he described in a letter as follows: -

> "I cannot tell you how extraordinarily distracted and spread out I am. I am trying to find various things in the archives; I look at old papers and hunt up unpublished documents. From these I hope to shed some light on the history of the [House of] Brunswick. I receive and answer a huge number of letters. At the same time, I have so many mathematical results, philosophical thoughts, and other literary innovations that should not be allowed to vanish that I often do not know where to begin."

Background

Leibniz was born in Leipzig, Saxony, towards the end of the Thirty Years' War. His father died when he was six and a half years old, and from that point on he was raised by his mother. His father had been a Professor of Moral Philosophy at the University of Leipzig, and when his father died Leibniz inherited his father's personal library. His schoolwork at the time was not that extensive, but the library enabled him to study a wide variety of advanced philosophical and theological works. Access to the library, largely written in Latin, also led to his proficiency in Latin, which he achieved by the age of 12.

He enrolled in his father's former university at age 15, completed his bachelor's degree in philosophy in 1662 and earned his master's degree in philosophy in 1664 before his 18th birthday. Leibniz then enrolled in the University of Altdorf where he earned a Doctorate in Law and obtained his license to practice law.

In 1672 he went to Paris as a diplomatic envoy of the Elector of Mainz, and here he met Dutch physicist and mathematician Christiaan Huygens. With Huygens as his mentor, he began a program of self-study that soon pushed him to making major contributions to both subjects, including discovering his version of the differential and integral calculus in 1675. He was unaware of Newton's work on calculus which was completed 10 years earlier. Leibniz published his work on calculus in 1684 and Newton published in 1687, and there ensued an unfortunate dispute, discreditable to all parties, as to who had the priority. It is today, however, the notation invented by Leibniz that is most used, and even though Newton got there first, they are both now usually credited with its discovery.

While in Paris Leibniz also met Nicolas Malebranche and Antoine Arnauld (the leading French philosophers of the day) and he studied the writings of Descartes and Pascal, both unpublished as well as published. In 1673 he visited London and met with the Royal Society, where he demonstrated a calculating machine that he had designed and had been building since 1670. The machine was able to execute all four basic operations (adding, subtracting, multiplying, and dividing), and the Society quickly made him an external member.

The last important influence on his philosophy was that of Spinoza, whom he visited in 1676. He spent a month in frequent discussions with him, and secured part of Spinoza's *Ethics* in manuscript form. In later years, however, he minimised this influence by saying he had met him once and Spinoza had told him some good anecdotes about politics.

In1673, he entered service with the House of Hanover, and remained working for them for the rest of his life, becoming their librarian from 1680 onwards. The only major works he published during his life were **The Theodicy** (1710), and **Monadology** (1714). He did, however, submit numerous papers to leading European journals of the time, including: -

- Meditations on Knowledge, Truth, and Ideas (1684)
- Brief Demonstration of a Notable Error of Descartes (1686)
- Whether the Essence of Body Consists in Extension (1691)
- New Systems in Nature (1695)
- On Nature Itself (1698)

He also wrote a book-length study of John Locke's empiricism, *New Essays on Human Understanding*, but decided not to publish it when he learned of Locke's death. Indeed, much of his writing remained unpublished at the time of his death including tens of thousands of letters and unpublished manuscripts. From conversations he had with other philosophers, most notably Arnauld, he thought that many of his ideas would be regarded as shocking, hence Russell says: -

> "There are two systems of philosophy which may be regarded as representing Leibniz: one, which he proclaimed, was optimistic, orthodox, fantastic, and shallow; the other, which has slowly been unearthed from his manuscripts by fairly recent editors, was profound, coherent, largely Spinozistic, and amazingly logical. It was the popular Leibniz who invented the doctrine that this is the best of all possible worlds... it was this Leibniz whom Voltaire caricatured as Doctor Pangloss. It would be unhistorical to ignore this Leibniz, but the other is of far greater philosophical importance."

Philosophy

His Monadology

Like Descartes and Spinoza, Leibniz based his metaphysical philosophy on the notion of substance, but he differed radically from them as regards the relation of mind and matter. Descartes allowed three substances, God, mind, and matter, whereas Spinoza admitted just God alone (remember he thought that everything was God). Also, for Descartes, extension (the property of existing in more than one dimension) is the essence of matter; but for Spinoza, both extension and thought are attributes of God.

Leibniz held that extension cannot be an attribute of a substance because that involves plurality, and therefore could only belong to an aggregate of substances. He believed that matter was an aggregate of an infinite number of substances, which he called **Monads**. Each of these would have some of the properties of a physical point, but only when viewed abstractly; in fact he believed each monad is a soul. This was to some extent a logical conclusion because if you reject extension as an attribute of substance, then the only remaining possible attribute seemed to be thought. Thus, he rejected matter and substituted in its place an infinite family of souls. Here are the first two paragraphs from the *Monadology*: -

1. The monad, which we shall discuss here, is nothing but a simple substance that enters into composites – simple, i.e. without parts.

2. And there must be simple substances, since there are composites; for the composite is nothing more than a collection, or aggregate, of simples.

The essence of a monad is its irreducible simplicity. Unlike atoms, monads possess no material or spatial character. They also differ from atoms by their complete mutual independence, so that interactions among monads are only apparent. Instead, by virtue of the principle of 'pre-established harmony', each monad follows a pre-programmed set of "instructions" peculiar to itself, so that a monad "knows" what to do at each moment. (These "instructions" could be seen as analogues of the scientific laws governing subatomic particles.) By virtue of these intrinsic instructions, each monad is like a little mirror of the universe. Monads need not be "small"; e.g., each human being constitutes a monad, in which case free will is problematic.

Monads are purported to have eliminated the following problems: -

- Interaction between mind and matter arising in the system of Descartes;
- Lack of individuation inherent to the system of Spinoza, which represents individual creatures as merely accidental.

Leibniz formulated several principles as part of his reasoning and these have been used, in different forms, by philosophers and mathematicians in logical arguments ever since. Here are the three most important ones: -

- **Identity/contradiction**. If a proposition is true, then its negation is false and vice versa.
- **Identity of indiscernibles**. Two distinct things cannot have all their properties in common. If every predicate possessed by x is also possessed by y and vice versa, then entities x and y are identical; to suppose two things indiscernible is to suppose the same thing under two names. Frequently invoked in modern logic and philosophy, the "identity of indiscernibles" is often referred to as **Leibniz's Law**.
- **Sufficient reason**. "There must be a sufficient reason for anything to exist, for any event to occur, for any truth to obtain."

The **Identity of indiscernibles** is fundamental to his idea of monads: -

"For in nature there are never two beings which are perfectly alike and in which it is not possible to find an internal difference, or at least a difference founded upon intrinsic quality."

Monads were created initially by God, and although they form larger structures, they don't really interact with each other. They only appear to interact because God endowed them with a 'pre-established harmony' (a bit like synchronised clocks). Each monad also has a degree of 'perception' or awareness of other monads around it, but that varies according to the dignity of the monad concerned. Monads form a hierarchy, in which some are superior to others, for example, a human body is entirely composed of monads, each of which is a soul, but there is one dominant monad which is what is called the soul of the person of whose body it forms a part.

Proofs of God

Leibniz arguments for the existence of God are four in number; they are (1) the ontological argument, (2) the cosmological argument, (3) the augment from eternal truths, and (4) the argument from pre-established harmony.

The ontological argument defines God as the most perfect being and then says if he does not exist, he is not perfect, therefore, to be perfect he must exist. The cosmological argument is that there must be a first cause, and Leibniz includes here his principle of 'sufficient reason': there must be a reason for the universe, and therefore, that reason must be God.

The argument from eternal truths is more involved. Some things are true only some of the time, like the statement "it is raining", but other things are always true e.g. two plus two equals four. All statements that are only about essence (not about existence) are either always true or never true, and those that are always true are 'eternal truths'. Leibniz says that the reason for the world must be found in the eternal truths, and that these must exist as thoughts in the mind of God.

The argument from pre-established harmony goes back to his synchronised monads and says that only God could have synchronised them. This is another version of the argument from design.

Leibniz's Theodicy

Theodicy is a term relating to any religious arguments that justify the existence of evil and suffering in a world created by a supposedly loving and benevolent God. It was in fact Leibniz who coined this term, although the arguments themselves have a long history stretching back through St Aquinas, Plotinus and earlier.

It was Leibniz's theodicy that Voltaire caricatured in *Candide,* via the character Doctor Pangloss who kept claiming, in the face of one disaster after another, that this was for the best in this the best of all possible worlds.

Leibniz actual arguments were, firstly, that a world was only possible if it did not contradict the laws of logic. Secondly, God, being good, decided to create the best of the possible worlds, and He considered that to be one that had the greatest excess of good over evil. Thirdly, He could have created one without evil, but that would not have been as good because some goods are logically bound up with certain evils (e.g. in the trivial case of being thirsty on a hot day, the drink of cold water is so much better because of the pain of the previous thirst). And fourthly Leibniz used his principle of 'sufficient reason', i.e. God must have had a reason for creating this particular world.

It seems logically impossible for God to bestow free will and at the same time decree that there should be no sin. The world that resulted, however, does seem to contain an excess of good over evil (according to Leibniz) hence demonstrating it is the best possible world.

In fact, Leibniz thought the world deterministic, but because it was so complex, the analysis required to deduce how someone will act is only possible for God. So, although human actions flow from prior causes that ultimately arise in God (and therefore are known as a metaphysical certainty to God) an individual's free will is exercised, he claims, within natural laws, where choices are merely contingently necessary, to be decided in the event by a "wonderful spontaneity" that provides individuals an escape from rigorous predestination.

Symbolic logic

Leibniz believed that much of human reasoning could be reduced to calculations of a sort, and that such calculations could resolve many differences of opinion: -

> "The only way to rectify our reasonings is to make them as tangible as those of the Mathematicians, so that we can find our error at a glance, and when there are disputes among persons, we can simply say: Let us calculate without further ado, to see who is right."

He took his speculations much further. Defining a character as any written sign, he then defined a "real" character as one that represents an idea directly and not simply as the word embodying the idea. Some 'real characters', such as the notation of logic, serve only to facilitate reasoning.

> "It is obvious that if we could find characters or signs suited for expressing all our thoughts as clearly and as exactly as arithmetic expresses numbers or geometry expresses lines, we could do in all matters insofar as they are subject to reasoning all that we can do in arithmetic and geometry. For all investigations which depend on reasoning would be carried out by transposing these characters and by a species of calculus."

All ideas, he says, are compounded from a very small number of simple ideas, and complex thoughts could therefore be represented by combining the characters for simpler thoughts using a uniform and symmetrical combination operator, analogous to arithmetical multiplication.

Legacy

When Leibniz died, his reputation was in decline. He was remembered for only one book, **The Theodicy**, whose supposed central argument Voltaire lampooned in *Candide*. Voltaire's depiction of Leibniz's ideas was so influential that many believed it to be an accurate description.

Leibniz's philosophical thinking appeared fragmented, because his philosophical writings consist mainly of a multitude of short pieces: journal articles, manuscripts published long after his death, and many letters to numerous correspondents. However, Russell says that Leibniz "is the best example of a philosopher who uses logic as a key to metaphysics".

Unlike Descartes and Spinoza, Leibniz had a thorough university education in philosophy. He was deeply interested in the new methods and conclusions of Descartes, Huygens, Newton, and Boyle, but viewed their work through a lens heavily tinted by the scholastic background of his early education. Yet it remains the case that Leibniz's methods and concerns often anticipate the logic, and analytic and linguistic philosophy of the 20th century. Indeed, Russell was so impressed that he went so far as to claim that Leibniz had developed logic in his unpublished writings to a level which was reached only 200 years later.

His idea of reasoning through a universal language of symbols and calculations remarkably foreshadows great 20th century developments in formal systems, such as Turing completeness, where computation was used to define equivalent universal languages.

Leibniz's reputation as a philosopher is now perhaps higher than at any time since he was alive, and analytic and contemporary philosophy continues to invoke his notions of identity, individuation, and possible worlds. This reputation, however, rests mainly on his ideas on logic and on writings unpublished during his lifetime rather than his two books ***The Theodicy*** and ***Monadology*** published before his death.

23

George Berkeley

Introduction

George Berkeley (1685 – 1753) is a bit of an enigma in that he seems to have one foot on each side of the empiricist/rationalist divide (i.e. does knowledge start with our experience of the world or does it come from reason?) Having said that, he is usually classified alongside the empiricists of the British tradition.

Berkeley picks up on the ideas of John Locke's philosophy of perception, but he then extends these to the point where perception itself is the only reality and denies the existence of matter altogether, thus making him the first of the so called 'Idealist' philosophers (i.e. the theory that everything that exists is mental). He was also a religious man and held that God was the source of our perceptions, perhaps a logical extension if you reject matter as the source.

In popular terms it is quite easy to make fun of someone who says that matter does not exist except when it's being perceived. What happens when no-one is looking, is it still there? For example, in the early twentieth century, the English priest, theologian and author of detective stories, Ronald Knox penned the following limerick making fun of Berkeley's philosophy: -

> There was a young man who said "God
> Must find it exceedingly odd
>   To think that the tree
>   Should continue to be
> When there's no one about in the quad."

Reply: -
> "Dear Sir:
> Your astonishment's odd;
> I am always about in the quad.
>   And that's why the tree
>   Will continue to be
> Since observed by,
>   Yours faithfully,
>   God."

We also have Boswell's account of Dr. Johnson's retort to Berkeley's ideas: -

> "After we came out of church we stood talking for some time together of Bishop Berkeley's ingenious sophistry to prove the non-existence of matter, and that everything in the universe is merely ideal. I observed, that though we are satisfied that his doctrine is not true, it is impossible to refute it. I shall never forget the alacrity with which Johnson answered, striking his foot with mighty force against a large stone, till he rebounded from it, 'I refute it thus!'"

Notwithstanding the above, however, a more detailed examination of Berkeley's philosophy can be very rewarding, especially regarding the question of how we give credence to that which we think we know, in other words the field of epistemology (the theory of knowledge).

Background

Firstly, a note on pronunciation: The English pronunciation is "Barkley", the Americans, however, pronounce it "Burkley", even though the town (and the university) of Berkeley, in California, is named in honour of George Berkeley.

Berkeley was born near the town of Kilkenny, in southern Ireland, in 1685, to a Protestant Irish family. At the age of fifteen he entered Trinity College, Dublin, and it was here that he read, and was inspired by, Descartes and John Locke. At the age of twenty-two he was elected a Fellow of the college, and it was during his years as a Fellow that he wrote his most important works: -

- A New Theory of Vision (1709)
- Treatise Concerning the Principles of Human Knowledge (1710)
- The Dialogues of Hylas and Philonous (1713)

Also in 1713, he went to London, and there he was the toast of the town, mentioned in works by Swift, Pope, and others, and debating before royalty. A year or two later, after a grand tour of the Continent, he set up a scheme for starting a college in Bermuda, from where the whole of

America was to be evangelized. He even won backing from both the king and parliament, with a promised grant of £20,000 for the venture. The romantic design actually came to nothing, but Berkeley's stay in Rhode Island, while waiting for the grant, was a very fruitful one for American education and for the infant universities of Yale and Harvard, who benefited from scholarships, libraries, and other gifts from him. And, of course, the Californians named a town after him.

Berkeley returned to England disappointed and was shortly afterwards appointed Bishop of Cloyne in Ireland. He continued to write, but his later worked lacked the force of what he produced in his twenties. He died at the age of 68 while on a visit to Oxford to install one of his sons there.

It seems no-one ever had a bad word to say about him, he treated everyone with respect and kindness. Pope attributed "To Berkeley every virtue under heaven", and his wife said of him that "he loved God and man" and he "silenced and confused atheists, disguised as mathematicians and fine gentlemen".

Philosophy

Berkeley had two main philosophical concerns, the first was how to deal with recent sceptical worries about the material world (i.e. how can we know that such a world exists), and second, he wanted to counter what he saw as the growing tendency of the scientists and philosophers of his day to push God to the periphery in their thinking about the world. With science describing an increasingly mechanistic view of how the universe worked, it seemed that God was only required to set the whole thing in motion.

The first concern is about how we perceive the world and what inferences we can legitimately draw from those perceptions. He starts by agreeing with Locke that all we have, present in our mind, are our perceptions, and these derive from sensation and reflection. This makes him an empiricist of the school of Locke. But he then went further than Locke in denying the ability of the mind to form abstract ideas.

Locke, remember, denied innate ideas, saying that everything we know comes from experience via perception and reflection. He said that all our simple ideas are involuntary ones (i.e. we cannot compel ourselves to have a perception of a tree or a boat or a person: they are either given or not given to the perception). Locke then went on to say that all our complex or abstract ideas are built up through combinations of simple ideas via the mind's reflection and self-criticism. Berkeley accepts the empiricist approach of knowledge, that of only being by perception and reflection, but he rejects Locke's doctrine of complex ideas.

An Introduction to Philosophy

In the introduction to his ***Principles of Human Knowledge***, Berkeley says: -

> It is indeed an opinion *strangely* prevailing among men, that houses, mountains, rivers, and in a word all sensible objects have an existence natural or real, distinct from their being perceived by the understanding. But with how great an assurance and acquiescence soever this principle may be entertained in the world; yet whoever shall find in his heart to call it into question, may, if I mistake not, perceive it to involve a manifest contradiction.

A word, he says, is not a complex or abstract idea, but a sign of several particular ideas. To some extent that sounds like a distinction without a difference. But he makes it clearer with the example of a geometrician demonstrating a method of cutting a line in half. The geometrician draws a line on the paper and demonstrates the method of bisecting it. The line itself is a particular line, however, for this demonstration it represents all lines because the method works on all lines in general. Therefore, that particular line becomes general by being made a sign, so the word *line*, which taken absolutely is *particular*, but by being made a sign is made general.

The elimination of complex or abstract ideas is important to him in order to keep his philosophy as unconfused as possible. He admits only a strictly empirical view of the objects of human knowledge as being: -

> Either *ideas* actually (1) imprinted on the senses, or else such as are (2) perceived by attending to the passions and operations of the mind, or lastly (3) formed by the help of memory and imagination, either compounding, dividing, or barely representing those originally perceived ideas in the aforesaid ways.

From this starting point, do we really know anything but the mind's ideas? Is not all, in some sense perception? From here we get his famous maxim "Esse is Percipi" i.e. "To Exist is to be Perceived".

He expands on this in his ***Dialogues of Hylas and Philonous***, where he has Hylas expounding the common-sense view and Philonous responding as Berkeley. Hylas starts by saying 'can anything be more fantastical than to believe there is no such thing as matter?' To which Philonous replies that 'by sight we perceive only light, colour, and shape;

George Berkeley

by hearing, only sounds; and so on. Consequently, apart from sensible qualities there is nothing sensible, and sensible things are nothing but sensible qualities or combinations of sensible qualities.'

Philonous then sets out to prove that "the reality of sensible things consist in being perceived." He examines the different senses, starting with heat and cold. Great heat, he says, is a pain, and must be in the mind. Therefore, heat is mental, and a similar argument applies to cold. He reinforces this with the example of lukewarm water. When one of your hands is hot and the other cold, if you put both hands into lukewarm water, one hand will feel it as cold and the other as hot, but the water can't itself be both hot and cold at the same time. Therefore, heat and cold are only sensations in our minds.

Hylas switches to sight and says that "the case of colours is different, Can anything be plainer than that we see them on objects?" But Philonous easily deals with that. He says, 'what about clouds at sunset which are red and golden, but if you get up close to such a cloud you will see it has no such colour'. He also goes on to deal with the other senses in the same way, showing that they are all subjective to the individual and his situation.

Hylas gives way on the senses but then says he made a mistake in not distinguishing the object from the sensation. Forget perception for a minute, colours for example must "have a real existence without the mind, in some unthinking substance". To this Philonous says "That any immediate object of the senses – that is any idea or combination of ideas – should exist in an unthinking substance, or exterior to *all* minds, is in itself an evident contradiction. ... Whatever is immediately perceived is an idea; and can any idea exist out of a mind?"

Locke, remember, distinguished between primary and secondary qualities, primary ones being bulk, figure, number, etc., which belong to an object itself, while secondary ones such as colour, heat, texture, etc., were attributes imputed by the mind. Berkeley, however, asks if some qualities occurred only in the mind, by what logical process is it possible to say that the remaining qualities, observed by the senses, were 'real' qualities? How can we attribute substantial reality to matter when all that is known is perceptual reality?

He goes on to say, however, that even though we know nothing about matter, that is not to say that we have no knowledge of anything beyond ideas. We have knowledge of: - "*that which experiences ideas*", i.e. of a self. (You can see here, of course, the influence of Descartes.) Also, this self is not just another idea, because ideas are passive, but the self is active. The self is a substance, but not a material one (because it has already been demonstrated that there are no material substances), it is, therefore, an active substance or *spirit*.

Our personal spirit, although it has inner activity, cannot by itself determine what sense impressions we receive, therefore there must be another source, outside ourselves, of these impressions. That source is the Supreme Spirit – God. His proof of God is as follows: -

> "Whatever power I may have over my own thoughts, I find the ideas actually perceived by Sense have not a like dependence on my will. When in broad daylight I open my eyes, it is not in my power to choose whether I shall see or no, or to determine what particular objects shall present themselves to my view; and so likewise as to the hearing and other senses; the ideas imprinted on them are not creatures of my will. There is therefore some other Will or Spirit that produces them."

Solipsism avoided.

Note here that in denying the existence of anything material in the world Berkeley come very close to solipsism, i.e. the idea that 'I am the only thing that exists, everything else is just ideas in my head, even other people'. Logically, it's impossible to refute this, but Berkeley avoids it by identifying spirit and God as the source of our sense impressions.

Berkeley is an '**Idealist** ', i.e. someone who says: -

- All we actually know about the world are sensations (colour, sound, taste, touch, the relative positions of things that we perceive). We cannot know about the world by any other means. For us, these sensations are what we mean by 'the world'.
- All these sensations are 'ideas': they are mental phenomena. (The colour red does not exist independent of the mind perceiving something of that colour.)
- Things are therefore collections of these ideas; they exist by being perceived. (A tree, for example, is a collection of perceptions: colours, shape, texture etc. and may well appear different to different people.)

What happens, however, if nobody looks at the tree, does it still exist? Berkeley's answer is that it does because it is being perceived by God.

Descartes revolutionised philosophy with his 'I think therefore I am'. But for him, the fact that he exists (in some undetermined form) is all he could logically say, because it was possible that an evil demon generated the thoughts he had, therefore he could not, with certainty, believe his perceptions of the world. Berkeley went beyond that by saying that objects (like a tree) did exist, but only as bundles, or collections, of perceptions in the mind.

Berkeley's Science and Mathematics

Berkeley's work covered more than just the science of perception, his interests were very wide ranging, and there is not space here to do them all justice. When he was fifty, for instance, he wrote a book titled *A Defence of Free-thinking in Mathematics*. In it he continues his criticism of complex or abstract ideas. And in defence of immaterialism, he attacks a number of the scientific ideas of his day, in particular those of Newton and Leibniz.

He argued against Isaac Newton's doctrine of absolute space, time, and motion. Time, for him, is simply generalised from the succession of ideas in our own minds, it has no existence apart from them. There is no absolute time behind the succession of ideas; duration and the measure of duration are one and the same thing. Absolute or pure space, that extension in which Newton lodged his atomic particles, is also for Berkeley an illusion. Space can only be relative to the position of perceived bodies, and it would be meaningless to consider space without bodies. Motion, too, could only be conceived in relative terms between bodies. These arguments of his were an amazing precursor to the views of Ernst Mach and Einstein.

He also attacks the idea of infinitesimals, Newton's, and Leibniz's mathematics of calculus. He did not object to the use to which this type of mathematics was put, only to its philosophical consequences. Because if you could divide reality into points so minute as to be below sense experience, and derive laws of nature from this, then knowledge would no longer be derived from sense experience. While the mathematics might work, the idea of physically breaking a line into ever smaller and smaller pieces was obviously impossible to him.

Legacy

Berkeley was famous in his day and his ideas were very influential to subsequent philosophers like Hume, Kant, and Schopenhauer. Interest in

An Introduction to Philosophy

Berkeley's work also increased after World War II because he tackled many of the issues of paramount interest to philosophy in the 20th century, such as the problems of perception, the difference between primary and secondary qualities, and the importance of language.

Philosophers like Russell and Wittgenstein used his ideas as a starting point for their own. Russell says of him that: - "He thinks he is proving that all reality is mental; what he is proving is that we perceive qualities, not things, and that qualities are relative to the percipient."

So, although his ideas might seem absurd to a common-sense view, his philosophy is well worth understanding, because it touches the heart of what it means to be alive and aware in the universe.

24

David Hume

Introduction

David Hume (1711 – 1776) is the third of the great empiricist philosophers of the British tradition. Writing in Edinburgh during the period called **The Enlightenment**, or **The Age of Reason** (which stretched from the 1650s through to the 1780s), Hume picked up on the ideas of Locke and Berkeley and expanded on them, producing, according to Russell: -

"A scepticism that no-one could deny, but no-one could accept".

We covered some of Hume's thinking in chapter 3 where we looked at **epistemology** (the theory of knowledge). This asks: -

- How do we know that those things that we think we know, are actually correct?
- (In other words: how do we give credence to our understanding of the world?)

Since then, we have looked back at the development of Western Philosophy, from Socrates through to Locke and Berkeley, so it seems relevant that we should now re-look at Hume in order to better understand how his ideas fit into that development (albeit at the expense, perhaps, of some duplication).

Background

Hume was born in Edinburgh in 1711. His father owned a small estate in Berwickshire, but his family was not rich. He was educated at home until, at the young age of 12, he entered Edinburgh University. His family wanted him to become a lawyer and after university they sent him to some merchants they knew in Bristol to learn business, but he failed to fit in there.

He decided to go to France to live frugally in a country retreat and continue his studies. It was during his time there that he produced his great work *A Treatise of Human Nature*. This was published in three volumes in 1739 and 1740, when he was 28. Unfortunately, this work did not sell well, possibly because he was not well known at that time. Being a naturally cheerful person however, he didn't dwell long on this setback. He returned to his family estate in Scotland and occupied himself with his political writings, and in 1741 he published **Essays, Moral, Political, and Literary**, which was much more successful and laid the ground for his subsequent literary fame.

After that, he applied for the Chair of Moral Philosophy at the University of Edinburgh but was unsuccessful because he was seen as being an atheist. From 1746, Hume served for three years as secretary to General James St Clair, who was envoy to the courts of Turin and Vienna. And it was during that time that he wrote *Philosophical Essays Concerning Human Understanding*, published in 1748 as **An Enquiry Concerning Human Understanding**. This was a revised and more accessible version of his earlier *Treaties of Human Nature*.

Hume's religious views were often regarded as suspect, and it was necessary in the 1750s for his friends to avert a trial against him on the charge of heresy. He returned to Edinburgh in 1751 and obtained the post of librarian at the university, which gave him access to a large selection of books. Here he continued his writing producing **An Enquiry Concerning the Principles of Morals** in 1751, and **The History of England** *(1754-62) a* series of books which went through 100 editions. This later work made him a rich man. He also produced **The Natural History of Religion** in 1757 and **Dialogues Concerning Natural Religion** which was published posthumously in 1779.

Philosophy

In chapter 3, when we looked at Hume, we just considered his theory of knowledge. He divided knowledge into two types: - deductive knowledge and inductive knowledge. Deductive knowledge comes from things like mathematics and logic, whereas inductive knowledge is everything else we think we know. All inductive knowledge comes from experience and perception of the world via our senses. Remember he gave the example of one billiard ball hitting another, it is only due to experience that we expect the second ball to move, a baby, for instance, would have no such expectation. Therefore, it is only through experience of the world that we build up knowledge, and, importantly, this knowledge can only be something we give probabilities to [please refer back to chapter 3 for a more detailed discussion of knowledge]. He also denied the existence of innate ideas, because, as demonstrated, experience of the world can only come via the senses.

> "The only existences, of which we are certain, are perceptions, which, being immediately present to us by consciousness, command our strongest assent, and are the first foundation of all our conclusions."

Berkeley, remember, was willing to suppose that, in addition to perception, we have a *notion* of spiritual things, including a *notion* of God, and that these two notions support the existence of an external reality (albeit not one of physical substance). Hume went further, he denied innate ideas and could find no evidence of anything other than ideas formed via perception.

Both Descartes and Berkeley identified a self or soul of some sort, but Hume could find no evidence for this. Whenever he examined the workings of his own mind, he could identify nothing other than the flow of thoughts and experiences. He says: -

> "For my part, when I enter most intimately into what I call *myself*, I always stumble on some particular perception or other, of heat or cold, light or shade, love or hatred, pain or pleasure. I never catch *myself* at any time without a perception." ... [The self he says is] "nothing but a bundle or collection of different perceptions, which succeed each other with inconceivable rapidity, and are in a perpetual state of flux and movement."

Russell comments that:

> "This conclusion is important in metaphysics, as getting rid of the last surviving use of 'substance'. It is important for theology, as abolishing all supposed knowledge of the 'soul'. It is important in the analysis of knowledge, since it shows that the category of subject and object is not fundamental. In this matter of the ego Hume made an important advance on Berkeley."

Hume divided the mind's contents into two categories: impressions – perceptions we have via our senses; and ideas – less vivid copies of impressions. If I see a red apple, for instance, I have a sensory impression of its colour: red. My mind can then take a copy of this sense impression of the colour red and use it as my idea or concept of red, but if I close my eyes and try to imagine a red door it will be less vivid than a direct sensation. This is called Hume's Copy Principle.

He then distinguishes between two sorts of ideas, simple ones and complex ones. The complex ideas we have are built from simple ones, e.g. we could imagine a snowball using the simple ideas of cold, hard, round and white, or even a unicorn by combining the simple ideas of horse and horn.

Cause and Effect

Another part of Hume's philosophy is his rejection of the idea of cause and effect. He says that if you repeatedly perceive one thing following another thing, then you conceive the idea that the first thing caused the second. But you have not actually perceived this causal relation, it is just an idea that you have conceived. He says that the power by which one object produces an effect in another is not discoverable from the ideas of the two objects; therefore, we can only know cause and effect from experience, not from reasoning or reflection.

He maintains that when we say A causes B, we mean only that A and B are constantly observed to be conjoined, not that there is some necessary connection between them: - "We cannot penetrate into the reason of the conjunction." "Necessity," he says, "is something that exists in the mind, not in objects." And "all our reasonings concerning causes and effects are derived from nothing but custom."

He also extends these ideas to claim that past experience is not a rational justification that the future will be the same, only that it increases the probability: the taste of an apple yesterday is not a guarantee that it will taste the same today. The conclusion is one of complete scepticism: -

> "All probable reasoning is nothing but a species of sensation. 'Tis not solely in poetry and music, we must follow our taste and sentiment, but likewise in philosophy."

David Hume

Morality and Politics

Hume also wrote on morality and on politics, but we don't have space here to cover all his output. In terms of morality, he denies that there is a moral law outside man, reducible to axioms like those of geometry. For him, morality is subjectivity; it is the result of a feeling. There is no wrong in the objective situation in external nature; it is within himself that man feels right or wrong.

He comes close to the Social Contract of Hobbes, but he rejects Hobbes' notion of a brutish state of nature from which men fled in fear to society. He argues that the social life of man involves some kind of agreement to accept the restrictions of society. This arises from a general sense of common interest. The disadvantages are the restrictions on individual liberty, but the advantages are the security and permanence of one's possessions, and the opportunity to add to them.

Religion

We covered some of Hume's ideas on religion in chapter 3. Remember one of the things he argued against was the plausibility of miracles, which he connected with his idea of knowledge being based on probability.

His last publication was the posthumous ***Dialogues Concerning Natural Religion.*** In this Hume has three philosophers named Demea, Philo, and Cleanthes debate the nature of God's existence. Between them they discuss all the arguments from previous philosophers for God's existence, but while all three agree that a god exists, they differ sharply in opinion on God's nature or attributes and how, or if, humankind can come to knowledge of a deity.

The Stanford Encyclopedia of Philosophy says: -

> Whatever interpretation one takes of Hume's philosophy as a whole, it is certainly true that one of his most basic philosophical objectives is to discredit the doctrines and dogmas of traditional theistic belief. There are, however, some significant points of disagreement about the exact nature and extent of Hume's irreligious intentions. One of the most important of these is whether Hume's sceptical position leads him to a view that can be properly characterized as "atheism".

It adds however: -

Hume lived and wrote at a time of severe religious persecution, by both the church and the state. Unorthodox religious views, and more especially any form of open atheism, would certainly provoke strong reactions from the authorities. Caution and subterfuge in these circumstances was essential if difficulties of these kinds were to be avoided.

The ***Dialogues*** were originally published with neither the author's nor the publisher's name.

Legacy

Hume's approach to philosophy places him with John Locke, George Berkeley, Francis Bacon, and Thomas Hobbes as a British Empiricist. He strove to create a total naturalistic science of man that examined the psychological basis of human nature, and, against the rationalists, he held that passion rather than reason governs human behaviour.

He argued against the existence of innate ideas, postulating that humans can have knowledge only of the objects of experience and the relations of ideas, calling the rest (especially including religious based philosophies) "nothing but sophistry and illusion". His compatibilist theory of free will takes causal determinism as fully compatible with human freedom, and has proved extremely influential on subsequent moral philosophy.

Hume's moral theory maintained an early commitment to naturalistic explanations of moral phenomena, and is usually taken to have first clearly expounded the 'is–ought problem', or the idea that a statement of fact alone can never give rise to a normative conclusion of what *ought* to be done.

His ***Treatise of Human Nature*** (begun when he was just 23) is now regarded as one of the most important works in the history of Western Philosophy. Hume has since proved extremely influential on subsequent Western thought, especially on utilitarianism, logical positivism, William James, Immanuel Kant, the philosophy of science, early analytic philosophy, and cognitive science.

Immanuel Kant credited Hume with awakening him from "dogmatic slumbers", and according to Schopenhauer, "there is more to be learned from each page of David Hume than from the collected philosophical works of Hegel, Herbart and Schleiermacher taken together".

A. J. Ayer claimed that his own views derived from doctrines which are themselves the logical outcome of the empiricism of Berkeley and

David Hume

David Hume. Albert Einstein, in 1915, wrote that he was inspired by Hume's positivism when formulating his theory of special relativity. Karl Popper said: "I approached the problem of induction through Hume. Hume, I felt, was perfectly right in pointing out that induction cannot be logically justified". Danish theologian and philosopher Søren Kierkegaard said: "Hume's suggestion that the role of reason is not to make us wise but to reveal our ignorance."

Hume also engaged with other contemporary intellectuals such as Jean-Jacques Rousseau, James Boswell, and Adam Smith (who acknowledged Hume's influence on his economics and political philosophy). Isaiah Berlin once said of Hume that "No man has influenced the history of philosophy to a deeper or more disturbing degree." And The Stanford Encyclopedia of Philosophy writes that Hume is "Generally regarded as one of the most important philosophers to write in English."

25

Thomas Reid

Introduction

Thomas Reid (1710 – 1796) was a Scottish philosopher best known for his philosophical method, his theory of perception and its wide implications on epistemology, and as the developer and defender of an agent-causal theory of free will. In these and other areas he offers perceptive criticisms of the philosophy of Locke, Berkeley and especially Hume.

Background

Reid was the son of a Scottish minister; he went to university in Aberdeen and later became the Librarian there. He founded the Aberdeen Philosophical Society (which became known as 'The Wise Club'), and in 1752 he became Professor of Philosophy at Kings College, Aberdeen. Then, in 1764, he succeeded Adam Smith as Professor of Moral Philosophy at Glasgow University.

His first important work was **Enquiry into the Human Mind on the Principles of Common Sense**, published in 1764. His other major work was the massive **Essays on the Intellectual Powers of Man**, which appeared in 1785. The *Essays* were a condensed and ordered form of his lectures spanning the previous twenty years.

He left his position at Glasgow University in 1781 and spent his retirement organising his notes and writing. He died of palsy in Glasgow and was buried at Blackfriars Church in the grounds of Glasgow College, and when the university moved to Gilmorehill in the west of Glasgow, his tombstone was inserted into the main building.

Philosophy

Reid's theory of knowledge had a strong influence on his theory of morals. He thought epistemology was an introductory part to practical ethics: When we are confirmed in our common beliefs by philosophy, all we have to do is to act according to them, because we know what is right. His moral philosophy is reminiscent of Roman stoicism in its emphasis on the agency of the subject and on self-control.

Reid's whole approach to philosophy was that of common sense, a position that, in philosophical terms today, we would call 'realistic'. He starts by making fun of the empiricists where they take perception as the only valid reality. Why should these 'impressions' and 'ideas' (that Locke and Hume talked about) not be subject to the same scepticism so vigorously applied to every other department?

Locke forced bodies to give up their secondary qualities to ideas: Berkeley thereafter stole their primary qualities: then Hume disposed of mental substance as readily as Berkeley disposed of material, and so spirits, too, surrendered, leaving ideas victorious alone upon an abandoned field. But what, asked Reid, if ideas have cannibalistic tendencies? Philosophers will be out of a job!

He devoted a great deal of time to the problem of perception, what do we mean by it, how does it work, and what is the relationship between perception and knowledge of the world? His ***Inquiry*** is a methodologically pioneering work due to its extensive and rigorous use of observational data to justify his claims about perception.

The problem is how we get from sensations, which are admittedly not identical with the objects that promote them, to a conviction of an external nature and an experiencing self? Reid says that sensation *suggests* to us present existence: memory *suggests* past existence; and any change in nature *suggests* a cause. He looks at each of the senses in turn, here is what he says of touch: -

> "And in like manner... certain sensations of touch, by the constitution of our nature, suggest to us extension, solidity, and motion, which are nowise like to sensations, although they have been hitherto confounded with them."

He says that the eye is the organ of sight, and we know how it forms a picture of visible objects upon the retina; but how that picture makes us 'see' the object is not known. We can give no reason why a picture on the retina should be followed by vision, while a picture on any other part of our body produces nothing. He concludes that we simply have this power, as given by God.

Sensations are signs of external objects. They are not the external objects themselves but carry immediate powerful conviction that these objects exist and possess such qualities of form, colour, texture and position as our senses read into them.

Reid also appeals to the authority of language in his *Essays*, he says: -

> "In the perception of an external object, all languages distinguish three things, the ***mind*** that perceives, the operation of that mind, which is called ***perception***, and the ***object*** perceived. Nothing appears more evident to a mind untutored by philosophy, than that these three are distinct things, which, although related, ought never to be confounded. The structure of all languages supposes this distinction, and is built upon it. Philosophers have introduced a fourth thing in this process, which they call the idea of the object, which is supposed to be an image, or representation of the object, and is said to be the immediate object. The vulgar know nothing about this idea."

According to Reid, the mind is so constituted that sensation automatically causes a belief in external objects. A sensation of smell, for example, causes the belief that there is an external cause of the sensation. This belief is neither inferred nor rational but is caused by the occurrence of the sensation. This is, he maintains, intuitively obvious to common sense.

Legacy

His *Essays* (based on his lectures) were widely used as textbooks, especially in America. He was also a supporter of the French Revolution (although disappointed at its excesses) and his work became an official part of the French university curriculum.

Reid hoped that Hume would reply to his criticisms, but Hume's disdainful response was to recommend him to avoid Scotticisms and improve his English. What seems to be missing in Reid's criticism of Hume is an understanding of Hume's induction method for how we develop concepts about the world from infancy onwards.

Schopenhauer, however, praised Reid for explaining that the perception of external objects does not result from the raw data that is received through the five senses.

Reid was also an important influence on the American philosopher Charles Sanders Peirce, who shared Reid's concern to revalue common sense and whose work links Reid to American Pragmatism.

26

Rousseau

Introduction

Jean-Jacques Rousseau (1712 – 1778) was not really a philosopher in the traditional sense, but he did have a powerful influence on subsequent philosophy, literature, taste, manners, and politics. He was the first of the school of philosophy now labelled as 'Romanticism and German Idealism' and is rightly considered the father of the Romantic Movement.

Background

Rousseau was born in Geneva, which was, at the time, a city-state, and a Protestant associate of the Swiss Confederacy. Geneva, in theory, was governed democratically by its male voting "citizens" although the citizens were a minority of the population when compared to the immigrants, referred to as "inhabitants". He was proud that his family had voting rights in the city, and throughout his life he generally signed his books "Jean-Jacques Rousseau, Citizen of Geneva".

His mother died just nine days after his birth, and he was brought up by an aunt. His father was a poor watchmaker who made extra money as a dancing master. Rousseau was educated as an orthodox Calvinist. He left school at the age of 12 and was apprenticed to various trades, but he hated them all.

At 16 he fled to neighbouring Savoy, which was at the time an independent state, but which is now divided between Switzerland, Italy and France. There he took shelter with a Catholic priest and asked to be converted to Catholicism. How sincere he was is unknown, in his *Confessions* he represents it as an 'act of a bandit', but that was written many years later, after he had reverted to Protestantism.

He drifted around Europe, finding work where he could, and seemingly able to charm a number of rich ladies into relationships. In 1745 he moved to Paris and there befriended and became the lover of Thérèse Levasseur, a seamstress who was the sole support of her mother and numerous ne'er-do-well siblings. At first, they did not live together, though later Rousseau took Thérèse and her mother in to live with him as his servants, and he assumed the burden of supporting her large family. He lived with her for the rest of his life (not to the exclusion of other affairs) and had five children by her, all of whom he persuaded her to take to the Foundling Hospital.

While in Paris, Rousseau became a close friend of French philosopher Diderot and, beginning with some articles on music in 1749, contributed numerous articles to Diderot and D'Alembert's great *Encyclopédie*, the most famous of which was an article on political economy written in 1755.

Philosophy

His first literary success came in 1750, when he won a prize for the best essay on the question: 'Have the arts and sciences conferred benefits on mankind?' Rousseau answered that they haven't, contending that they are the worst enemies of morals, and, by creating wants, are the sources of slavery. He held up for admiration the 'noble savage' as being free from the corrupting influences of civilisation.

This was really the start of the Romanticism Movement. It was also, remember, an outlook opposite to Hobbes who had said that men are driven by their passions, and without a social contract to bind them into a civilised society, it would be a 'war of all against all'.

Rousseau returned to Geneva in 1754, reconverted to Calvinism and regained his official Genevan citizenship. He then elaborated on his ideas in a second essay in 1755 entitled 'Discourse on Inequality', holding that "man is naturally good, and only by institutions is he made bad." Rousseau does not object to natural inequality, in respect of age, health, intelligence, etc., but only to inequality resulting from privileges authorised by convention. According to him, the origin of civil society and its consequent social inequalities is to be found in private property: -

> "The first man who, having enclosed a piece of land, bethought himself of saying 'this is mine,' and found people simple enough to believe him, was the real founder of civil society."

He dedicated his second essay to the City Fathers of Geneva, but they were not too pleased, they didn't want to be considered as the equals to ordinary citizens. He also sent a copy of his new essay to Voltaire, who was living in Geneva at that time, and Voltaire replied: -

"I have received your new book against the human race, and thank you for it. Never was such cleverness used in the design of making us all stupid. One longs, in reading your book, to walk on all fours. But as I have lost that habit for more than sixty years, I feel unhappily the impossibility of resuming it. Nor can I embark in search of the savages of Canada, because the maladies to which I am condemned render a European surgeon necessary to me; because war is going on in those regions; and because the example of our actions has made the savages nearly as bad as ourselves."

In 1761 Rousseau published an 800-page novel, ***Julie, ou la nouvelle Héloïse***. It was an immense success; the book's rhapsodic descriptions of the natural beauty of the Swiss countryside struck a chord with the public in terms of romantic scenery, feelings of sentiment, and behavioural manners. In it he illustrates the principle that one should do what is imposed upon him by society only insofar as it would seem congruent with one's "secret principles" and feelings, being constituent of one's core identity.

Then, in 1762, he published both ***Emile*** and ***The Social Contract***. *Emile* was a treatise on education according to 'natural' principles and might have been considered harmless had it not contained a section entitled 'The Confession of Faith of a Savoyard Vicar', which set forth his principles of natural religion. This upset both the Catholic and Protestant orthodoxies. *The Social Contract* was even more dangerous, for it advocated democracy and denied the divine right of kings.

Both books greatly increased his fame, but both were eventually banned. The French Government even ordered his arrest, and few places would give him asylum. At last Fredrick the Great took pity on him and allowed him to live in the village of Motiers. That lasted three years but then the villagers, led by their pastor, accused him of poisoning and tried to murder him.

He fled to England where Hume had offered to help him, and there he initially had great success. George III granted him a pension, and he saw Burke almost daily. That friendship didn't last, however, with Burk, in the end, saying that Rousseau was a man ruled by vanity. Hume was longest faithful to him, but by that time Rousseau had come to suffer from persecution mania, which ultimately drove him insane, and he even argued with Hume. His last years were spent back in Paris in great poverty, and when he died, suicide was suspected.

Russell says that there is much in Rousseau's work which, however important in other respects, does not concern philosophy, and he thereafter only considers his theology and his political theory.

Theology

Russell says that in theology Rousseau made an innovation which has now been accepted by the great majority of Protestant theologians. Before him, every philosopher from Plato onwards, if he believed in God, offered intellectual arguments in favour of his belief. The arguments may not, to us, seem very convincing, but the philosophers who advanced them certainly believed them to be logically valid. Modern Protestants, for the most part, don't use the old 'proofs', and base their faith on things like emotions of awe, of mystery, and of our sense of right and wrong. This way of defending religious belief was invented by Rousseau, but it has become so familiar that his originality may not easily be appreciated by a modern reader.

> "Ah, Madame!" Rousseau writes to an aristocratic lady, "sometimes in the privacy of my study, with my hands pressed tight over my eyes or in the darkness of night, I am of the opinion that there is no God. But look yonder: the rising sun, as it scatters the mists that cover the earth, and lays bare the wondrous glittering scene of nature, disperses at the same moment all cloud from my soul. I find my faith again, and my God, and my belief in Him."

In the 'Confession of Faith of a Savoyard Vicar', from the book *Emile*, Rousseau has his priest saying that he cares nothing for the wisdom of the old philosophers, also that he has no need of a revelation. Instead, he espouses what he calls 'Natural Religion', which is listening to what God says to the heart. In considering the rules of conduct he says that he does not deduce these rules from 'high philosophy' but finds them in the depths of his heart. Conscience is in all circumstances an infallible guide to right action; we have only to follow feeling rather than reason in order to be virtuous.

One can see how these ideas would have upset the establishment. When reason was on the side of religion, no-one would have thought of rejecting it. But in Rousseau's day reason (as represented by Voltaire) was opposed to religion, therefore we should do away with it. The noble savage knows nothing of the ontological argument, he has a natural religion of the heart.

Russell comments, rather scathingly, that: -

> "For my part, I prefer the ontological argument, the cosmological argument, and the rest of the stock-in-trade, to the sentimental illogicality that has sprung from Rousseau. The old arguments at least were honest: if valid, they proved their point; if invalid, it was open to any critic to prove them so. But the new theology of the heart dispenses with argument; it cannot be refuted, because it does not profess to prove its points. At bottom, the only reason offered for its acceptance is that it allows us to indulge in pleasant dreams. This is an unworthy reason, and if I had to choose between Thomas Aquinas and Rousseau, I should unhesitatingly choose the Saint."

Political Theory

This is set down in his ***Social Contract***, published in 1762. It is very different in style from his other writings, containing little sentimentality and much close intellectual reasoning. He says that democracy is best in small states, aristocracy in middle-sized ones, and monarchy in large ones.

When he speaks of democracy, he means it as the Greeks meant it, direct participation of every (eligible) citizen. Since this is not possible in larger states, his praise of democracy always implies praise of a city state. He acknowledges that this is not really possible however, because people cannot be always assembled and always occupied with public affairs: -

> "Were there a people of gods, their government would be democratic. So perfect a government is not for men."

The book starts with: - "Man is born free, and everywhere he is in chains. One man thinks himself the master of others, but remains more of a slave than they are." Russell says that: - "Liberty is the nominal goal of Rousseau's thought, but in fact it is equality that he values, and that he seeks to secure even at the expense of liberty."

His conception of the social contract seems at first to be like Locke's, but in the end it turns out to be closer to Hobbes. There comes a time when individuals can no longer maintain themselves in primitive independence, and they have to unite in some sort of society, but how can they give up some of their liberty without harming their interests? Rousseau says that: -

> "The problem is to find a form of association which will defend and protect with the whole common force the person and goods of each associate, and in which each, while uniting himself with all, may still obey himself alone, and remain as free as before. This is the fundamental problem of which the Social Contract provides the solution."

The Contract consists in: -

> "The total alienation of each associate, together with all his rights, to the whole community; for, in the first place, as each gives himself absolutely, the conditions are the same for all; and this being so, no one has any interest in making them burdensome to others."

Although this is a complete abrogation of liberty to the sovereign power, he goes on to say that the "sovereign cannot impose upon its subjects any fetters that are useless to the community, nor can it even wish to do so." The sovereign, however, is the sole judge of what is useful to the community. It should be noted here that "sovereign" means, in Rousseau's terms, not the monarch or the government, but the community in its collective and legislative capacity. [One can see how these ideas might be attractive to communists of the future.]

Rousseau spends a lot of time defining something he calls the 'general will' and he contrasts that with the 'will of all'. Here is an example of this difference. It may be, within a group of car drivers, each individual would like to be able to drive as fast as their car will allow, say 90 mph. So, driving at 90 mph is the 'will of all'. But if they all drove that fast there could be mayhem. Let's say that traffic flows best if a speed limit of 50 mph is imposed. Rousseau would say that a 50 mph limit is the 'general will'. It is not the will of each individual driver, but it is in the best interests of society as a whole, so it turns out to be in the best interest of individuals. As a member of society, your interests are the interests of the state; therefore, the state is, in Rousseau's terms, "forcing you to be free". The same argument applies to other state impositions such as paying taxes.

The problem arises as to how to get the people to agree to these terms, and Rousseau offers two solutions here.

1. To the extent that class and inequality in wealth are obstacles to people agreeing to be ruled by the state, they should be abolished, and then there would be no self-interest to be protected.
2. We should raise new citizens so that they identify strongly with the state. Education should aim to strengthen social bonds and should emphasise civic virtue.

He also thinks that religion should be obligatory because it promotes virtue and social adhesion, and he says that there should be a State religion. In addition, he recommends having an official censor to discourage anti-social behaviour and encourage conformity.

Legacy

Rousseau's legacy is twofold; his ideas on politics had profound consequences throughout Europe and beyond, and, as the father of Romanticism, his influence on art, literature, and manners of behaviour have been immense.

During the period of the French Revolution, Rousseau was the most popular of the philosophers among members of the Jacobin Club. He was later interred as a national hero in the Panthéon in Paris, in 1794, 16 years after his death.

In terms of his politics, Russell says that: -

> "The social Contract became the Bible of most of the leaders in the French Revolution... Its first-fruits in practice were the reign of Robespierre; the dictatorships of Russia and Germany (especially the latter) are in part an outcome of Rousseau's teaching."

It is also said that Jefferson derived the Declaration of Independence from Rousseau as well as from Locke and Montesquieu. As ambassador to France (1785-89) he absorbed much from both Voltaire and Rousseau, and the success of the American Revolution raised the prestige of Rousseau's philosophy.

The German writers Goethe, Schiller, and Herder have stated that Rousseau's writings inspired them. Herder regarded Rousseau to be his "guide", and Schiller compared Rousseau to Socrates. Goethe, in 1787, stated: *"Emile and its sentiments had a universal influence on the cultivated mind."* The elegance of Rousseau's writing is also held to have inspired a significant transformation in French poetry and drama— freeing them from rigid literary norms.

Other writers who were influenced by Rousseau's writings included Leopardi in Italy; Pushkin and Tolstoy in Russia; Wordsworth, Southey, Coleridge, Byron, Shelly, and Keats in England; and Hawthorne and Thoreau in America.

And Tolstoy has been quoted as saying: - *"At fifteen I carried around my neck, instead of the usual cross, a medallion with Rousseau's portrait."*

27

Immanuel Kant

Introduction

Immanuel Kant (1724 – 1804) was the second philosopher of the school of philosophy now labelled 'Romanticism and German Idealism'. He was greatly influenced by Rousseau (who was the first in this school), and especially by Rousseau's *Emile, which* was a treatise on education according to 'natural' principles, and which also set forth his principles of natural religion. In temperament, however, Kant was the complete opposite. Whereas Rousseau was self-educated, flamboyant, impulsive, and travelled widely, Kant was purely academic, disciplined and never ventured more than 50 miles from his hometown. He was indeed a man of such regular habits that people would set their watches by him as he passed by their doors on his morning constitutional.

The other great influence on his work was Hume. He claimed that Hume had awakened him from his dogmatic slumbers. And much of Kant's work was actually written as a direct answer to Hume's empiricism, and to Hume's ideas on the subject of cause and effect.

Background

Kant was born into poverty in 1724 in Konigsberg, East Prussia (now Kaliningrad, in Russia). After his schooling he spent some time as a tutor, then as a university lecturer, and finally he became Professor of Logic and Metaphysics at the University of Konigsberg. He taught geography, anthropology, physics, and philosophy there. He had originally been educated in the philosophy of Leibniz, but he abandoned that due to the influences of Rousseau and Hume.

He never married; his whole life was academic and fairly uneventful, even though he lived through the Seven Years' War (during part of which the Russians occupied East Prussia), the French Revolution, and the early part of Napoleon's career.

Hume's writings were not published in German translation until 1754, when Kant was in his thirties and was just starting his lecturing at the university. During this time, he published a number of scientific papers on subjects like astronomy and geology. He became the Professor of Logic and Metaphysics there at the age of 46, and that same year he published his Inaugural Dissertation entitled ***On the Form and Principles of the Sensible and the Intelligible Worlds***.

His main works however, for which he is most famous, were written and published when he was in his late fifties and early sixties. They were his ***Critique of Pure Reason*** (1781) and his ***Critique of Practical Reason*** (1788), the former being on metaphysics and the latter on morals.

He published a few things after that, but these were mainly expansions on his two Critiques. His last lecture at the university was in 1796 at the age of 72, and he died eight years later at the age of 79.

Philosophy

In his works Kant argued that: -

a) Fundamental concepts of the human mind structure human experience.
b) Space and time are forms of our sensibility.
c) The world as it is "in-itself" is unknowable.
d) Reason is the source of morality.
e) Aesthetics arises from a faculty of disinterested judgment.

Rather audaciously, he described himself as having effected a Copernican revolution in philosophy, akin to Copernicus' reversal of the age-old belief that the sun revolved around the earth.

Kant later admitted to a friend that, in his *Inaugural Dissertation*, he had failed to account for the relation between our sensible and our intellectual faculties. After reading Hume he realized that he needed to explain how we combine sensory knowledge with reasoned knowledge. He spent the next twelve years working out his answer, and then a year writing his ***Critique of Pure Reason.***

Critique of Pure Reason

In this work Kant attempted to explain the relationship between reason and human experience, and to move beyond the failures of traditional philosophy and metaphysics. Kant wanted to put an end to an era of 'futile and speculative theories of human experience', while at the same time resisting the scepticism of thinkers such as David Hume.

He regarded himself as showing the way beyond the impasse between the **Rationalists,** the view that regards 'reason' as the chief source and test of knowledge, (e.g. Descartes, Leibniz, and others) and the **Em**piricists, the view that knowledge comes only or primarily from sensory experience, (e.g. Locke, Berkeley and Hume).

Hume says that some things can be known by Deduction but only very few, i.e. those of logic and mathematics. The rest of what we know is from Induction via experience and, as such, can only take a probability of some degree of being certain. Kant says we can go further than this, and claims that "*a priori*" propositions (i.e. knowledge or justification independent of experience) can be arrived at after having learnt general rules from examples.

For instance, in mathematics we learn that two marbles and another two marbles make four marbles, and having learnt the specific case we can generalize it so that two plus two is always four even without marbles. In the same way, says Kant, we can learn about things like cause and effect from specific examples, but having learnt the general principle it then becomes "*a priori*" knowledge.

Hume had said that we can never know completely about cause and effect because one thing coming after another might just be coincidence, all we can do is assign a probability to it. Kant, however, claims to have got round that problem with his analysis above, and says that this resolves the dichotomy between the Rationalists and the Empiricists.

In terms of our perception of the world, Kant makes a distinction between things we perceive and the external causes of those perceptions. The external causes he terms as "things-in-themselves", and he says that we can never directly experience them, (i.e. the world as it is "in-itself" is unknowable). All we have are our perceptions of the world and those perceptions are shaped by the mind using its organising capacity and its "*a priori*" knowledge. [Hume would have agreed that all we have are our perceptions of the world, but he would say that all knowledge thus gained is a) inductive knowledge and b) is shaped by experience alone.]

One of Kant's main ideas here is that space and time are not substances in the external world, they are subjective, and are part of our *a priori* apparatus of perception. For space he gives four reasons why he thinks this: -

1. Space is presupposed in referring sensations to something external, and external experience is only possible through the presentation of space.
2. We can imagine that there could be space with nothing in it, but we can't imagine that there could be no space.
3. There is only one space. When we talk of "spaces" these are parts, not instances.

4. Space is infinite, and holds within itself all the parts of space; this relationship is different from that of a concept to its instances; therefore, space is not a concept but a form of intuition.

He provides similar arguments for time. For him, the external "things-in-themselves" do not exist in space and time. Space and time are part of our mental apparatus that allow us to experience and order things in the world, they are not concepts, they are forms of 'intuition'. [Though the word 'intuition' is the accepted translation it is not altogether satisfactory, a more literal translation is "looking at" or "view"].

Although space and time are *a priori* intuitions and not concepts, Kant does identify a number of other *a priori* capacities which are concepts; these are the twelve "categories" which he identifies, and which can be grouped in four sets of three: -

- **Of Quantity**: unity, plurality, totality
- **Of Quality**: reality, negation, limitation
- **Of Relation**: substance-and-accident, cause-and-effect, reciprocity
- **Of Modality**: possibility, existence, necessity

These are all part of our mental constitution, and as such are applicable to whatever we experience, but he says that there is no reason to suppose that they are applicable to 'things-in-themselves', they are only *'a priori'* capacities of the mind.

In fact, Kant argues that all possible objects of our experience are provably dependent on our mind supplying the base framework of: space; time; concepts; and principles, within which these objects of our experience exist and behave. And that these 'a priori' capacities make our experiences possible. Therefore, no recourse to experience can be employed in their proof: on the contrary, these principles must be established independently of experience.

His conclusion is that metaphysics can justify our 'a priori' concepts, and the principles containing them, in so far as they can be shown to make our experience of the world possible.

In the face of it, this looks like a circular argument, but he says that unless we embrace this idea it can be shown that there are pairs of arguments that are mutually self-contradictory (or 'Antinomies' as they are known). Only by accepting his system can metaphysics be saved from self-contradiction.

For example: - 'The world has a beginning in time and is limited as regards space', and its antithesis: - 'The world has no beginning in time and no limits in space'. Kant gives several such contradictions, which, he says, are effectively bypassed by adopting his system. This part of his argument greatly impressed Hegel, whose dialectic proceeds wholly by way of antinomies.

Kant's Religion

In a famous section of the *Critique of Pure Reason* Kant sets out to demolish all the purely intellectual proofs of the existence of God. He makes it clear, however, that he has other reasons for believing in God; these he sets forth in his *Critique of Practical Reason* which was published some six years later.

There are, he says, only three proofs of God's existence by pure reason: -

1. **The ontological proof**: - Imagine the most perfect thing, if it does not exist then there is something more perfect that does exist.
2. **The cosmological proof**: - There must have been a time when no physical thing existed, but since physical things exist now, there must have been some non-physical thing to bring them into existence.
3. **The physico-theological proof**: - This is the argument from design: the universe exhibits order, which is evidence of purpose and hence of a designer or creator.

He argues against these thus: -

1. The ontological proof defines God as the most real being, i.e. the subject of all predicates that belong to being absolutely. People who assert this say that 'existence' is itself a predicate, but Kant says that 'existence' is not a predicate because the predicates for something imaginary are the same as for a real such something.
2. As far as the cosmological proof goes, Kant says that the last step in the argument is the ontological argument over again, and hence is refuted by his previous argument.
3. The design argument, he says, could at best only prove an Architect, not a Creator, and therefore cannot give an adequate conception of God.

He concludes that: -

> "The only theology of reason which is possible is that which is based upon moral laws or seeks guidance from them."

God, freedom, and immortality, he says, are the three "ideas of reason". But although reason leads us to form these ideas, it cannot itself prove their reality. The practical use of reason is developed near the end of the ***Critique of Pure Reason***, and more fully developed in the ***Critique of Practical Reason***. The argument is that moral law demands justice i.e. happiness proportional to virtue. Only Providence can ensure this and has evidently not ensured it in this life. Therefore, there is a God and a future life; and there must be freedom, since otherwise there would be no such thing as virtue.

Critique of Practical Reason

According to some philosophers, Hume for instance, morality is ultimately rooted in our sentiments, and reason has little, if anything, to do with right and wrong. Kant, by contrast, says that how we feel is morally irrelevant – what matters is that we do our moral duty, which reason alone can establish.

> *"Two things fill the mind with ever increasing wonder and awe... the starry heavens above me and the moral law within me."*

He says that what matters about an action, so far as its moral worth is concerned, is the 'intention' with which it is performed, the outcome is irrelevant. But what is the right intention? Kant says it is our moral duty to do the right thing; he calls it the '**Categorical Imperative**'.

Whenever we perform an action, we are guided by one or more principles, which he calls 'maxims'. A greedy person, for instance, might always act on the maxim 'always act to maximize your wealth', whereas a hedonist might be guided by 'always act to increase your happiness'. In each case the maxim gives the reason for acting.

The examples above are of the form: - 'if you want to achieve Z then do Y'. A categorical imperative on the other hand simply says: - 'do Y'. He says that moral principles have this categorical character. Our moral duty is: - 'don't steal', period. It's not: - 'don't steal if you don't want to get caught'.

How do we establish what our moral duty is? Kant says: -

> *"Act only according to a maxim by which you can at the same time will that it shall become a general law."*

A second moral principle he gives is: -

Immanuel Kant

> *"Act in such a way that you always treat humanity, whether in yourself or in another, never simply as a means, but always at the same time as an end."*

In other words, you give respect to other people, for instance you don't lie to them in order to get them to do something for you. You tell them the truth and let them, as rational moral agents themselves, decide whether they will help you or not.

Another aspect of this moral system is that it would not be right to help someone just because you felt sorry for them; you should help them simply because it is your moral duty to do so.

Kant's Politics

Kant was still writing into his seventies, and one of these works was his treatise entitled ***Perpetual Peace***. In this he advocates a federation of free states, bound together by a covenant forbidding war. Reason, he says, utterly condemns war, and only an international government can prevent it. The civil constitution of the component states should be 'republican', and he defines this to mean that the executive and the legislative branches of government are separated. Most philosophers up to then only seemed to consider the best way to govern states in isolation; Kant actually seems to look forward towards bodies like the E.E.C. or the U.N. as a way of making the world safer.

Legacy

Many people consider Kant to be one of the great philosophers of all time; someone who found a middle way between the extremes of Rationalism and Empiricism; and someone who bought reason to morality with his 'Categorical Imperative'.

Others disagree, however, pointing out the awkwardness of the 'thing-in-itself' concept of objects in the external world, and the lack of emotion in his system of morality. Also, while accepting that our experiences of space and time are subjective, making them purely 'a priori' components of the mind seems to be taking this subjectiveness too far. Russell says, for instance, that he 'cannot agree that Kant is the greatest, but that it would be foolish not to recognize his importance'.

One influence, however, is that very little philosophy these days is done in the pre-Kantian style; he changed the framework within which philosophical inquiry is carried out. He greatly influenced subsequent philosophers like Hegel, and some philosophers even today use his moral philosophy to argue against relativism, supporting the view that universality is essential to moral philosophy.

28

Jeremy Bentham

Introduction

Jeremy Bentham (1748 – 1832) is best known as one of the founding fathers of an ethical system called **Utilitarianism**. With Bentham we return to the British Empiricists, his ideas are a natural continuation from Hobbes, Locke, Hume, and Adam Smith, and he virtually ignores Rousseau, Kant and German idealism. The importance of Bentham and his successors is not so much philosophical as political; as leaders of British radicalism; and as the men who unintentionally paved the way for the doctrines of socialism.

Adam Smith, following upon the ideas of the empiricists and the scientists of the day, had discovered self-interest to be the mainstay of the economic life of man. Bentham then expanded this notion of self-interest, first into a theory of jurisprudence, and thereafter into a more general political philosophy.

Background

Bentham was born in 1748, at the beginning, therefore, of the new age marked by the French Revolution, the American Revolution, and the Industrial Revolution. His father was a well-to-do lawyer who had great ambitions for his infant son, and they lived in the then prosperous, residential neighbourhood of Spitalfields in London.

His father had visions of him as a future Lord Chancellor, and almost immediately began to mould the boy for that destiny. Indeed, the young Bentham turned out to be something of an infant prodigy, at the age of three he was found seated at a table reading a huge book, by candlelight because it had got dark while he was reading. The book was Rapin's *History of England*.

He learnt Greek and Latin at his father's knee, and at the age of five was scraping away at Corelli and Handel on a miniature violin. At seven he went to Westminster School, which he heartily disliked, and at 13 he matriculated and went up to Queen's College, Oxford. By that time, he had already mastered Locke's *Essay concerning Human Understanding*, and was so rationalist in his outlook that he experienced a severe attack of conscience over the 39 articles of religion to which he had to adhere as a condition of entry to the college.

Bentham took his master's degree at 18 and then entered the legal profession, but to his father's great disappointment he had little interest in the practicing of law. At Oxford he had become very interested in the advances in science of that age, and if the law was to be his profession, then he proposed to approach it in the same spirit that Newton examined the relationships of solid bodies, and with, he began to hope, as profound and revolutionary results for the world. He decided to put his talents to work in forming legislation rather than the practicing of it, and he justified his stance thus: -

> "All the principles and measures of law, if they are just and proper now, would at any time have been so, and will be so everywhere, and to the end of time. They will hold good, so long as pleasure is pleasure, and pain is pain; so long as steel wounds, fire burns, water seeks a level, bread nourishes, inanition destroys... so long as men derive credit or fortune from their ancestors, or feel affection for their children."

This sense of vocation filled him from early manhood, but for a long time his labour at the principles of law-making earned him neither money nor recognition, and certainly didn't please his father.

His first published work, however, caused quite a stir and brought him some powerful friends. This was his **Fragment on Government**, published anonymously in 1776 when he was 29. When he had been at Oxford Bentham had attended some lectures given by **Sir William Blackstone**. He was an English jurist, judge, and Tory politician, and is most noted for writing a book called *Commentaries* about the Laws of England, which was very influential. Bentham's **Fragment on Government** was really a book of commentaries on Blackstone's *Commentaries*.

After publication of the *Fragment,* recognition came rather faster in the rest of the world than in Britain. He became an international figure (he himself actually invented the word 'international') long before fame came to him in Britain. He was made a French citizen in 1792 and much of his work was first printed abroad, including his most famous work **Rationale of Punishment and Rewards**, which was published in French 14 years before its appearance in England.

Jeremy Bentham

In his 38th year he made the grand tour, part of which involved spending time in Russia. While there he wrote his ***Defence of Usury***, which laid out the economics behind the ideas of utilitarianism. On his return to England, he tried to make a political career but was disappointed in this, so he went back to his writing again on the principles of legislation. In 1789 he published his great work ***Introduction to the Principles and Morals of Legislation***.

He also spent many years, and much of the fortune his father left him, on a scheme for prison reform, but was embittered by the failure of the government to take it up. In the end parliament awarded him £23,000 by way of compensation for it, but this hardly repaid him for the time he spent on it. His design for a prison was called a panopticon, a type of prison in which all prisoners could be viewed by guards at all times, without the prisoners knowing whether they were observed or not. The fact that the inmates cannot know when they are being watched means that all inmates must act as though they are always watched, effectively controlling their own behaviour constantly.

No true prisons of this design have ever been built although one or two have come close, notably the Presidio Modelo in Cuba, and the Allegheny County Courthouse and Jail in Pittsburgh, Pennsylvania. Part of the reason is just the technical difficulties of the design, but also the idea has been criticized for the reductive, mechanistic, and inhumane approach to human lives.

To some extent such a prison design has a similar purpose to the idea that you must be good because God is watching you all the time. Ironically, we get the same effect today with the 20th-century technology of closed-circuit television, only this is not just in jails, it's in offices, shops, parks, the high street, motorways, stadiums, and numerous other public places.

Bentham was the acknowledged, although somewhat unlikely, leader of the "Philosophical Radicals". He was a shy man, and although dedicated to his writing, actually published little himself during his lifetime. In many cases it was his friends who published for him, and much of his work was published posthumously. Russell says that he did not become truly radical until he was 60, and that was partly due to his friend James Mill, who was 25 years younger and the father of John Stuart Mill.

Bentham lived until he was 82, and on his death in 1832, he left instructions for his body to be first dissected, and then to be permanently preserved as an "auto-icon" (or self-image), which would be his memorial. This was done, and the auto-icon is now on public display, in a glass case, at University College London. The body is, on occasion, taken to meetings of the College Council, where he is recorded as attending but not voting.

Philosophy

Utilitarianism

This is actually one form of a broader theory called consequentialism, which says that the extent to which an action is morally right or wrong is determined by its consequences alone, nothing else matters. [Note that this is virtually the opposite of Kant's idea. Remember that Kant said it is the intention behind the act that makes it morally right or wrong, not its consequences.]

If then we agree with consequentialism, the question next becomes 'what consequence should we aim to achieve?' The answer according to utilitarianism is '**happiness**', Bentham argues that we should act to maximise pleasure and minimise pain: -

> "Nature has placed mankind under the governance of two sovereign masters, pain and pleasure. It is for them alone to point out what we ought to do..."

And: -

> "...the greatest happiness of the greatest number is the foundation of morals and legislation."

Utilitarianism, therefore, is not just selfishness, everyone's happiness must count equally. The difficulty that arises, however, is how to compare one person's suffering with another's happiness, e.g. would it be right to steal food from one person in order to give it to a starving person?

Part of Bentham's argument is that it is not which particular pleasures or pains we suffer that matter, but their intensity and duration. And for this he developed a theory called '**felicific calculus**'. According to him, the sum total pleasure an action brings about is calculated by taking into account the following: -

- How intensely the pleasure/pain is felt.
- How long that pleasure/pain lasts.
- How certainly the pleasure/pain is to follow the action.
- How quickly the pleasure/pain will follow.

- How likely the pleasure/pain is to be followed by experiences of the same kind.
- How likely the pleasure/pain is to be followed by experiences of the opposite kind.
- How many people experience it.

In terms of Government, he says that instead of legislating for other purposes (such as the support of existing institutions or the protection of trade) government ought simply to legislate to increase the sum of human happiness. But the question then arises 'who is to be the judge of happiness?' In the last analysis, it's the individual concerned, so governments, other things being equal, need only ask themselves what individuals would demand. Leave the individual alone and he will pursue his own good, that is the law of his nature. The net result of the universal pursuit of individual good is the greatest common measure of happiness. Government was best when it interfered least.

His ***Defence of Usury*** sought the abolition of laws against usury on the grounds that they interfere with individual freedom. All oppressive and restrictive legislation made it impossible for man to follow his natural bent, and so increased the sum of human misery. He says, "all punishment is mischief... upon the principle of utility, if it ought to be admitted, it ought only to be admitted so far as it promised to exclude some greater evil".

As well as the principle of 'greatest happiness', Bentham's philosophy rested on a second principle, that of psychology based on the 'association of ideas'. This part of his thinking emanated from Locke via Hume. He recognises association of ideas and language, and association of ideas and ideas. By means of this principle he aims at a deterministic account of mental occurrences.

To Bentham, determinism in psychology was important because he wished to establish a code of laws (and, more generally, a social system) which would automatically make men virtuous. And of course, his happiness principle became necessary in order to define 'virtue'. Much of this already exists in Locke, but Bentham's merit (according to Russell) was in his vigorous application of it to various practical problems.

According to Bentham, the business of the legislator is to produce harmony between public and private interests. He says that: – it is to the interest of the public that I should abstain from theft, but it is not in my interest except in the case where there is an effective criminal law. Thus, criminal law is a method of making the interests of the individual coincide with those of the community; that is its justification.

Men are punished to prevent crime, not because we hate criminals. Indeed, it is more important that punishment should be certain rather than it should be severe. In his day, many minor offences were subject to the death penalty, with the result that juries often refused to convict because they thought the penalty excessive. Bentham advocated the abolition of the death penalty for all but the worst offences, and before he died the criminal law had been mitigated in this respect.

Civil law, he says, should have four aims: subsistence, abundance, security, and equality. It will be observed that he does not mention liberty. He cared little for liberty and actually had great contempt for the rights of man. The rights of man, he said, 'are plain nonsense; the imprescriptible rights of man are nonsense on stilts'. When the French revolutionaries made their "declaration of the rights of man" Bentham called it "a metaphysical work – the ne plus ultra of metaphysics". Its articles, he said, "could be divided into three classes: (1) Those that are unintelligible, (2) those that are false, (3) those that are both".

Russell says that: - "Bentham's ideal, like that of Epicurus, was security, not liberty".

His gradual evolution towards Radicalism had two sources: on the one hand, a belief in equality, deduced from the calculus of pleasures and pains; on the other hand, an inflexible determination to submit everything to the arbitrator of reason. His love of equality led him to advocate equal division of a man's property among his children, and in later years to oppose monarchy and hereditary aristocracy. He also advocated complete democracy, including votes for women. His refusal to believe without rational grounds led him to reject religion, including a belief in God. He would not excuse anything on the ground that it was traditional, he was opposed to imperialism, whether British, American, or other, and he considered colonies a folly.

Many people thought that the rejection of God by the Utilitarians was shocking, because how could you have morality without God. But Bentham sought legal and social reform because he saw that many of the laws and customs of his day were clearly a cause of great misery to lots of people. Utilitarianism suggests not just that it is desirable to alleviate such suffering where we can, but that it is a moral requirement to do so. Bentham felt this moral obligation acutely, and he acted on it.

Animal rights

Bentham was one of the earliest thinkers to suggest that animals might have rights too. If what matters, morally speaking, is pleasure and pain, then because animals also experience this, they too are deserving of moral consideration. Many philosophers had previously deemed animals less worthy because it was supposed that they lacked the faculty of reason, both Descartes and Kant took this view for instance. But Bentham disagrees, for him, it's the ability to suffer that matters, not the ability to reason.

> "The question is not, Can they reason?, nor Can they talk? but, Can they suffer?"

Legacy

Bentham died on the day before the royal assent to the Reform Bill, the passing of which marked a triumph of his views, and of the British middle class, of which he was a member. So much was he to dominate the century in which he died that one historian, at the end of that century, said that he did not know a single law or reform effected since Bentham's day which could not be traced to his influence. And Russell comments on Bentham that: -

> "He seems to have thought that, by means of democracy combined with adequate supervision, legislators could be so controlled that they could only further their private interests by being useful to the general public. There was in his day not much material for forming a judgment as to the working of democratic institutions, and his optimism was therefore perhaps excusable, but in our more disillusioned age it seems somewhat naive."

His influence, however, was very wide ranging. He provided the principle and draft legislation affecting laws, and the constitutions of the United States, Canada, and other countries on five continents, by which they included such phrases as "the pursuit of happiness".

He also made a major contribution to International Law which provided the legal foundation for The League of Nations, the United Nations and the United Nations International Court at The Hague, offering the framework by which nations today can - indeed must - go to court not to war.

Bentham's radicalism was based on his wish for equality, and his practical, legal reforms were directed against the landed oligarchy of the day, which he wanted replaced by a democracy working for the 'greatest happiness for the greatest number'. These ideas of Bentham, and thereafter his successors, almost inevitably led the way to British Socialism.

29

Georg Hegel

Introduction

Georg Wilhelm Friedrich Hegel (1770 – 1831) was the natural successor to Immanuel Kant in the German Idealist School of philosophy. His main interest was in the historical development of philosophy. Most philosophers focus on ideas and concepts, believing, for example, that the task of a philosopher is to arrive at knowledge of ideas, which are considered to be timeless and unchanging entities. Hegel, however, says that our ideas are historically conditioned, a product of their time, and that you need to understand history to understand the development and growth of the mind.

> *"The history of the world is none other than the progress of the consciousness of freedom."*

He obtained wide recognition in his day and was very influential within the continental tradition of philosophy. Hegel's principal achievement was his development of a distinctive version of idealism sometimes termed "absolute idealism," in which the dualisms of, for instance, mind and nature, and subject and object are overcome. Also, via his concept of "spirit", he attempts to integrate psychology, the state, history, art, and religion into one overriding philosophy.

Background

Hegel was born in August 1770 in Stuttgart, in the Duchy of Württemberg in south-western Germany. At the age of three he went to the "German School", and then, two years later, when he entered the "Latin School", he already knew the first declension, having been taught it by his mother.

Georg Hegel

During his adolescence Hegel read voraciously, especially any writers associated with the Enlightenment.

At the age of 18 Hegel entered a Protestant seminary attached to the local University, where two fellow students were to become vital to his development: poet Friedrich Hölderlin, and philosopher-to-be Friedrich Wilhelm Schelling. Sharing a dislike for what they regarded as the restrictive environment of the Seminary, the three became close friends and mutually influenced each other's ideas. All greatly admired Hellenic civilization and Hegel additionally steeped himself in Rousseau and Lessing. At this time, they watched the unfolding of the French Revolution with shared enthusiasm. Schelling and Hölderlin immersed themselves in theoretical debates on Kantian philosophy, from which Hegel remained aloof; his own need to engage critically with the central ideas of Kantianism did not come until he was 30.

Having received his theological certificate from the Seminary, he became a tutor for a few years, and during this time wrote several papers on Christianity. In 1801, Hegel moved to Jena at the encouragement of his old friend Schelling, who held a position at the University there. Hegel also secured a position at the University, but it was initially unsalaried. He supported himself with his writing and was putting the finishing touches to his main work ***The Phenomenology of Mind*** just three days before Napoleon conquered the city in the battle of Jena.

After that he moved around Germany taking a number of university posts until, in 1818, he accepted the chair of philosophy at the University of Berlin, where he stayed until his death in 1831. As well as ***The Phenomenology of Mind***, his other main works were ***The Science of Logic*** and ***The Philosophy of Right***. He also produced an encyclopaedia and numerous articles and papers, and after his death many of his lecture notes were published in book form.

Hegel has a reputation of being a difficult philosopher (indeed Russell says "the hardest to understand of all the great philosophers") and his obscure writing style does not help. He has few followers today, but he did produce a few original insights and arguments.

Philosophy

Hegel's philosophy is a natural extension of Kant's, but he did also criticise some of Kant's thinking quite severely. Kant, remember, held that the concepts of both space and time were purely subjective, they were, he said, creations of the mind which we use to make sense of the universe. The reason they had no external reality is because, if they were real, you would have pairs of antitheses or opposites that did not make sense, i.e. 'the universe has a beginning and is finite' and 'the universe exits forever and is boundless'. Kant also, however, believed in something he (rather clumsily) called 'things-in-themselves', i.e. some kind of 'ultimately unknowable' reality external to mind.

Hegel liked, and used himself, the ideas of antitheses, but he didn't like Kant's 'unknowable' 'things-in-themselves'. Hegel expanded on the idea of arguing using antitheses in his book *The Science of Logic.* This was not the Syllogistic logic of Aristotle, but his own idea of moving from ***thesis*** to ***antithesis*** to ***synthesis***, which is often referred to as dialectic logic. And indeed, the synthesis of one argument can then become the thesis of the next.

He applies this logic to abstract concepts as well as practical ones. For instance, take the bare notion of 'existence' or 'being'; since this bare notion of being has no content at all, it cannot be anything. Therefore, it must be nothing, the antithesis of being. Being and nothing, however, are opposites, constantly moving in and apart from each other; they require to be brought together under the synthesis 'becoming'. Hegel then moves this dialectic on through many more obscure stages until, in the end, he believes he is able to demonstrate the necessity of absolute idealism, i.e. that the only thing that is ultimately real is the absolute idea, which is Mind, knowing itself as all reality.

The word 'Mind' in the previous paragraph needs more explanation. Hegel uses the German word 'Geist' which has no real single equivalent in English. It can sometimes be translated as Mind and sometimes as 'Spirit' and is sometimes used as referring to a mixture or combination of the two. So, it can have religious connotations, or it might be used as purely the mental or intellectual side of our being but as distinct from the physical. Because in German it has both meanings Hegel is able to use it in a way that suggests an overarching collective Mind that is some sort of active force throughout history that all human beings, in terms of their mental aspect, are a part of. Because of this ambiguity, translators often use the capitalized term 'Mind' to express Hegel's concept of Geist.

From his early interest in mysticism, he retained a belief in the connectedness of everything. The apparent existence of separate things in the world, people, atoms, souls etc. was, he thought, an illusion. But he differed from Spinoza by conceiving the whole, not as a simple substance, but as a complex system, what we might think of today as an organism. Take, for instance the idea of an uncle and a nephew, we might think of that as a simple, individual relationship. But it can't exist by itself because it implies that the uncle has a brother or sister, and that this sibling married another person and had a son with them, and this other person would have had parents, etc... Everything in the world is connected into a complex Whole, which Hegel calls the 'Absolute', and this Absolute is spiritual.

Georg Hegel

Two things distinguish Hegel from others who have had similar outlooks. One is the emphasis on logic: Hegel thought that the nature of reality could be deduced from the sole consideration that it must not be self-contradictory. The other distinguishing feature (which is closely connected to the first) is the triadic movement called the 'dialectic'. Logic, for Hegel, is (according to Russell) "the same thing as metaphysics, it is quite different from what is commonly called logic".

In another example of Hegel's logic, he begins with the assumption that "the Absolute is Pure Being", we assume that it just is, without assigning any qualities to it. But pure being without any qualities is nothing; therefore, we are led to the antithesis: "the Absolute is Nothing". From this thesis and antithesis, we are led on to the synthesis: the union of Being and Not-Being is Becoming, and so we say: "the Absolute is Becoming". But this also won't do, because there must be something that becomes. In this way our view of Reality develops by the continual correction of previous errors, all of which arose from undue abstraction, by taking something finite or limited as if it could be the whole.

> *"The limitations of the finite do not come merely from without; its own nature is the cause of its abrogation, and by its own act it passes into its counterpart."*

The process, according to Hegel, is essential to the understanding of the result. Each later stage of the dialectic contains all earlier stages, as it were in solution; none of them is wholly superseded but is given its proper place as a movement in the Whole. It is, therefore, impossible to reach the truth except by going through all stages in the dialectic.

Knowledge, for Hegel, has a triadic movement. It begins with sense-perception, in which there is only awareness of the object. Then, through sceptical criticism of the senses, it becomes purely subjective. At last, it reaches the stage of self-knowledge, in which subject and object are no longer distinct. Thus, self-consciousness is the highest form of knowledge. The highest kind of knowledge must be possessed by the Absolute, and as the Absolute is the Whole there is nothing outside of itself to know. "The truth is the whole" he says, and nothing partial is quite true.

The Absolute Idea is something like Aristotle's God; it is thought thinking about itself. We are told that Spirit is the only reality, and that its thought is reflected into itself by self-consciousness.

> *"**The Absolute Idea**. The idea, as unity of the **Subjective** and **Objective Idea**, is the notion of*

An Introduction to Philosophy

> the **Idea** – a notion whose object is the **Idea** as such, and for which the objective is **Idea** – an **Object** which embraces all characteristics in its unity".

[Maybe something's lost in translation, but it is said that the original German is even more difficult!]

He goes on to say that although ultimate reality is timeless, and time is merely an illusion generated by our inability to see the Whole, yet the time-process has an intimate relation to the purely logical process of the dialectic. This time-process is from the less to the more perfect, both in an ethical and in a logical sense, indeed these two senses are, for him, not really distinguishable.

This idea of a time-process and of the development of the Spirit is central to Hegel's philosophy and is the reason he was so interested in and wrote so much about world history.

Hegel's Conception of History

According to Hegel, Spirit, and the course of its development, is the substantial object of the philosophy of history. The nature of Spirit may be understood by contrasting it with its opposite, namely Matter. The essence of Matter is gravity; the essence of Spirit is Freedom. Matter is outside itself, whereas Spirit has its centre in itself. "Spirit is self-contained existence".

> "But what is Spirit? It is the one immutably homogeneous Infinite – pure Identity – which in its second phase separates itself from itself and makes this second aspect its own polar opposite, namely existence for and in Self as contrasted with the universal."

In the historical development of Spirit, he claims, there have been three main phases: The Orientals, the Greeks and Romans, and the Germans.

> "The history of the world is the discipline of the uncontrolled natural will, bringing it into obedience to a universal principle and conferring subjective freedom. The East knew, and to the present day knows, only that **One** is free; the Greek and Roman world, that **some**

*are free; the German world knows that **All** are free."*

You might then suppose that democracy would be the appropriate form of government where all are free, but not so. He says that democracy and aristocracy belong to the stage where some are free, despotism to that where one is free, and monarchy to that where all are free. Hegel uses the term 'freedom' in an odd sense. He says that there is no freedom without law, but he then turns this round to say that wherever there is law there is freedom. Russell says that "freedom, for him, means little more than the right to obey the law". Hegel praises Rousseau in this respect for distinguishing between the 'general will' and the 'will of all'.

He spent a lot of time and analysis on history in order to demonstrate the development of the State, which he holds as almost sacred. We are told that "the State is the actually existing realised moral life", and that all the spiritual reality possessed by a human being he possesses only through the State.

"For Truth is the unity of the universal and subjective Will, and the universal is to be found in the State, in its laws, its universal and rational arrangements. The State is the Divine Idea as it exists on Earth."

He goes on to argue against any sort of League of Nations by which the independence of separate States might be limited. The duty of a citizen is entirely confined to upholding the independence and sovereignty of his own State. It follows from this that war is not wholly evil because it is part of the purpose of the State to protect the life and property of the citizens, and this provides the moral justification for war.

But Hegel goes further than this. He is opposed to an organisation such as a world government which would prevent conflicts arising because he thinks it a good thing that there should be wars from time to time. War has a positive moral value: -

"War has the higher significance that through it the moral health of peoples is preserved in their indifference towards the stabilizing of finite determinations."

If we think back to Hegel's metaphysics, we see that his logic led him to believe that there is more reality or excellence (the two terms for him are synonymous) in wholes than in parts, and that the whole increases in reality and excellence as it becomes more organised. This obviously led to prefer a State to a collection of individuals.

Some of Russell's Analysis of Hegel's ideas

Is there more reality, and is there more value, in a whole than in its parts? Hegel answers yes to both questions. The question of reality is metaphysical, but the question of value is ethical. These are often treated as almost the same, but it is important to keep them apart.

Hegel's view is that any portion of the universe is so profoundly affected by its relations to the other parts and the whole, that no true statement can be made about any part except to assign it its place in the whole. And its place in the whole depends on all the other parts. That is the metaphysical position.

However, from an ethical standpoint, if we take the eye, for example, it is worthless outside a living body; by itself it has no value. But for Hegel, this is the same kind of relationship as a citizen to the State, he would say the citizen has no value outside a State, but that is more questionable! Just because there might be a metaphysical analogy does not mean an ethical analogy can automatically be drawn.

Even the metaphysical logic of Hegel can be questioned. Yes, undoubtedly, everything is connected in some way to everything else, but that does not mean you can't create true statements about parts. For instance, to say something correct about John you don't need to know *all* about John, you only need to specify enough about him to correctly identify him.

Legacy

Hegel's influence was immense both within philosophy and in the other sciences. Throughout the 19th century many chairs of philosophy around Europe were held by Hegelians.

Marx and Engels gave Hegel's idea of dialectic a material basis; hence **dialectic materialism**, which is the official name given to Marxist philosophy by its proponents in the Soviet Union.

Russell says that: - "It will be seen that Hegel claims for the State much the same position as St Augustine and his Catholic successors claimed for the Church. There are, however, two respects in which the Catholic claim is more reasonable than Hegel's. In the first place, the Church is not a chance geographical association [...]. In the second place, there is only one Catholic Church, whereas there are many States." He further says: -

"Such is Hegel's doctrine of the State – a doctrine which, if accepted, justifies every internal tyranny and every external aggression that can possibly be imagined."

Popper makes the claim that Hegel's system formed a thinly veiled justification for the absolute rule of Frederick William III, and that Hegel's idea of the ultimate goal of history was to reach a state approximating that of 1830s Prussia. Popper further proposed that Hegel's philosophy served as an inspiration for communist and fascist totalitarian governments of the 20th century, whose dialectics allow for any belief to be construed as rational.

Isaiah Berlin listed Hegel, along with Rousseau, as one of the architects of modern authoritarianism who undermined liberal democracy.

30

Schopenhauer

Introduction

Arthur Schopenhauer (1788 – 1860) was the next philosopher in the German Idealist tradition after Hegel, but although a contemporary of Hegel he didn't think much of him, calling his work "castles of abstraction", and saying that Hegel used deliberately impressive but ultimately vacuous verbiage. Instead, taking as his starting place the transcendental idealism of Immanuel Kant, Schopenhauer developed an atheistic metaphysical and ethical system that has been described as an 'exemplary manifestation of philosophical pessimism'.

Rejecting the contemporaneous post-Kantian philosophies of German idealism, Schopenhauer was among the first thinkers in Western philosophy to share and affirm significant tenets of Eastern, and especially Indian, philosophy.

Though his work failed to garner substantial attention during his lifetime, Schopenhauer has had a posthumous impact across various disciplines, including philosophy, literature, and science, with many subsequent philosophers, artists and intellectuals citing his influence.

Background

Schopenhauer was born on 22 February 1788, in the city of Danzig (then part of the Polish–Lithuanian Commonwealth; present day Gdańsk, Poland). His parents were both descendants of wealthy German commercial families, and his father, who was a follower of Voltaire, regarded England as the land of liberty and intelligence.

At the age of nine he was sent to school in Paris for two years, and on his return his father was pleased to find that he had nearly forgotten German. At fifteen he spent some time at a boarding school in England and then, on his return, to please his father, he became a clerk in a commercial house in Hamburg. He hated the idea of a business career, however, and longed for a literary and academic life.

This became possible when his father died, and his mother was willing that he abandon commerce to become a student. He entered the University

Schopenhauer

of Göttingen in 1809 and there he studied metaphysics and psychology. His mother was a lady of literary aspirations who wrote books and enjoyed friendships with men of culture, but she and Schopenhauer did not get on. He was annoyed by her philandering and Russell says that his subsequent low opinion of women was no doubt due in part to his quarrels with his mother.

He wrote his first book, ***On the Fourfold Root of the Principle of Sufficient Reason***, while at university. His mother informed him that the book was incomprehensible, and it was unlikely that anyone would ever buy a copy. In a fit of temper Schopenhauer told her that his work would be read long after the "rubbish" she wrote had been totally forgotten. In fact, although they considered her novels of dubious quality, her publishing firm held her in high esteem because they consistently sold well.

In 1814, Schopenhauer began his seminal work ***The World as Will and Representation*** and it was published in 1818. In 1820, he became a lecturer at the University of Berlin, and he decided to schedule his lectures to coincide with those of Hegel, whom Schopenhauer described as a "clumsy charlatan." However, only five students turned up to Schopenhauer's lectures, and he thereafter dropped out of academia.

He had several relationships with women but never married any of them, living as a bachelor until his death at the age of 72. He kept a pet poodle named Atma (the world-soul), smoked a long pipe, read the London Times, and walked for two hours every day. He was anti-democratic and hated the revolution of 1848; he believed in spiritualism and magic; and in his study he had a bust of Kant and a bronze figure of the Buddha.

Philosophy

Schopenhauer's starting point was Kant's transcendental idealism. Kant, remember, makes a distinction between the world as we experience it (called the phenomenal world) and the world as it actually is (called the noumenal world). The world as we experience it is a construction of our own making; even space and time are mental artefacts we use to make sense of the world, the world as it is being ultimately unknowable to us.

For an analogy: - Suppose a fisherman repeatedly casts his net into the sea and discovers that all the fish he catches are bigger than five centimetres wide. He then concludes that the sea contains few, if any, fish less than five centimetres wide, but he has ignored the fact that the mesh in his net is five centimetres wide! From a Kantian view, the net has imposed some sort of order on the fisherman's knowledge of the sea, just like our senses limit and order our knowledge of the world.

Schopenhauer accepts the division of the world into phenomenal and noumenal, however, unlike Kant, he is less sceptical about our ability to know anything positive about the 'world-in-itself'. He thinks that we possess at least some clues as to the underlying nature of reality.

He says that our cognitive faculties construct the world based on four versions of the 'principle of sufficient reason', to which all phenomena much conform. This is elaborated most fully in his first book, written when he was just 25.

On the Fourfold Root of the Principle of Sufficient Reason

The four principles our minds use to construct our view of the world are:

1. **Sensibility**
   Our sensibility operates with the principle that everything is situated in space according to a Euclidean geometry, and in time via the temporal nature of counting.

2. **Understanding**
   Our understanding works with the law of causality and yields perception of a physical world which it pictures as the cause of our sensations.

3. **Reason**
   Our reason (which is secondary to understanding) works on the principle that every judgment must have its justification.
   [Schopenhauer is very critical of other philosophers who, he says, either confuse these two principles or, like Hegel, treat concepts as primary.]

4. **Motive**
   The fourth principle bids us conceive of human action as being necessarily determined by motive.

He maintains that the world constructed on these principles can only exist for the subject of knowledge to whose faculties they correspond. Schopenhauer expands on this in his main work, published in 1818 when he was 30.

Schopenhauer

The World as Will and Representation

Kant's greatest merit, for Schopenhauer, was the distinction of the phenomenon from the 'thing-in-itself'. He agrees with Kant that the 'thing-in-itself' is not the cause of our sensations or of phenomenon, since causation applies only within the phenomenal world (i.e. in the mind). Where he disagrees with Kant, however, is in saying that there is a way in which we can form some understanding of the nature of the 'thing-in-itself' (for Kant that was totally unknowable).

Schopenhauer says that our perceptual experience of the phenomenal world of things in space and time is not our only experience. We are aware of ourselves, both in the perceptual fashion by which we know external things, and, quite differently, 'from within' as 'Will', or more specifically as 'Will to Live'.

Our behaviour, he says, presents itself to us not only as the movements of a physical object but more intimately as the phases of a 'Will'. This 'Will' is not the cause of our behaviour; rather the experience of the 'Will' and the experience of the physical phenomenon of our behaviour are the same thing known inwardly and outwardly.

> *"My body is the only object of which I know not merely from one side, that of representation, but also the other, that is called will."*

He continues by saying that from knowledge of my own nature as a 'thing-in-itself' I can then infer something of the nature of the physical world in general. For while I cannot prove that the rest of nature is more than mere appearance, we must suppose (disregarding solipsism) that everything in the world is the appearance of what in itself is 'Will' in the same sense as is my body and its behaviour.

The natural world, then, is the appearance of 'Will' to itself, but is this one 'Will' or many? Schopenhauer says it is all one 'Will', because the idea of number, he says, is an operation of the mind, a way in which we impose order on reality. We perceive things to be individual only because we don't have the full picture, as in the analogy of the net cast into the sea. His conclusion, then, is that the universe is a single, vast, cosmic 'Will to Exist' which experiences itself through an apparent diversity of conscious beings in a spatio-temporal and deterministic world.

So far, says Russell, we might expect Schopenhauer to identify his cosmic 'Will' with God, and teach a pantheistic doctrine not unlike Spinoza's, in which virtue would consist in conformity to the divine 'Will'. But at this point his pessimism leads to a different development.

An Introduction to Philosophy

The cosmic 'Will' is wicked; 'Will', altogether, is wicked, or at any rate is the source of all our endless suffering. Suffering is essential to all life and is increased by every increase of knowledge. 'Will' has no fixed end, which if achieved would bring contentment. There is no such thing as happiness; an unfulfilled wish causes pain, and attainment brings on satiety. Instinct urges men to procreation, but this just brings into existence new occasions for suffering and death.

All this is very sad, but there is a way out, and it was discovered, Schopenhauer claims, in India. The best of the Indian myths is that of Nirvana, which Schopenhauer interprets as extinction. This, he agrees, is contrary to the Christian doctrine, but he says: -

> "The ancient wisdom of the human race will not be displaced by what happened in Galilee."

The cause of suffering is intensity of 'Will'; the less we exercise 'Will', the less we shall suffer. And here knowledge turns out to be useful after all, provided it is knowledge of a certain sort. The distinction between one man and another is part of the phenomenal world and disappears when the world is truly seen. To the good man, the veil of Maya (illusion) has become transparent; he sees that all things are one, and that the distinction between himself and another is only apparent. He reaches this insight by love, which is always sympathy, and has to do with the pain of others. When the veil of Maya is lifted, a man takes on the suffering of the whole world. In the good man, knowledge of the whole quiets all volition; his 'Will' turns away from life and denies his own nature.

> "There arises within him a horror of the nature of which his own phenomenal existence is an expression, the kernel and inner nature of that world is recognised as full of misery."

The good man will practice complete chastity, voluntary poverty, fasting and self-torture. In all things he will aim at the breaking down of his individual 'Will'. But he does not do this, as do the Western mystics, to achieve harmony with God; the good that is sought is wholly negative.

> "We must banish the dark impression of that nothingness which we discern behind all virtue and holiness as their final goal, and which we fear as children fear the dark; we must not even evade it like the Indians,

> *through myths and meaningless words, such as reabsorption in Brahma or the Nirvana of the Buddhists. Rather we do freely acknowledge that what remains after the entire abolition of 'Will' is for ... those in whom the 'Will' has turned and has denied itself, this our world, which is so real, with all its suns and milky ways – is nothing."*

Schopenhauer's Ethics

In 1841 he published two more books: ***On the freedom of the Will,*** and ***On the Basis of Morality***. In the second of these he expounded his ethical system, which is closely related to his metaphysics.

He starts with a critique of Kant's ideas on morality. Kant, remember said it was our moral duty to do the right thing; he called it the 'Categorical Imperative'. For Schopenhauer, the very idea of a categorical, as opposed to a hypothetical, imperative, is an absurdity. An imperative is normally an order of some kind, given by someone who can impose sanctions on those who do not conform to it. He believed that a 'categorical Imperative' only made sense to Kant because, unconsciously he took it as a command from God.

In contrast, moral goodness is identified by Schopenhauer with unselfish compassion for others. The good man is one who, not making the usual distinction between himself and others, is filled with universal compassion. Thus, he acts on the principle 'Injure no one; on the contrary, help everyone as much as you can.'

This compassion, which constitutes moral worth, manifests itself in its lesser form in justice, based on the principle of non-interference with anyone obtaining things legitimately, i.e. not at the expense of someone else. It manifests itself in its fullest form, however, as the loving kindness which inspires an active concern to help others when in need.

It should be noted that, for Schopenhauer, the goal of compassion is the relief of misery and does not include the creation of positive happiness. This is partly because his pessimistic view of life implies that positive happiness, as opposed to relief from the worst sort of unhappiness, is impossible. And partly because he thinks that the kind of identification with others, which constitutes compassion, can only occur when one becomes aware of another as a fellow sufferer.

Legacy

Russell says that two things are important about Schopenhauer; his pessimism, and his idea that 'Will' is superior to knowledge. His pessimism is perhaps an important balance to most other Western philosophers, who tend to be optimistic, Science, Russell points out is neither. More important, however, was the doctrine of the primacy of the 'Will'. In one form or another, this has gone on to strongly influence several subsequent philosophers, most notably Nietzsche, Henri Bergson, William James, and John Dewey. It has, moreover, acquired a vogue outside the circles of professional philosophers. Russell goes on to say: -

> *"In spite of inconsistency and a certain shallowness, his philosophy has considerable importance as a stage in historical development."*

Other sources note that: - although his work failed to garner substantial attention during his life, Schopenhauer had a posthumous impact across various disciplines, though more so in the arts (especially literature and music) and psychology than in philosophy. His popularity peaked in the early twentieth century, especially during the Modernist era, and has waned somewhat thereafter.

Nevertheless, several recent publications have reinterpreted his work, and his theories are also being explored by some modern philosophers as a precursor to evolutionary theory and modern evolutionary psychology.

Tolstoy said that one summer he was in "Constant raptures over Schopenhauer and a whole series of spiritual delights which I've never experienced before". Wagner claimed that Schopenhauer had "a radical influence on my whole life". And Friedrich Nietzsche owed the awakening of his philosophical interest to reading **The World as Will and Representation**.

As a teenager, Ludwig Wittgenstein adopted Schopenhauer's 'epistemological idealism'. However, after his study of the philosophy of mathematics, he rejected this, turning instead to 'conceptual realism'. And in later years, Wittgenstein was highly dismissive of him, saying: - "Schopenhauer has quite a crude mind... where real depth starts, his comes to an end."

One interesting legacy, however, is that Schopenhauer was the first Western philosopher to be openly atheist. He specifically asks people to reflect on the "cruelties to which religions, especially the Christian and Mohammedan, have given rise", and "the misery they have brought to the world".

31

John Stuart Mill

Introduction

John Stuart Mill (1806 – 1873) was an English philosopher, political economist, feminist, and one of the most significant thinkers in the history of liberalism. He contributed widely to social theory, political theory, and political economy, and has been called "the most influential English-speaking philosopher of the nineteenth century".

His conception of **liberty** justified the freedom of the individual in opposition to unlimited state control. He was a proponent of utilitarianism (the ethical theory developed by his predecessor Jeremy Bentham) and he also contributed significantly to the theory of the 'scientific method'.

Background

Mill was born in London, in 1806, as the eldest son of James Mill, the Scottish philosopher, historian and economist. James Mill was a close friend of the English philosopher Jeremy Bentham and adopted many of Bentham's principles in their entirety. In particular, he followed Bentham's ideas on education. John Mill, therefore, was given an extremely rigorous upbringing, and was deliberately shielded from association with children his own age other than his siblings. His father had as his explicit aim to create a genius intellect that would carry on the cause of utilitarianism and its implementation after he and Bentham had both died.

Whether he would have been a genius without this hothouse environment can never be known but he was a certainly a precocious child. He began learning Greek at the age of three, and by the age of eight he had read *Aesop's Fables*, Xenophon's *Anabasis*, and the whole of Herodotus, and was acquainted with Lucian, Diogenes Laërtius, Isocrates and six dialogues of Plato. He had also read a great deal of history in English and had been taught arithmetic, physics, and astronomy.

At the age of eight, Mill began studying Latin, the works of Euclid, and algebra, and was appointed schoolmaster to the younger children of the family. His main reading was still history, but by the age of ten he had read all the commonly taught Latin and Greek authors. His father also thought that it was important for Mill to study and compose poetry. One of Mill's earliest poetry compositions was a continuation of the Iliad. In his spare time, he also enjoyed reading about natural sciences and popular novels, such as *Don Quixote* and *Robinson Crusoe*.

About the age of 12, Mill began a thorough study of the scholastic logic, while at the same time reading Aristotle's logical treatises in the original language. In the following year he was introduced to political economy and studied Adam Smith and David Ricardo. John and his father were great walkers, and during their walks in the hills of Hampstead and Highgate each day, John had to give his father an account of what he had read and submit to a searching inquisition about it.

At the age of fourteen, Mill stayed a year in France with the family of Sir Samuel Bentham, brother of Jeremy Bentham. The mountain scenery he saw led to a lifelong taste for mountain landscapes. In Montpellier, he attended the winter courses on chemistry, zoology, and logic at the *Faculté des Sciences*, as well as taking a course of the higher mathematics.

In early adolescence, although his education had already been conducted in adherence to Benthamite principles, Mill started reading Bentham's political writings, and he was immediately entranced. He says that, from the very first pages, Bentham's ideas: -

> "Burst upon me with all the force of novelty. ... The feeling rushed upon me, that all previous moralists were superseded ... here indeed... was a new era in thought."

His enthusiasm for Benthamism was almost religious in nature and he decided that his task was to reform the world along these lines. But five years later, at the age of twenty, he went through a crisis of doubt and melancholia. He asked himself the following question: -

> "Suppose that all your objects in life were realised; that all changes and institutions and opinions which you were looking forward to, could be completely effected at this instant: would this be a great happiness to you?"

His answer to himself was "No!" And at this his heart sank, the whole foundation on which he had constructed his life fell down. It seemed to him as if he had nothing left to live for. He blamed his collapse on the severity and aridity of his early education at the hands of his father. This, he thought, had sharpened his powers of analysis but had eroded his capacity for feeling. He described it as being in possession of a well-equipped ship and rudder, but with no sail.

Poetry, he said, saved him, especially Wordsworth's poetry. It was not just the outward beauty of the poems, but the states of feeling and of thought coloured by feeling under the excitement of beauty, that became medicine for his state of mind.

> "They seemed to be the very culture of the feelings which I was in quest of. In them I seemed to draw from a source of inward joy, of sympathetic and imaginative pleasure, which could be shared by all human beings; which had no connection with struggle or imperfection, but would be made richer by every improvement in the physical or social condition of mankind."

This led him to both question the educational methods of his father and to modify the general theory of Bentham so as to conclude that the *direct* pursuit of happiness is a mirage. In his subsequent writings he maintained that the cultivation of an ideal nobleness of will and conduct should be, to individual human beings, an end, to which the specific pursuit either of their own happiness or that of others should, in any case of conflict, give way.

At 17 he had received an appointment under his father in the East India Company, and he stayed with the company for 35 years, retiring only when the company closed down for good. He didn't think that he could make a living as a writer, so he pursued his writing while still working. He rose through the company, becoming an accomplished statesman in charge of relations between the company and native Indian states. A few years after his retirement he briefly became a member of parliament, where he took a most active part in debates: his proposals for the representation of women and for reform of government were far ahead of his time. He died at his house in France in 1873, to the last busying himself with social questions.

Mill wrote numerous books and articles, both political and scientific, but his main works were: -

- *A System of Logic* (1843)
- ***Essays on Some Unsettled Questions of Political Economy*** (1844)
- ***The Principles of Political Economy: with some of their applications to social philosophy*** (1848)
- *On Liberty* (1859)

- ***Considerations on Representative Government*** (1861)
- ***Utilitarianism*** (1863)
- ***The Subjection of Women*** (1869).

Philosophy

A System of Logic

Mill's first main work, and the one which initially made him famous in his day, was his book on logic, published in 1843 when he was 27. Little attention had been paid to this subject since Locke and Hume, and many still considered Aristotle to be the master in this area. With the rise of science, however, a number of people were revisiting the subject, indeed Mill's aim was clearly described in the subtitle of the book: - 'Being a connected view of the principles of evidence and the methods of scientific investigation'.

The work starts with a critical examination of Aristotelian logic in which his father trained him. He aims to show that, in using logic, we are not simply reasoning about our ideas of things, but what we assume are the things themselves.

> "When I say that fire causes heat, do I mean that my idea of fire causes my idea of heat? No: I mean that the natural phenomenon, fire, causes the natural phenomenon, heat."

He believed that the notion of a logical proposition as a relationship between ideas (as opposed to between phenomena) was a fatal error in the philosophy of logic and had held back the advancement of science.

Having established that logic is not word-spinning but a method of arriving at proof about reality, it was possible for him to embark on his own contribution to the subject, which was about the importance of induction as a method. He did not diminish the importance of deduction but argued that induction, especially in its connection with experimentation, is of equal importance.

What then is induction? It is a process of inference from established instances to all other identical cases. He argues for instance that if we say that all animals have nervous systems and we mean no more than all known animals have nervous systems, no induction is involved. If, however, we mean to infer that a nervous system will be found even in animals not yet discovered, then that is induction.

The underlying assumption here is that the universe is orderly and subject to definable laws. Then, if what determines one case will determine identical cases, it follows that the notion of 'Cause' is at the root of the theory of induction. This he saw as answering Hume's sceptical notion of 'Cause' as being concerned with 'efficient' causes while science is concerned with 'physical' ones.

It is a little strange that Russell, in his great **'History of Western Philosophy'** does not give a chapter to John Stuart Mill, especially given Russell's love of logic. Instead, he just gives the odd reference to Mill in other places. With respect to Mill's system of logic, all Russell says is that it can be usefully employed so long as the law of causality is assumed, but this law, as Mill admits, can only be accepted on the basis of induction itself.

On Liberty

Mill's *On Liberty* (1858) addresses the nature and limits of the power that can be legitimately exercised by society over the individual. However, Mill is clear that his concern for liberty does not extend to all individuals and all societies. He states that "Despotism is a legitimate mode of government in dealing with barbarians".

He states that it is acceptable to harm oneself as long as the person doing so is not harming others. He also argues that individuals should be prevented from doing lasting, serious harm to themselves or their property. This is his harm principle. Because no one exists in isolation, harm done to oneself may also harm others, and destroying property deprives the community as well as oneself. Mill excuses those who are "incapable of self-government" from this principle, such as young children or those living in "backward states of society". It is important to bear in mind that the arguments in *On Liberty* are grounded on the principle of Utility, and not on appeals to natural rights.

On Liberty also includes an impassioned defence of free speech. Mill argues that free discourse is a necessary condition for intellectual and social progress. We can never be sure, he contends, that a silenced opinion does not contain some element of the truth. He also argues that allowing people to air false opinions is productive for two reasons. First, individuals are more likely to abandon erroneous beliefs if they are engaged in an open exchange of ideas. And second, by forcing other individuals to re-examine and re-affirm their beliefs in the process of debate, these beliefs are kept from declining into mere dogma. It is not enough for Mill that one simply has an unexamined belief that happens to be true; one must understand why the belief in question is the true one.

Utilitarianism

Jeremy Bentham's famous formulation of utilitarianism is known as the "greatest-happiness principle". It holds that one must always act so as to produce the greatest aggregate happiness among all sentient beings, within reason. Mill's major contribution to utilitarianism is his argument for the qualitative separation of pleasures. Bentham treats all forms of happiness as equal, whereas Mill argues that intellectual and moral pleasures (higher pleasures) are superior to more physical forms of pleasure (lower pleasures). Mill distinguishes between happiness and contentment, claiming that the former is of higher value than the latter, a belief encapsulated in the statement that: -

> "It is better to be a human being dissatisfied than a pig satisfied; better to be Socrates dissatisfied than a fool satisfied. And if the fool, or the pig, is of a different opinion, it is because they only know their own side of the question."

Sometimes it is difficult to decide on what to do to obtain the 'greatest happiness'. Suppose a white man kills a black person in an area torn by racial strife, and as a result there are daily riots of escalating violence. Suppose too that you could secure the arrest of an innocent white person for the crime by testifying against him. The riots and further violence would stop; a much happier outcome for most of the people.

Some Utilitarians deal with these kinds of conflicts by distinguishing between act and rule utilitarianism. 'Act utilitarian' says each action should be judged solely on its ability to produce the greatest happiness, but 'Rule utilitarian' says we should follow those rules that will produce the greatest happiness. For instance, a 'Rule utilitarian' might say that 'Do not kill the innocent' is a rule that increases happiness overall in the long run.

Bentham is an 'Act utilitarian', but Mill believes we should be 'Rule utilitarians' except where we face a dilemma generated by two rules, for example the rule 'Do not steal' and the rule 'Do not allow people to starve'. If I can only feed a starving person by stealing food for them, I must break one of the two rules. Under these circumstances, says Mill, I must revert to being an 'Act utilitarian' and judge the case solely on what will produce the greatest happiness in that situation.

Slavery

In 1850, Mill sent an anonymous letter (which came to be known under the title "The Negro Question"), in rebuttal to Thomas Carlyle's anonymous letter to *Fraser's Magazine for Town and Country* in which Carlyle argued for slavery. Mill supported abolition in the United States. He later wrote about slavery that: -

> "This absolutely extreme case of the law of force, condemned by those who can tolerate almost every other form of arbitrary power, and which, of all others, presents features the most revolting to the feeling of all who look at it from an impartial position, was the law of civilized and Christian England".

Women's Rights

Mill's view of history was that right up until his time "the whole of the female" and "the great majority of the male sex" were simply "slaves". He argued that relations between sexes simply amounted to "the legal subordination of one sex to the other". He thought it was "one of the chief hindrances to human improvement; and that it ought to be replaced by a principle of perfect equality." His book ***The Subjection of Women*** (1861, published 1869) is one of the earliest written on this subject by a male author.

Political Democracy

Mill's major work on political democracy, ***Considerations on Representative Government***, defends two fundamental principles, extensive participation by citizens, and the enlightened competence of rulers. The two values are obviously in tension with each other, and some readers have concluded that he is an elitist democrat, while others count him as an earlier participatory democrat. But in chapter three he presents what is still one of the most eloquent cases for the value of participation by all citizens. He believed that the incompetence of the masses could eventually be overcome if they were given a chance to take part in politics, especially at the local level.

Legacy

As probably the most gifted and certainly the most outstanding of Jeremy Bentham's philosophical disciples, Mill stands out as a key figure in nineteenth century liberalism. It is in Mill that we find the most fully developed and best articulated statement of utilitarianism.

Russell, however, is a lot more critical, saying that "Mill, in his *Utilitarianism*, offers an argument which is so fallacious that it is hard to understand how he can have thought it valid. He says: Pleasure is the only thing desired; therefore, pleasure is the only thing desirable. He argues that only things visible are things seen, similarly the only things desirable are things desired. He does not notice that a thing is visible if it *can* be seen, but desirable if it *ought* to be desired."

As noted with Bentham, utilitarianism led inexorably to British Socialism, and as expounded by Mill with his ideas of progress within society, it influenced every progressive movement of the century.

32

Soren Kierkegaard

Introduction

Soren Kierkegaard (1813 – 1855) was a Danish philosopher, theologian, poet, social critic and religious author who is widely considered to be the first existentialist philosopher. He wrote critical texts on organized religion, Christendom, morality, ethics, psychology, and the philosophy of religion, displaying a fondness for metaphor, irony, and parables. Much of his philosophical work deals with the issues of how one lives as a "single individual", giving priority to concrete human reality over abstract thinking and highlighting the importance of personal choice and commitment.

> "The greatest hazard of all, losing one's self, can occur very quietly in the world, as if it were nothing at all. No other loss can occur so quietly..."

'Existentialism' is a loose term for the reaction, led by Kierkegaard, against the abstract rationalism of Hegel's philosophy. Remember Hegel's conception of 'absolute consciousness', within which all oppositions are supposedly reconciled via successive levels of thesis and antithesis. Kierkegaard, however, insisted on the irreducibility of the subjective, personal dimension of human life. He characterised this in terms of the perspective of the 'existing individual', and it is from this use of the term 'existence', describing a distinctive human mode of being, that existentialism gets its name (although it was Sartre and Marcel who, much later, actually coined the term).

Background

Born into a prosperous family in 1813, in Copenhagen, Denmark, Kierkegaard was the youngest of seven children. His father was a very strict Christian and was convinced that, because of his own sins, none of his children would survive him, or even live beyond 33, the age Christ died. Only Soren and his brother Peter did. His mother was very protective of him. His father encouraged him to become a priest, and his brother did actually become a bishop, but after his father died in 1838, he completed his university degree in theology and then, supported by a large inheritance, he began a career as an independent thinker and writer.

Kierkegaard didn't want to be a philosopher in the traditional or Hegelian sense, and he didn't want to preach a Christianity that was an illusion. Philosophy dissatisfied him: - he couldn't envisage "dedicating himself to Speculation." He noted in one of his journals (which, incidentally, are the source of many aphorisms credited to the philosopher): -

> "What I really need is to get clear about what I must do, not what I must know, except insofar as knowledge must precede every act. What matters is to find a purpose, to see what it really is that God wills that I shall do; the crucial thing is to find a truth which is truth for me, to find the idea for which I am willing to live and die."

He wanted to: - "lead a completely human life and not merely one of knowledge." And said: - "Not until a man has inwardly understood himself and then sees the course he is to take does his life gain peace and meaning."

An important aspect of Kierkegaard's life – generally considered to have had a major influence on his work – was his broken engagement to Regine Olsen. Kierkegaard and Olsen met in 1837 and were instantly attracted to each other. They became engaged in 1840, but a year later he broke off the engagement. In his journals, Kierkegaard mentions his belief that his "melancholy" made him unsuitable for marriage, but his precise motive for ending the engagement remains unclear.

Like his father, Kierkegaard was consumed by inner torment, by feelings of guilt and dread. He considered himself a permanent outsider. He seems to have broken his engagement with Olsen (who was ten years his junior) to save her from his own brooding and miserable nature, but also, partly as an act of sacrifice, so that he could pursue his own work with greater intensity.

Kierkegaard also became involved in a spat with the satirical paper *The Corsair*, which was in the habit of ridiculing the great and the good of Danish society. The paper had printed an article by its editor, criticizing one of Kierkegaard's essays ***Stages on Life's Way***. The article complimented Kierkegaard for his wit and intellect, but questioned whether he would ever be able to master his talent and write coherent, complete works. Kierkegaard responded with two pieces, one insulting the editor's integrity, and the other a directed assault on *The Corsair*, in which Kierkegaard, after criticizing the journalistic quality and reputation of the paper, openly asked *The Corsair* to satirize him. This it duly did, and he then found himself the laughingstock of Copenhagen society.

He travelled little and, other than a few trips to Germany and Sweden, he spent his entire life in the city of Copenhagen. Kierkegaard's final years were taken up with a sustained, outright attack on the Church of Denmark by means of newspaper articles published in *The Fatherland* and a series of self-published pamphlets called *The Moment*, also translated as "The Instant".

Kierkegaard collapsed on the street in 1855. He stayed in the hospital for over a month and refused communion. At that time he regarded pastors as mere political officials, a niche in society who were clearly not representative of the divine. He died in the hospital, possibly (it is said) from complications from a fall he had taken from a tree in his youth.

Kierkegaard's Writings

In terms of his writings, Kierkegaard published some of his works using pseudonyms and others under his own name. Whether being published under a pseudonym or not, Kierkegaard's central writings on religion have included **Fear and Trembling** and **Either/Or**, the latter of which is considered to be his magnum opus.

Pseudonyms were used often in the early 19th century as a means of representing viewpoints other than the author's own. Kierkegaard employed the same technique as a way to provide examples of indirect communication. In writing under various pseudonyms to express sometimes contradictory positions, Kierkegaard is sometimes criticized for playing with various viewpoints without ever committing to one in particular, though he himself has testified to all his work deriving from a service to Christianity.

His output was prolific, including many books, pamphlets, and articles. As well as the two mentioned above his main works were **Philosophical Fragments, The Concept of Anxiety, Concluding Unscientific Postscript to Philosophical Fragments, The Concept of Irony** and **The Sickness Unto Death**.

Many of his discourses, written under his own name, he dedicated to the: - "single individual" who might want to discover the meaning of his works. Notably, he wrote: "Science and scholarship want to teach that becoming objective is the way. Christianity teaches that the way is to become subjective, to become a subject." While scientists can learn about the world by observation, Kierkegaard emphatically denied that observation could reveal the inner workings of the world of the spirit.

Philosophy

Kierkegaard's philosophy was driven by two dislikes. Firstly, he reacted against the prevailing Hegelian philosophy, which he regarded as abstract and hedonistic. And secondly, he reacted against the established church. Organised religion he saw as merely finite institutions which catastrophically usurp the true role of religion. He upheld what he considered to be an authentic Christian faith, as opposed to the diluted 'Sunday Christianity' that he thought many of his contemporaries professed.

He pointed out that most people who describe themselves as Christians are born into their faith, and that their involvement extends little beyond attending church on a Sunday. He thought Danish Christians were churned out by the Danish state church "with the greatest possible uniformity of a factory product", and that this, according to him, is not the true faith.

Nor is the true Christian one who **rationally** recognizes the truth of religious claims, in the way that many Christian philosophers (including Thomas Aquinas) have thought possible. Faith is not some sort of 'second-rate' form of belief for those not clever and well educated enough to recognise proofs of God's existence. True faith is not inferior to, but is higher than, reason.

An authentic Christian faith, thinks Kierkegaard, involves making a deeply passionate and personal commitment to accept divine authority above all else. It involves making a fearful, life-transforming leap beyond what is reasonable and rational, to accept what is profoundly paradoxical. And it is a leap that must be made, not once, but repeatedly.

In his book *Fear and Trembling* he writes about the biblical story of Abraham. God tells him to take his only son Isaac into the mountains and sacrifice him as an offering to God. Abraham obeys and only when he has the knife in his hand ready to strike does an angel appear to revoke God's instructions.

Kant thought Abraham wrong in intending to do something so immoral as to kill an innocent child, but Kierkegaard on the other hand considers Abraham's faith a rare example of authentic Judeo-Christian faith. The true Christian is one who realises that there is a higher duty than a moral one which usually governs society; it is a duty to the higher authority of God himself.

> "Faith is the highest passion in a human being.
> Many in every generation may not come that far,
> but none comes further."

There is obviously a sense here, in which this makes such an individual an outsider, someone who stands apart from conventional, rule-based morality.

A critic might suggest, at this point, that Kierkegaard is giving people license to kill innocent people in the name of whatever God they believe in. But Kierkegaard tries to anticipate this criticism by pointing out that Abraham also acts out of love for his son, and that Abraham had faith that his son would be restored to him by God.

Kierkegaard also stresses the importance of the self, and the self's relation to the world, as being grounded in self-reflection and introspection. He argued in ***Concluding Unscientific Postscript to Philosophical Fragments*** that "subjectivity is truth" and "truth is subjectivity." This has to do with a distinction between what is objectively true and an individual's subjective relation (such as indifference or commitment) to that truth.

For instance, people who in *some sense* believe the same things may relate to those beliefs quite differently. Two individuals may both believe that many of those around them are poor and deserve help, but this knowledge may lead only one of them to decide to actually help the poor.

The Seeds of Existentialism

Kierkegaard rejected the claim, which he took (perhaps unfairly) to be Hegel's, that we can look forward to a time when the different interests and concerns of people can be satisfied through their comprehension within an all-embracing objective understanding of the universe. According to Kierkegaard, no such synthesis can do justice to an individual's concern for their own life.

Hence, he argues, even though Kantian epistemology correctly implies that we should recognize that our own subjective perceptions are just the manifestations of our objective situation in the world, we cannot similarly resolve ethical questions by subjecting our moral consciousness to an impersonal analytic perspective. For ethical questions essentially concern ourselves. In asking ourselves how we are to lead our lives, we deceive ourselves if we pretend that the adoption of an objective, impersonal understanding of our situation will by itself provide an answer.

Kierkegaard takes it that this relationship between ethics and subjectivity is a two-way relationship. Not only are ethical questions essentially first-person, the 'real subject' is also 'the ethically existing subject', as he puts it. He also says that we should not think of our existence as 'real subject' as something to take for granted. Instead, it is an aspect of our lives that needs to be developed if we are to achieve our full potential as individuals. The fact of our 'existence' implies that we cannot avoid first person practical questions, but we may well lack a coherent conception of ourselves by reference to which we can begin to answer them.

How then is such a conception to be acquired? How is one to 'become an individual'? Not, he says, by acquiring more knowledge of the world. Instead, we have to engage the will: it is by making choices and commitments (such as marriage) which enable us to develop long-term interests that we give our lives an ethical structure.

When Kierkegaard writes that "it is impossible to exist without passion", he means that it is only by entering into engagements whose fate can arouse the passions that we gain a sense of our own identity and in that way become an 'existing individual'. The basic idea here is that one can make sense of one's life as a whole only through personal conduct and relationships with others.

Legacy

For obvious reasons, rationalists (followers of Hegel, Kant, and the like) have dismissed Kierkegaard as being irrational, but that in Kierkegaard's writings which repels rationalists has drawn sympathy from circles later regarded as fascist. Equally, democrats are put off him by his contempt for public opinion, the crowd, and parliamentary institutions. Also, his religious thinking, together with his focus on the individual, made him an obvious target for the Marxist.

The tendency to ascribe extreme views to Kierkegaard may be due in part to the perceived anti-humanism of his later rejection of all bourgeois forms of human association, including marriage and the family, which he saw as always becoming merely forms of self-indulgence, rather like his views on organised religion in which the conventions matter more than the individual's search for truth.

Many modern philosophers have found, in the religious framework of his writings, an impediment to any serious appreciation of his thought, although Wittgenstein did once refer to Kierkegaard as "by far the most profound thinker of the last century".

The American philosopher William James attended some lectures on Kierkegaard, and although he had not read Kierkegaard's works, as they were not yet translated into English, he agreed with much of what he heard. James' favourite quote from Kierkegaard was: "We live forwards but we understand backwards". James wrote in 1909: -

> "We live forward, we understand backward, said a Danish writer; and to understand life by concepts is to arrest its movement, cutting it up into bits as if with scissors, and, immobilizing these in our logical herbarium where, comparing them as dried specimens, we can ascertain which of them statically includes or excludes which other. This treatment supposes life to have already accomplished itself, for the concepts, being so many views taken after the fact, are retrospective and post mortem. Nevertheless we can draw conclusions from them and project them into the future."

Many 20th-century philosophers, both theistic and atheistic, and theologians drew concepts from Kierkegaard, including the notions of angst, despair, and the importance of the individual. His fame as a philosopher grew tremendously in the 1930s, in large part because the ascendant existentialist movement pointed to him as a precursor, although some later writers celebrated him as a highly significant and influential thinker in his own right.

In 1964 Life Magazine traced the history of existentialism, describing its origins as being with some of the early Greek philosophers, but then went on to say: -

> "The orthodox, textbook precursor of modern existentialism was the Danish theologian Søren Kierkegaard (1813–1855), a lonely, hunchbacked writer who denounced the established church and rejected much of the then-popular German idealism – in which thought and ideas, rather than things perceived through the senses, were held to constitute reality. He built a philosophy based in part on the idea of permanent cleavage between faith and reason. This was an existentialism which still had room for a God whom Sartre later expelled, but which started the great pendulum-swing toward the modern concepts of the absurd."

Russell, however, almost completely ignores Kierkegaard; in his great '*A History of Western Philosophy*' there are only a few odd references to him here and there. This is probably because he thought Kierkegaard was not a philosopher in the traditional sense, Kierkegaard did not write about such concepts as logic, time, space and the phenomenon of matter and perception. Also, at the time Russell was writing, existentialism was probably too new a concept to cover in depth.

33

Karl Marx

Introduction

Karl Heinrich Marx (1818 – 1883) was a radical social theorist, and organiser of the working class, whose thought is widely regarded as the chief inspiration for all forms of social radicalism. He is also thought of as the man who claimed to have made Socialism scientific.

Much of his work concerns economics and political history rather than pure philosophy, although it is hard to draw the line around any of these subjects, and certainly politics, in an academic sense, comes within the remit of philosophy. Russell says he is difficult to classify: -

> "In one aspect, he is the outcome ... of the Philosophical Radicals, continuing their rationalism and their opposition to the romantics. In another aspect he is a reviver of materialism, giving it a new interpretation and a new connection with human history. In yet another aspect he is the last of the great system builders, the successor of Hegel, a believer, like him, in a rational formula summing up the evolution of mankind. Emphasis on any one of these aspects at the expense of the others gives a false and distorted view of his philosophy."

It is also not possible to study Marx without identifying the influence of his long-term friendship and collaboration with Friedrich Engels (1820 – 1895), a German social theorist, working-class organizer, and philosopher.

Background

Marx was born, in 1818 in the German city of Trier, to a successful, conservative, Jewish middle-class family. His parents converted to Christianity in 1824, when Marx was six, because his father, a lawyer, could not practice law due to Prussia's anti-Semitic laws. Largely non-religious, however, his father was a man of the Enlightenment, interested in the ideas of the philosophers Immanuel Kant and Voltaire.

Marx was the third of nine children but became the eldest when his brother died in 1819 when Marx was just one. He was baptized into the Lutheran Church in August 1824 along with his surviving siblings. He was home educated until he was 12 and then attended a school where the headmaster was a friend of his father.

At seventeen he went to the University of Bonn to study law. Due to a condition referred to as a "weak chest" he was excused from military duty when he turned 18. While at the University at Bonn, he joined the Poets' Club, a group containing political radicals that were monitored by the police. Although initially good, his grades deteriorated, and so his father sent him to the more serious University of Berlin in 1836. At Berlin, however, he discovered philosophy and changed his course of study to that as well as law.

Also, in 1836 he became more serious about his studies and his life. He became engaged to Jenny von Westphalen, an educated baroness of the Prussian ruling class who had known Marx since childhood. She actually broke off her engagement with a young aristocrat to be with Marx. Their relationship was socially controversial due to the differences between their religious and class origins, but Marx befriended her father, and later dedicated his doctoral thesis to him. Seven years after their engagement Marx and Jenny married and, despite their exceedingly hard life after 1850, the marriage was a happy one and lasted until her death in 1881.

At Berlin, Marx became interested in the recently deceased German philosopher G. W. F. Hegel, whose ideas were then widely debated among European philosophical circles. In 1837 he became involved with a group of radical thinkers known as the Young Hegelians. They were critical of Hegel's metaphysical assumptions but adopted his dialectical method in order to criticize established society, politics, and religion from a leftist perspective.

His doctoral thesis, ***The Difference Between the Democritean and Epicurean Philosophy of Nature***, which he completed in 1841, was described as "a daring and original piece of work in which Marx set out to show that theology must yield to the superior wisdom of philosophy". The essay was controversial, particularly among the conservative professors at the University of Berlin, so Marx decided, instead, to submit his thesis to the more liberal University of Jena, whose faculty awarded him his PhD in April 1841

Marx was considering an academic career, but this path was barred by the government's growing opposition to classical liberalism and the Young Hegelians. He moved to Cologne in 1842, where he became a journalist, writing for the radical newspaper *"Rhineland News"*, expressing his early views on socialism and his developing interest in economics. He criticized both right-wing European governments as well as figures in the liberal and socialist movements whom he thought ineffective or counterproductive.

In 1843, however, Prussia's government banned the paper, so in that year he moved to Paris and took a job as co-editor of a new, radical leftist Parisian newspaper. While in Paris, in 1844, Marx became reacquainted with the German socialist Friedrich Engels, and this was the beginning of a lifelong friendship and writing collaboration. Engels convinced Marx that the working class would be the agent and instrument of the final revolution in history.

During his time in Paris Marx engaged in an intensive study of "political economy", the study of which he would pursue for the rest of his life and would result in his major economic work—the three-volume series called *Capital*. Marxism is based in large part on three influences: Hegel's dialectics, French utopian socialism, and English economics. Together with his earlier study of Hegel's dialectics, the studying that Marx did during this time in Paris meant that all major components of "Marxism" were in place by the autumn of 1844.

When, in 1845, the French government, at the request of the Prussian government, shut down the paper he worked for, Marx moved to Brussels, where he was allowed to stay as long as he didn't publish anything on contemporary politics. Engels joined him there, and in late 1847, Marx and Engels began writing what was to become their most famous work, **The Communist Manifesto,** which was first published on 21 February 1848.

Later that year, Europe experienced a series of protests, rebellions, and often violent upheavals that became known as the **Revolution of 1848**. In France, a revolution led to the overthrow of the monarchy and the establishment of the French Second Republic. Marx was supportive of such activity and so the Belgian government arrested him, he was then forced to flee back to France, where, with a new republican government in power, he believed that he would be safe.

In 1849 Paris was in the grip of both a reactionary counter-revolution and a cholera epidemic, so Marx moved to London, where he stayed for the rest of his life. While in London, he devoted himself to the task of organizing the working class in preparation for revolution. His main source of income was his colleague, Engels, who derived much of his money from his family's business. Most of Marx's journalistic writing, however, was as a European correspondent for the *New York Daily Tribune*.

An Introduction to Philosophy

His life in London was one of poverty, three of his six children died from the effects of this. Apart from his journalism, he spent most of his time (up to 10 hours a day) in the Reading Room of the British Museum, studying and pursuing his writing in failing health. In 1859 Marx published *A Contribution to the Critique of Political Economy*, his first serious economic work. This work was intended merely as a preview of his three-volume ***Das Kapital*** (English title: ***Capital: Critique of Political Economy***). Volume 1 of his seminal work *Capital* was published in 1867, but it was left to Engels to edit and publish the remaining two volumes after Marx's death in 1883. During his life, Marx published many books and articles on philosophy, history and economics, including: -

- The Philosophical Manifesto of the Historical School of Law, 1842
- Critique of Hegel's Philosophy of Right, 1843
- "Notes on James Mill," 1844
- Economic and Philosophic Manuscripts of 1844, 1844
- The German Ideology, 1845
- "Wage Labour and Capital," 1847
- Manifesto of the Communist Party, 1848
- A Contribution to the Critique of Political Economy, 1859
- Theories of Surplus Value, 3 volumes, 1862
- "Value, Price and Profit," 1865
- Capital, Volume I (Das Kapital), 1867
- Capital, Volume II (posthumously published by Engels), 1885
- Capital, Volume III (posthumously published by Engels), 1894

Philosophy

Marx, like Bentham and James Mill, would have nothing to do with romanticism; it is always his intention to be scientific. His economics is an outcome of British classical economics, changing only the motive force. Classical economics, consciously or unconsciously, was aimed at the welfare of the capitalist, as opposed to both the landowner and the wage-earner. Marx, on the contrary, set to work to represent the interests of the wage-earner.

He called himself a materialist, but not of the eighteenth-century sort. His sort, which under Hegelian influence, he called "dialectical", differed in an important way from the traditional materialism. The older materialism, he said, mistakenly regarded sensation as passive, and thus attributed activity primarily to the object. In Marx's view, all sensation or perception is an interaction between subject and object; the bare object, apart from the activity of the percipient, is a mere raw material, which is transformed in the process of becoming known. Knowledge in the old sense of passive contemplation is an unreal abstraction; the process that really takes place is one of *handling* things.

> "The question whether objective truth belongs to human thinking is not a question of theory, but a practical question. The truth, i.e. the reality and power, of thought must be demonstrated in practice. The contest as to the reality or non reality of a thought which is isolated from practice, is a purely scholastic question. ... Philosophers have only *interpreted* the world in various ways, but the real task is to *alter* it."

I.e. what philosophers have called the 'pursuit of knowledge' is not one where the object is constant, and adaptation is on the part of the knower. On the contrary, both knower and object are in a continual process of mutual adaption. He calls this 'dialectical' because it is never fully completed.

Russell says that: - "it is essential to this theory to deny the reality of 'sensation' as conceived by British empiricists. What happens, when it is most nearly what they mean by 'sensation', would be better called 'noticing', which implies activity. In fact – so Marx would contend – we only notice things as part of the process of acting with reference to them, and any theory which leaves out action is a misleading theory."

Marx's ideas on History

Marx's philosophy of history is a blend of Hegel and British economics. Hegel thought there was a logic to the way history unfolds and that the fundamental engine of change is the dialectic (successive levels of thesis and antithesis). The fundamental difference between Hegel and Marx is that Hegel thought that this process towards a better society occurred at the level of mind and ideas, whereas Marx thought it was fundamentally one of material change.

Hegel is a ***dialectic idealist***; he believes all change is ultimately change to what he calls *Geist* (mind or spirit) while Marx is a ***dialectical materialist***. He dispenses with Hegel's mysterious *Geist* and insists that it is our material situation – in particular, the way in which production takes place – that shapes what is going on at the level of ideas, including political and religious thought. In this way Marx's materialism becomes economics.

In Marx's view society passes through great epochs that are characterized by their particular economic structure. First there was the feudal society, then came the capitalist society, and that will eventually be replaced by a communist society. Each of these economic systems is shaped by the dominant productive forces of the day. Marx wrote that: -

> "The hand-mill gives you a society with the feudal lord; the steam-mill, a society with the industrial capitalist."

As technology advances and the forces of production continue to develop, so they eventually outstrip and become cramped by relations of production. Ultimately, the strain becomes too much and the system ruptures, giving birth to a new system better suited to the advancing forces of production. And so the cycle continues.

Under a capitalist system, the productive output of the vast majority (the proletariat) is harnessed to a system over which they have no control, it is owned by the capitalist class (the bourgeoisie). So, the proletariat are trapped in an endless cycle of meaningless activity just to survive, they are 'alienated' both from each other and from what they produce.

According to Marx, true freedom requires the development of a society in which man is genuinely self-determined and able to engage in forms of production through which he can properly express his humanity. He thought that the forces of production had developed to the extent that this has now become a genuine possibility. Although he didn't describe a communist society in detail, he is clear that, within it, the mechanism that currently traps people in this alienated existence – private property – is gone.

Hegel had earlier conceived of alienation in the form of the 'unhappy consciousness', i.e. a misunderstood Christian religiosity which experiences the human self as empty and worthless, and places everything of value in a supernatural 'beyond'. The cure, Hegel thought, was the recognition that finite nature is not the absence of infinite spirit but its expression.

To Marx, however, alienation becomes intelligible when we see that the alienated consciousness tells the truth in its laments, not in its consolations. Religion, according to Marx, gives expression to a mode of life which is really; empty, unfulfilled, degraded, and devoid of dignity. Religious illusions have hold on us because they provide a false semblance of meaning and fulfilment for a mode of life which without this illusion would be seen for the unredeemed meaninglessness that it is. For Marx, religious misery is both an expression of actual misery and an attempt to flee from it into a world of imagination. It is, in his words: - "The opium of the people."

The way out of alienation is not, as Hegel thought, a new philosophical interpretation of life, but a new form of earthly existence, a new society in which the material conditions for fulfilling human life would no longer be lacking.

Engels' Influence

Friedrich Engels was already a young Hegelian when he first met Marx in Berlin in 1842, but it was not until they met again in Paris two years later that they became friends. It was Engels who introduced Marx both to the working-class movement and the study of political economy. After participating in the unsuccessful revolution in 1848 in Germany he moved to Manchester where he worked in the family business. He produced a series of his own writings on history, politics, and philosophy, but he also co-wrote many works with Marx, and he spent the last ten years of his life on the posthumous publication of the second and third volumes of Marx's *Capital*.

Always acknowledging Marx's mind to be more original and profound than his own, Engels nevertheless was an able writer of encyclopaedic learning, whose output covers a much broader range than Marx's. It is also said that it was Engels who gave Marx's ideas a more scientific basis, and that the philosophy of dialectical materialism actually owes more to his writings than to Marx's.

Legacy

Marx's ideas have had a profound impact on world politics and intellectual thought. Followers of Marx have frequently debated amongst themselves over how to interpret Marx's writings, and each branch sees itself as Marx's most accurate interpreter. In the political realm, these tendencies include Leninism, Marxist–Leninism, Trotskyism, Maoism, and numerous others. Throughout the twentieth century, revolutions in dozens of countries labelled themselves 'Marxist', and many major world leaders have cited Marx as an influence.

Russell, however, says that: - "Considered purely as a philosopher, Marx has grave shortcomings. He is too practical, too much wrapped up in the problems of his time. His purview is confined to this planet, and, within this planet, to Man. Since Copernicus, it has been evident that Man has not the cosmic importance which he formerly arrogated to himself. No man who has failed to assimilate this fact has a right to call his philosophy scientific. There goes with this limitation to terrestrial affairs a readiness to believe in progress as a universal law. ... It is only because of this belief in the inevitability of progress that Marx thought it possible to dispense with ethical considerations. If Socialism was coming it must be an improvement. ... Marx professed himself an atheist, but retained a cosmic optimism which only theism could justify."

From an academic perspective, Marx's work contributed to the birth of modern sociology. His ideas have also had a profound influence on subsequent artists, authors, musicians, and film makers.

34

William James

Introduction

William James (1842 – 1910) was the first, significant American philosopher. Although primarily a psychologist (who was also trained as a physician), he became important to philosophy for two main reasons. Firstly, he invented the doctrine which he called "radical empiricism", and secondly, he was one of the three main protagonists of the theory called "pragmatism" or "instrumentalism", the other two being F.C.S. Schiller (1864 – 1937) and Dr John Dewey (1859 – 1952).

James was one of the leading thinkers of the late nineteenth century and is believed by many to be one of the most influential philosophers the United States has ever produced, while others have labelled him the "Father of American psychology". He was also the first educator to offer a psychology course in the United States.

James wrote widely on many topics, including epistemology, education, metaphysics, psychology, religion, and mysticism. One of his most influential books is *The Principles of Psychology*, which was a groundbreaking text in the field of psychology. However, for our purposes, we will only consider his contribution to philosophy.

Background

William James was born in New York in 1842, the son of Henry James Sr., a noted and independently wealthy theologian, who was well acquainted with the literary and intellectual elites of his day. The whole family was talented and his brother, Henry James, became a celebrated author. William James received an eclectic trans-Atlantic education, developing fluency in both German and French, indeed the family made two trips to Europe while he was still a child, setting a pattern that resulted in thirteen more European journeys during his life. His early artistic bent led to an apprenticeship in the studio of William Morris Hunt in Newport, Rhode Island, but he switched, in 1861, to scientific studies at Harvard University.

An Introduction to Philosophy

In early adulthood, James suffered from a variety of physical ailments, including those of the eyes, back, stomach, and skin. He was also tone deaf. He was subject to a variety of psychological symptoms which were diagnosed at the time as neurasthenia, and which included periods of depression, during which he contemplated suicide for months on end.

He took up medical studies at Harvard Medical School in 1864, but he took a break in the spring of 1865 to join naturalist Louis Agassiz on a scientific expedition up the Amazon River, although he aborted this trip after eight months, as he suffered bouts of severe seasickness and mild smallpox. His studies were interrupted once again due to illness in April 1867. He travelled to Germany in search of a cure and remained there until November 1868; at that time, he was 26 years old. During this period, he began to publish, and reviews of his works appeared in literary periodicals such as the North American Review.

James finally earned his M.D. degree in June 1869, but he never practiced medicine. What he called his "soul-sickness" would only be resolved in 1872, after an extended period of philosophical searching. He married Alice Gibbens in 1878, and in 1882 he joined the Theosophical Society.

James's time in Germany proved intellectually fertile, helping him find that his true interests lay not in medicine but in philosophy and psychology. Later, in 1902 he would write: -

> *"I originally studied medicine in order to be a physiologist, but I drifted into psychology and philosophy from a sort of fatality. I never had any philosophic instruction, the first lecture on psychology I ever heard being the first I ever gave".*

James interacted with a wide array of writers and scholars throughout his life, including his godfather Ralph Waldo Emerson, also Charles Sanders Peirce, Bertrand Russell, Ernst Mach, John Dewey, Mark Twain, Henri Bergson and Sigmund Freud, to mention just a few. He spent almost his entire academic career at Harvard and was appointed instructor in physiology in 1873, assistant professor of psychology in 1876, assistant professor of philosophy in 1881. Then full professor in 1885, and emeritus professor of philosophy in 1907. He was drawn to the scientific study of the human mind at a time when psychology was constituting itself as a science.

He wrote a huge number of books and articles throughout his life; a non-exhaustive bibliography of his writings, compiled by John McDermott, actually stretches to 47 pages. Among this list, perhaps his most important philosophical works are: -

- An essay called ***The Will to Believe*** 1897
- ***The Varieties of Religious Experience*** 1902
- An essay called ***Does 'Consciousness' Exist?*** 1904
- ***Pragmatism*** 1907
- ***The Meaning of Truth: A Sequel to "Pragmatism"*** (Posthumously) 1912
- ***Essays in Radical Empiricism*** (Posthumously) *1*912

Philosophy

In his essay ***Does 'Consciousness' Exist?*** James laid out his theory of consciousness. This involved a radical reassessment of the subject-object relationship which until then had been a fundamental cornerstone of philosophical thinking. It had been taken for granted that there was a kind of occurrence called 'knowing', which involved one entity, the knower or subject, being aware of another entity, the thing known or object. The knower was regarded as the mind or soul; the object known might be a material object, an abstract idea, another mind, or the self, as in the case of self-consciousness. Almost everything in philosophy, says Russell, was at that time bound up with the dualism of subject and object; if this relationship changes then everything needs to be radically reconsidered.

Consciousness, says James: -

> *"[I]s the name of a nonentity, and has no right to a place among first principles. Those who still cling to it are clinging to a mere echo, the faint rumour left behind by the disappearing 'soul' upon the air of philosophy.'*

There is, he continues: -

> *"[N]o aboriginal stuff or quality of being, contrasted with that of which material objects are made, out of which our thoughts of them are made."*

He explains that he is not denying that our thoughts perform a function which is that of knowing, and that this function may be called "being conscious". What he is denying is that consciousness is a "thing". He holds that there is "*only one primal stuff or material,*" out of which everything in the world is composed, and that 'stuff' he calls "*pure experience"*. This he defines as *"the immediate flux of life which furnishes the material to our later reflection."* There is no *"inner duplicity"* here, a given undivided portion of experience can be in one context the knower and in another something known.

It will be seen, says Russell, that this doctrine abolishes the distinction between mind and matter, if regarded as a distinction between two different kinds of what James calls 'stuff'. Those who agree with James in this advocate what they call "neutral monism", according to which, the material of which the world is constructed is neither mind nor matter, but something anterior to both. James himself did not develop this implication; on the contrary, his use of the phrase "pure experience" points more to some kind of Berkeleian idealism.

Pragmatism

The second philosophical position for which James is remembered is his pragmatism. This starts as a position in philosophy but then carries over into his ideas on religion.

James proposed a world view, which he called pragmatism, which declared that the value of any truth was utterly dependent upon its use to the person who held it. Additional tenets of James's pragmatism include the view that the world is a mosaic of diverse experiences that can only be properly interpreted and understood through an application of "radical empiricism." Radical empiricism (not related to the everyday scientific empiricism) asserts that the world and experience can never be halted for an entirely objective analysis; if nothing else, the mind of the observer and simple act of observation will affect the outcome of any empirical approach to truth because the mind and its experiences, and nature are inseparable.

The principle of pragmatism was (according to James) first developed by C. S. Peirce (1839 – 1914), who maintained that, to attain clearness in our thoughts of an object, we need only consider what conceivable effects of a practical kind the object involves. James enlarged on this by adding that the function of philosophy is to find what difference it makes to you or me if this or that world-formula is true. In this way theories become instruments, not answers to enigmas.

James defined true beliefs as those that prove useful to the believer. He was prepared to advocate any doctrine which tends to make people virtuous and happy; if it does so it is 'true' in the sense in which he uses that word.

> *"An idea is 'true' so long as to believe it is profitable to our lives."*

It is correct to say that an idea must agree with reality, but 'agreeing' does not mean 'copying'.

> *"To 'agree' in the widest sense with a reality can only mean to be guided either straight up to it or into its surroundings, or to be put into such working touch with it as to handle either it or something connected with it better than if we disagreed."*

Peirce was not happy with James' changes. Peirce had developed the idea as a scientific road to impersonal and objective standards, but James gave it a personalised and subjective twist.

James' Ideas on Religion

Probably his best-known book is his ***The Varieties of Religious Experience***, which actually began as a series of lectures he gave. It is distinctive in treading a fine line between being respectful to religion while at the same time telling the stark truth as he saw it. The historian Peter Watson says: -

> "The book takes as its main theme the various psychological states and emotions that he took to be at the centre of religious experience. He considered whether religious leaders in the past had been frankly pathological in their religious concerns... he looked at the role of fear in religious belief, at surrender and passivity... He touched on yoga, Buddhism, Loa-tzu and Vedanta... he looked at conversion, at saintliness, at mysticism and martyrdom, at the phenomenon of cosmic consciousness. And at root, he said, religion was about 'emotionality', religion was a 'massive chapter' in human egotism, born of a core uneasiness within us, a sense that there is something wrong about us with religion providing the solution to that unease. He believed that there is always something solemn about religion – solemn, serious and tender – that satisfies a need we have, a solemnity which we feel enlarges us, produces a 'gladness', an inner unity.
>
> At the same time James noted that many people go through the same emotional journey but without turning to religion, so that while religion 'works' for people who are religious, this says nothing about whether any one set of

religious beliefs are 'true', and he thought that mystics have no right to impose their view on the rest of us. In fact, he went so far as to argue that 'we must say goodbye to dogmatic theology'."

What James did was to provide the first pragmatic argument for those who believe in God; He is real because belief in him produces real effects, like, for instance, living a more satisfying life. James refers to an experiment in which chickens learnt that pecking at a lever opened a door to some food. He said that, to all intents and purposes, the chickens *believed* that if they pecked the lever the door would open. As he put it, "Their beliefs were rules for action." He went on to say that: -

> "If behaving as though we have free will, or as if God exists, gets us the results we want, we will not only come to believe those things; they will be, pragmatically true ... 'The Truth' is the name of whatever proves itself to be good in the way of belief."

The nineteenth century mathematician and philosopher W. K. Clifford had argued that it is morally wrong to believe anything on insufficient evidence, and hence considered religious belief to be immoral. James, however, rejects that view, he says it can be legitimate to believe when the evidence is inconclusive, and he uses the following analogy: -

Suppose you are climbing a mountain. To return home safely you must leap a wide chasm, but your chance of making it is not particularly strong. To succeed, you must feel confident, hesitate and all may be lost. So, even though you are not entirely justified in believing that you will make it safely across, it is nevertheless sensible for you to believe it, particularly as belief will make it more likely that you will succeed. He said that it is sometimes sensible to allow our "*passional nature*" (interests, hopes, desires and fears) to influence our beliefs, even though there is insufficient evidence to warrant that belief.

When is it legitimate to believe something without evidence? James posits that the following three conditions must be satisfied: -

1. We must be faced with a choice between options that are '*live*'. A live option is one that is a genuine possibility; one we can take seriously, for instance most contemporary adults would not consider a belief in Zeus or Santa Claus a live option.
2. The choice must be '*forced*'. A forced choice is one where you have no option but to make a choice one way or the other, e.g. shall I visit my mother today (it's got to be one or the other). But

the choice between travelling to Africa or India is one I don't have to make.
3. The choice must be *'momentous'* - one that will have a major impact on your life.

These three conditions are met in the mountain example i.e. the choice is live, it is forced, and the consequences are momentous. According to James we face a similar choice when it comes to religious belief, the choice is forced, it is momentous and for many it is a live choice.

James is interested in religion as a human phenomenon, but actually shows little interest in the objects which religion contemplates. He wants people to be happy, and if belief in God makes them happy, let them believe in Him. Russell notes that this, so far, is only benevolence, not philosophy; it becomes philosophy when it is said that if the belief makes them happy it is "true".

Legacy

American pragmatism was further developed by Dr John Dewey; while Peirce's pragmatism was scientifically elitist, and James' was psychologically personalistic, Dewey's became democratically populist.

Pragmatism had a mixed reception in Europe. In Italy it was turned into a party platform for Italian philosophers of science. In Britain several philosophers were followers of James, and his ideas were put to work on issues of logic and the philosophy of language. Others however were more critical, especially in the light that the utility of a belief is changeable over time. Pragmatism also came to be looked down upon as a quintessentially American philosophy – a philosophical expression of the American go-getter spirit with its success-orientated ideology.

While liking his ideas on consciousness, Russell is strongly critical of James' pragmatism on the following grounds: - The moral duty of understanding is usually held to comprise two equal precepts, 'believe truth' and 'shun error'. The sceptic is often criticised for only attending to the second, and thus fails to believe various truths which a less cautious person will believe. If believing truth and avoiding error are of equal importance then, when presented with two possibilities, there is an even chance of believing the truth. James, however, never mentions probability, yet there is almost always some discoverable consideration of probability regarding any question.

He continues by saying that James' doctrine is an attempt to build a superstructure of belief upon a foundation of scepticism, but it is dependent on the fallacy of ignoring all extra-human facts. Berkeleian idealism, he says, combined with scepticism causes him to substitute belief in God for God, and to pretend that this will do just as well.

Russell also notes (dryly) that he always found that the hypothesis of Santa Claus "works satisfactorily in the widest sense of the word" and that therefore the phrase "Santa Claus exists" is true! On the same lines, the Pope, at that time, condemned the pragmatic defence of religion.

James' ideas on consciousness and on the subject/object relationship also fell on fertile ground. Later developments in science used the idea of the observer influencing the experiment, and the British philosopher Gilbert Ryle (1900 – 1976), in his classic book **The Concept of Mind** (1949), agreed with James that the mind is not a thing (either material or non-material). That, he said, was a category mistake; the mind is not a thing, he says, it is a process.

James' biggest legacy, however, is in psychology, but that is another subject, (albeit with overlaps).

35

Nietzsche

Introduction

Friedrich Nietzsche (1844 – 1900) regarded himself as the successor to Schopenhauer, and rightly so says Russell, who thought Nietzsche's philosophy was the more consistent and coherent of the two.

Schopenhauer, remember, says that our perceptual experience of the phenomenal world of things in space and time is not our only experience. We are aware of ourselves, both in the perceptual fashion by which we know external things, and, quite differently, 'from within' as 'Will', or more specifically as 'Will to Live'.

> *"My body is the only object of which I know not merely from one side, that of representation, but also the other, that is called will."*

Schopenhauer then supposed that everything in the world is the appearance of what in itself is 'Will', in the same sense as his body and its behaviour is; and therefore, that the universe is a single, vast, cosmic 'Will to Exist' which experiences itself through an apparent diversity of conscious beings. Instead of identifying this cosmic 'Will' with God, however, Schopenhauer concluded it was a wicked thing because it allowed, and indeed was the source of, all our suffering. At this point, Schopenhauer claimed that the only way out was one discovered in India; this was the idea of 'Nirvana', which he says leads to the extinction of the will.

Nietzsche picks up on both this idea of the 'Will', and the problem of suffering, but he ignores the mystical, Eastern influence, bringing a more rational and scientific analysis to his philosophy, and focusing mainly on the ethical question of how best to live one's life.

An Introduction to Philosophy

Background

Born in 1844, Nietzsche grew up in the small town of Röcken, near Leipzig in Germany where his father was a Lutheran pastor. He had a sister, Elizabeth, two years younger than him and a brother, Ludwig, three years younger. When Nietzsche was five his father died of a degenerative brain disease, going slowly mad over a period of a year, then, six months later his brother died at the age of two. These losses had a large influence on him and helped shape his thinking on suffering in the years to come. He also worried that he too might inherit his father's madness.

He was a serious boy and earned the nickname 'little pastor'; it was always assumed that he would become a priest, and indeed he initially studied theology with that intention. At school Nietzsche received an important grounding in languages—Greek, Latin, Hebrew, and French, all of which later enabled him to read the primary sources of the old philosophers.

At the age of 20 he entered the University of Bonn where he began by studying theology and classical philology. (Philology is the study of language in written historical sources; it is a combination of literary criticism, history, and linguistics and is more commonly defined as the study of literary texts and written records, the establishment of their authenticity, and the determination of their meaning.)

During his first year there he came across the new idea of applying the study of strict literary criticism to the bible and began to understand that much of its content was largely myth. This intellectual understanding, together with his emotional feelings about suffering, led him more and more to doubt religion, and at the end of his first year there he dropped theology completely and concentrated his studies on philology alone.

His mother was angry about his loss of faith, and around this time Nietzsche wrote a long letter to his sister Elizabeth, who was deeply religious, explaining his thinking and which ended with the sentence: -

> *"Hence the ways of men part: if you wish to strive for peace of soul and pleasure, then believe; if you wish to be a devotee of truth, then inquire..."*

About that time, he came across a book by Schopenhauer called **"The World as Will and Representation"**. This had a huge influence on him, and he accepted much of Schopenhauer's thinking on the idea of suffering but disagreed with his idea of putting up with it. Nietzsche wanted to find a solution to the problem.

In 1867, Nietzsche signed up for one year of voluntary service with the Prussian army. However, in March 1868 he had a riding accident and tore two muscles in his left side, leaving him exhausted and unable to walk for months. Consequently, he turned his attention to his studies again.

In 1869 Nietzsche became professor of classical philology at the University of Basel in Switzerland. He was only 24 years old and had neither completed his doctorate nor received a teaching certificate. He was awarded an honorary doctorate by the University of Leipzig. Even though the offer came at a time when he was considering giving up philology for science, he accepted and to this day, Nietzsche is still among the youngest of the tenured Classics professors on record.

At this time, he had become great friends with Richard Wagner and was greatly struck by the idea of music and the arts as a way of overcoming the problem of suffering, but he eventually fell out with Wagner when he began to feel that the composer was just pandering to the great and good of society.

During his time at Basel, he published his first major work **The Birth of Tragedy**. Academically, this was not well received, and this probably put a halt to his career. He became depressed with academia and his health was also starting to fail him, so in 1879 he quit his post and for the rest of his life he travelled round Europe living on his pension. One of his favourite places was a little village called Sils Maria in Switzerland, and it was here, in 1883, that he wrote his famous **Thus Spoke Zarathustra**. This was a productive time, and he wrote a number of books and essays, including **Beyond Good and Evil** in 1886 and **On the Genealogy of Morality** in 1887. Because of his illnesses, however, a lot of what he wrote is in the form of short, pithy sentences, aphorisms, and predictions for which he is now most often known, and which, to some extent, masks his genius and deep understanding of his subjects. Nietzsche never married. He proposed to one lady he became infatuated with three times, but his proposal was rejected each time, and he saw this as another part of his suffering to be overcome, indeed he contemplated suicide due to this rejection.

In 1889 Nietzsche suffered a mental collapse, and was writing to people, signing his letters as 'Dionysus' and the 'antichrist', he also suffered at least two strokes. At the age of 44 he was put into an asylum where he stayed for 10 years. Then, for the last three years of his life he stayed with his sister, unable to talk at all.

Unfortunately, she made somewhat of an exhibition of him, dressing him in white robes and inviting people to see him, including, among others, the philosopher and social reformer Rudolf Steiner. She also inherited his notebooks and subsequently edited and published them, under the title '**The Will to Power**', but also giving them her own anti-

An Introduction to Philosophy

Semitic bias. There is no evidence that Nietzsche himself was anti-Semitic however, but this coloured his reputation for many years.

Philosophy

Nietzsche's philosophy was driven by two main forces, his loss of faith, and his need to come to terms with suffering. It was also informed, however, through his extraordinary intellect, his intensive study of philology, and his deep knowledge of ancient texts.

He saw that society as a whole was becoming more secular, but he worried that it still retained a Christian morality, which he viewed as pernicious for a number of reasons: -

- a) Christian morality focused mainly on the next life.
- b) It fostered the idea that life was to be endured and suffered.
- c) It robbed life of its sublime meaning.
- d) It robbed this life of its happiness.

Also, however, while the age he was living in was dominated by the rise of science (which he loved) he saw that the triumph of objectivity might deprive humanity of something fundamental, leading to: - a lack of moral code; no solution to the fear of death; and the total absence of any higher purpose. Nietzsche wanted to find new meaning in a world deprived of God.

His first main work, **The Birth of Tragedy,** was an attempt to deal with the problem of suffering in a world without the consolation of a belief in God. It was art, he said, that made life worthwhile, and specifically it was best delivered via different forms of Greek Tragedy, plays, operas, books etc. These tragedies explored the themes of Apollo versus Dionysus, i.e. light and logic versus confusion, dance and chaos. Suffering is an affirmation of life, and this can be a group collective experience.

After his falling out with Wagner, however, and the adverse academic reception of his first book, he started to change his thinking from the idea that the transformation of the masses would change society to the idea that it would only be achieved through the transformation of the individual.

In 1883, while walking in the mountains, depressed, split with his mother, rejected in love, suffering with ill health, and contemplating suicide, he suddenly had what he claimed was his best idea: -

If a demon whispered in your ear that you had to live your life the same again and again with all its pain and

> *suffering, would you fall to the ground and curse that demon or would you say that he was a God and that his utterances were divine?*

This idea has become known as 'The eternal recurrence of the same'. Nietzsche decided we should say an emphatic YES to this. We should embrace our mistakes and suffering as part of our life, and we should become the hero of our own life.

> *"To live life most fully one had to risk suffering and overcome it."*

> *"What doesn't kill you makes you stronger."*

It was then that he wrote perhaps his most famous work ***Thus Spoke Zarathustra,*** which is made up of four books, and is a parable on the importance of self-overcoming. Zarathustra is a prophet who comes down the mountain to talk to people about the idea that God is dead, and about how we should live our lives in the knowledge of this idea. He also, in this book introduces his notion of the 'overman' or 'superman'.

The superman is not someone with superhuman powers, it is someone who is self-reliant and sets his own goals; he does not rely on society, parents or religion. Happiness, he says, is not the absence of suffering; it is the passing through suffering and overcoming obstacles. The superman, therefore, is really a symbol of man's potential.

The historian Peter Watson says that Nietzsche's core insight "was that there does not exist any perspective external to or higher than life itself. There cannot exist any privileged viewpoint, any abstraction or force outside the world as we know it; there is nothing beyond reality, beyond life itself, nothing 'above'; there is no transcendence, nothing metaphysical. As a result, we can make no judgement on existence that is universally valid or 'objective'". As Nietzsche said: -

> *"The value of life cannot be assessed."* and *"There are no facts, only interpretations."*

Watson goes on to say that, from this, certain things follow. We are solely the product of historical forces. The world is a chaos of multiple forces and drives and we must learn to situate ourselves in the chaos. The way we do this is via the 'will to power', by which we seek control over inanimate nature. Our history, especially that of the religions (Christianity in particular), has given us a hidden prejudice in favour of the 'beyond' at the expense of the 'here and now', and this must be changed. We must *"select to live only those instances that we would be willing to live with over and over again, in infinite recession."* In this way we will be saved – saved from fear.

These few years were a productive period for Nietzsche, and he produced two more books, **Beyond Good and Evil** and **On the Genealogy of Morality,** both of which are about how to live without values given by God. Also, because he was dismayed at the persistence of Christian values, these books presented his analysis as to where and how these Christian values arose in the first place.

Nietzsche goes back to the ancient Greek and Roman societies and says that they valued strength and self-reliance. We have drives, he says, like aggressiveness and sexuality, and the Greeks and Romans were masters who celebrated such drives and affirmed themselves. Christian values originated in the slaves around that time. They had no choice but to put up with their lot, and so to rationalise their situation they started to claim that our strong drives were wrong – they were an affront to God. They became obsessed with ideas like compassion, and this leads, he says, to just being contented with life, and putting our hope into the next life.

The slaves made a virtue out of self-denial, and this somehow became a strength which overturned our traditional ideas of strength, and it is these ideas that persist in society now even after the death of God. This leads to a herd mentality where our basic instincts are constantly being put down and suppressed, we are made to feel guilty about ourselves. If humanity is to survive, he says, we need great individuals and men of genius; Christian morality holds us down, it is a slave morality.

> *"Christianity is called the religion of pity. Pity stands opposed to the tonic emotions which heighten our vitality: it has a depressing effect. We are deprived of strength when we feel pity. That loss of strength which suffering as such inflicts on life is still further increased and multiplied by pity. Pity makes suffering contagious."*

Nietzsche admires strength of will above all things. "*I test the power of a will,*" he says, "*according to the amount of resistance it can offer and the amount of pain and torture it can endure and know how to turn to its own advantage.*" Christianity, he argues, aims at taming the heart in man, but this is a mistake. A wild beast has a certain splendour, which it loses when it is tamed.

Legacy

Russell (writing of course at the end of the Second World War) was not a fan. He says that: -

> *"It is undeniable that Nietzsche has had a great influence, not among technical philosophers, but among people of literary and artistic culture. ... Nevertheless there is a great deal in him that must be dismissed as merely megalomaniac. ...It is obvious that in his day-dreams he is a warrior, not a professor; all the men he admires were military".*

As Russell comments, Nietzsche had a huge influence on the artistic community during the early part of the twentieth century: writers, composers, artists, and poets, all struggling to find meaning in a world devoid of God. H. L. Mencken produced the first book on Nietzsche in English in 1907, **The Philosophy of Friedrich Nietzsche**, and in 1910 another a book of translated paragraphs from Nietzsche was published, increasing the knowledge of his philosophy in the United States. Nietzsche is known today as a precursor to expressionism, existentialism, and postmodernism.

W. B. Yeats described Nietzsche as the intellectual heir to William Blake, and he tried to raise awareness of Nietzsche in Ireland. A similar notion was espoused by W. H. Auden who wrote of Nietzsche: - "O masterly debunker of our liberal fallacies [...] all your life you stormed, like your English forerunner Blake". Thomas Mann's novel **Death in Venice** shows a use of Apollonian and Dionysian themes. And Freud, of course, was very interested in Nietzsche's analysis of the origins of Christian morality and hence the nature of guilt in our psyche.

Nietzsche's growing prominence suffered a severe setback, however, when his works became closely associated with Adolf Hitler and the Third Reich. It is debated among scholars whether Hitler read Nietzsche, although if he did his reading of him may not have been extensive. He was, however, a frequent visitor to the Nietzsche Museum in Weimar and he did use expressions of Nietzsche's, such as "lords of the earth" in *Mein Kampf*.

These days, with a more distant perspective from the two world wars, it is possible to provide a somewhat more objective analysis of his philosophy. The historian Peter Watson, for instance, says of Nietzsche: -

> *"He was a thoroughly unusual man – quixotic, contradictory, a young meteor who shone with an*

incandescent writing style but who burned out quickly and went mad at the age of forty-five. His aphoristic style lent itself to easy assimilation, by the public as well as by other philosophers, and was designed to be provocative and incendiary. ... The uses to which his ideas have been put, or have said to have been put, since his death, are also a source of continuing notoriety. Nietzsche's concept of nihilism caught the imagination of the world, one of its consequences being that he is the only person whose ideas ... have been blamed for two world wars. This is a burdensome – and enduring – legacy."

36

Edmund Husserl

Introduction

Edmund Husserl (1859 – 1938) was a German philosopher who established the concept of phenomenology within philosophy. In his early career he worked on logic based on an analysis of 'intentionality', and in his later, mature work, he sought to develop a systematic foundational science of conscious awareness based on 'phenomenological reduction'.

He argued that 'transcendental consciousness' sets the limits of all possible knowledge, and he re-defined phenomenology as a 'transcendental-idealist philosophy'. Husserl's ideas went on to profoundly influence the landscape of twentieth-century philosophy, and he still remains a notable figure in contemporary philosophy and beyond.

Background

Husserl was born in 1859, in Prossnitz, Moravia, then part of Austria, (now known as Prostejov in the Czech Republic.) He was born into a Jewish family; the second of four children, and his father was a milliner. His childhood was spent in Prossnitz, where he attended the elementary school, and then he travelled to Vienna to study at a secondary school there.

At the University of Leipzig, from 1876 to 1878, Husserl studied mathematics, physics, and astronomy, and while there, he was inspired by philosophy lectures given by Wilhelm Wundt, one of the founders of modern psychology. Then, in 1878, he moved on to a University in Berlin, where he continued his study of mathematics, and, while there, he attended more philosophy lectures.

In 1881 he left Leipzig for the University of Vienna to complete his mathematics studies, and there, in 1883, he obtained his PhD with his work "***Contributions to the Calculus of Variations***".

Following his PhD in mathematics he decided to devote his attention to philosophy. In 1884 at the University of Vienna he attended the lectures of Franz Brentano on philosophy and philosophical psychology. Brentano introduced him to the writings of many past and current philosophers and is often credited as being his most important influence, especially with regard to 'intentionality'.

His father died in 1884, and in 1887 Husserl converted to Christianity, being baptised into the Lutheran Church. "While outward religious practice never entered his life any more than it did that of most academic scholars of the time, his mind remained open for the religious phenomenon as for any other genuine experience" wrote one of his biographers. Also, in 1887 he married Malvine Steinschneider, a union that would last over fifty years. They had three children together, but their son, Wolfgang, later became a casualty of the First World War.

Following his marriage, Husserl had a long teaching career in philosophy, mainly at the universities of Halle, Gottingen, and Freiburg. In 1887 he wrote a paper entitled "*On the Concept of Number*", which would serve later as the basis for his first important work, "*The Philosophy of Arithmetic*" published in 1891. Other major works of his were "*Logical Investigations*" (1901), and "*Ideas Pertaining to a Pure Phenomenology*" (1913).

After his retirement in 1928, he continued to use the library at the University of Freiburg until banned because of his Jewish origins; under the Nazis he became the victim of anti-Semitic attacks, and his works were banned. Shortly after his death in 1939, his archives were found, and a Franciscan monk managed to take all his manuscripts, library, and correspondence (some 40,000 pages) to safety in Belgium.

Philosophy

Maths and logic

In his first works Husserl tries to combine mathematics, psychology, and philosophy with a main goal to provide a sound foundation for mathematics. He analyses the psychological process needed to obtain the concept of number and then tries to build up a systematic theory on this analysis.

In this six-volume work he starts by criticising the doctrine that logical entities such as propositions, universals, and numbers can be reduced to mental states or activities. He insists that such targets of consciousness are objective, and that the attempt to reduce them to activities of mind is incoherent.

Husserl maintains that mathematical laws are not empirical laws that describe the workings of the mind, but ideal laws whose necessity is intuited *a priori*.

He says that we generate the concept of number by counting certain collections of objects. He then makes a distinction between proper and improper presenting. In an example Husserl explains this in the following way: if you are standing in front of a house, you have a proper, direct presentation of that house, but if you are looking for it and ask for directions, then these directions are an indirect, improper presentation. In other words, you can have a proper presentation of an object if it is actually present, and an improper (or symbolic as he calls it) if you only indicate that object through signs, symbols, etc. Husserl's *Logical Investigations* (1901) is considered the starting point for the formal theory of wholes and their parts, which is known as mereology.

Intentionality

Another important element (that Husserl took over from Brentano) is intentionality, i.e. the relationship between mental acts and the external world is that our conscious thoughts are always '**about**' something. You are never merely conscious, you are always conscious of something: a book, a tree, or a headache, for example.

Intentionality is the main characteristic of mental phenomena, and it is this aspect by which they can be distinguished from physical phenomena. Every mental phenomenon, every psychological act, has a content, i.e. it is directed at an object (the intentional object). Every belief, desire, etc. has an object that it is about, i.e. the believed, or the desired. Brentano used the expression "intentional inexistence" to indicate the status of the objects of thought in the mind.

The property of being intentional, of having an intentional object, was the key feature to distinguish mental phenomena from physical phenomena, because physical phenomena lack intentionality altogether. To help make this clear, a cigarette is not intentional; it is not by itself 'about' smoking, but a thought about smoking the cigarette in front of you is intentional, and the cigarette becomes the 'intentional object'.

Note also, an interesting feature of intentional states is that they can be directed towards things that either do, or do not, exist. Therefore, God is defined as an 'intentional object' whether he exists or not! Similarly, the dagger that Macbeth hallucinates in the air before him is an 'intentional object', despite not being real. Another aspect of intentional objects is that they can be out of sight, e.g. the dark side of the moon, or the nucleus of an atom.

An Introduction to Philosophy

Phenomenology

Husserl's radical approach to the study of consciousness is to try and investigate it by studying the objects of conscious awareness, (the above mentioned 'intentional objects'). And it is this discipline that he calls phenomenology.

Some years after the publication of his *Logical Investigations*, Husserl made some key conceptual elaborations which led him to assert that to study the structure of consciousness, one would have to distinguish between the act of consciousness and the phenomena at which it is directed (the 'intentional objects').

Knowledge of 'essences' (i.e. the attribute or set of attributes that make an entity or substance what it fundamentally is) would, he says, only be possible by "bracketing" all assumptions about the existence of an external world.

> *"...the whole world, when one is in the phenomenological attitude, is not accepted as actuality, but only as actuality-phenomenon."*

These new concepts prompted the publication of his *Ideas Pertaining to a Pure Phenomenology* in 1913, in which they were at first incorporated. From the *Ideas* onward, Husserl concentrated on the ideal, essential structures of consciousness. The metaphysical problem of establishing the reality of what we perceive, as distinct from the perceiving subject, was of little interest to him.

Husserl says that the world of objects and ways in which we direct ourselves toward and perceive those objects is normally conceived of in what he called the "natural standpoint", which is characterized by a belief that objects exist, distinct from the perceiving subject, and exhibit properties that we see as emanating from them.

He proposed a radical new phenomenological way of looking at objects by examining how we, in our many ways of being intentionally directed toward them, actually "constitute" them. In the Phenomenological standpoint, the object ceases to be something simply "external" and ceases to be seen as providing indicators about what it is and becomes instead a grouping of perceptual and functional aspects that imply one another under the idea of a particular object or "type".

The notion of objects as real is not expelled by phenomenology, but "bracketed" as a way in which we regard objects. In order to better understand the world of appearances and objects, phenomenology attempts to identify the features of how objects are perceived, and it pushes attributions of reality into a role as attributions about the things we perceive.

Suppose I look at a cup on the table in front of me. I observe the cup, or at least I think I do. Of course, a sceptic will insist that there may be no cup there at all, as in a dream or a hallucination, or even if it is there he may say that I'm not seeing all its actual attributes. Husserl, however, says that at least I can be sure the cup exists as an 'intentional object'. The cup, as an object of my awareness, is simply given, and so I can *bracket* such thorny philosophical questions as whether there really is a cup present, and focus my attention solely on the 'intentional object'. I can study the content of my conscious awareness without having to make any assumptions about external reality.

With this new science of phenomenology, Husserl hopes it will be possible to reveal and systematically classify the basic structures of consciousness. He believes he can build up a valuable taxonomy of our conscious states and the many different ways they are directed towards objects.

The science of phenomenology

From *Logical Investigations* (1901) to *Experience and Judgment* (published in 1939), Husserl expressed clearly the difference between meaning and object. He identified several different kinds of names. For example, there are names that have the role of properties that uniquely identify an object. Each of these names expresses a meaning and designates the same object.

Examples of this are "the victor in Jena" and "the loser in Waterloo", or "the equilateral triangle" and "the equiangular triangle"; in both cases, both names express different meanings, but designate the same object.

There are names which have no meaning but have the role of designating an object: "Aristotle", "Socrates", and so on. And finally, there are names which designate a variety of objects. These are called "universal names"; their meaning is a "concept" and refers to a series of objects (the extension of the concept). The way we know sensible objects is called "sensible intuition".

Husserl also identifies a series of "formal words" which are necessary to form sentences and have no sensible correlates. Examples of formal words are "a", "the", "more than", "over", "under", "two", "group", and so on. Every sentence must contain formal words to designate what Husserl calls "formal categories".

There are two kinds of categories: meaning categories and formal-ontological categories: -

An Introduction to Philosophy

- Meaning categories relate judgments; they include forms of conjunction, disjunction, and forms of plural, among others.
- Formal-ontological categories relate objects; and include notions such as set, cardinal number, ordinal number, part and whole, relation, and so on.

The way we know these categories is through a faculty of understanding he calls "categorical intuition".

Through sensible intuition our consciousness constitutes what Husserl calls a "situation of affairs". It is a passive constitution where objects themselves are presented to us. To this situation of affairs, through categorical intuition, we are able to constitute a "state of affairs". One situation of affairs through objective acts of consciousness can serve as the basis for constituting multiple states of affairs.

For example, suppose a and b are two sensible objects in a certain situation of affairs. We can use it as basis to say, "$a<b$" and "$b>a$", two judgments which designate the same state of affairs. For Husserl a sentence has a proposition or judgment as its meaning and refers to a state of affairs which has a situation of affairs as a reference base.

In a later period, Husserl also began to wrestle with the complicated issues of intersubjectivity, specifically, how communication about an object can be assumed to refer to the same ideal entity. Indeed, it should be noted that one of the major dividing lines in Husserl's thought is the turn to a version of Kantian transcendental idealism (i.e. things known a-priori in our brain).

Husserl, like Descartes, advocated 'philosophy as rigorous science' (the title of an article of his in 1911), because philosophy is the undoubtable basis of our doubtable (but for the most part correct) beliefs about the empirical world.

Husserl disagreed with Descartes, however, in one crucial respect. Whereas Descartes moved swiftly from the proposition 'I think' to the conclusion 'I am a thinking thing', Husserl claims that the belief 'I am a thinking thing' itself needs to be bracketed. I, who am conscious of objects, am neither a thinking substance, nor an embodied person, nor even the stream of my experiences. I am conscious of, and in that sense distinct from, my experiences; I am (in Kantian terms) pure transcendental ego.

The Crisis of the European Sciences is Husserl's unfinished work, and in it, Husserl attempts a historical overview of the development of Western philosophy and science, emphasizing the challenges presented by their increasingly (one-sidedly) empirical and naturalistic orientation. He declares that mental and spiritual reality possess their own reality, independent of any physical basis, and that a science of the mind must be established on as scientific a foundation as the natural sciences have managed.

Legacy

All fields of study have their own lexicon of technical terms, and philosophy is no exception. Words like epistemology, ontology, empiricism, idealism and others can be a little off-putting to start with, but such terms also provide a path into the field, because, if you learn the word, you then have an understanding of the concept involved, and such words then become hooks on which to hang other concepts.

Although Husserl did not himself coin the words ***Intentionality*** and ***Phenomenology***, it was his work on these terms that made them truly part of philosophy's lexicon. Husserl himself was always a little disappointed at the tendency of his students to go their own way, to embark upon fundamental revisions of phenomenology rather than engage in the communal task as originally intended by the radical new science. Notwithstanding, however, he did attract many philosophers to phenomenology.

Martin Heidegger is the best known of Husserl's students, the one whom Husserl chose as his successor at Freiburg University, and Heidegger's magnum opus ***Being and Time*** was dedicated to Husserl. Subsequently, however, they had a number of differences of opinion. Edith Stein was Husserl's student at Göttingen while she wrote her ***On the Problem of Empathy*** (1916). She then became his assistant at Freiburg (1916–1918). Later, however, she adapted her phenomenology to the modern school of Thomas Aquinas.

Jean-Paul Sartre was largely influenced by Husserl, although he later came to disagree with key points in his analyses. Sartre rejected Husserl's transcendental interpretations begun in his ***Ideas*** (1913) and instead followed Heidegger's ontology.

Many other philosophers were influenced by him, including Kurt Gödel, and Rudolf Carnap. Indeed, the influence of the Husserlian phenomenology now extends beyond the confines of the West, it has even started to impact (indirectly) scholarship in Eastern and Oriental thought, including Islam.

37

Dr John Dewey

Introduction

Dr John Dewey (1859 – 1952) was a leading proponent of the American school of thought known as pragmatism, a view that rejected the dualistic epistemology and metaphysics of modern philosophy at that time in favour of a naturalistic approach that viewed knowledge as arising from an active adaptation of the human organism to its environment.

On this view, inquiry should not be understood as consisting of a mind passively observing the world and drawing from this ideas that if true correspond to reality, but rather as a process which starts with a check or an obstacle to successful human action, proceeds to active manipulation of the environment to test hypotheses, and results in a re-adaptation of the organism to its environment that allows once again for human action to proceed.

With this view as his starting point, Dewey developed a broad body of work encompassing virtually all the main areas of philosophical concern in his day. He also wrote extensively on social issues in such popular publications as the *New Republic*, thereby gaining a reputation as a leading social commentator of his time. And he was a major educational reformer within the 20th century.

Although he is probably best known for his publications on education, he wrote on many topics, including epistemology, metaphysics, aesthetics, art, logic, social theory, and ethics. The overriding theme of all his works was his profound belief in democracy, be it in politics, education or communication and journalism.

Background

John Dewey was born on October 20, 1859, the third of four sons born to Archibald Dewey and Lucina Rich of Burlington, Vermont. He attended public school and then went on to the University of Vermont in Burlington. While at the University of Vermont, Dewey was exposed to evolutionary theory through the teaching of G.H. Perkins, and ***Lessons in Elementary Physiology***, a text by T.H. Huxley, the famous English evolutionist. The theory of natural selection continued to have a life-long impact upon Dewey's thought, suggesting the barrenness of static models of nature, and the importance of focusing on the interaction between the human organism and its environment when considering questions of psychology and the theory of knowledge.

The formal teaching in philosophy at the University of Vermont was confined for the most part to the school of Scottish realism, a school of thought that Dewey soon rejected, but his close contact both before and after graduation with his teacher of philosophy, H.A.P. Torrey, a learned scholar with broader philosophical interests and sympathies, was later accounted by Dewey himself as "decisive" to his philosophical development.

After graduation in 1879, Dewey taught high school for two years, during which time the idea of pursuing a career in philosophy took hold, so he gave up teaching and traveled to Baltimore to enroll as a graduate student at Johns Hopkins University. While there he came under the tutelage of two powerful and engaging intellects who were to have a lasting influence on him: George Sylvester Morris, a German-trained Hegelian philosopher, who exposed Dewey to the organic model of nature characteristic of German idealism; and G. Stanley Hall, one of the most prominent American experimental psychologists at the time, who provided Dewey with an appreciation of the power of scientific methodology as applied to the human sciences. The confluence of these viewpoints propelled Dewey's early thought and established the general tenor of his ideas throughout his philosophical career.

Upon obtaining his doctorate in 1884, Dewey accepted a teaching post at the University of Michigan, and thus began a lifelong academic career at different American universities, and his reputation grew as a leading philosopher and educational theorist. He retired from active teaching in 1930 but continued to write and give public lectures until his death in June 1952 at the age of ninety-two. During his life he wrote nearly 30 books and many articles.

Philosophy

Pragmatism

Dewey further developed the philosophy of pragmatism originated by C.S. Peirce and William James, which declared that the value of any truth was utterly dependent upon its use to the person who held it. While Peirce's pragmatism was scientifically elitist, and James' was psychologically personalistic, Dewey's became democratically populist.

Dewey sometimes referred to his philosophy as instrumentalism rather than pragmatism and would have recognized the similarity of these two schools to the newer school named consequentialism. He was concerned that some criticisms of his ideas resulted from a misunderstanding of the terms he used, and so in his book *Logic: The Theory of Inquiry* (1938), he defined with precise brevity the proper interpretation of "pragmatic" as: -

> "... the function of consequences as necessary tests of the validity of propositions, provided these consequences are operationally instituted and are such as to resolve the specific problem evoking the operations..."

His concern for precise definition also led him to detailed analysis of careless word usage, reported in the journal *Knowing and the Known* in 1949.

Theory of Knowledge

In Dewey's view, traditional epistemologies, whether rationalist or empiricist, had drawn too stark a distinction between thought (the domain of knowledge) and the world of fact to which thought purportedly referred: thought was believed to exist apart from the world.

He saw that Rationalism, stemming from Descartes, led to a doctrine of innate ideas, ideas constituted from birth in the very nature of the mind itself, and this produced a dichotomy between the self and the world. Empiricism, on the other hand, had, beginning with Locke, done the same just as markedly by its commitment to an introspective methodology and a representational theory of ideas. But if thought constitutes a domain that stands apart from the world, how can its accuracy as an account of the world ever be established?

For Dewey a new model, rejecting traditional presumptions, was wanting, and this is what he strived to develop throughout his years of writing and reflection. He wanted to use the ideas of pragmatism to develop a better theory of knowledge, and in this he was heavily influenced by the ideas of Hegel, William James, and Charles Darwin.

Darwin accounted for the origins of species as a product of the adaptation of organisms to their environments. In a similar way, Dewey came to believe that a productive, naturalistic approach to the theory of knowledge must begin with a consideration of the development of knowledge as an adaptive human response to the environment.

Dr John Dewey

Unlike traditional approaches in the theory of knowledge, which saw thought as a subjective primitive out of which knowledge was composed, Dewey's approach understood thought genetically, as the product of the interaction between organism and environment, and knowledge as having practical instrumentality in the guidance and control of that interaction. Thus, Dewey adopted the word "instrumentalism" as a descriptive term for his new approach.

The implication for the theory of knowledge was clear: - the world is not passively perceived and thereby known; active manipulation of the environment is involved integrally in the process of learning from the start.

Russell, a contemporary of Dewey, goes a long way to endorsing this view, but in the end he can't fully agree. He says some things known are just facts, such as Columbus crossed the ocean in 1492. But Dewey does not aim at judgments that are absolutely 'true' or condemn their contradictions as absolutely 'false'. In his opinion there is a process called "inquiry", which is one form of mutual adjustment between an organism and its environment. Ideas, suppositions, and theories, etc. are entertained as hypothetical solutions to the originating impediment of the problematic situation. The final test of the adequacy of these solutions comes with their employment in action.

Dewey thought that the issues surrounding the conditions of truth, as well as knowledge, were hopelessly obscured by the traditional, and in his view misguided, meanings to the terms, resulting in confusing ambiguity. He later abandoned these terms in favor of "**warranted assertiblity**" to describe the distinctive property of ideas that results from successful "inquiry". He makes "inquiry" the essence of logic and defines it in this way: -

> "Inquiry is the controlled or directed transformation of an indeterminate situation into one that is so determinate in its constituent distinctions and relations as to convert the elements of the original situation into a unified whole."

As the organism or human interacts more with its environment it will, with successive 'inquiries' and tests, become more and more adapted to its environment. And for humans, intelligent inquiry is facilitated by the use of language, which allows, by its symbolic meanings and implication relationships, the hypothetical rehearsal of adaptive behaviours before their employment under actual, prevailing conditions for the purpose of resolving problematic situations.

An Introduction to Philosophy

Dewey accepted the conditional nature of knowledge that was characteristic of the school of pragmatism: - the view that any proposition accepted as an item of knowledge has this status only provisionally, contingent upon its adequacy in providing a coherent understanding of the world as the basis for human action.

He defended this general outline of the process of inquiry throughout his long career, insisting that it was the only proper way to understand the means by which we attain knowledge, whether it be the commonsense knowledge that guides the ordinary affairs of our lives, or the sophisticated knowledge arising from scientific inquiry. The latter is only distinguished from the former by the precision of its methods for controlling data, and the refinement of its hypotheses.

Metaphysics

Dewey disagreed with William James' assessment that pragmatic principles were metaphysically neutral. In Dewey's view, the central aim of traditional metaphysics had been the search for knowledge of reality, and the two competing theories were Idealism or Empiricism. The pragmatic theory, however, showed that knowledge is a product of an activity directed to the fulfilment of human purposes, and that a true (or warranted) belief is known to be such by the consequences of its employment rather than by any psychological or ontological foundation. This rendered the longstanding aim of metaphysics, in Dewey's view, moot, and opened the door to renewed metaphysical discussion grounded firmly on a pragmatic empirical basis.

Dewey asserts that things experienced empirically "are what they are experienced as." He uses as an example a noise heard in a darkened room that is initially experienced as fearsome. Subsequent inquiry (e.g., turning on the lights and looking about) reveals that the noise was caused by a shade tapping against a window, and thus innocuous. But the subsequent inquiry, Dewey argues, does not change the initial status of the noise: it was experienced as fearsome, and in fact *was* fearsome.

The point stems from the naturalistic roots of Dewey's logic. Our experience of the world is constituted by our interrelationship with it, a relationship that is imbued with practical import. The initial fearsomeness of the noise is the experience of the uncertain, problematic character of the situation, an uncertainty that is not merely subjective or mental, but a product of the potential inadequacy of previously established modes of behaviour to deal effectively with the pragmatic demands of present circumstances.

The subsequent inquiry does not, therefore, uncover a reality (the harmless nature of the noise) underlying a mere appearance (its fearsomeness), but by settling the demands of the situation, it effects a change in the inter-dynamics of the organism-environment relationship of the initial situation – a change in reality.

Thus, rather than understanding the mind as a primitive and individual human endowment, and a precondition of conscious and intentional action, as was typical in the philosophical tradition since Descartes, Dewey offers a genetic analysis of mind as an emerging aspect of cooperative activity mediated by linguistic communication. Consciousness, in turn, is not to be understood as a domain of private awareness, but rather as the fulcrum point of the organism's readjustment to the challenge of novel conditions where the meanings and attitudes that formulate habitual behavioural responses to the environment fail to be adequate.

Dewey offers a response to the traditional mind-body problem of the metaphysical tradition, a response that understands the mind as an emergent issue of natural processes, more particularly as the web of interactive relationships between human beings and the world in which they live.

Ethics, social theory, and education

Dewey's mature thought in ethics and social theory is linked to his theory of knowledge in its conceptual framework and naturalistic standpoint with its emphasis on the social dimension of inquiry both in its processes and its consequences. In fact, it would be reasonable to claim that Dewey's theory of inquiry cannot be fully understood either in the meaning of its central tenets or the significance of its originality without considering how it applies to social aims and values, the central concern of his ethical and social theory.

He rejected the atomistic understanding of society of the Hobbesian social contract theory, according to which the social, cooperative aspect of human life was grounded in the logically prior and fully articulated rational interests of individuals. Dewey claims in ***Experience and Nature*** (1925) that the collection of meanings that constitute the mind have a social origin. This expresses the basic contention that the human individual is a social being from the start, and that individual satisfaction and achievement can be realized only within the context of social habits and institutions that promote it.

Moral and social problems, for Dewey, are concerned with the guidance of human action to the achievement of socially defined ends that are productive of a satisfying life for individuals within the social context. The central focus of his criticism of the tradition of ethical thought is its tendency to seek solutions to moral and social problems in dogmatic principles and simplistic criteria which in his view were incapable of dealing effectively with the changing requirements of human events. He located the motivation of the traditional dogmatic approaches in philosophy to the forlorn hope for security in an uncertain world. He maintains that ideals and values must be evaluated with respect to their social consequences, either as inhibitors or as valuable instruments for social progress.

The social condition for the flexible adaptation that Dewey believed was crucial for human advancement is a democratic form of life, not instituted merely by democratic forms of governance, but by the inculcation of democratic habits of cooperation and public spiritedness, productive of an organized, self-conscious community of individuals responding to society's needs by experimental and inventive, rather than dogmatic, means. The development of these democratic habits, Dewey argues, must begin in the earliest years of a child's educational experience. Dewey rejected the notion that a child's education should be viewed as merely a preparation for civil life, during which disjointed facts and ideas are conveyed by the teacher and memorized by the student only to be utilized later. The school should rather be viewed as an extension of civil society and continuous with it, and the student encouraged to operate as a member of a community, actively pursuing interests in cooperation with others. It is by a process of self-directed learning, guided by the cultural resources provided by teachers, that Dewey believed a child is best prepared for the demands of responsible membership within the democratic community.

Legacy

Dewey's philosophical work received varied responses from his philosophical colleagues during his lifetime. There were many philosophers who saw his work, as Dewey himself understood it, as a genuine attempt to apply the principles of an empirical naturalism to the perennial questions of philosophy. Dewey's critics, however, often expressed the opinion that his views were more confusing than clarifying, and that they appeared to be more akin to idealism than the scientifically based naturalism Dewey expressly avowed.

Russell has fun at Dewey's expense by saying that if asked if he had coffee with his breakfast this morning he would have to say, 'wait a while, I must try two experiments before I answer you. First, I will make myself believe that I did have coffee and observe the consequences, if any, and then I will make myself believe I did not have coffee and again observe the consequences, if any. Then I will compare the two sets of consequences to see which I found more satisfactory.'

Russell was concerned with what he saw as the severing of the relation between belief and the fact or facts which would be commonly said to verify the belief. He says that Dewey: -

> "… considers a belief "true", or as nearly "true" as we can make it, if it has a certain kind of relation (sometimes very complicated) to it causes. Dr John Dewey holds that it has "warranted assertability" – which he substitutes for "truth" – if it has certain kinds of effects."

Dewey was sensitive and responsive to the criticisms brought against his views. He often attributed them to misinterpretations based on the traditional, philosophical connotations that some of his readers would attach to his terminology.

The influence of Dewey's work, along with that of the pragmatic school of thought itself, although considerable in the first few decades of the 20th century, was gradually eclipsed during the middle part of the century as other philosophical methods, such as those of the analytic school in England and America, and phenomenology in continental Europe, grew to ascendency.

Recent trends in philosophy, however, leading to the dissolution of these rigid models, have led to approaches that continue and expand on the themes of Dewey's work: -

- W. V. O. Quine's project of naturalizing epistemology works upon naturalistic presumptions anticipated in Dewey's own naturalistic theory of inquiry.
- The social dimension and function of belief systems, explored by Dewey and other pragmatists, has received renewed attention by such writers as Richard Rorty and Jürgen Habermas.
- American phenomenologists such as Sandra Rosenthal and James Edie have considered the affinities of phenomenology and pragmatism.
- And Hilary Putnam, an analytically trained philosopher, has recently acknowledged the affinity of his own approach to ethics with that of Dewey's.

The renewed openness and pluralism of recent philosophical discussion has meant a renewed interest in Dewey's philosophy, an interest that promises to continue for some time to come.

38

Bertrand Russell

Introduction

Bertrand Russell (1872 - 1970) was probably the most important, and most famous, philosopher of the twentieth century. His output was prolific and his interests wide ranging. He was equally at home writing about mathematics, logic, language, epistemology, and metaphysics as he was writing about ethics, religion, psychology and politics.

He led the British "revolt against idealism", and he is considered one of the founders of analytic philosophy, along with his predecessor Gottlob Frege, colleague G. E. Moore, and protégé Ludwig Wittgenstein.

A lifelong atheist and socialist, he was a pacifist during the First World War, and late in life was the founding president of the Campaign for Nuclear Disarmament.

Background

Bertrand Russell was born on 18 May 1872, in the Welsh village of Trellech, Monmouthshire, into an influential and liberal family of the British aristocracy. His parents, Viscount and Viscountess Amberley, were radical for their times. Lord Amberley was an atheist, and his atheism was evident when he asked the philosopher John Stuart Mill to act as Russell's secular godfather. Mill died the year after Russell's birth, but his writings had a great effect on Russell's life.

His paternal grandfather, Earl Russell, had been asked twice by Queen Victoria to form a government, serving her as Prime Minister in the 1840s and 1860s. Lady Amberley was the daughter of Lord and Lady Stanley of Alderley. Russell often feared the ridicule of his maternal grandmother, one of the campaigners for the education of women.

Russell's mother died of diphtheria when he was two, and his father of bronchitis when he was four. Bertrand and his brother Frank (who was seven years older than him) went to live with his paternal grandparents in Richmond Park, London. His grandfather, former Prime Minister Earl Russell, died in 1878, and was remembered by Russell as a kindly old man in a wheelchair. His grandmother, Countess Russell, was the dominant family figure for the rest of Russell's childhood and youth.

The countess was from a Scottish Presbyterian family, and successfully petitioned the Court of Chancery to set aside a provision in Amberley's will requiring the children to be raised as agnostics. Despite her religious conservatism, she held progressive views in other areas (accepting Darwinism and supporting Irish Home Rule), and her influence on Russell's outlook on social justice, and standing up for principle, remained with him throughout his life.

He was educated at home by a series of tutors. When he was eleven years old, his brother Frank introduced him to the work of Euclid, which transformed his life. During these formative years he also discovered the works of Percy Bysshe Shelley. In his autobiography, he writes: "I spent all my spare time reading him, and learning him by heart, knowing no one to whom I could speak of what I thought or felt, I used to reflect how wonderful it would have been to know Shelley, and to wonder whether I should meet any live human being with whom I should feel so much sympathy".

Russell claimed that from age 15, he spent considerable time thinking about the validity of Christian religious dogma, which he found very unconvincing. He came to the conclusion that there is no free will and, two years later, that there is no life after death. Finally, at the age of 18, after reading Mill's "Autobiography", he abandoned the "First Cause" argument and became an atheist.

Russell won a scholarship to read Mathematics at Trinity College, Cambridge, and commenced his studies there in 1890. While there he became acquainted with the younger George Edward Moore, and came under the influence of Alfred North Whitehead. He quickly distinguished himself in mathematics and philosophy, graduating in 1893 and becoming a Fellow in 1895.

He wrote several papers on maths and logic, and then, between 1910 and 1913, in collaboration with Alfred North Whitehead, he published perhaps his most important philosophical work - The three-volume *Principia Mathematica*, in which they aimed to put all of mathematics onto secure logical foundations.

During World War I, Russell was one of the few people to engage in active pacifist activities and in 1916, he was dismissed from Trinity College following his conviction under the Defence of the Realm Act 1914. A later conviction for publicly lecturing against inviting the US to enter the war on the United Kingdom's side resulted in six months' imprisonment in Brixton prison. While there he read widely and wrote his book *Introduction to Mathematical Philosophy*.

An Introduction to Philosophy

In August 1920, Russell travelled to Russia as part of an official delegation sent by the British government to investigate the effects of the Russian Revolution, and thereafter wrote a number of articles on Soviet Russia. Although a socialist, he condemned totalitarianism in every form, left or right.

He spent some time lecturing in the United States and was appointed professor at the City College of New York in 1940, but after a public outcry the appointment was annulled by a court judgment that pronounced him "morally unfit" to teach at the college due to his opinions, especially those relating to sexual morality detailed in his book ***Marriage and Morals*** (1929). [During his life he was married four times and was rumoured to have had numerous affairs.] Many intellectuals, led by Dr. John Dewey, protested at his treatment, and Einstein wrote an open letter in his defence which included his now well quoted phrase: - "great spirits have always encountered violent opposition from mediocre minds".

During the Second World War, he reluctantly concluded that Adolf Hitler taking over all of Europe would be a permanent threat to democracy: "War was always a great evil, but in some particularly extreme circumstances, it may be the lesser of two evils."

In 1945, he published his ***A History of Western Philosophy*** which was based on a series of his lectures in the States. It became a best-seller and provided Russell with a steady income for the remainder of his life.

Russell participated in many broadcasts by the BBC, particularly *The Brains Trust* and the *Third Programme*, on various topical and philosophical subjects. By this time Russell was world-famous outside academic circles. In 1948, he was invited by the BBC to deliver the inaugural Reith Lectures — what was to become an annual series of lectures, still broadcast by the BBC. His series of six broadcasts, titled *Authority and the Individual*, explored themes such as the role of individual initiative in the development of a community and the role of state control in a progressive society.

In September 1961, at the age of 89, Russell was jailed for seven days in Brixton Prison for "breach of peace" after taking part in an anti-nuclear demonstration in London. The magistrate offered to exempt him from jail if he pledged himself to "good behaviour", to which he replied: "No, I won't." Russell died of influenza on 2 February 1970 at his home in Wales.

Philosophy

Russell is generally credited with being one of the founders of analytic philosophy. He was deeply impressed by Gottfried Leibniz (1646–1716), and he wrote on almost every major area of philosophy. He was particularly prolific in the fields of: metaphysics; the logic and the philosophy of mathematics; the philosophy of language; ethics; and epistemology.

Logic

He thought that that mathematics and logic are one and the same field of study and was very interested in the new ideas of 'Set Theory'. Indeed, he discovered a flaw in the theory which has since become known as 'Russell's Paradox', described as follows: -

> According to set theory, any definable collection is a set. Then, let R be the set of all sets that are not members of themselves. If R is not a member of itself, then its definition dictates that it must contain itself, and if it contains itself, then it contradicts its own definition as the set of all sets that are not members of themselves.

Some people tried to get round this by altering the axioms of set theory, but Russell solved it by altering the logical language itself and by employing an analysis called a 'theory of types', which is a kind of Meta set theory.

Mathematics

The *Principia Mathematica* (often abbreviated *PM*) is a three-volume work on the foundations of mathematics, written by Alfred North Whitehead and Bertrand Russell and published in 1910, 1912, and 1913. *PM* was an attempt to describe a set of axioms and inference rules, in symbolic logic, from which all mathematical truths could in principle be proven. As such, this ambitious project is of great importance in the history of mathematics and philosophy, it being one of the foremost products of the belief that such an undertaking may be achievable.

One of the main inspirations and motivations for *PM* was the earlier work of Gottlob Frege on logic, which Russell discovered allowed for the construction of paradoxical sets. *PM* sought to avoid this problem by ruling out the unrestricted creation of arbitrary sets. This was achieved by replacing the notion of a general set with the notion of a hierarchy of sets of different 'types', a set of a certain type only being allowed to contain sets of strictly lower types.

PM has long been known for its typographical complexity. Famously, several hundred pages are required in PM to prove the validity of the proposition 1+1=2.

The Principia covered only set theory, cardinal numbers, ordinal numbers, and real numbers. Deeper theorems from real analysis were not included, but by the end of the third volume it was clear to experts that a large amount of known mathematics could in principle be developed in the adopted formalism. But it was also clear how lengthy such a development would be.

A fourth volume on the foundations of geometry had been planned, but the authors admitted to intellectual exhaustion upon completion of the third.

Analytic Philosophy

In much the same way that Russell used logic to try and clarify issues in the foundations of mathematics, he also used logic in an attempt to clarify issues in philosophy. As one of the founders of analytic philosophy, Russell made significant contributions to a wide variety of areas, including metaphysics, epistemology, ethics, and political theory.

According to Russell, it is the philosopher's job to discover a logically ideal language — a language that will exhibit the nature of the world in such a way that we will not be misled by the accidental, imprecise surface structure of natural language. As Russell writes: -

> "Ordinary language is totally unsuited for expressing what physics really asserts, since the words of everyday life are not sufficiently abstract. Only mathematics and mathematical logic can say as little as the physicist means to say."

Just as atomic facts combine to form molecular facts in the world itself, such a language will allow for the description of such combinations using logical connectives such as "and" and "or."

The reason Russell believes many ordinarily accepted statements are open to doubt is that they appear to refer to entities that may be known only through inference. Thus, underlying Russell's various projects was not only his use of logical analysis, but also his long-standing aim of discovering whether, and to what extent, knowledge is possible. He writes in 1911: -

"There is one great question: can human beings *know* anything, and if so, what and how? This question is really the most essentially philosophical of all questions."

Motivating this question was the traditional problem of the external world. If our knowledge of the external world comes through inferences to the best explanation, and if such inferences are always fallible, what guarantee do we have that our beliefs are reliable? Russell's response to this question was partly metaphysical and partly epistemological.

On the metaphysical side, Russell developed his famous theory of **logical atomism**, in which the world is said to consist of a complex of logical atoms (such as "little patches of colour") and their properties and relations. (The theory was crucial for influencing Wittgenstein's theory of the same name.) Together these atoms and their properties form the atomic facts which, in turn, combine to form logically complex objects. What we normally take to be inferred entities (for example, enduring physical objects) are then understood as logical constructions formed from the immediately given entities of sensation.

On the epistemological side, Russell argues that it is also important to show how each questionable entity may be reduced to, or defined in terms of, another entity (or entities) whose existence is more certain.

It is in this context that Russell also introduces his famous distinction between two kinds of knowledge of truths: that which is direct, intuitive, certain, and infallible, and that which is indirect, derivative, uncertain and open to error. To be justified, every indirect knowledge claim must be capable of being derived from more fundamental, direct, or intuitive knowledge claims. The kinds of truths that are capable of being known directly include both truths about immediate facts of sensation, and truths of logic.

Examples of this analysis are discussed in ***The Problems of Philosophy*** (1912) where Russell states that propositions with the highest degree of self-evidence (what he here calls "intuitive knowledge") include "those which merely state what is given in sense, and also certain abstract logical and arithmetical principles, and (though with less certainty) some ethical propositions".

Russell's Theory of Descriptions

In his analysis of language, one of the things Russell addresses is an ambiguity between names and descriptions. For example, we can say 'John is tall', this refers to the individual John and an assertion about him that he is tall. This can then be evaluated as being either true or false.

An Introduction to Philosophy

However, there is the problem of the empty reference. If names and descriptions are 'referring expressions', how can we succeed in using them to say something is true or false in the case where they don't refer to anything? E.g. in the sentence 'The golden mountain does not exist'.

This sentence is true, but there is nothing for the description (golden) or name (mountain) to refer to, so those parts of the sentence can't do their usual jobs. This puzzle occurs when you try to break the sentence down into it logical parts, in order to analyse it mathematically.

Russell's theory gets round this. When we say - 'the F is G', we are actually making three distinct claims: -

- At least one thing is F;
- At most one thing is F; and
- Whatever is F is G.

For the three claims to be true, all that is required is that something be uniquely F, and that whatever is F also be G. It doesn't matter what is uniquely F or G as long as something is. So, the phrase 'the golden mountain' does not refer to a name and a description, it can be taken as a single reference. Going back to 'John is tall', we should not think of 'John' as a name but as a description of a unique individual.

Russell's Neutral Monism

Another of Russell's major contributions is his defence of neutral monism, the view that the world consists of just one type of substance which is neither exclusively mental nor exclusively physical. Like idealism (the view that nothing exists but the mental) and physicalism (the view that nothing exists but the physical), neutral monism rejects dualism (the view that there exist both distinct mental and physical substances). However, unlike both idealism and physicalism, neutral monism holds that this single existing substance may be viewed in some contexts as being mental and in others as being physical. As Russell puts it: -

> "Neutral monism"—as opposed to idealistic monism and materialistic monism—is the theory that the things commonly regarded as mental and the things commonly regarded as physical do not differ in respect of any intrinsic property possessed by the one set and not by the other, but differ only in respect of arrangement and context."

The whole duality of mind and matter, according to this theory, is a mistake; there is only one kind of stuff out of which the world is made, and this stuff is called mental in one arrangement, physical in the other.

Russell's Teapot

In an article titled "Is There a God?" commissioned, but never published, by Illustrated magazine in 1952, Russell wrote: -

> "Many orthodox people speak as though it were the business of sceptics to disprove received dogmas rather than of dogmatists to prove them. This is, of course, a mistake. If I were to suggest that between the Earth and Mars there is a china teapot revolving about the sun in an elliptical orbit, nobody would be able to disprove my assertion provided I were careful to add that the teapot is too small to be revealed even by our most powerful telescopes. But if I were to go on to say that, since my assertion cannot be disproved, it is intolerable presumption on the part of human reason to doubt it, I should rightly be thought to be talking nonsense. If, however, the existence of such a teapot were affirmed in ancient books, taught as the sacred truth every Sunday, and instilled into the minds of children at school, hesitation to believe in its existence would become a mark of eccentricity and entitle the doubter to the attentions of the psychiatrist in an enlightened age or of the Inquisitor in an earlier time."

The idea here is to illustrate that the philosophic burden of proof lies upon a person making scientifically unfalsifiable claims, rather than shifting the burden of *disproof* to others.

Russell's ethics and politics

As mentioned in the biography above, he was a socialist, a humanist, a utilitarian (as influenced by his godfather John Stuart Mill), and he hated totalitarian regimes. Unfortunately, however, there is not room here to cover all his philosophy.

Legacy

According to Russell, analytical empiricism differs from that of Lock, Berkley, and Hume by its incorporation of scientific findings, mathematics and logic. Questions such as what is number, what is space and time, what is mind and what is matter are moving from philosophy to science. While full answers are not yet in, it is the 'scientific method' that represents the honest way forward rather than the grand invented philosophical systems of the past. This leaves to philosophy questions of value, ethics, and politics.

Russell and Whitehead's ***Principia Mathematica*** was groundbreaking and put the logic of mathematics onto a completely new level. In 1931, however, Kurt Gödel published his incompleteness theorem, which proves that no formal system extending basic arithmetic can be used to prove its own consistency. This was a problem for the idea of completely proving all of mathematics, but still, the techniques specified in the ***Principia*** were a very powerful addition to both logic and mathematics.

In 1950 Russell was awarded the Nobel Prize in Literature "in recognition of his varied and significant writings in which he champions humanitarian ideals and freedom of thought". Since his death in 1970, Russell's reputation as a philosopher has continued to grow, not only in the areas of mathematics and logic, but also with regard to his pacifism and a lifetime spent opposing war.

39

Wittgenstein

Introduction

Ludwig Wittgenstein (1889 – 1951) was an Austrian-British philosopher who worked primarily in logic, the philosophy of mathematics, the philosophy of mind, and the philosophy of language. During his lifetime he only published one book on philosophy; his remaining manuscripts were edited and published posthumously.

His teacher, Bertrand Russell, described Wittgenstein as "the most perfect example I have ever known of genius as traditionally conceived; passionate, profound, intense, and dominating".

His philosophy is often divided into an early period and a later period. The early Wittgenstein was concerned with the logical relationship between propositions and the world, and he believed that by providing an account of the logic underlying this relationship, he had solved all philosophical problems. The later Wittgenstein rejected many of the assumptions of his earlier writings, arguing that the meaning of words is best understood as their use within a given 'language-game' as he called it.

Background

Wittgenstein was born in Vienna in 1889 to one of Europe's richest families, where he was one of nine children, four girls and five boys. The children were baptized as Catholics, received formal Catholic instruction, and raised in an exceptionally intense environment. The family was at the centre of Vienna's cultural life; both Brahms and Mahler gave regular concerts in their numerous music rooms for instance.

It was their father's aim to turn his sons into captains of industry; they were not sent to school lest they acquire bad habits but were educated at home to prepare them for work in their father's industrial empire. Three of his brothers committed suicide, however, and Wittgenstein himself contemplated it too. At the age of 14 he was allowed to go to school, but he never really fitted in there. It was there, however, that he lost his faith in God (although he was later to return to it).

He also discovered Schopenhauer in school and was strongly influenced by his book **The World as Will and Representation**. As a teenager, he adopted Schopenhauer's epistemological idealism. However, after his study of the philosophy of mathematics, he abandoned this for Gottlob Frege's conceptual realism. And in later years, Wittgenstein was highly dismissive of Schopenhauer, describing him as an ultimately "shallow" thinker: "Schopenhauer has quite a crude mind ... where real depth starts, his comes to an end."

There is much debate about the extent to which Wittgenstein and his siblings, who were of 3/4 Jewish descent, saw themselves as Jews. The issue has arisen in particular regarding Wittgenstein's schooldays, because Adolf Hitler was at the same school for part of the same time (they were actually born within six days of each other). Laurence Goldstein argues it is "overwhelmingly probable" the boys met each other: that Hitler would have disliked Wittgenstein, a "stammering, precocious, precious, aristocratic upstart ...". Other commentators have dismissed as irresponsible and uninformed any suggestion that Wittgenstein's wealth and unusual personality may have fed Hitler's anti-Semitism.

Wittgenstein studied mechanical engineering in Berlin and then went on to the University of Manchester, studying aeronautics. It was at this time that he became interested in the foundations of mathematics, particularly after reading Bertrand Russell's **The Principles of Mathematics**. He then decided that he needed to study logic and the foundations of mathematics.

So, on 18 October 1911 Wittgenstein arrived unannounced at Russell's rooms in Trinity College, Cambridge, while Russell was having tea with a friend. He was soon not only attending Russell's lectures but dominating them. Russell wrote in November 1911 that he had at first thought Wittgenstein might be a crank, but soon decided he was a genius. Three months after Wittgenstein's arrival Russell told a friend: "I love him and feel he will solve the problems I am too old to solve."

In 1913 Wittgenstein inherited a large fortune from his father. He initially made some donations to artists and writers and then, in a period of severe personal depression after the First World War, he gave away his entire fortune to his brothers and sisters.

He left academia several times—serving as an officer on the front-line during World War I, where he was decorated a number of times for his courage; teaching in schools in remote Austrian villages; and working as a hospital porter during World War II in London, while largely managing to keep secret the fact that he was one of the world's most famous philosophers. He described philosophy as "the only work that gives me real satisfaction."

Wittgenstein

The only philosophy book published in his lifetime was his ***Tractatus Logico-Philosophicus*** (1921) which he wrote while serving as a soldier in the First World War. This made him famous. He returned to Cambridge in 1929 to take up a teaching post and was made a fellow of Trinity College.

In 1939 Wittgenstein was elected to the chair in philosophy at Trinity, and he acquired his British citizenship soon afterwards. By this time, Wittgenstein's view on the foundations of mathematics had changed considerably. In his early 20s, Wittgenstein had thought logic could provide a solid foundation, and he had even considered updating Russell and Whitehead's *Principia Mathematica*. Now he denied there were any mathematical facts to be discovered. At Cambridge he met the young Alan Turing, who described Wittgenstein as "a *very* peculiar man", and the two had many discussions about the relationship between computational logic and everyday notions of truth.

Wittgenstein resigned the professorship at Cambridge in 1947 to concentrate on his writing but by 1949 he was too tired to work, and it was discovered that he had inoperable cancer. He died in April 1951 at the age of 62. His second great work (published posthumously in 1951) was called ***Philosophical Investigations***. It was based on his notes and manuscripts, some of which have also been published separately as ***The Blue Book*** and ***The Brown Book***. Another posthumous book published from his papers was called ***On Certainty***.

Wittgenstein's archive of unpublished papers comprised 83 manuscripts, 46 typescripts and 11 dictations, amounting to an estimated 20,000 pages.

Philosophy

Wittgenstein's philosophy takes as its starting point Russell's analysis of language. Russell thought that ordinary language was too imprecise to be logical about the world. He used his ideas from logic and mathematics to try to build logical, unambiguous sentences from smaller 'atomic like' facts combined with logical connectives such as 'and' and 'or'.

Both Russell and Wittgenstein wanted to discover how language connects with the world, and thereby how language can have meaning.

Tractatus Logico-Philosophicus

This book is written in short, carefully numbered paragraphs of extreme compression. It is an attempt to analyse our knowledge of the world starting from basic principles (much like Descartes with his "I think therefore I am"). At the same time, it is an analysis of the structure of language and how language relates to the world and acquires meaning.

Here is how it starts: -

> 1   The world is all that is the case.
> 1.1 The world is the totality of facts, not of things.
> 1.11 The world is determined by the facts, and by their being all the facts.
> 1.12 For the totality of facts determines what is the case, and also whatever is not the case.
> 1.13 The facts in logical space are the world.
> 1.2   The world divides into facts.
> 1.21 Each item can be the case or not the case while everything else remains the same.
>
> 2   What is the case—a fact—is the existence of atomic facts.
> 2.01 An atomic fact is a combination of objects (entities, things).
> ......and so on....

The whole book is essentially a series of propositions that build into more and more complex ideas; it is, in effect, one long logical argument.

It can be quite difficult to read the whole book from start to finish keeping the whole argument in your head as you do it, so here instead is a summary.

- Both the world and language are complex structures, both are made of parts or elements or atoms or symbols at the bottom of the structure.
- The two structures parallel each other.
- The world is not just things (like shoe or hill or bird) it is also facts or relationships between things (such as 'it is raining').
- Language is made of propositions i.e. thoughts or claims about the world.
- Propositions describe facts.
- Elementary propositions describe 'states of affairs'.
- Names describe objects.
- It is at this lowest state that the connection between world and language occurs because the arrangement of names in an elementary proposition is a picture of a state of affairs.

Wittgenstein

This idea of language as a picture of the world is central to Wittgenstein's thinking here and he gives an example from another type of language, that of music. Musical notes on a page are a picture of the notes played on a piano. There is an intimate connection between reading the music on a page and listening to it being played on the piano.

This, he says, is how language has meaning. There is a direct mapping between words and the world at the lowest elementary level. And here he claims to have solved all the previous problems of philosophy with this logical analysis. He is, of course, only talking about the metaphysical problems.

He notes that science best provides facts in the world, but he also notes it says nothing about ethics and morality. He says that that is the other half of philosophy which is not covered in the Tractatus.

"Whereof we cannot speak, thereof we must remain silent."

Ethics and religion can't be analysed, we should not try because that attempt would have to take the form of propositions and assertions and, he claims, this can't be done in that field.

Philosophical Investigations

This book (published posthumously from his notes and manuscripts) shows that over the intervening years his thinking had changed quite a lot. He starts this by criticising the Tractatus with respect to how language acquires meaning. Both books regard philosophical problems as spurious, they only occur, he says, because we misunderstand the way language works.

In the Tractatus he says language acquires meaning through its relational mapping to the world. In Philosophical Investigations, however, he says language acquires meaning through the way we use it. Language doesn't just make assertions (such as it is raining), we use it in many other ways, e.g. asking questions, giving commands, making expressions of desire, play acting, or even quoting poetry. Where we make mistakes is when we try to apply language used in one area to a different area.

He called these different areas of language 'language games'. That's not games in a frivolous sense of the word, but games as in the idea of a structured, rule-based activity. And there would be different rules in different language areas. Meaning is then set by the tradition of use in any given area. Language is no longer dependent on the world; it is dependent on its use within a given area.

An Introduction to Philosophy

These games (the different areas in which language is used) are similar to each other but there is no underlying thing in common connecting them, so they can't be directly mapped to each other, or to the world, and hence they can't be logically analysed.

Note here that ethics and religion constitute their own game, i.e. any meaning arises purely within its own area, and through how the language is used within that area. This then supports his aim to protect ethics and religion from a reductive scientific approach.

On Certainty

His posthumously published book **On Certainty** continued these themes. It's a book about epistemology, i.e. how can we be certain about those things that we think we know. It is structured as a collection of aphorisms discussing the relationship between knowledge and certainty.

Here are some extracts from **On Certainty** (the book also uses numbered propositions).

> 65. When language-games change, then there is a change in concepts, and with the concepts the meanings of words change.

> 95. The propositions describing this world-picture might be part of a kind of mythology. And their role is like that of rules of a game; and the game can be learned purely practically, without learning any explicit rules.

> 97. The mythology may change back into a state of flux, the river-bed of thoughts may shift. But I distinguish between the movement of the waters on the river-bed and the shift of the bed itself; though there is not a sharp division of the one from the other.

> 599. ... To say: in the end we can only adduce such grounds as we hold to be grounds, is to say nothing at all. I believe that at the bottom of this is a misunderstanding of the nature of our language-games.

Legacy

In these later books Wittgenstein is considered to have added two main ideas to philosophy: -

1. How do you know any given rule is consistent?
2. Language has to be a shared activity.

There is no such thing as a private language. If I say I know how tall I am, and then measure myself by putting my hand on my head, there is no real reference or cross check. In his terms, if I have a sensation and give it the name 'S', I possess no 'criterion of correctness' by which I might apply the term in future. If I later have another sensation that I think is 'S', all I have is my memory, there is no external measure of correctness.

If you grew up with nobody around and started to name things yourself, how would you know you were being consistent? This shows the impossibility of a *logically* private language. Therefore, there can't be a Cartesian theory of knowledge (e.g. I think therefore I am). Rules can only exist in a public setting; they have to be a shared activity.

In 1999 a survey among American university and college teachers ranked the **Investigations** as the most important book of 20th-century philosophy, standing out as "the one crossover masterpiece in twentieth-century philosophy, appealing across diverse specializations and philosophical orientations."

Oxford philosopher Peter Hacker argues that Wittgenstein's influence on 20th-century analytical philosophy can be attributed to his early influence on the Vienna Circle and later influence on the Oxford "ordinary language" school and Cambridge philosophers.

A grouping called 'New Wittgenstein scholars' advance "an understanding of Wittgenstein as aspiring, not to advance metaphysical theories, but rather to help us work ourselves out of confusions we become entangled in when philosophizing."

Dan Dennett says that Wittgenstein "showed us new ways of being suspicious of our own convictions when confronting the mysteries of the mind."

And Wittgenstein himself said "Philosophy is a battle against the bewitchment of our intelligence by means of language".

40

Heidegger

Introduction

Martin Heidegger (1889 – 1976) was, like Husserl (under whom he studied), a phenomenologist in the German tradition. His philosophy is also largely thought of as a precursor to existentialism, although he himself denied the affinity.

He is widely acknowledged to be one of the most original and important philosophers of the 20th century, and his first and best-known book, ***Being and Time*** (1927), although unfinished, is one of the central philosophical works of the last century.

He made critical contributions to the philosophical conceptions of truth (arguing that its original meaning was un-concealment); to the philosophical analyses of art as a site of the revelation of truth; and to the philosophical understanding of language as the "house of being".

Heidegger is a controversial figure, largely for his affiliation with Nazism, for which he never publicly expressed regret, although later, in private, he said it was "the biggest stupidity of his life".

Kant had called the inability to prove the existence of an external world the "scandal" of philosophy, but Heidegger thinks the only scandal is that philosophers keep looking for a proof of its existence.

Background

Heidegger was born in 1889 in the village of Messkirch, Germany. The son of a sexton, he was raised as a Roman Catholic. His family could not afford to send him to university, so he entered a Jesuit seminary, though he was turned away within weeks because of the health requirement and what the director and doctor of the seminary described as a psychosomatic heart condition.

After that, supported by the church, he went to study theology at the University of Freiburg on the understanding that he would defend the church's doctrine. While there, however, Heidegger broke with Catholicism and switched his field of study to philosophy. He studied under Edmund Husserl and was greatly influenced by Husserl's phenomenology.

He completed his doctoral thesis on psychologism in 1914 and then stayed on as an unsalaried teacher for two years. He served as a soldier during the final year of World War I – but working behind a desk and never leaving Germany.

In 1923, Heidegger was elected to an extraordinary Professorship in Philosophy at the University of Marburg, and while there he began to develop, in his lectures, the main theme of his philosophy: - the question of the sense of being.

In 1927, Heidegger published his main work, ***Being and Time***. Then, when Husserl retired as Professor of Philosophy in 1928, Heidegger accepted the University of Freiburg's election to be his successor.

Heidegger was elected rector of the University in April 1933, and joined the National Socialist German Workers' (Nazi) Party in May of that year. After the war he was blocked from teaching for a while because of his Nazi associations, but this was later rescinded, and he started teaching again at Freiburg University in 1950. He retired in 1958 but continued teaching by invitation until 1967.

He died on 26 May 1976, and was buried in the Messkirch cemetery, beside his parents and brother.

Philosophy

Heidegger's philosophy is founded on the attempt to join together what he considers are his two fundamental insights: -

- The first insight derives from the influence of Edmund Husserl who argued that: – all that philosophy could and should be is a description of experience (hence the phenomenological slogan, "to the things themselves"). Heidegger's version of phenomenology, however, meant understanding that 'experience' is already situated in the world, and in ways of being.

- The second insight is Heidegger's observation that, in the course of over 2,000 years of history, philosophy has attended to all the beings that can be found in the world (including the world itself) but has forgotten to ask what Being itself is.

Phenomenology

Husserl's radical approach to the study of consciousness was to try to investigate it by studying the objects of conscious awareness, and this discipline he called phenomenology. He noted that consciousness never just 'is' but is always directed 'to' something, it is always 'about' something. This 'aboutness' is termed in philosophy as 'intentionality', and therefore, the objects of our awareness are called 'intentional objects'. Husserl then went on to say that we can't (as yet) study reality itself, so we should 'bracket' the study of reality (keeping that for a later time perhaps) and just study these mental 'intentional objects' as a way of learning more about consciousness.

Like Husserl, Heidegger is also a phenomenologist, and he too offers a descriptive philosophy of experience. Heidegger's version of phenomenology, however, differs markedly from that of Husserl.

Heidegger rejects Husserl's approach to the study of consciousness. Like Husserl, he believes that consciousness is essentially 'intentional' (i.e. it is about, or directed towards, objects). But what generates this intentionality, according to Heidegger, is precisely our activity in the world. It is through our engagement with the world that meaning and intentionality are created. Accordingly, for Heidegger, conscious experience is itself essentially rooted in the world; hence we cannot 'bracket' the world and study consciousness in isolation.

Thus, Husserl's understanding that all consciousness is "intentional" is transformed in Heidegger's philosophy, becoming the thought that all experience is grounded in "care". This is the basis of Heidegger's "existential analytic", as he develops it in ***Being and Time***. Heidegger argues that describing experience 'properly entails finding the being for whom such a description might matter'. Heidegger thus conducts his description of experience with reference to something he calls "***Dasein***": - the being for whom Being is a question.

According to Heidegger, the fundamental mode of human consciousness (*Dasein* – literally meaning '*being there*') is not, as Descartes supposed, a kind of detached separate existence, but something firmly located in the world. Since Descartes' time, philosophers have tended to view the human condition as essentially one of *subject* in a world of *objects*. What marks us out as subjects was thought to be our conscious awareness (i.e. we have conscious experiences, and engage in conscious reflection). Once we begin to view ourselves in this way, as subjects divided from a world of objects, we become disembodied observers of the world, and we then face the problem of explaining how we might come to know about the world, or even interact with it.

Heidegger, on the other hand, engages in an analysis of the kind of 'being' that is specific to human beings. He believes that this analysis reveals that the human condition is not, as Descartes supposes one of detached reflection of the world, but one of actually *"being in the world"*.

Heidegger's hammer

One of Heidegger's favourite illustrations of this point is a man using a hammer. If the man is competent with the tool, he will typically use it, not with conscious deliberation, but unthinkingly. If he is consciously aware of, or thinking about, anything at all, it may well be something entirely unrelated.

Heidegger does not deny that we can attend consciously and deliberately to what we are doing, but that is not how we normally use the hammer for instance. Conscious reflective engagement typically arises only when something goes wrong. If, where I'm walking, the pavement is broken and uneven, then I will probably give it my full attention, otherwise I hardly give it a second glance.

From Descartes' view, which divides us from the world, the fundamental problem is epistemological, how can we *know* anything of the world? But the world is not separated from us, as if by some sort of screen, so it is not something we need to infer the existence of. Neither is it something we should 'bracket' and ignore. Rather, says Heidegger, it is the place we start from.

Being and knowledge

The primary form of discourse, for Heidegger, is not an explicit assertion, such as 'This hammer is too heavy', but utterances such as 'too heavy! Give me a lighter one', made in the work situation.

Truth too is not primarily the correspondence between an assertion, or proposition, and a state of the world, but a disclosure of the world to and by **Dasein**. Also, meaning, like truth, is something that is extruded from the mind. This following is taken from a 1927 work of his called ***The Basic Problems of Phenomenology***: -

> *Names, words in the broadest sense, have no a priori fixed measure of their significant content. Names, or again their meanings, change with transformations in our knowledge of things, and the meanings of names and words always change according to the predominance of a specific line of vision towards the thing somehow named by the name. All significations,*

> *including those that are apparently mere verbal meanings, arise from reference to things.*

The representative theory of perception is rejected along with the correspondence theory of truth: -

> *What we 'first' hear is never noises or complexes of sounds, but the creaking wagon, the motor-cycle ... It requires a very artificial and complicated state of mind to 'hear' a 'pure noise'.*

What he is saying here is our perception of the world is not just sense-data, but is based on our built in, or learnt, pre-processing that has already taken place prior to conscious awareness. Similarly, the idea that something is true only if it corresponds to the facts, also ignores our mental pre-processing based on our previous experience of the world.

Being, death and time

Dasein must be considered as a whole, and this requires an account of death. *Dasein* can be genuinely authentic only in its 'being towards death', since here it accepts finitude. *Dasein* is individualised by death: it dies alone, and no one else can die in its place. Thus, death is the criterion for authenticity: I must recognize that I will die, not simply that 'one' dies.

There is, Heidegger believes, a pervasive tendency to conceal the inevitability of one's own death. Like Kierkegaard and Tolstoy, he refers to the old syllogism 'All men are mortal, Caius is a man, so Caius is mortal': 'That Caius, man in the abstract, was mortal', mused Tolstoy's Ivan, 'was perfectly correct, but he was not Caius, not an abstract man, but a creature quite separate from all others'.

Authentic being towards death is related to something he calls 'resoluteness': it is only if I am aware of my finitude that I have reason to act now, rather than procrastinate, and it is the crucial decision made with a view to the whole course of my future life that gives my life its unity and shape.

The future is thus the primary aspect of time. But a decision is also constrained by a situation inherited from the past (the second aspect of time) and the more important the decision is, the more it will be taken in view of the past. The third aspect of time is the present, and this is now the moment of decision.

> *To the anticipation which goes with resoluteness, there belongs a present in accordance with which a*

> *resolution discloses the situation. In resoluteness, the present is not only brought back from distraction with the objects of one's closest concern, but it gets held in the future and in having been. That **present** which is held in authentic temporality and which thus is **authentic** itself, we call 'the moment of vision'.*

Although he published many papers, mostly taken from his lectures, ***Being and Time*** was Heidegger's first real academic book. It was published in 1927 when had been under pressure to publish in order to qualify for Husserl's (to whom he dedicated the work) chair at the University of Freiburg. The success of this work ensured his appointment to the post. It is actually called an unfinished work, however, because he planned to write a second part to it expanding his thinking on his idea of the "existential analytic". The fact that he didn't write this second part, and that his subsequent writings hardly mention the "existential analytic", might be interpreted as him being unable to fully join his ideas of individual experience with the vicissitudes of the *collective* human adventure that he understands the Western philosophical tradition to be.

Heidegger's later thinking

His late philosophy emerges for the most part in discussions of past thinkers. For instance, in 1942 he published a work called ***Plato's Doctrine of Truth***, in which he argues that in Plato's allegory of the cave, truth ceased to be 'unhiddenness' and became mere 'correctness'. This, he claims, set in motion the degeneration of thought about being into metaphysics: the history of Western philosophy is a history of decline.

The appropriate response to being is thinking. The early Greeks did it, he says, but we have forgotten it. Thinking contrasts with assertion, logic, science, metaphysics, philosophy itself, and especially technology (which is merely an instrument for calculation and domination of entities). Language, which played a subordinate part in ***Being and Time***, now becomes central.

Not language as an instrument of manipulation (into which it has degenerated under the auspices of metaphysics) but language as the 'abode of being': -

> *Language speaks, not man. Man only speaks when he fatefully responds to language.*

Art, and especially poetry, are of crucial importance for thinking and language. Poetry is not a secondary phenomenon: it has a special relation to being and truth. Poetry is 'founding of truth': it discloses the (or 'a') world, and it creates a language for its adequate expression. When a painting, such as Van Gogh's peasant shoes, 'sets up' a world, the world of the peasant, it is essentially poetry. Poetry is close to the sacred: -

The thinker says being. The poet names the holy.

Heidegger regularly denied, however, that his early thought differed significantly from his later thought, or that either bore any similarity to Sartre's existentialism.

Legacy

Because Heidegger's discussion of ontology (the study of being) is rooted in an analysis of the mode of existence of individual human beings, his work has often been associated with existentialism. The influence of Heidegger on Sartre's ***Being and Nothingness*** is marked. However, even though Heidegger is considered by many observers to be the most influential philosopher of the 20th century in continental philosophy (especially in France), aspects of his work have been criticized by those who nevertheless acknowledge this influence.

Much of the criticism of Heidegger's philosophy has come from analytic philosophy, beginning with logical positivism. In ***"The Elimination of Metaphysics Through Logical Analysis of Language"*** (1932), Rudolf Carnap accused Heidegger of offering an "illusory" ontology, criticizing him for wrongly dismissing the logical treatment of language which, according to Carnap, can only lead to writing "nonsensical pseudo-propositions."

The British logical positivist A. J. Ayer was strongly critical of Heidegger's philosophy. In Ayer's view, Heidegger proposed vast, overarching theories regarding existence, which are completely unverifiable through empirical demonstration and logical analysis.

Expressing the sentiments of many mid-20th-century analytic philosophers, Bertrand Russell commented that: -

> *Highly eccentric in its terminology, his philosophy is extremely obscure. One cannot help suspecting that language is here running riot.*

Roger Scruton stated that: "His major work *'Being and Time'* is formidably difficult—unless it is utter nonsense, in which case it is laughably easy."

Recently however, Heidegger's reputation within English-language philosophy has slightly improved in philosophical terms. This is, in some part, through the efforts of Hubert Dreyfus, Richard Rorty, and a newer generation of analytically oriented phenomenology scholars.

41

Jean-Paul Sartre

Introduction

Jean-Paul Sartre (1905-1980) was the quintessential, twentieth century intellectual philosopher, playwright, novelist, and political activist. He, together with Simone de Beauvoir, Albert Camus, Maurice Merleau-Ponty and others formed the basis of the French intelligentsia before, during and after the Second World War, and had a profound effect on modern philosophy and modern culture.

Sartre took the phenomenology of Husserl and Heidegger, added perhaps a touch of Nietzsche, American pragmatism, and modern science, and created the philosophy of 'Existentialism'.

Having done that, however, few could actually define its meaning, even the French group themselves differed on its interpretation, and indeed its definition seemed to change as they lived through the war years and beyond. Still, the world had been given a new outlook and the world wanted to learn more.

Background

Jean-Paul Sartre was born on 21 June 1905 in Paris as the only child of Jean-Baptiste Sartre, an officer of the French Navy, and Anne-Marie Schweitzer.

When Sartre was two years old, his father died of a fever in Indochina. Anne-Marie moved back in with her parents, where she raised Sartre with help from her father, a teacher of German who taught Sartre mathematics and introduced him to classical literature at a very early age. When he was twelve, Sartre's mother remarried, and the family moved to La Rochelle.

He attended a private school in Paris where he earned certificates in psychology, history of philosophy, logic, general philosophy, ethics and sociology, and physics. He then went on to the École Normale Supérieure, an institution of higher education in Paris, where he graduated.

In 1929 at the École Normale, he met Simone de Beauvoir, who studied at the Sorbonne and later went on to become a noted philosopher, writer, and feminist. The two became inseparable and lifelong companions, initiating a romantic relationship, though they were not monogamous.

Sartre was drafted into the French Army from 1929 to 1931 and served as a meteorologist for them. Thereafter he became a schoolteacher, first in La Havre and then in Paris.

In 1932 a friend, Raymond Aron, introduced Sartre to the ideas of Edmund Husserl, the founder of phenomenology, and Sartre was immediately taken with it. According to Beauvoir he rushed to the nearest bookshop and asked for everything they had on phenomenology.

In the summer of 1933 Sartre moved to Berlin and lived there for a year studying the phenomenology of Husserl and Heidegger, then he returned to teaching back in France. He also started writing more; his first novel *Nausea* came out in 1938 and this is considered one of the canonical works of existentialism.

Sartre was a prolific writer of plays, screenplays, novels, essays, critical essays, philosophy books and papers, including his most famous book on existentialist philosophy ***Being and Nothingness*** published in 1943 during the war. The title pays homage to Heidegger's great book ***Being and Time***.

In 1939 Sartre was again drafted into the French army, where he again served as a meteorologist. He was captured in 1940 and held as a prisoner of war for about a year.

In 1941, however, persuaded the authorities to release him by claiming his eyesight (which had always been bad) was a lot worse than it really was. During those two years he never fired a shot, but he did spend a lot of time reading and writing.

When back in Paris, with Beauvoir and the others, they carried on in an unreal world under occupation, still going to cafes and still writing. He had some contact with the intellectual side of the resistance and wrote some anti-occupation plays, which (oddly enough) were not censored by the Germans.

After the war he became a worldwide celebrity and spent some time in the United States. Everybody wanted to know about existentialism.

With the onset of the Cold War, however, Sartre's philosophy became more Marxist, although he also attacked what he saw as abuses of freedom and human rights by the Soviet Union. Also, at this time he fell out with his former friend Camus. Camus' version of existentialism was less politically active and more interested in the absurdity of human experience; Sartre thought he had sold out.

In 1964 Sartre was awarded the Nobel Prize for Literature but refused it, saying that he always declined official honours and that "a writer should not allow himself to be turned into an institution".

An Introduction to Philosophy

Though his name was by then a household word (as was "existentialism" during the tumultuous 1960s), Sartre remained a simple man with few possessions. He was actively committed to causes right up to the end of his life, for instance the strikes in Paris in the summer of 1968, during which he was arrested for civil disobedience.

He died on 15 April 1980 in Paris from oedema of the lung, and at his funeral on Saturday, 19 April, 50,000 Parisians lined the route of his cortege.

Sartre's Influences

Although well versed in traditional philosophy, Sartre wanted something more from the subject, something meaningful to the individual about how to live and how to make sense of life. On hearing about the new ideas of phenomenology he immediately saw that here was an approach that might bring philosophy alive for the individual.

Edmund Husserl (1859 – 1938) invented the concept of phenomenology. He took over from Brentano the idea of intentionality, i.e. the relationship between mental acts and the external world is that our conscious thoughts are always **'about'** something. You are never merely conscious, you are always conscious of something: a book, a tree, or a headache, for example. The property of being intentional, of having an intentional object in mind, was the key feature to distinguish mental phenomena from physical phenomena.

Husserl was interested in how consciousness works, and his radical approach to the study of consciousness was to try and investigate it by studying the objects of conscious awareness, (the above mentioned 'intentional objects'). It is this discipline that he calls phenomenology. He claims that we cannot completely know the external world and that real knowledge is only possible by "bracketing" all assumptions about the existence of an external world and by just studying our intentional objects.

Martin Heidegger (1889 – 1976), who studied under Edmund Husserl, picked up on the idea of phenomenology and expanded it. He agreed with the idea of studying conscious awareness via our intentional objects, but his version of phenomenology included an understanding that 'experience' is already situated in the world, and in ways of being.

He also pointed out that, in the course of over 2,000 years of history, philosophy had attended to all the beings that can be found in the world (including the world itself) but had forgotten to ask what Being itself is.

Thus, Husserl's understanding that all consciousness is "intentional" is transformed in Heidegger's philosophy, becoming the thought that all experience is grounded in "care". This is the basis of Heidegger's "existential analytic", as he develops it in his great book ***Being and Time***. He argues that describing experience 'properly entails finding the being for whom such a description might matter'. And his discussion of ontology (the study of being) is rooted in an analysis of the mode of existence of individual human beings.

Philosophy

Sartre picks up on intentionality, phenomenology, and the being for whom experience matters, and, adding a touch of Nietzsche, makes freedom the centre of his philosophy.

His primary idea is that people, as humans, are "condemned to be free". This theory relies upon his position that there is no creator, and is illustrated using the example of the paper cutter. Sartre says that if one considered a paper cutter, one would assume that the creator would have had a plan for it: an "essence". Sartre said that human beings have no essence before their existence because there is no Creator. Thus, his phrase: - "existence precedes essence".

This freedom can be an enormous burden and responsibility, which we do not always wish to acknowledge. So, we deceive ourselves, pretending that, like most mere physical objects, we are wholly predetermined to be what we are and to behave the way we do. When we deceive ourselves like this, we are guilty of "bad faith".

Sartre famously illustrates this with the example of a waiter. The waiter plays his part in an exaggerated, clichéd way, balancing his tray and pouring drinks as if he were merely a puppet playing the role of a waiter. He is, says Sartre, guilty of bad faith. The truth is he is free either to carry on being a waiter, or to quit his job and find another career, but this freedom weighs heavily on his shoulders, and so he deceives himself by acting as if he is a mere thing.

As humans, we exist, but not for any particular purpose (as for instance an egg-timer does). What purpose we have, and how we act, must be freely chosen by us. This responsibility to choose is unavoidable, he claims. You are able, right now, to choose different values, to find new goals, to forge yourself anew.

Of course, we don't choose the particular circumstances into which we are born, I might be part of a wealthy family, or I might find myself a slave, and these circumstances will restrict what I can do. Nevertheless, I am free to choose how I respond to these circumstances. This freedom, he says, is hard to bear, we make our choices "in anguish abandonment, and despair", which is why we fall into 'bad faith', and why we end up deceiving ourselves about this radical freedom.

An Introduction to Philosophy

Sartre's book ***Being and Nothingness*** is an in-depth exploration of the metaphysics of existentialism based on the philosophy of phenomenology. It is notoriously difficult to read, indeed Camus claimed that he had never got much further than page 179 (it is well over 600 pages long).

In the introduction, Sartre sketches his own theory of consciousness, being, and phenomena through criticism of the phenomenologists (Husserl and Heidegger) as well as the idealists, rationalists, and empiricists. According to him, one of the major achievements of modern philosophy is phenomenology because it disproved the kinds of dualism that set the existent up as having a "hidden" nature (as proclaimed by Immanuel Kant and Descartes); Phenomenology has removed "the illusion of worlds behind the scene".

Based on an examination of the nature of phenomena, he describes the nature of two types of being, being-in-itself (the being of things) and being-for-itself. While being-in-itself is something that can only be approximated by human beings, being-for-itself is the being of consciousness.

From Sartre's phenomenological point of view, nothingness is an experienced reality and cannot be a merely subjective mistake. The absence of a friend and absence of money hint at a *being* of nothingness. It is part of reality. He goes on to develop a theory of nothingness which is central to the whole book, especially to his account of bad faith and freedom. By bringing nothingness into the world, consciousness does not annihilate the being of things, but changes its relation to it.

Another idea in the book is that the mere possible presence of another person causes one to look at oneself as an object and see one's world as it appears to the other. This is not done from a specific location outside oneself, but is non-positional. This is a recognition of the subjectivity in others.

Sartre also expands on the idea that consciousness does not make sense by itself: it arises only as an awareness of objects. Consciousness is therefore always, and essentially, consciousness *of something*, whether this "something" is a thing, a person, an imaginary object, etc. Phenomenologists refer to this quality of consciousness as "intentionality". Sartre's contribution, then, is that in addition to always being consciousness *of something*, consciousness is always consciousness *of itself*. In other words, all consciousness is, by definition, *self-consciousness*. By "self-consciousness", Sartre does not mean being aware of oneself thought of as an object (e.g., one's "ego"), but rather that, as a phenomenon in the world, consciousness both appears, and appears *to itself*, at the same time. By appearing to itself, Sartre argues that consciousness is fully transparent; unlike an ordinary "object" (a house, for instance, of which it is impossible to perceive all the sides at the same time), consciousness "sees" all aspects of itself at once. This non-positional quality of consciousness is what makes it a unique type of being, a being that exists *for itself*.

The book includes a critique of Sigmund Freud's theory of the unconscious, based on the claim that consciousness is essentially self-conscious. Sartre also argues that Freud's theory of repression is internally flawed, where people block out traumatic memories. He views Freud's unconscious to be a scapegoat for the paradox of simultaneously knowing and not knowing the same information. But instead of alleviating the paradox, Freud simply moves it to a censor, establishing **"between the unconscious and consciousness an autonomous consciousness in bad faith"**. Sartre thinks that the postulation of a censor within the psychic economy is therefore redundant: at the level of the censor, we still encounter the same problem of a consciousness that hides something from itself.

Over the years Sartre (and de Beauvoir) became more Marxist in outlook. In particular, Sartre supported the FLN (National Liberation Front) in Algeria in their resistance to the harsh French colonial rule there. This was a further point of conflict with Camus, who was himself from Algeria.

Sartre also came in for a lot of criticism at this time, from the intellectual left, for being too slow to condemn human rights abuses in the Soviet Union.

Existentialism

It is difficult to precisely define existentialism, partly because different philosophers have slightly different ideas about it, and partly due to the involved premises of phenomenology on which it is based. Indeed, even Sartre himself once said: "Existentialism? I don't know what that is." And yet at another time he said that existentialism was just humanism by another name.

In simple terms, however, existentialism is the belief that philosophical thinking begins with the human subject—not merely the thinking subject, but the acting, feeling, living human individual. While the predominant value of existentialist thought is commonly acknowledged to be freedom, its primary virtue is authenticity.

It is, at root, a philosophy concerned with finding self, and the meaning of life, through free will, choice, and personal responsibility. In the view of the existentialist, the individual's starting point is characterized by what has been called **"the existential attitude"** or a sense of disorientation, confusion, or dread in the face of an apparently meaningless or absurd world. At the same time, however, it includes the recognition that others are probably experiencing the same angst, and in Sartre's hands existentialism becomes an ethical theory.

Legacy

Sartre's huge range of output including philosophy books, plays, novels, screenplays, critical essays, and letters make him one of the most important intellectual figures of the twentieth century. But over and above that his philosophy of existentialism had an immense effect on both other philosophers and popular culture.

Existentialism became popular in the years following World War II, and strongly influenced many disciplines besides philosophy, including theology, drama, art, literature, and psychology. We now have: - existential Marxism, existential sociology, existential psychoanalysis, existential theology and so on. The general feature of these hybrids is an emphasis on the irreducibility of the perspectives of human agents, their activities, emotions, and thoughts. Even the word 'existential' itself has become almost part of our everyday language.

Sartre does have his critics, some philosophers, for instance, argue that Sartre's thought is contradictory. Specifically, they believe that Sartre makes metaphysical arguments despite his claim that his philosophical views ignore metaphysics. Others have said his attack on Freud was based on a misunderstanding of Freud's theories. He has also been criticized for supporting dictators like Stalin and Castro and Mao. It cannot be denied, however, that he has given people a new way of looking at themselves and at their lives.

42

Maurice Merleau-Ponty

Introduction

Maurice Merleau-Ponty (1908-1961) was a French phenomenological philosopher, strongly influenced by Edmund Husserl and Martin Heidegger. The formation and structure of meaning in human experience was his main interest, but he also wrote on perception, art, and politics.

He was a friend of Jean Paul Sartre, Simone de Beauvoir, and Albert Camus, together forming part of the French intelligentsia in Paris before, during and after the Second World War.

At the core of Merleau-Ponty's philosophy is a sustained argument for the foundational role perception plays in both understanding the world and engaging with the world. Like the other major phenomenologists, Merleau-Ponty expressed his philosophical insights in writings on art, literature, linguistics, and politics. He was the only major phenomenologist of the first half of the twentieth century to engage extensively with the sciences, and especially with descriptive psychology. His major work on this was his 1945 book **Phenomenology of Perception**. It is through this engagement that his writings have become influential in the recent project of naturalizing phenomenology, in which phenomenologists use the results of psychology and cognitive science.

Merleau-Ponty emphasized the body as the primary site of knowing the world (a corrective to the long philosophical tradition of placing consciousness as the source of knowledge) and he maintained that the body, and that which it perceived, could not be disentangled from each other. The articulation of the primacy of **embodiment** led him away from phenomenology towards what he was to call "indirect ontology" or the ontology of "the flesh of the world" (*la chair du monde*), seen in his final and incomplete work, *The Visible and Invisible*, and his last published essay, "**Eye and Mind**".

Background

Maurice Merleau-Ponty was born in 1908 in Rochefort-sur-Mer, France. His father died in 1913 when Merleau-Ponty was five years old. After secondary schooling at the lycée Louis-le-Grand in Paris, Merleau-Ponty became a student at the École Normale Supérieure, where he studied alongside Jean-Paul Sartre and Simone de Beauvoir.

He attended Edmund Husserl's "Paris Lectures" in February 1929, and in that year, he also received his DES degree (roughly equivalent to an MA thesis) from the University of Paris, on the basis of the (now-lost) thesis "*Plotinus's Notion of the Intelligible Many*". He then passed the 'agrégation' in philosophy in 1930, which allowed him to become a high school teacher. Around this time he also published a novel under the pseudonym of Jacques Heller.

Merleau-Ponty taught first at the Lycée de Beauvais (1931–33) and then got a fellowship to do research from the Caisse nationale de la recherche scientifique. From 1934–1935 he taught at the Lycée de Chartres. He then, in 1935, became a tutor at the École Normale Supérieure, where he was awarded his doctorate based on two important books: **The Structure of Behaviour** (1942) and **Phenomenology of Perception** (1945).

After teaching at the University of Lyon from 1945 to 1948, Merleau-Ponty lectured on child psychology and education at the Sorbonne from 1949 to 1952. He was awarded the Chair of Philosophy at the Collège de France from 1952 until his death in 1961, making him the youngest person to have been elected to a Chair.

Besides his teaching, Merleau-Ponty was also political editor for **Les Temps Modernes** from the founding of the journal by Sartre in October 1945 until December 1952.

In his youth he had read Karl Marx's writings, and Sartre even claimed that Merleau-Ponty converted him to Marxism. Their friendship ended, however, over a quarrel as he became disillusioned about communism, while Sartre still endorsed it.

Merleau-Ponty died suddenly of a stroke in 1961 at age 53, apparently while preparing for a class on René Descartes. He is buried in Père Lachaise Cemetery in Paris.

Merleau-Ponty's Influences

Like Sartre, Merleau-Ponty was influenced by the German phenomenologists Husserl and Heidegger. To recap briefly...

Edmund Husserl (1859 – 1938) invented the concept of phenomenology. He took over from Brentano the idea of intentionality, i.e. the relationship between mental acts and the external world is that our conscious thoughts are always '**about**' something. You are never merely conscious, you are always conscious of something: a book, a tree, or a headache, for example. The property of being intentional, of having an intentional object in mind, was the key feature to distinguish mental phenomena from physical phenomena.

Husserl was interested in how consciousness works, and his radical approach to the study of consciousness was to try and investigate it by studying the objects of conscious awareness, (the above mentioned 'intentional objects'). It is this discipline that he called phenomenology. He claims that we cannot completely know the external world, and that real knowledge is only possible by "**bracketing**" all assumptions about the existence of an external world and by just studying our intentional objects.

Martin Heidegger (1889 – 1976), who studied under Edmund Husserl, picked up on the idea of phenomenology and expanded on it. He agreed with the idea of studying conscious awareness via our intentional objects, but his version of phenomenology included an understanding that 'experience' is already situated in the world, and in ways of being.

Thus, Husserl's understanding that all consciousness is "intentional" is transformed in Heidegger's philosophy, becoming the thought that all experience is grounded in "care". This is the basis of Heidegger's "existential analytic", as he develops it in his great book ***Being and Time***. He argues that describing experience 'properly entails finding the "being" for whom such a description might matter'. And his discussion of ontology (the study of being) is rooted in an analysis of the mode of existence of individual human beings.

Philosophy

From these influences, and together with Sartre, de Beauvoir, and Camus, the philosophy of existentialism was created. It is difficult to precisely define existentialism, partly because different philosophers have slightly different ideas about it, but in simple terms it is the belief that philosophical thinking begins with the human subject, not merely the thinking subject, but the acting, feeling, living human individual.

While the predominant value of existentialist thought is commonly acknowledged to be freedom, its primary virtue is authenticity.

Existentialism is, at root, a philosophy concerned with finding self, and the meaning of life, through free will, choice, and personal responsibility. In the view of the existentialist, the individual's starting point is characterized by what has been called "**the existential attitude**" or a sense of disorientation, confusion, or dread in the face of an apparently meaningless or absurd world. At the same time, however, it includes the recognition that others are probably experiencing the same angst, and it then becomes an ethical theory. So far this is Sartre's perspective.

To this, however, Merleau-Ponty brings a scientific perspective, making the primacy of perception central to his thinking. He constantly argued against the subject-object dualism of Cartesian philosophy, which still continued to dominate Sartre's existentialism.

Drawing on Husserl's notion of a pre-predictive intentionality, and on Heidegger's exposition of human existence as 'being-in-the-world', Merleau-Ponty developed a description of the world as 'the field of experience in which I find myself'.

Descartes' "I think therefore I am" was transformed to read 'I belong to myself while belonging to the world'. Any attempt to constitute the world as an object of knowledge is always derivative in relation to that primary access to the world that Merleau-Ponty located in the body.

Perception

With his book ***Phenomenology of Perception*** (1945) Merleau-Ponty became established as the pre-eminent philosopher of the body. The body is neither subject nor object, but an ambiguous mode of existence that infects all knowledge. He drew on the critical examination of contemporary psychology and physiology, presented in his first book ***The Structure of Behaviour*** (1942), to argue the primacy perception.

He questioned the attempt of traditional philosophy to look to perception to provide some guarantees that mark its difference from hallucination. What is given in perception is ambiguous. However, this does not lead to scepticism any more than does the experience of being disillusioned. The discovery that one was the victim of an illusion does not challenge faith in perception altogether. It is only in the light of a new perception that the previous perception was doubted.

He wanted to show, in opposition to the traditional ideas that began with John Locke, that perception was not the causal product of atomic sensations. This atomist-causal conception was being perpetuated in certain psychological currents of the time, particularly in behaviourism. According to Merleau-Ponty, perception has an active dimension, in that it is a primordial openness to the "lifeworld".

As a difference from Husserl's thinking, Merleau-Ponty develops the thesis according to which "all consciousness is perceptual consciousness". In doing so, he establishes a significant turn in the development of phenomenology, indicating that its conceptualisations should be re-examined in the light of the primacy of perception when weighing up their philosophical consequences.

Maurice Merleau-Ponty

Taking the study of perception as his point of departure, Merleau-Ponty was led to recognize that one's own body is not only a thing, a potential object of study for science, but is also a permanent condition of experience, and an essential ingredient of the perceptual openness to the world. He therefore underlines the fact that there is an inherence of consciousness and of the body of which the analysis of perception should take account. The primacy of perception signifies a primacy of experience, insofar as perception becomes an active and essential dimension.

> "Insofar as I have hands, feet; a body, I sustain around me intentions which are not dependent on my decisions and which affect my surroundings in a way that I do not choose".

Prior to this point there had been two main themes in the philosophy of our understanding of the world; Empiricism, which holds that knowledge is based on observation and experimentation; and Idealism (sometimes known as Rationalism) which base knowledge on reason, introspection, and intuition, saying that all we can rely on is the mind.

Merleau-Ponty says both these camps are wrong. Empiricists think that attention is like the beam of a searchlight illuminating a pre-existing landscape. Whereas Rationalists think that, if consciousness finds, for instance, the geometrical circle when looking at a dinner plate, it is because consciousness already put it there (for instance Kant's synthetic *"a priori"* knowledge).

Perception, he says, is not just seeing, it is not like looking through a window; it is how the body responds to sensation. It is not just what meets the eye, a large amount of pre-processing takes place prior to conscious awareness, and it includes a vast background of assumptions, memories, associations, and anticipations that combine to make up one's experience. Also, its expression is made possible because we are situated within a linguistic world just as we are embedded in a perceptual world; the language we use interposes between our experience and its expression.

Radical reflection

Merleau-Ponty also distinguished what reflection reveals from what is given in an unreflective experience. This led him to the idea of a 'radical reflection'. Radical reflection was Merleau-Ponty's alternative to analysis, which he consistently criticized. Analytic thought, in his view, breaks up experience into constituent parts, for example sensations and qualities, and is thus obliged to invent a power of synthesis, of some sort, in an attempt to rebuild the world of experience. (In spite of this, however, his work has found a more receptive audience among analytic philosophers than other phenomenologists have managed to receive.)

Throughout his writings Merleau-Ponty sought ways to explore the body's primordial contact with the world prior to the impact of analysis. In doing so, he was resisting a tendency of contemporary scientific and philosophic thought to enhance the value of autonomous knowledge arrived at under experimental conditions.

Merleau-Ponty understood science to be an *ex post facto* abstraction. Causal and physiological accounts of perception, for example, explain perception in terms that are only arrived at after abstracting from the phenomenon itself. Merleau-Ponty chastised science for taking itself to be the area in which a complete account of nature may be given. The subjective depth of phenomena cannot be given in science as it is; he wanted to institute a "return to the phenomena."

Language and Art

Expression, particularly in language and the arts, plays an increasingly central role in Merleau-Ponty's thought in the years following his book **Phenomenology**, when he aimed to formulate a general theory of expression as the grounding for a philosophy of history and culture. This interest is first reflected in a series of essays addressing painting and literature. These include Merleau-Ponty's first essay on painting, "***Cézanne's Doubt***", which finds in Cézanne a proto-phenomenological effort to capture the birth of perception through painting.

Cézanne epitomizes the paradoxical struggle of creative expression, which necessarily relies on the idiosyncrasies of the artist's individual history and psychology, as well as the resources of the tradition of painting, but can succeed only by risking a creative appropriation of these acquisitions in the service of teaching its audience to see the world anew.

Similarly, Leonardo da Vinci's artistic productivity is explicable neither in terms of his intellectual freedom, nor his childhood, but as the dialectic of spontaneity and sedimentation by which Merleau-Ponty had formerly defined history.

In a manuscript partially completed during his later years, and published posthumously as *The Prose of the World,* he pursues these themes through a phenomenological investigation of literary language and its relationship with scientific language and painting. Critiquing our commonsense ideal of a pure language that would transparently encode pre-existing thoughts, Merleau-Ponty argues that instituted language—the conventional system of language as an established set of meanings and rules—is derivative from a more primordial function of language as genuinely creative, expressive, and communicative. He was very interested in how children acquire language as they develop and learn to effectively communicate with others.

Political Philosophy

From the first issue of ***Les Temps Modernes*** in October 1945 until his death, Merleau-Ponty wrote regularly on politics, including reflections on contemporary events as well as explorations of their philosophical underpinnings and the broader political significance of his times.

Always writing from the left, Merleau-Ponty's position gradually shifted from a qualified Marxism, maintaining a critical distance from liberal democracy, as well as from Soviet communism, to the rejection of revolutionary politics in favour of a "new liberalism". Drawing on the extended example of the French revolution, Merleau-Ponty argues that every revolution mistakes the structure of history for its contents, believing that eliminating the latter will absolutely transform the former.

> "The very nature of revolution is to believe itself absolute and to not be absolute precisely because it believes itself to be so".

The alternative that Merleau-Ponty endorses is the development of a "non-communist left", an "a-communism", or a "new liberalism", the first commitment of which would be to reject the description of the rivalry between the two powers as one between "free enterprise" and Marxism.

This non-communist left would occupy a "double position", "posing social problems in terms of [class] struggle" while also "refusing the dictatorship of the proletariat". This pursuit must welcome the resources of parliamentary debate, in clear recognition of their limitations, since Parliament is "the only known institution that guarantees a minimum of opposition and of truth". By exercising "methodical doubt" toward the established powers and denying that they exhaust political and economic options, the possibility opens for a genuine dialectic that advances social justice while respecting political freedom.

Legacy

Merleau-Ponty's critical position with respect to science was stated in his Preface to the *Phenomenology*— he described scientific points of view as "always both naive and at the same time dishonest". Despite, or perhaps because of, this view, his work influenced and anticipated the strands of modern psychology known as post-cognitivism. In addition, Merleau-Ponty's work has influenced researchers trying to integrate neuroscience with the principles of chaos theory.

Several authors on feminism cite Merleau-Ponty's influence. In particular, Merleau-Ponty's phenomenology of the body was taken up by Iris Young in her essay "***Throwing Like a Girl***." And Sara Heinämaa has argued for a rereading of Merleau-Ponty's influence on Simone de Beauvoir.

Also, in her highly recommended book "***At the Existentialist Cafe***" Sarah Bakewell says of him: -

> "He put together the fullest description he could of how to live from moment to moment, and thus of what we are... Merleau-Ponty arguably left the most lasting intellectual legacy of all [of the existentialists], not least in his direct influence on the modern discipline of 'embodied cognition', which studies consciousness as a holistic social and sensory phenomenon rather than as a sequence of abstract processes."

43

Alfred Jules Ayer

Introduction

Sir Alfred Jules Ayer (1910 – 1989) was a British philosopher, best known for his promotion of the philosophy called 'Logical Positivism', as articulated in his books ***Language, Truth, and Logic*** (1936) and ***The Problem of Knowledge*** (1956).

In ***Language, Truth, and Logic*** (published when he was just 24) he put forward what were understood to be the major theses of Logical Positivism, and so established himself as that movement's leading English representative. In endorsing these views Ayer saw himself as continuing in the line of British empiricism, established by Locke and Hume, an empiricism whose most recent representative was Russell.

Throughout his subsequent career he remained true to this tradition's rejection of the possibility of synthetic *a priori* knowledge, and so he saw the method, and purpose, of philosophy to be the analysis of the meaning of key terms, such as 'causality', 'truth', 'knowledge', 'freedom', and so on.

The major portion of his work was devoted to exploring different facets of our claims to knowledge, particularly perceptual knowledge and knowledge that depended on inductive inference for its credence.

He always wrote with stylish crispness and clarity, and it is said that he could lay bare the bones of a philosophical difficulty in a few paragraphs of strikingly simple prose. On many a philosophical problem Ayer cannot be bettered for providing a lucid, informative, and revealing description of its contours. Amongst British philosophers of the 20th Century, he has often been ranked as second only to Russell.

Background

Ayer was born in St John's Wood, in Northwest London, to a wealthy family from continental Europe. His mother, Reine Citroën, was from the Dutch-Jewish family who founded the Citroën car company in France. His father, Jules Ayer, was a Swiss Calvinist financier who worked for the Rothschild family.

An Introduction to Philosophy

He was educated at Ascham St Vincent's School, a former boarding preparatory school for boys in Eastbourne, in which he started boarding at the comparatively early age of seven for reasons to do with the First World War. He then went on to Eton in Berkshire. It was at Eton that Ayer first became known for his characteristic bravado, although primarily interested in furthering his intellectual pursuits he was very keen on sports, particularly rugby. Ayer nevertheless felt an 'outsider', and it is clear that his fellow-students did not warm to him very much, perhaps due to the excessive zeal with which he attempted to convert them to atheism. Feeling 'an outsider' was something that remained with him all his life.

During his last year there, as a member of Eton's senior council, he unsuccessfully campaigned for the abolition of corporal punishment at the school. In his final examinations at Eton Ayer came second in his year, and first in classics, and he won a classics scholarship to Christ Church, Oxford.

At Oxford he studied both Greek and philosophy, one of his tutors being Gilbert Ryle. It was Ryle who suggested that Ayer read Wittgenstein's *Tractatus*, a work that immediately impressed him. After graduation Ryle was also instrumental in getting Ayer to go to Vienna in 1933 to study with the philosophers of the Vienna Circle for a year.

When he returned to England he wrote and published his first book, **Language, Truth and Logic** in 1936, this being the first exposition in English of Logical Positivism as newly developed by the Vienna Circle. This made Ayer, at age 26, the 'enfant terrible' of British philosophy.

In the Second World War he served as an officer in the Welsh Guards, chiefly in intelligence (Special Operations Executive and MI6). After the war he briefly returned to Oxford University where he became a fellow and Dean of Wadham College. He thereafter taught philosophy at London University from 1946 until 1959, when he also started to appear on radio and television.

He was an extrovert and social mixer who liked dancing and attending the clubs in London and New York. He was also obsessed with sport: he had played rugby for Eton and was a noted cricketer and a keen supporter of the Tottenham Hotspur football team. For an academic, Ayer was an unusually well-connected figure in his time, with close links to 'high society' and the establishment. Presiding over Oxford high-tables, he is often described as charming, but at times he could also be intimidating.

Ayer was married four times to three women. His first marriage was from 1932–1941 to (Grace Isabel) Renée (d. 1980), who subsequently married philosopher Stuart Hampshire, Ayer's friend and colleague. In 1960 he married Alberta Constance (Dee) Wells, with whom he had one son. Ayer's marriage to Wells was dissolved in 1983 and that same year he married Vanessa Salmon, former wife of politician Nigel Lawson. She died in 1985 and in 1989 he remarried Dee Wells, who survived him. Ayer also had a daughter with Hollywood columnist Sheilah Graham Westbrook.

From 1959 to his retirement in 1978, Sir Alfred held the Wykeham Chair, Professor of Logic at Oxford, and he was knighted in 1970. Ayer died on 27 June 1989.

Philosophy

Like other philosophers, Ayer is interested in epistemology (the theory of knowledge) and his method of approach is via a branch of philosophy called 'Logical Positivism', sometimes also called Logical (or Linguistic) empiricism. Central to this doctrine is the principle of the verifiability of sentences or statements.

Ayer holds that there are just two sorts of cognitively meaningful statements, those which are, in principle, empirically verifiable (i.e. observationally testable) and those which are analytic (i.e. true simply in virtue of linguistic rules). Scientific statements, and statements of ordinary fact, belong to the first class, while statements of mathematics and of logic belong to the second. Religious and metaphysical statements, such as 'God exists' (or, indeed, that he does not), or that there is a realm of things in themselves behind phenomena, are meaningless because they belong to neither class.

Basic ethical statements are regarded similarly as factually meaningless, but are allowed as emotive meanings (that is, they express emotional attitudes). Ayer does not disfavour them in the same way as he does religious or metaphysical ones, this is made clearer in his later works.

Here is a section from the preface to ***Language, Truth and Logic:*** -

> The views which are put forward in this treatise derive from the doctrines of Bertrand Russell and Wittgenstein, which are themselves the logical outcome of the empiricism of Berkeley and David Hume. Like Hume, I divide all genuine propositions into two classes: those which, in his terminology, concern 'relations of ideas', and those which concern 'matters of fact'. The former class comprises the a priori propositions of logic and pure mathematics, and these I allow to be necessary and certain only because

> they are analytic. That is, I maintain that the reason why these propositions cannot be confuted in experience is that they do not make any assertion about the empirical world, but simply record our determination to use symbols in a certain fashion. Propositions concerning empirical matters of fact, on the other hand, I hold to be hypotheses, which can be probable but never certain.

He then goes on to argue that anything expressed in metaphysical terms is 'literally' meaningless.

> To test whether a sentence expresses a genuine empirical hypothesis, I adopt what may be called a modified verification principle. For I require of an empirical hypothesis, not indeed that it should be conclusively verifiable, but that some possible sense-experience should be relevant to the determination of its truth or falsehood. If a putative proposition fails to satisfy this principle, and is not a tautology, then I hold that it is metaphysical, and that, being metaphysical, it is neither true nor false but literally senseless. It will be found that much of what ordinarily passes for philosophy is metaphysical according to this criterion, and, in particular, that it can not be significantly asserted that there is a non-empirical world of values, or that men have immortal souls, or that there is a transcendent God.

He follows Russell in his analysis of language structure. For instance, take the proposition 'Unicorns are fictitious'. Here we see a superficial grammatical resemblance to the proposition 'Dogs are faithful', and this creates the assumption that they are of the same logical type. But dogs have to exist to be faithful and so it is held that unicorns must exist in some way in order to possess the property of being fictitious. However, it is plainly self-contradictory to say fictitious objects exist, so it leads to the belief that they are real in some non-empirical sense – that they have a mode of being which is different from the being of existent things. But since there is no way of testing for that non-empirical mode of being, it becomes devoid of all literal significance. He therefore maintains that the postulation of non-existent entities results from superstition.

He asserts that the job of philosophy is to provide definitions. That is not the 'explicit' definitions you would find in a dictionary, it is more the definitions of descriptive phrases in their use. For example, in a dictionary you will find 'oculist' defined as an 'eye doctor', so these two definitions could be used synonymously to give two sentences meaning the same thing.

When we look at '*in use*' definitions, however, we are looking for two ideas that are equivalent. For example, the sentence 'The round square cannot exist' is equivalent to the sentence 'No one thing can be both square and round'. They are not exactly the same, but the second sentence includes the first as a subset, it is a more general case.

Empiricism

As an admitted empiricist, he confronts head on the objection that it is impossible, on empiricist principles, to account for our knowledge of necessary truths. For, as Hume conclusively showed, no general proposition whose validity is the subject of the test of actual experience can ever be logically certain. No matter how many times it is confirmed by a test, there is no logical guarantee that it will be substantiated in the next test.

This means that no general proposition referring to a matter of fact can ever be shown to be necessarily and universally true; at best it can only be a probable hypothesis. However, the fact that the validity of a proposition cannot be logically guaranteed in no way entails that it is irrational to believe it. On the contrary, he says, what is irrational is to demand certainty where probability is all that is obtainable. All the views of science (and common sense) are hypotheses, and this is the basis of the empiricist thesis.

Moral theories

When we make a statement such as 'Killing is wrong', we seem to be attributing to acts of killing a certain property – the moral property of it being wrong. Presumably, what we say will then be *true* or *false* depending on whether or not acts of killing possess that property.

However, Ayer says this appearance is deceptive. True, 'Killing is wrong' looks superficially similar to (say) 'Unicycling is easy', or 'Running is healthy', but these other two statements are used to make claims, and so might be true or false. Ayer says that the statement 'Killing is wrong' is not making a claim, it is asserting our attitude towards killing. And because no claim is being made then the statement is neither true nor false.

An Introduction to Philosophy

> If I say to someone, 'You acted wrongly in stealing that money', I am not stating anything more than if I had simply said, 'You stole that money'. In adding that this action is wrong I am not making any further statement about it. I am simply evincing my moral disapproval of it. It is as if I had said, 'You stole that money', in a particular tone of horror, or written it with the addition of some special exclamation marks.

This follows from his views that a) a sentence can have factual significance only if it is possible empirically to verify it, and b) moral sentences such as 'Killing is wrong' are not empirically verifiable. It follows then that 'Killing is wrong' lacks factual significance.

Ethically he espoused a qualified utilitarianism, though interpreting the 'greatest happiness' principle as the expression of an optional fundamental attitude.

Epistemology

With his later book *The Problem of Knowledge* he sees epistemology as primarily an effort to justify ordinary claims to knowledge against philosophical scepticism. Scepticism arises (he says) when there appears to be a gap between our only possible evidence for the existence and character of things of a certain sort and our ordinary confident claims of knowledge about them.

For example, our access to the physical world seems to be only via our own sense-data, to the minds of others via their behaviour, and to the past via our memories. He lists four types of possible solution to this: -

1. **Naive realism** – which holds that the problematic things are, after all, directly given to us, so that we somehow directly perceived physical objects, other minds, or the past, without the intermediary of any sense-data, behaviour, or memories which are mere representations of them.

2. **Reductionism** – this reduces the existence of problematic things to the holding of suitable patterns among the evidential data, e.g. sense-data, behaviour, or memory images and historical records.

3. **The scientific approach** – which tries to show that the inference from evidence to conclusion has a scientifically respectable inductive character. The difficulty here is that there can be no

inductive grounds for moving from Xs to Ys if we have no possible access to the latter except by the former.

4. **The method of descriptive analysis** – simply describes how we do, in fact, base our beliefs on the evidence, and shows that the complaint that these are not well based is unreasonable because it makes an impossible demand. It is this option that Ayer favours.

Despite his iconoclasm, Ayer had no truck with some of the wilder assaults upon traditional philosophical thought, such as ordinary-language philosophy on the one hand, and behaviourism and physicalism on the other.

Legacy

Ayer once described himself as "Horatio to Russell's Hamlet." But, while Russell was the superior logician, Ayer was arguably the more penetrating and imaginative epistemologist. Asked to assess his contribution at the end of his life, Ayer responded, "I suppose that I care more about having got something right in philosophy, if I have got anything right, than having written elegantly. Although I like that too."

The members of the Vienna Circle had little knowledge of traditional philosophy and less use for it; but they loathed and feared the German idealistic philosophies which appeared to be legitimating the rise of irrationalism in continental politics. Their goal was to replace the dangerous philosophic mystifications of Europe with a tough, empirical 'scientific mentality', and this they called logical positivism. A.J. Ayer is chiefly responsible for bringing this philosophy to the English-speaking world, and it continued to have a significant effect on the English-speaking world for decades to come.

In 1983, Washington University Professor of Philosophy Thelma Lavine said – "In writing '*Language, Truth and Logic*,' Ayer was an enfant terrible who cleverly placed a lighted stick of dynamite under all traditional philosophies. The old philosophic landscape has never been fully rebuilt since then". That book, she continued, "is generally conceded to be one of the most influential books of 20th-century philosophy."

Ayer wrote almost fifty books on philosophy and many papers and articles. As well as his own ideas he wrote widely on other philosophical movements and other individual philosophers, both current and historical. And many of these are used as standard texts in university philosophy courses. He was also a frequent guest on TV and radio.

In the later twentieth century, logical positivism fell a little out of favour, but it is very difficult to find fault with his ideas, and the clarity they are presented with is beyond question. The only real criticism is perhaps that he does not go far enough with questions like how words 'hook onto' the world, and how the brain generates the mind. But that is said with the hindsight of late twentieth and early twenty-first century scientific perspective.

44

Daniel C. Dennett

Introduction

Daniel Clement Dennett III (born March 28, 1942) is an American philosopher, writer, and cognitive scientist whose research centres on the philosophy of mind, philosophy of science, and philosophy of biology; and particularly as those fields relate to evolutionary biology and cognitive science.

As of 2018, he is the co-director of the Center for Cognitive Studies, and the Austin B. Fletcher Professor of Philosophy at Tufts University, Medford, Massachusetts. He has authored several highly influential books, has written numerous articles and essays published in scientific journals, and has joint authored books with other prominent scientists and philosophers.

Dennett is an atheist and secularist, a member of the Secular Coalition for America advisory board, and a member of the Committee for Skeptical Inquiry. He is sometimes also referred to as one of the "**Four Horsemen of New Atheism**", along with Richard Dawkins, Sam Harris, and the late Christopher Hitchens.

Background

Dennett was born on March 28, 1942, in Boston, Massachusetts, the son of Ruth Marjorie (née Leck) and Daniel Clement Dennett, Jr. Dennett spent part of his childhood in Lebanon, where, during World War II, his father was a covert counter-intelligence agent with the Office of Strategic Services posing as a cultural attaché to the American Embassy in Beirut. When he was five, his mother took him back to Massachusetts after his father died in an unexplained plane crash. Dennett's sister is the investigative journalist Charlotte Dennett. Dennett says that he was first introduced to the notion of philosophy while attending summer camp at age 11, when a camp counsellor said to him, "You know what you are, Daniel? You're a philosopher."

Dennett graduated from Phillips Exeter Academy in 1959 and spent one year at Wesleyan University before receiving his Bachelor of Arts in philosophy at Harvard University in 1963. At Harvard University he was a student of W. V. Quine. In 1965, he received his Doctor of Philosophy degree from the University of Oxford, where he studied under Gilbert Ryle as a member of Hertford College. His dissertation was entitled "**The Mind and the Brain: Introspective Description in the Light of Neurological Findings; Intentionality**".

Dennett describes himself as: -

> "*An autodidact—or, more properly, the beneficiary of hundreds of hours of informal tutorials on all the fields that interest me, from some of the world's leading scientists*".

He is the recipient of a Fulbright Fellowship, two Guggenheim Fellowships, and a Fellowship at the Center for Advanced Study in the Behavioral Sciences. He is a Fellow of the Committee for Skeptical Inquiry and a Humanist Laureate of the International Academy of Humanism. He was also named '2004 Humanist of the Year' by the American Humanist Association.

In February 2010, he was named to the Freedom From Religion Foundation's Honorary Board of distinguished achievers. And In 2012, he was awarded the Erasmus Prize: - an annual award for a person who has made an exceptional contribution to European culture, society, or social science, "for his ability to translate the cultural significance of science and technology to a broad audience."

Dennett married Susan Bell in 1962. They currently live in North Andover, Massachusetts, and have a daughter, a son, and four grandchildren. He is also an avid sailor.

Philosophy

Dennett's main interests are in understanding consciousness and understanding our place in the universe and how we developed into that place.

The methods and approach he brings to this are threefold: -

1. Firstly, as a philosophy lecturer, he has at his disposal, not only all the writings from past great philosophers, but also all the analysis and criticisms of those ideas by numerous other thinkers. Dennett often says that "the reason we teach the history of philosophy is that it is the history of very smart people making

very tempting mistakes." Also, as a philosophy lecturer of many years standing, he has been able to test and debate his own ideas with thousands of university undergraduates in his classes and many other university colleagues.
2. Secondly, he fully acknowledges the importance of science. He has a strong interest in neurology and how the brain works, and an equally strong interest in biology and evolution. In these areas he has sought out the leading experts in their fields, both in person and via their scientific literature. All of Dennett's own books and papers, giving his philosophical analysis of the implications in these areas, include very extensive references and bibliographies to the published scientific findings he talks about.
3. Thirdly, he brings to his analysis a very rigorous and honest approach. Any idea is discussed and analysed from multiple sides; and especially he presents any counter arguments to his own in their fullest and most forceful position, before demonstrating what he believes are their errors in logic. If, however, a question can't yet be decided, then he says so, while at the same time presenting the latest research and the possible future direction on the issue. He never advocates something without evidence; indeed, this is the main issue he takes with faith and religion. And all this is done in an accessible and entertaining style, making his books both a pleasure and an education to read.

Dennett's philosophy has a number of separate themes running through it: scientific evidence, evolutionary development, how the mind and consciousness work and the interaction between culture and evolution. These are interlinked and mutually supportive themes in all his books, but perhaps the easiest approach to an understanding of his work is to consider these themes separately.

Phenomenology

Edmund Husserl (1859 – 1938) invented the concept of phenomenology. He took over from Brentano the idea of intentionality, i.e. the relationship between mental acts and the external world is that our conscious thoughts are always '**about**' something. You are never merely conscious, you are always conscious of something: a book, a tree, or a headache, for example. The property of being intentional, of having an intentional object in mind, was the key feature to distinguish mental phenomena from physical phenomena.

Husserl was interested in how consciousness works, and his radical approach to the study of consciousness was to try and investigate it by studying the objects of conscious awareness, (the above mentioned 'intentional objects'). It is this discipline that he called phenomenology.

Husserl claimed that we cannot completely know the external world and that real knowledge is only possible by "bracketing" all assumptions about the existence of an external world and by just studying our intentional objects.

This approach to an understanding of consciousness was picked up by others and it most famously became the basis of existentialism, which is, of course, a very individual and subjective philosophy.

Dennett picks up on intentionality and phenomenology as a good basis for understanding consciousness, but asks why should we "bracket" other ways of attaining knowledge? Science has progressed enormously since Husserl's day; we now have a much better understanding of neurology; plus we have brought a scientific approach to the study of behaviour and psychology.

He then coins the new term **Heterophenomenology** for this wider and more inclusive study of consciousness that takes in not just one's own consciousness but the consciousness of others too. The prefix 'Hetero' coming from the Greek meaning "other party" or "another". This approach is explained fully in his groundbreaking book ***Consciousness Explained*** (1991), an ambitious title, but the book fully lives up to it.

Phenomenology has usually seemed to be a matter of pooling shared, first-person-singular observations. Descartes did it with his 'I think therefore I am', and so did the British Empiricists, Locke, Berkeley and Hume, all writing from introspection. But is introspection just a matter of 'looking and seeing'? Dennett says: -

> "I suspect that when we claim to be just using our powers of inner observation, we are always actually engaging in a sort of impromptu theorizing."

Heterophenomenology (the phenomenology of another, not just oneself) is a term to describe an explicitly third-person, scientific approach to the study of consciousness and other mental phenomena. It consists of applying the scientific method with an anthropological bent, combining the subject's self-reports with all other available evidence to determine their mental state. The goal is to discover how the subject sees the world himself or herself, without taking the accuracy of the subject's view for granted.

The method requires a researcher to listen to the subjects, and take what they say seriously, but to also look at everything else available to them, including the subject's bodily responses and environment, evidence provided by relevant neurological or psychological studies, the researcher's memories of their own experiences, and any other scientific data that might help to interpret what the subject has reported.

The key role of heterophenomenology in Dennett's philosophy of consciousness is that it defines all that can or needs to be known about the mind. For any phenomenological question "why do I experience X", there is a corresponding heterophenomenological question "why does the subject say 'I experience X'". To quote Dennett: -

> "The total set of details of heterophenomenology, plus all the data we can gather about concurrent events in the brains of subjects and in the surrounding environment, comprise the total data set for a theory of human consciousness. It leaves out no objective phenomena and no subjective phenomena of consciousness."

Consciousness

One of Dennett's main objectives in ***Consciousness Explained*** is to enable people to understand the error that Descartes made when he fell for (what is now known in his honour as) 'Cartesian Dualism'; the idea that the brain has both physical and non-physical parts to it.

Related to this is the idea that there is some special part within the brain (either a non-physical soul in religious terms, or some central physical brain structure) which is identified with our inner "I", our conscious self; i.e. some inner observer collecting and analysing all the data that enters via the senses. This traditional model of the mind Dennett calls the "Cartesian Theatre", and this model persists even after any ideas of a ghostly dualism have been exorcized. He says: -

> "The idea of a special centre in the brain is the most tenacious bad idea bedevilling our attempts to think about consciousness."

The brain does not take in all sensory inputs and display them in some inner Cartesian Theatre for another part of the brain to watch and think about. If that was the case, you would have the same problem of understanding how that watching part of the brain worked. It would have to take in information from this first Cartesian Theatre and display it in some smaller inner Cartesian Theatre, and so on ad infinitum. So obviously there is no central location or inner watcher; it is the whole brain that experiences the world.

Another idea Dennett deals with in this book is a famous series of experiments that neurologist Benjamin Libet performed in the 1980s. By careful measurements Libet showed that the decision to move a wrist by a subject occurred in the subject's subconscious prior to the subject's conscious decision to do so. This result has been used by religious people in support of Cartesian Dualism, but also by Determinists claiming that therefore free will does not exist. Dennett disagrees with both camps. It is, he says, just how the mind works, consciousness is not immediate, it takes a finite amount of time to construct our picture of the world, and so our conscious awareness is always a fraction behind real time. It's too small amount of time to matter, and anyway it's easily compensated for when catching a ball for instance.

On these lines Dennett also discusses another experiment. A subject watches two lights close together where first one is on then the other. The subject reports this as seeing the light move from the first position to the second. Then this is repeated with the first light as white and the second as red. The subject reports that the light moved and changed to red halfway along the line from the first to the second. The problem here is that the subject has reported seeing red before the second light actually comes on. How is this possible?

In a Cartesian Theatre model Dennett says that you have to assume that either history has been edited (which Dennett calls the Orwellian solution, re 1984) or that false testimony has been accepted (which Dennett calls the Stalinesque method). Dennett's solution to this is his Multiple Drafts Model. The brain is constantly at work coming up with possible theories about what is happening at any given moment, discarding those that don't work, but then immediately moving on to the next moment in time and the next issue to understand.

He also views 'the self' as a construction of the mind. It is, he says, the "Centre of Narrative Gravity" for the individual. We put into words what is happening to us, and how we feel about what is happening, and how that fits with the story of our lives as we experience it.

Free Will

In his book ***Freedom Evolves*** (2003) Dennett examines the problem of where free will comes from if the world is fully deterministic. That is, if we imagine being able to know where every particle in the universe is and how it is moving then we would be able to work out what is going to happen in the future. In fact, from this point of view the future would be completely determined, hence we would not really be 'free' to act because everything we did would be pre-determined.

He points out two problems with this view: -

- Firstly, there is a question as to the possibility of ever doing this because you would have to deal with things like chaos, and the uncertainty principle in quantum mechanics (i.e. that it is impossible to determine both the exact position of a particle and its velocity at the same time).
- Secondly, there is the difficulty that any model of the universe would itself be part of the universe and so would have to model itself, and then to model itself modelling itself... ad infinitum.

So, although we can consider the universe to be deterministic, with effect following cause for instance, it is impossible to know what will happen in the future.

Now obviously organisms in the world could not know what is going to happen but they will certainly survive better if they avoid predators and other dangerous situations. So, they do best when they take in information about the world and make decisions based upon that information; run, fight, eat or mate. Simple instincts can do very well for many creatures. The biologist Stephen Jay Gould tells the story of when he was a youngster in the US navy, an older seaman gave him the following advice 'if it moves salute it, if it doesn't, paint it', a good way to keep your head down and survive without getting into trouble. Gould went on to show how simple, hard-wired instincts serve many animals very well, especially where the cost of running a large brain is prohibitive.

However, the more brain power you can bring to such decisions the more freedom you have to choose a good path. In other words, as per the title of Dennett's book, freedom evolves, even in a deterministic world. To Dennett, evolutionary theory, not physics, is the key to understanding freedom; it explains how we can be free when our parts aren't free.

Religion

Some people claim that God is needed to tell us what is right and wrong (for instance the Ten Commandments) but in his book ***Darwin's Dangerous Idea*** (1996), Dennett clearly demonstrates that evolution can account for the origin of morality. He also rejects the concept of the 'naturalistic fallacy' as the idea that ethics exist in some free-floating realm, this fallacy, he says, is a rush from facts to values.

In ***Breaking the Spell: Religion as a Natural Phenomenon*** (2006), Dennett shows how we can account for religious belief naturalistically, explaining possible evolutionary reasons for the phenomenon of religious adherence. The book includes a comprehensive look at the origins and evolution of religion itself, from the earliest beliefs up to the present day, where he says that 'belief in belief' has become a virtue in its own right.

An Introduction to Philosophy

The "spell" that requires "breaking" is not religious belief itself but the belief that it is off-limits to or beyond scientific inquiry.

Intuition Pumps

Dennett has long been a champion of Intuition Pumps as an aid to philosophical thinking, and his book ***Intuition Pumps and Other Tools for Thinking*** (2013) is a valuable resource in this respect.

Intuition Pumps are thought experiments (stories or scenarios) that are designed to help us think about a given issue. Note that they don't have to be true (or even possible); they are just structured to enable us to think more clearly about an idea. These stories or scenarios can be long and complex or very short, also they are given names or titles in order that we can easily remember them.

An example of a short Intuition Pump (given by Dennett) is the one called '**Daddy is a Doctor**'. A five-year-old girl is asked what daddy does, and she replies that daddy is a doctor. Does she know what a doctor is? Perhaps she just thinks daddy helps people if they get sick. When she is eight, her concept of a doctor will have become more complex and so on. But does the person asking the question know what a doctor is, as well as say a doctor himself or herself does? And anyway, does it matter? Useful meaning has been imparted.

This story helps us to understand where meaning comes from, and that words are not definite things. Words (like doctor) are concepts, created by our brains and developed, modified, and refined over time from the experiences and information we are exposed to. Each one of us might have a slightly different concept of any given word, but we can still communicate with each other and impart useful meaning, even though the words we use are not definite.

A second aspect that this particular intuition pump helps us to think about is the idea of belief. How much does the girl need to know in order to understand the proposition? If understanding comes in degrees, as this example shows, then belief, which depends on understanding, must also come in degrees. We could say that she '**sort of**' understands that her daddy is a doctor, which is not the same as saying that she has any reservations or doubts. This helps us to think more clearly about belief, meaning and mental concepts, all neatly encapsulated, and made easy to remember, by the intuition pump 'Daddy is a Doctor'.

Memes

The term meme was coined by Richard Dawkins and was conceived to be analogous to a gene. A meme is defined as a "unit of culture", i.e. an idea, a word, a belief, or even a pattern of behaviour. It becomes "hosted" in the minds of one or more individuals and can reproduce itself in the sense of jumping from the mind of one person to the mind of another.

Thus, what would otherwise be regarded as one individual influencing another to adopt a belief can be seen as an 'idea-replicator' reproducing itself in a new host, and, as with genetics, a meme's success may be due to its contribution to the effectiveness of its host.

Many people have picked up on the idea of memes and expanded on it, one of them being Dan Dennett. In his book ***From Bacteria to Bach and Back*** (2017) he is particularly interested in language and the origin of consciousness.

While biological evolution is a very slow method of change (of the order of thousands of years), cultural evolution is extremely quick. Some people often confuse to the two, thinking for instance, that people in the West are more highly evolved than say tribes in the jungles around the world. This is obviously wrong; genetically we are exactly the same (except for minor surface features like skin colour), the actual difference is only cultural.

Having said that, however, the interaction between cultural evolution and biological evolution is a fascinating one. Take language for instance, the capacity for this involves genetic changes to the mouth and the larynx, as well as to the structure of the brain for processing and understanding words and language.

These genetic changes would not be preserved and handed down unless they provided good survival capabilities, and what better tool for survival is there than language. To be able to discuss ideas and cooperate with others is of tremendous value.

These changes still took thousands, perhaps millions, of years but it is possible to see the interaction between cultural evolution and biological evolution driving our use of words, language, and ideas, and contributing to the development of the human mind and our human consciousness. And this book by Dennett (heavily referenced in a large bibliography to the latest scientific research papers and books) is a fascinating analysis of these ideas.

Legacy

Being a living philosopher, it is perhaps too early to talk about Dennett's legacy, but it is true to say his influence has been huge, both among other philosophers and scientists, and among anyone else interested in philosophy. He is a champion of rationality, and of applying the latest science to any philosophical questions. Richard Dawkins, who knows him well, has said of him that it is like having a wise older brother to discuss ideas with, and the British philosopher A.C. Grayling has worked with him and greatly admires his approach to philosophy.

Many current philosophers refer to him, and if any philosopher proposes anything different then they must take Dennett's analysis into consideration. This is particularly so with issues such as the (so called) "hard problem" of consciousness, and the notion of "Qualia", both of which, says Dennett, don't really exist.

Philosophers like John Searle, Thomas Nagel, and David Chalmers (who coined the phrase 'the hard problem of consciousness') all contend that there is an aspect of consciousness that can never be explained via third party objective science. Dennett obviously disagrees; indeed, he thinks it is a defeatist attitude to *start* with a definition that says such an understanding is beyond reach. And his book ***Consciousness Explained*** with its approach of Heterophenomenology, and its analysis of scientific results clearly demonstrates the way forward.

In ***Consciousness Explained***, and in later books, Dennett spends a lot of time analysing and refuting the concept of Qualia in human consciousness. Qualia are meant to refer to feelings or sensations in the mind, as when we experience the colour blue for instance. The problem is, however, that there is no clear or definite definition of the concept, and certainly no brain structure or mechanism associated with it. 'Qualia' is just Latin for quality, but of recent times it has been re-purposed and associated with the 'hard problem' of consciousness, and together they seem to be re-introducing dualism by the back door. As a concept it is probably better to just think of qualia as a poetic term describing perhaps our emotional and psychological response to something. For a detailed analysis of why it's a bad intuition pump one can do no better than to read the chapter 'Qualia Disqualified' in ***Consciousness Explained.***

Dennett has also been criticised for being too materialistic. His answer, however, is that he fully recognises we have a spiritual side, but he defines this as approaching the world's complexities with an attitude of humble, awestruck curiosity, trying to stay both centred and engaged, while letting go of the self.

45

Other Ideas in Recent Western Philosophy

Introduction

A number of other, more recent, philosophers and their ideas are often referred to in philosophical papers and discussions. The intention here is just to give a brief summary of some of the most cited ones together with any relevant criticisms.

Karl Popper (1902 – 1994)

Mainly noted as the initiator of the discipline of 'The Philosophy of Science', Popper is known for his rejection of the classical inductivist views on the scientific method in favour of empirical falsification. According to Popper, a theory in the empirical sciences can never be proven, but it can be falsified, meaning that it can (and should) be scrutinised with decisive experiments. Popper was opposed to the classical justificationist account of knowledge, which he replaced with 'critical rationalism'. This approach, however, seems to ignore probability in the field of knowledge.

In political discourse, he is known for his vigorous defence of liberal democracy and the principles of social criticism that he believed made a flourishing open society possible.

In thinking about knowledge Popper famously proposed three worlds: World One, being the physical world, or physical states; World Two, being the world of mind, or mental states, ideas and perceptions; and World Three, being the body of human knowledge expressed in its manifold forms, or the products of the Second World made manifest in the materials of the First World (i.e., books, papers, paintings, symphonies, and all the products of the human mind). World Three, he argued, was the product of individual human beings in exactly the same sense that an animal's path is the product of individual animals, and thus has an existence and is evolution independent of any individually known subjects. The influence of World Three, in his view, on the individual human mind (World Two) is at least as strong as the influence of World One. In other words, the knowledge held by a given individual mind owes at least as much to the total, accumulated, wealth of human knowledge made manifest, comparable to the world of direct experience. As such, the growth of human knowledge could be said to be a function of the independent evolution of World Three.

Many contemporary philosophers, such as Daniel Dennett, have not embraced Popper's Three World conjecture, mostly due to its resemblance to mind–body dualism.

Another way to look at this is to note that Popper's third world just comprises many elements of his first world to which we can attribute a higher probability of being true. This is because, when we each build our mental concepts of the physical world, we can compare them with other people's ideas, either directly or via books etc. and this increases our confidence in them.

Thomas Kuhn (1922 – 1996)

Kuhn was an American philosopher of science whose 1962 book *The Structure of Scientific Revolutions* was influential in both academic and popular circles, introducing the term paradigm shift, which has since become an English-language idiom.

Kuhn made several claims concerning the progress of scientific knowledge: that scientific fields undergo periodic "paradigm shifts" rather than solely progressing in a linear and continuous way, and that these paradigm shifts open up new approaches to understanding what scientists would never have considered valid before; and that the notion of scientific truth, at any given moment, cannot be established solely by objective criteria but is defined by a consensus of a scientific community.

There is a criticism that his account of science from The Structure of Scientific Revolutions results in relativism. Kuhn attempted to address this but never completely succeeded. Years after the publication of *The Structure of Scientific Revolutions* Kuhn dropped the concept of a paradigm and began to focus on the semantic aspects of scientific theories. In particular he focuses on the taxonomic structure of scientific terms. As a consequence, a scientific revolution is not defined as a 'change of paradigm' anymore, but rather as a change in the taxonomic structure of the theoretical language of science.

Apart from dropping the concept of a paradigm, Kuhn also began to look at the process of scientific specialisation. In a scientific revolution,

45

Other Ideas in Recent Western Philosophy

Introduction

A number of other, more recent, philosophers and their ideas are often referred to in philosophical papers and discussions. The intention here is just to give a brief summary of some of the most cited ones together with any relevant criticisms.

Karl Popper (1902 – 1994)

Mainly noted as the initiator of the discipline of 'The Philosophy of Science', Popper is known for his rejection of the classical inductivist views on the scientific method in favour of empirical falsification. According to Popper, a theory in the empirical sciences can never be proven, but it can be falsified, meaning that it can (and should) be scrutinised with decisive experiments. Popper was opposed to the classical justificationist account of knowledge, which he replaced with 'critical rationalism'. This approach, however, seems to ignore probability in the field of knowledge.

In political discourse, he is known for his vigorous defence of liberal democracy and the principles of social criticism that he believed made a flourishing open society possible.

In thinking about knowledge Popper famously proposed three worlds: World One, being the physical world, or physical states; World Two, being the world of mind, or mental states, ideas and perceptions; and World Three, being the body of human knowledge expressed in its manifold forms, or the products of the Second World made manifest in the materials of the First World (i.e., books, papers, paintings, symphonies, and all the products of the human mind). World Three, he argued, was the product of individual human beings in exactly the same sense that an animal's path is the product of individual animals, and thus has an existence and is evolution independent of any individually known subjects. The influence of World Three, in his view, on the individual human mind (World Two) is at least as strong as the influence of World One. In other words, the knowledge held by a given individual mind owes at least as much to the total, accumulated, wealth of human knowledge made manifest, comparable to the world of direct experience. As such, the growth of human knowledge could be said to be a function of the independent evolution of World Three.

Many contemporary philosophers, such as Daniel Dennett, have not embraced Popper's Three World conjecture, mostly due to its resemblance to mind–body dualism.

Another way to look at this is to note that Popper's third world just comprises many elements of his first world to which we can attribute a higher probability of being true. This is because, when we each build our mental concepts of the physical world, we can compare them with other people's ideas, either directly or via books etc. and this increases our confidence in them.

Thomas Kuhn (1922 – 1996)

Kuhn was an American philosopher of science whose 1962 book *The Structure of Scientific Revolutions* was influential in both academic and popular circles, introducing the term paradigm shift, which has since become an English-language idiom.

Kuhn made several claims concerning the progress of scientific knowledge: that scientific fields undergo periodic "paradigm shifts" rather than solely progressing in a linear and continuous way, and that these paradigm shifts open up new approaches to understanding what scientists would never have considered valid before; and that the notion of scientific truth, at any given moment, cannot be established solely by objective criteria but is defined by a consensus of a scientific community.

There is a criticism that his account of science from The Structure of Scientific Revolutions results in relativism. Kuhn attempted to address this but never completely succeeded. Years after the publication of *The Structure of Scientific Revolutions* Kuhn dropped the concept of a paradigm and began to focus on the semantic aspects of scientific theories. In particular he focuses on the taxonomic structure of scientific terms. As a consequence, a scientific revolution is not defined as a 'change of paradigm' anymore, but rather as a change in the taxonomic structure of the theoretical language of science.

Apart from dropping the concept of a paradigm, Kuhn also began to look at the process of scientific specialisation. In a scientific revolution, a new paradigm (or a new taxonomy) replaces the old one; by contrast, specialisation leads to a proliferation of new specialties and disciplines. This attention to the proliferation of specialties would make Kuhn's model less 'revolutionary' and more 'evolutionary'.

Willard Quine (1908 – 2000)

Willard Van Orman Quine was an American philosopher who mainly worked in theoretical philosophy and logic. He is perhaps best known for his arguments against Logical Empiricism, in particular against its use of the analytic-synthetic distinction.

In the 1930s and 40s, discussions with Rudolf Carnap (a Logical Positivist of the Vienna Circle) and others, led Quine to doubt the tenability of the distinction between "analytic" statements (those true simply by the meanings of their words, such as "All bachelors are unmarried") and "synthetic" statements (those true or false by virtue of facts about the world).

In 1951 Quine published a paper entitled ***Two Dogmas of Empiricism*** and this paper has been widely cited ever since. The paper is an attack on two central aspects of the logical positivists' philosophy: the first being the analytic–synthetic distinction, and the second being reductionism (the theory that each meaningful statement gets its meaning from some logical construction of terms that refers exclusively to immediate experience).

Quine concluded his "*Two Dogmas of Empiricism*" as follows:

> As an empiricist I continue to think of the conceptual scheme of science as a tool, ultimately, for predicting future experience in the light of past experience. Physical objects are conceptually imported into the situation as convenient intermediaries not by definition in terms of experience, but simply as irreducible posits comparable, epistemologically, to the gods of Homer .... For my part I do, qua lay physicist, believe in physical objects and not in Homer's gods; and I consider it a scientific error to believe otherwise. But in point of epistemological footing, the physical objects and the gods differ only in degree and not in kind. Both sorts of entities enter our conceptions only as cultural posits.

An Introduction to Philosophy

The terms analytic and synthetic are used to put knowledge into different categories based on the language used to describe the world. This approach tends to try and analyse meaning by looking at language. Both Russell and (early) Wittgenstein spent years trying to put together some form of algebra around language so that statements could be proved correct of false, but they never succeeded. The later Wittgenstein turned away from this approach. This terminology is also complicated by the inclusion of Kant's controversial 'synthetic *a priori*' category of knowledge.

It is easy to become bogged down in language, definitions and meaning. For all these reasons it might be best to avoid these terms altogether and instead use categories that correspond to how the knowledge is obtained. This refers back to chapter 3 on Epistemology which defines knowledge as being Deductive (mainly maths and logic) or Inductive (everything else we consider to be knowledge). Deductive knowledge would be 100% correct, Inductive less than 100% but can get very close (e.g. if I drop something I expect it to fall.) Inductive knowledge is how we as individuals come to understand the world, and (as Quine understood) this occurs via the building of concepts through our experience of the world. Induction is also the basis of all science, and here it becomes much stronger, with people working together and checking each other's results.

John Rawls (1921 – 2002)

John Rawls was an American moral and political philosopher in the liberal tradition. He has often been described as one of the most influential political philosophers of the 20th century.

His 1971 book ***A Theory of Justice*** is a work of political philosophy and ethics, in which he attempts to provide a moral theory alternative to Utilitarianism, and which addresses the problem of distributive justice (the socially just distribution of goods in a society). The theory uses an updated form of Kantian philosophy and a variant form of conventional social contract theory. Rawls's theory of justice is fully a political theory of justice as opposed to other forms of justice discussed in other disciplines and contexts.

In his 1985 essay "***Justice as Fairness***", and a subsequent book under the same title, Rawls further developed his two central principles for his discussion of justice. Together, they dictate that society should be structured so that the greatest possible amount of liberty is given to its members, limited only by the notion that the liberty of any one member shall not infringe upon that of any other member. Secondly, inequalities – either social or economic – are only to be allowed if the worst off will be better off than they might be under an equal distribution. Finally, if there is such a beneficial inequality, this inequality should not make it harder for those without resources to occupy positions of power – for instance, public office.

Rawls's argument for these principles of social justice uses a thought experiment called the "**original position**," (also known as "**the veil of ignorance**"). In the original position, you are asked to consider which principles you would select for the basic structure of society, but you must select as if you had no knowledge ahead of time what position you would end up having in that society. This choice is made from behind a veil of ignorance, which prevents you from knowing your ethnicity, social status, gender and, crucially, your individual idea of how to lead a good life. Ideally, this would force participants to select principles impartially and rationally.

It's a good idea, but in practice, the people designing those systems are probably fairly rich and powerful and are probably being lobbied by the same. Politics is always about compromise. Indeed, there have been a number of criticisms of Rawls' idea based on the impossibility of people ignoring their own beliefs and convictions.

Having said that however, Rawls' ideas of justice and fairness are well received, and he does have the unusual distinction among contemporary political philosophers of being frequently cited by the courts of law in both the United States and Canada.

Richard Rorty (1931 – 2007)

Rorty was an American philosopher who advocated a novel form of American Pragmatism (sometimes called neopragmatism) in which scientific and philosophical methods form merely a set of contingent "vocabularies" that people abandon or adopt over time according to social conventions and usefulness.

Rorty believed that abandoning representationalist accounts of knowledge and language would lead to a state of mind he referred to as "ironism", in which people become completely aware of the contingency of their placement in history and of their philosophical vocabulary.

In his major work, *Philosophy and the Mirror of Nature* (1979), Rorty argues that the central problems of modern epistemology depend upon a picture of the mind as trying to faithfully represent (or "mirror") a mind-independent, external reality. If we give up this metaphor, then we see that the entire enterprise of foundationalist epistemology is misguided. A foundationalist believes that in order to avoid the regress inherent in claiming that all beliefs are justified by other beliefs, some beliefs must be self-justifying and form the foundations to all knowledge.

This fits with both Quine's critique of the distinction between analytic and synthetic sentences, and Kuhn's account of the standard phases of the progress of disciplines, oscillating through normal and abnormal periods.

Rorty abandons specifically analytic modes of explanation in favour of narrative pastiche in order to develop an alternative conceptual vocabulary. This schema is based on the belief that there is no worthwhile theory of truth, aside from a non-epistemic semantic one (the theory in the philosophy of language which holds that truth is a property of sentences).

Rorty is among the most widely discussed and controversial of contemporary philosophers. His neopragmatism has been criticised by some as being both anti-philosophical and anti-intellectual, and by others for his rejection of the idea that science can depict the world. That being said however, it cannot be ignored that language does, to a large extent, shape our view of the world; remember Wittgenstein, for instance, and his belief that the meaning of words is best understood as their use within a given 'language-game'.

Robert Nozick (1938 – 2002)

Nozick was an American libertarian philosopher, best known for his books ***Anarchy, State, and Utopia*** (1974) and ***Philosophical Explanations*** (1981), in which he argues against Rawls' theories of justice and fairness in society.

Libertarianism is a political philosophy and movement that upholds liberty as a core principle. Libertarians seek to maximize autonomy and political freedom, emphasizing free association, freedom of choice, individualism, and voluntary association. Libertarians share a scepticism of authority and state power, but some of them diverge on the scope of their opposition to existing economic and political systems.

Nozick concludes that Rawls fails to consider how wealth is acquired, and therefore the injustice of taking someone's earnings and giving people who did not earn it. Doing so violates the rights to life, liberty and property of the people from whom it is being taken; he argues that it is wrong to harm people without their consent.

Nozick's ideas have attracted a lot of criticisms, mainly along the lines that he does not clearly define the premises his theories are built on; it is not clear that people who earn a lot actually deserve everything they earn; and he seems to propose nothing to help those less fortunate in society.

John Searle (1932 –)

John Searle is an American philosopher. He was Professor Emeritus of the Philosophy of Mind and Language and Professor of the Graduate School at the University of California, Berkeley, and is widely noted for his contributions to the philosophy of language, philosophy of mind, and social philosophy.

His approach to an understanding of consciousness is to argue that there is an aspect of consciousness that can never be explained via third party objective science, in effect endorsing the idea of the 'hard problem of consciousness', a phrase coined by Australian philosopher David Chalmers. Searle thinks there are certain phenomena (including all conscious experiences) that are ontologically subjective, i.e. can only exist as subjective experience.

He extends this view to argue against the possibility of a conscious artificial intelligence, and as part of that argument he created his famous **Chinese Room** thought experiment which goes as follows: -

> Searle supposes that he is in a closed room and has a book written in English that has instructions of what to do with Chinese characters, along with sufficient papers, pencils, erasers, and filing cabinets. Searle could receive Chinese characters through a slot in the door, process them according to the book's instructions, and produce Chinese characters as output. If the output passes the Turing test, it follows, says Searle, that he would do so as well, simply by following the instructions manually.
>
> Searle asserts that there is no essential difference between the roles of a computer performing the task and himself in the experiment. Each simply follows a program, step-by-step, producing a behaviour which is then interpreted by the user as demonstrating intelligent conversation. However, Searle himself would not be able to understand the conversation. ("I don't speak a word of Chinese, he points out.) Therefore, he argues, it

follows that the computer would not be able to understand the conversation either.

Although the Chinese Room argument was originally presented in reaction to the statements of artificial intelligence researchers, philosophers have come to consider it as an important part of the discussion around the philosophy of mind. It is a challenge to both functionalism and the computational theory of mind, and is related to such questions as the mind–body problem, the problem of other minds, the symbol-grounding problem, and the hard problem of consciousness.

These views have been strongly criticised as a) being a return to some form of dualism, and b) as defining the problem of consciousness as being unsolvable from the start. Probably the most effective of these criticisms are from the philosophers Douglas Hofstadter and Daniel Dennett.

Also, the philosopher Jack Copeland points out that the Chinese Room argument commits the fallacy of composition. Searle concludes that there is no understanding of Chinese because no individual part, including the human inside the room, understands Chinese. But the fact that individual parts lack a property does not mean that the whole lacks that property.

Thomas Nagel (1937 –)

Thomas Nagel is an American philosopher and a University Professor of Philosophy and Law, Emeritus, at New York University, where he taught from 1980 to 2016. His main areas of philosophical interest are legal philosophy, political philosophy, and ethics.

He is well known for his critique of material reductionist accounts of the mind, and this was most clearly expounded in his famous, and often cited, essay *What Is It Like to Be a Bat?* (1974). This endorses the notion of the 'hard problem of consciousness' by observing that even if we understood everything there is to know about how a bat's brain works, we would still never know what it's like to be a bat.

As with Searle's Chinese Room, there have been numerous criticisms of Nagel's ideas. These are, however, not simplistic arguments, and a full understanding of the issues involved requires almost book level analysis of how the mind works. One of the best, and most accessible, of these is Daniel Dennett's 1991 book *Consciousness Explained*.

Part Three

Eastern Philosophy

This section of the book provides an introduction to the field of Eastern Philosophy.

This is in no way meant to be either comprehensive or detailed. It is provided as a complement or counterbalance to Western Philosophy, and hopefully includes enough of an overview to provide a flavour of this different perspective.

46

Introduction to Eastern Philosophy

> *Accept what is in front of you without wanting the situation to be other than what it is. Study the natural order of things and work with them rather than against them, for to try to change what is only sets up resistance.*
>
> **The Philosophy of Lao Tzu**

Overview

First a note about the term 'Eastern Philosophy'. This is used, not as a definitive classification of one set of ideas, but more as a way of highlighting a difference from the Western variety, even though there are some overlaps and similarities. One would expect similarities; we all live in the same world and have the same problems to face, things such as survival and security, politics, and interpersonal relationships. Perhaps the main differences are just ones due to different cultural developments providing different histories, different outlooks, and different ways of thinking.

The term does, of course, have a geographical element, with Western Philosophy originating in Greece and spreading mainly in Europe and North America. It should be noted too that there are other non-Western philosophies based in Africa, South America, native North America, and Aboriginal Australia. But the term Eastern Philosophy is usually applied to India, China, and other Asian countries such as Japan and Korea; it can also be applied to parts of the Middle East. That said, although the term is being used here fairly loosely in a general sense, a few specific individual philosophies will be looked at in a bit more detail in the following chapters.

Eastern philosophy in general has a very different feel to it than the Western variety. There is less focus on science and less on cold logical analysis, instead it is usually more centred around how best to live one's life, how to relate to nature, and on our relationships with both each other and our community. Another difference is to do with religion. In the West, although early philosophy included religion, philosophy and theology soon became different areas of thought. But in the East philosophy and religion are more closely intertwined. This book is, however, a book on philosophy, and so what is covered in the next few chapters is only (as far as possible) those branches of Eastern philosophies that can be considered as philosophical systems in their own right as opposed to being systems of religion. This distinction is perhaps one only seen through Western eyes that are more used to dissection and classification, so it should be kept in mind that the reality is one of many overlaps and intertwining cultural perspectives.

One interesting historical aspect of philosophy in general is that it seems to have appeared around the same time in both the East and the West (give or take a few hundred years). Note that Homo sapiens as a species have been largely genetically distinct for about 200,000 to 300,000 years, yet the earliest philosophies we know about are only 2,500 to 3,000 years old. The Upanishads, for example, are a body of morality stories from India that appeared between 800 and 600 BC. This means that we only know about any philosophical thinking from about the last 1% of our history as a species, 99% of any of our philosophical thinking is unknown to us!

Several reasons have been suggested for this, not least being the absence of written documents of any source. Also, maybe it was not until farming of some kind developed which allowed a more settled type of existence together with more leisure time and larger communities where ideas could be exchanged and added to. Trade with other communities would also lead to a mixing of ideas.

Customs and rituals bind communities together, and ways of thinking become culturally inheritable. We are curious about the world we find ourselves in, and we are nothing if not story tellers. All cultures around the world have their origin stories, gods are invented to explain natural events, and superstitions arise, together with rituals to please or appease the gods. Again, this binds communities together and becomes incorporated with the authoritarian control of the society.

Much of these origins are lost to the depths of time, but it seems that around two and a half thousand years ago, in both the East and the West, a number of more comprehensive and systemised distinct philosophies emerged, initially incorporating religious ideas, and each displaying large aspects of their cultural heritage.

Indeed, it is one of the most astounding facts of human history that three different cultures produced, within about one hundred years of each

Introduction to Eastern Philosophy

other, four unique philosophical geniuses, each of whom went on to influence culture and philosophy, throughout the world, for the next 2,500 years. These were; Socrates in Greece, Lao Tzu and Confucius in China, and the Buddha in India.

The first two parts of this book covered the development of Western philosophical thinking, and this will be returned to in part four, but here we look at Eastern philosophy. We start with a few general Eastern concepts or outlooks, and then we will look in a little more detail at three specific Eastern based philosophies, Taoism, Confucianism, and Buddhism.

General Concepts

The following ideas are not exclusively Eastern, they do not define Eastern philosophy, and they are not all involved in any individual Eastern philosophy. They are just presented here as part of the cultural background to Eastern philosophy, and to provide a counterpoint to Western modes of thinking. Also, the following ideas are not definitive, black and white differences between East and West, they are just subtle biases in the spectrum of each concept.

The Self

In the West we value individuality, and, as individuals, we are almost defined by our differences. We talk about the freedom of the individual, individual rights, and the rights of man. These individual rights are often the basis for our laws: think of Magna Carta in England or The Bill of Rights in America. When we talk of the 'Social Contract' it is in terms of giving up some of our individual rights in order to be stronger together, and when we do something for the community we speak in terms of making sacrifices.

In the East, the perspective is different. People are virtually defined by their family and their community; individuality is almost frowned upon. The state is there to look after you, you owe everything to the state, and it is your duty to do whatever the state tells you to do. This is obviously an exaggeration and there is tension for the individual to prosper within any state requirements.

These ideas on the self have become incorporated into Eastern philosophies, with some of them aiming to banish the self completely, and others aiming at an understanding that the self is part of a universal self, or of us being 'at one' with the universe or nature. The idea (in Western terminology) is the dissolution of the ego, and the recognition that all disappointments only come from having wants and desires in the first place. If you recognise this then you accept what is, you go with nature rather than raging against it.

Harmony

The Western notion of harmony stems back to Plato and Pythagoras, with the idea of everything being in order in the universe, being in its right place, and being in the best ratio with each other. Indian thought is on the same lines, but the Chinese idea of harmony is different, it stems back to Confucian thinking, and it permeates Chinese society today. Here the idea is like a balance of opposites, yin and yang, black with white.

One thing on its own is out of balance, out of harmony, two or more things, combining to make a whole, creates harmony, even if the two things involved are opposite to each other. And this is reflected in the way the Chinese live; again, the idea of the individual with their own needs and wants is inharmonious, when people work together, both in a family and in society, then that is seen as striving for harmony. This is an important concept in Chinese society, and it is a strong element of their philosophies.

Karma

The superstitious and simple element to this is the idea that any immoral deed done in this life will bring you back in the next life as a lower being via reincarnation. The concept of karma however, which originated in India but is now quite widespread in the East, is often much more complex and subtle in its use than the basic superstitious version.

Different schools of thought and different religions (e.g. Hinduism, Buddhism, Jainism, Sikhism, Taoism, Shinto, etc) all have slightly different definitions or interpretations of the concept, indeed there is an ongoing debate regarding whether karma is a theory, a model, a paradigm, a metaphor, or a metaphysical stance.

Basically, the word karma means action, work, or deed, but there is also an element of cause and effect to it. By acting with good intent one builds up an accumulation of good karma, and bad intent builds up bad karma for you, and this then influences your future. In a less religious, less fatalistic, and more philosophical interpretation, we get the idea that if we act selfishly and badly to others this might well both influence our general outlook on life to be cynical and invite retaliation against us, giving us a bad future. And conversely, if we act well to others this will bring its own rewards. As with most concepts, there is no real definition, but people who use it seem to know what they mean when they employ it! [Note: - See the chapter on concepts in part four of this book].

Enlightenment

In the West, the term 'The Enlightenment' is applied to the period of European history, which started in the eighteenth century, in which philosophy finally split from religion and developed its understanding of the natural world based on rationality and scientific investigations.

In Eastern philosophy, however, 'enlightenment' is the English translation used for several different but related more spiritual concepts. Most notably the Buddhist terms: -

- **Bodhi**: literally meaning "to have woken up and understood".
- **Kensho**: a term from the Zen tradition usually translated as "seeing one's (true) nature".
- **Satori**: awakening, "comprehension; understanding".

And related terms from Asian religions such as: -

- **Moksha** in Hinduism: Liberation, or freedom from the cycle of death and rebirth, or freedom from ignorance through self-realization, self-actualization, and self-knowledge.
- **Kevala Jnana** in Jainism: complete understanding or supreme wisdom.

Translations are difficult things, using a word from one language as a translation for a word in another often does not convey the full meaning. Words do not stand alone; they have a whole baggage of related concepts, alternative uses, and cultural history. This will be the case in both the language being translated from and the language being translated into. The only way to gain more understanding of a foreign concept is to read as much about it as you can from a variety of different sources.

In the West, the word philosophy means 'love of wisdom', and this is usually thought of as being rational and basing knowledge on shared evidence. In the East, enlightenment is also seen as the goal of achieving wisdom, but this is more in terms of an individual losing their ego so as to understand the world as it actually is, and hence to accept it as such without wishing it to be different.

Impermanence

An Introduction to Philosophy

In the West we feel security in our daily lives, and if change occurs it is often a shock and is felt as a loss of something. Change, however, is the one thing that we know will happen, it's virtually a law of nature however much we try to resist or ignore it.

Eastern culture seems to recognise this, and its philosophies embrace the fact that things change, everything is impermanent, both within our lives and indeed our life itself. This is another aspect of accepting what is. The Japanese tradition, for instance, of almost a pilgrimage to visit a cherry orchard in spring to see the cherry blossom, is not just about the beauty of the blossom itself, it is also a reminder of the transient nature of beauty, and indeed of everything, as the wind blows the blossom from the trees. The seasons change, everything changes, and mortality is a fact of life.

A Final Word of Introduction

The few general concepts outlined above are just some of the ideas that pervade Eastern culture and that are enshrined into Eastern philosophy. It is said that learning a different language actually changes how we perceive the world, the same is true for learning about different cultures.

As noted above, Eastern Philosophy in general is more focused on ethics, on how to live one's life, and on our relationships with nature, with family and with community. It is also much more intertwined with religion than Western philosophy. That being said, the next three chapters of this book look in a little more detail at three of the Eastern philosophies that have perhaps the least religious aspects to them, having, as they do, more of a philosophical outlook as their main component.

47

Taoism

Introduction

Taoism or Daoism is a philosophical tradition of Chinese origin which emphasizes living in harmony with the Tao (the 'Way'). The Tao is a fundamental idea in most Chinese philosophical schools; in Taoism, however, it denotes the principle that is the source, pattern, and substance of everything that exists.

Taoism differs from Confucianism by not emphasizing rigid rituals and social order, but it is similar in the sense that it is a teaching about the various disciplines for achieving "perfection" by becoming one with the unplanned rhythms of the universe called "the way" or "Tao".

Taoist ethics vary depending on the particular school, but in general they tend to emphasize something called "wu wei" (action without intention), along with "naturalness", simplicity, spontaneity, and the Three Treasures: - "compassion", "frugality" and "humility".

History

The exact origins of Taoism are disputed and are probably lost to the depths of time, but the figure most associated with it is Lao Tzu (sometimes referred to as Laozi). He is a semi-legendary figure usually portrayed as a 6th-century B.C. contemporary of Confucius, but some modern historians think he might have lived during the Warring States period of the 4th century B.C.

Lao Tzu is considered to be the author of the main text of Taoism called the Tao Te Ching, although this too may have been added to over the years. This ancient book, as well as being the basis of Taoism, has influenced culture, philosophy, and religion throughout history in the East with many incoming philosophies and religions being interpreted through the words and concepts in its text.

Initially in China, Taoists were thought of as hermits or recluses who did not participate in political life, but over time a number of different schools of Taoism emerged, and at different times became adopted by the then ruling Chinese dynasty.

An Introduction to Philosophy

Today Taoism is one of five religions recognised by the People's Republic of China, it also has many millions of followers in Taiwan, and in other countries round the world. This book, however, is about philosophy, and so the populist religious aspects of Taoism today will be set aside in favour of just looking at the basic philosophical ideas of Taoism.

Philosophy

One of the main ideas in Taoism is the acceptance of what is in front of you without wanting the situation to be different. The natural order of things should be studied so that you can work with it rather than against it, because if you try to change what is, that only sets up resistance.

Other ideas include: treating all men as equals however they behave; when acting we should stop trying, then what we are doing will come more easily; understanding comes when we have a still and open mind; and we should serve whoever stands before us without any thought for ourselves.

The Tao, or the way or the path, is the universe in balance, it embodies the harmony of opposites; there would be no love without hate, no light without dark, no male without female.

The concept of a personal deity is foreign to Taoism, as is the concept of the creation of the universe. A Taoist seeks answers to life's problems through inner meditation and outer observation. The most efficient and effective 'way' to overcome problems is by non-contention or yielding, which is not the same as submission or capitulation, but exercising control by taking the 'way' of least resistance.

This can be seen in the discipline of T'ai Chi which is a kind of meditation in movement practiced by many in China and elsewhere. T'ai Chi exemplifies the Taoist principle known as wu-wei, literally translated as "not doing", but its proper meaning is to act without forcing – to move in accordance to the flow of nature.

The main text of Taoism, the Tao Te Ching, is a series of 81 very short poems talking about paradoxes, about the unknown, about nature. There are good English translations, but it must be remembered that translations are difficult at the best of times and so translations of paradoxes (which include, puns, triple meanings and plays on words) are even more problematic.

Here is one translation of the first verse of the Tao Te Ching: -

The Tao that can be told is not the eternal Tao.
The name that can be named is not the eternal Name.

Taoism

> The nameless is the beginning of heaven and earth.
> The named is the mother of ten thousand things.
> Ever desireless, one can see the mystery.
> Ever desiring, one can see the manifestations.
> These two spring from the same source but differ in name;
>   this appears as darkness.
> The gate to all mystery.

And here is another translation of the same verse: -

> The tao that can be told is not the eternal Tao.
> The name that can be named is not the eternal Name.
> The unnamable is the eternally real.
> Naming is the origin of all particular things.
> Free from desire, you realize the mystery.
> Caught in desire, you see only the manifestations.
> Yet mystery and manifestations arise from the same source.
> This source is called darkness.
> Darkness within darkness. The gateway to all understanding.

In the original Chinese the word Tao is repeated three times in the first line, the first as a noun meaning 'the way', the second as a verb meaning to speak or express, and the third as a noun again but this time alongside a character meaning 'always' or 'natural'. Even in the Chinese there are a number of different interpretations; ambiguities and double meanings abound.

Also, Chinese pictogram characters often actually look like stylised representations of things, so further meanings might be implicit. And this is what poetry does, in any language, it approaches its subject and its meanings obliquely, it uses double meaning, any or all of which might be intended. It induces in the reader different ways of looking at something based on stimulating tangent ideas from the reader's own experiences.

If we look again at this first verse, we see that the verse itself is trying to say that language is not the truth, if you can name a thing and say 'this is it' then you are wrong! Experiencing a thing is more real than naming it, names or words are only defined in terms of other names or words, and this multiplies to 'ten thousand things' (the Chinese way of saying many or all). If you put a name to something it puts a barrier between you and the thing, it fools you into thinking you understand it.

The verse then talks about our wants and desires; these too get in the way of experiencing reality. If we can let go of our 'self' we would get closer to the mystery. But it goes on to say that our desires spring from the same source as the mystery; this is the jin and yang of life. If we can

An Introduction to Philosophy

both let go of the self to be nearer to pure experience while at the same time be aware of the self, its wants and desires, then this is the gateway to understanding.

The 81 verses of the Tao Te Ching all use these ideas: of opposites creating harmony; letting go of the self; ambiguities and double meanings as a way of inducing understanding; and non-action producing action through working with nature instead of trying to control it.

Here is verse 48 for instance: -

> In the pursuit of learning, every day something is acquired.
> In the pursuit of Tao, every day something is dropped.
>
> Less and less is done
> Until non-action is achieved.
> When nothing is done, nothing is left undone.
>
> The world is ruled by letting things take their course.
> It cannot be ruled by interfering.

And here is verse 11: -

> Thirty spokes share the wheel's hub;
> It is the centre hole that makes it useful.
> Shape clay into a vessel;
> It is the space within that makes it useful.
> Cut doors and windows for a room;
> It is the holes which make it useful.
> Therefore profit comes from what is there;
> Usefulness from what is not there.

There are some beautiful insights and some real philosophical understandings here. The combination of T'ai Chi and the Tao Te Ching provides a balance in life, a quietness, and perhaps a re-evaluation of what's important. How far we can ignore our self, and our use of language, might be problematical, there is no such thing as pure perception, perception involves processing by the brain, but the attempt itself is certainly rewarding.

48

Confucianism

Introduction

Confucianism, also known as Ruism, is a system of thought and behaviour originating in ancient China. It has been variously described as tradition, a philosophy, a religion, a humanistic or rationalistic religion, a way of governing, or simply a way of life.

With particular emphasis on the importance of the family, and on social and political harmony, rather than on otherworldly sources of spiritual values, the core of Confucianism is humanistic. So, whereas Taoism was inward looking for the enlightenment of the individual, Confucianism is outward looking for a peaceful and happy society.

Many Chinese classical works have been attributed to Confucius, but most scholars agree that the best representation of his ideas is a book called *Analects* which is a collection of notes and quotations written down by his disciples and compiled into a book after his death. The reality is probably more complicated however, and it is thought that some chapters towards the end of the book may well have been added at a later date or dates.

History

Confucius (551 B.C. – 479 B.C.) was born in the state of Lu (now Shandong) China. He was raised by his mother in hardship and poverty because his father died when he was three. When he was 15, he decided to be a scholar. He married at 19 and started a career in government, hoping to put his ideas on governance to good use, and he rose to the position of chief of police in the local Department of Justice. He left after a short time, however, in order to devote himself to teaching.

He then spent several years travelling round China with a following of students. He tried but failed to get local rulers to implement his political ideas, and so eventually he settled to his teaching and to editing books. These books have become known as the "Confucian Classics" and include *The Book of Poetry*, *The Book of History*, and *The Book of Changes* (better known as the *I Ching*).

An Introduction to Philosophy

As a teacher he was a great success, over three thousand people studied with him, many becoming respected scholars in their own right. His teachings spread widely in China and the Far East, and were adopted as a national ideology during the Han dynasty. In modern times Confucian movements still exist but during the Cultural Revolution his ideas were attacked by the Communist Party as being too much like traditional servitude.

Philosophy

The *Analects*, of which two main versions exist, are split into 20 (or 22 chapters, depending on the version) with each chapter comprising a selection of numbered short paragraphs, stories, or aphorisms. Each chapter has a title which in some cases (but not all) indicates a general theme of the chapter, but the themes of adjacent chapters are unrelated to each other. Interestingly, chapter ten contains detailed descriptions of Confucius's behaviours in various daily activities, quite a unique picture of the times.

Despite the fragmentary appearance of the *Analects*, Confucius's philosophy is clearly held together by a single key concept called *ren* (or *jen*) in Chinese. This term appears over 100 times in the text. Again, we are faced with the difficulties of translation, any given word in either language may well be used in different ways at different times, and so not all variant uses of the word in one language would match all the variant uses of the concept in the other language. Having said that however, the surrounding text will often give more context to the usage implied at any given time.

The usual translation for *ren* is 'love', and in Confucian terms it means 'love of man'. This is not a romantic love, as celebrated by poets, and it is not love in any religious sense, it is a humanistic love based on natural feelings, but importantly, also cultivated through education. Another translation used for *ren* in some parts of the *Analects*, is 'a general and all-encompassing state of virtue'.

A second significant concept is *li,* which is to do with rituals and social norms; it is through *li* that *ren* is attained. Associated with *li* is *yi* which is righteousness or proper character. Through rituals, one practices the habit of expressing one's cultivated feelings at the appropriate time and place.

Analects Chapter four, paragraph 10: -

> A superior person's attitude towards the society is neither one of a conformist nor one of a rebel but one in accordance with yi.

Education is the path to a peaceful, ordered society. This is doubly true for a ruler, and, as such, he becomes an example for all his people. Confucius argued that the best government is one that rules through *li* (rights and rituals) and people's natural morality, not by using bribery and coercion.

> "If the people be led by laws, and uniformity sought to be given them by punishments, they will try to avoid the punishment, but have no sense of shame. If they be led by virtue, and uniformity sought to be given them by the rules of propriety, they will have the sense of the shame, and moreover will become good."
>
> From ***The Great Learning*** (one of the 'Four Books' in Confucianism)

The idea of educating people through *li* (rights, rituals, and moral codes) might be thought of as imposing conformity and restricting individuality. Confucian philosophy, however, sees people not as isolated individuals, rather as individuals who only exist in terms of their relationships to others and to their community, and people need to realise this in order to fully develop.

Analects Chapter 10, paragraph 3: -

> He who does not know *li* cannot establish himself (attain self-realisation).

The sage-king governs without restrictive laws, instead he uses *ren* (love of people) and makes himself an ethical model for his people.

Analects Chapter two, paragraph 1: -

> ... one governs with morality, as if he were the Northern Star, staying in his position, surrounded by all other planets.

The best form of government is via *wuwei* (non-action). This is achieved through education, and moral education starts in the family: first you learn to love and respect your parents and siblings; then you can learn to love and respect your community. Ethics is at the heart of Confucianism, and this is true even in business.

Analects Chapter seven, paragraph 15: -

> The attainment of wealth and honour through the violation of *yi* is as remote from me as clouds floating in the sky.

Confucius teaches that if people attain *ren* (love of others) through li (rituals and social norms) then society will become free from violence and crimes. There is even a version of the 'golden rule' in the Analects (treat others as you have them treat you).

Analects Chapter 15, paragraph 24: -

> Zi Gong [a disciple] asked: "Is there any one word that could guide a person throughout life?"
> The Master replied: "How about 'reciprocity'! Never impose on others what you would not choose for yourself."

His ethical and moral system relied on cultivating people's natural empathy for understanding others rather than any imposed laws or divinely ordained rules. He asserts that virtue is a mean between extremes. For example, the properly generous person gives the right amount—not too much and not too little.

The key to his philosophy is *ren* (human-heartedness), it should be a part of everything in life. For example: courage with *ren* is real courage, not just bravery; justice with *ren* is humane justice, not just justice; and wisdom with *ren* is being wise, not just being smart. The cultivation of *ren* is never ending, it is a continuous process of struggle. In Western terms this is 'Virtue Ethics', i.e. instead of using ethical rules to live by, one cultivates goodness of character, then good acts will follow.

Influence

The works of Confucius were translated into European languages through the agency of Jesuit missionaries stationed in China. These translations influenced European thinkers of the period, particularly the Deists and other philosophical groups of the Enlightenment.

Confucianism

The German philosopher Gottfried Wilhelm Leibniz was attracted to the philosophy because of its perceived similarity to his own, and the French philosopher Voltaire was also influenced by Confucius, seeing the concept of Confucian rationalism as an alternative to Christian dogma.

> "Confucius has no interest in falsehood; he did not pretend to be prophet; he claimed no inspiration; he taught no new religion; he used no delusions; flattered not the emperor under whom he lived..."
>
> **Voltaire**

49

Buddhism

Introduction

Buddhism today is noted as the world's fourth largest religion (after Christianity, Islam, and Hinduism in order of number of followers). However, it is much closer to philosophy than many other religions. It encompasses a variety of traditions, beliefs and spiritual practices largely based on original teachings attributed to the Buddha (born Siddhartha Gautama in the 5th or 4th century B.C.)

Two major extant branches of Buddhism are generally recognized: Theravada (Pali: "The School of the Elders") and Mahayana (Sanskrit: "The Great Vehicle"). Also, one of the subbranches of the Mahayana school is Zen Buddhism.

The goal of Buddhism is to overcome suffering (duhkha) caused by: - desire; attachment to a static self; and ignorance of the true nature of reality (avidya). Most Buddhist traditions emphasize transcending the individual self through the attainment of Nirvana or by following the path of Buddhahood, ending the cycle of death and rebirth.

History

There are several myths surrounding the Buddha's early life, some of them claiming he was a prince, but it seems likely he was born into a well-to-do family, perhaps around 563 B.C., in a small town in the foothills of the Himalayas. His family name was "Gautama" and he was called Siddhartha, and during his early life he was given a sheltered and scholarly upbringing.

His father's attempt to shelter Siddhartha from suffering in the world was, however, unsuccessful. He became strongly moved by the suffering of hardship, illness, and death, and by the common notion at that time that this suffering is endlessly repeated through the cycle of rebirths. So, as a young man, he left home in a quest to find and understand more about the world, and to find an answer to this endless cycle of suffering.

His journey through Northern India initially led him to two teachers of yogic meditation and he studied with them achieving high levels of

Buddhism

meditative consciousness, but despite his proficiency he became dissatisfied with this as an answer to the suffering in the world. He left them and next practiced ascetic techniques involving severe austerities such as suspension of breathing and extreme fasting. In fact, during this period, he came very close to death. This too he eventually rejected as an answer to suffering in the world.

He finally decided that, to achieve awakening, meditation was the best middle way of moderation between the extremes of self-indulgence and self-mortification. He sat down under a pipal tree (now known as "the Bodhi tree") and meditated all day and night, finally achieving awakening, at which point he became the Buddha or the "Awakened One".

After some deliberation with himself as to whether people were ready for this knowledge, he eventually decided to start teaching others his technique of Dharma meditation and his middle way of achieving awakening via his 'four noble truths' and his 'noble eightfold path'.

Initially he taught his disciples, and they established some monasteries, but Buddhism spread only slowly throughout India until the time of the Mauryan emperor Ashoka (304 B.C. – 232 B.C.), who was a public supporter of the religion. The support of Ashoka and his descendants led to the construction of more temples and to its spread throughout the Maurya Empire and into Central Asia and Sri Lanka. It later spread to China and other parts of the Far East.

At some point, the Mahayana version of Buddhism arose, probably from a strict forest ascetic movement, between the 2nd and 1st century B.C. and this became the dominant version in China and Japan by the 5th century A.D. Over this time a number of different versions of Buddhism emerged throughout India and Asia, including Zen Buddhism, which initially arose in China around the 5th century A.D. and then spread to Japan around the 12th century A.D.

Philosophy

Compassion is the heart of Buddhism, a care for others and a search for a way to alleviate suffering. The question is not "is there a God?" but instead it is "how should we behave?" whether God exists or not. And these problems should be resolved by examination and critical reflection. Buddhism does not require a leader; it just involves following the Buddha's teachings.

It is not a dogma with sacred texts, it is really just a method, a guide to a way of acting and thinking in order to achieve awakening. As it spread through Asia it cross pollinated with other cultures giving several variants, but its outlook is always humanistic and a care for life. While change in the world is inevitable, by gaining wisdom we can affect change and reduce suffering.

The Buddha was looking for a way out of superstition and a way to come out of the endless cycle of birth, pain, and death. And he saw that self-discovery comes from your own experiences and then drawing your own conclusions. All we can know is how we experience the world, and our minds determine what kind of experiences we have.

The world is constantly changing, but we are constantly changing too, therefore a permanent self does not exist. In fact, the idea of a permanent self is the cause of our problems, we become selfish, and this enslaves us. We can, he teaches, overcome suffering by rediscovering our 'non self' nature; liberation comes from within, there is no need for Gods or Heaven. Note here that suffering is not just pain and death, it includes anxieties, disappointments, and depression.

The Buddha recognised, however, that not all people had the time to spend on perfecting his version of Dharma meditation, and so, as a middle way of moderation between the extremes of self-indulgence and self-mortification, he provided another way of achieving awakening via his 'four noble truths' and his 'noble eightfold path'.

He also took the existing eastern concept of Karma, which at the time emphasised rituals to influence the next life, and subtly changed it to be about making individual choices to do good. This took Karma away from the priests and showed that doing good had real consequences in people's lives. It also meant people were less likely to blame the Gods for their suffering; their lot in life is more influenced by their own actions. This teaching had great appeal to all under classes in India, which at the time was heavily divided with the caste system.

The Middle Way

The Buddha proposed a middle way between Eternalism and Annihilationism. The Eternalists, following the Vedic teachings, said that man's true self (atman) is eternal. The Buddha, however, argued that, not only was there no evidence for this, but if it was true it set up a situation where the self was important and therefore contributed to human cravings and wants, and this created suffering.

The Annihilationists, on the other hand, claimed that everything was impermanent and that there was no connection between events, all was chance. Again, the Buddha said this was false, there is obviously such a thing as cause and effect. If the Annihilationists were correct there would be no hope, no cure for any disease and no path to liberation, because everything occurs by chance.

Buddhism

The middle way, he says, is that there is no permanent self because everything changes, but that because of cause and effect we can change ourselves, and this involves his new conception of Karma, that acts have consequences and therefore right acts give a better future.

The Four Noble Truths

1. The truth of pain (duhkha). The clinging and craving to impermanent states and things causes duhkha. This is more than just pain, anxiety, and suffering, it includes the intrinsically unsatisfactory nature of the temporary states and things.
2. The cause of duhkha is craving for things and trying to cling to changing phenomena. This ties us to samsara, the cycle of death and rebirth.
3. Duhkha ceases when craving and clinging cease or are confined. This also means that no more karma is being produced, and rebirth ends.
4. By following the Noble Eightfold Path, one starts to disengage from craving and clinging to the impermanent states and things.

The Noble Eightfold Path

The Noble Eightfold Path comprises: right views; right intention; right speech; right action; right livelihood; right effort; right mindfulness; and right concentration.

These eight headings summarise the more detailed teachings one must follow to detach from cravings and attain peace of mind. The first two, right views and right intention, are about wisdom. The next three, right speech, right action and right livelihood are about morality. And the last three, right effort, right mindfulness, and right concentration, are about awareness. One moves up through these stages, eventually leading to nirvana (a state of perfect quietude, freedom, and highest happiness as well as the liberation from, or ending of samsara, the repeating cycle of birth, life, and death).

A number of canonical Buddhist texts expand on these teachings showing how-to live-in accordance with the path: - renouncing possessions and practicing mindfulness and meditation. The goal of enlightenment is non-attachment; where there is no craving, and no wish for things to be different, there can be no suffering. But you can't get there through metaphysical questioning, that distracts the mind with unanswerable questions; the Buddha's philosophy is based on observation, experience, and reasoning, hence his rejection of such metaphysical questions. And one of the main experiences he bases his philosophy on is the effectiveness of meditation.

Again, in Western terms this is a version of 'Virtue Ethics', but whereas the Confucian version aimed at the good of society, the Buddhist version aims at moving the individual closer to nirvana through karma; the resultant good society is a secondary, welcome addition.

The split in Buddhism between the Theravada and Mahayana schools seems to have occurred within just 200 years of the Buddha's death. The main difference is that the Mahayana school aims not just at an end to one's own suffering, but to the enlightenment and happiness of others, even after achieving one's own nirvana. This is still not directly aimed at producing a good society, it is more an overall reverence for life in general.

Zen Buddhism

One version of Buddhism that has been popularised in the West by several authors is Zen Buddhism. This version originated in China around the 5th century A.D. through the mixing of Buddhism with other Chinese philosophies, especially Taoism. It spread to Vietnam, Korea and then to Japan in the 12th century A.D. In fact, the word 'Zen' is derived from the Japanese pronunciation of the Middle Chinese word 'Chan', an abbreviation of 'channa', which is a Chinese transliteration of the Sanskrit word of 'dhyana' (meditation). Again, there is not just one version of Zen, it has gone through several variations, some now lost but others still practiced. [It is the nature of both philosophies and religions that they change, absorb other influences, and splinter into numerous different versions.]

The idea of Zen in the west has achieved almost cult status. Either as the image of a lone monk meditating to achieve superpowers of some sort (levitation, or fighting skills), or as a description of a particular meditative approach to a task – 'he used a Zen like concentration'. More serious approaches to Zen Buddhism in the West have been taken by authors like Alan Watts and Paul Reps, but perhaps the best English language exposition of this philosophy can be found in a book called *'The Zen Doctrine of No-Mind'* by D.T. Suzuki.

Cult status aside, this is still a Buddhist philosophy. Its aim is an end to suffering through the awareness that suffering can only occur when we have wants and desires in the first place. This does not mean trying to get rid of those wants and desires, it is more the realisation that they are the cause of any suffering, and by so realising raise above them, awakening to see the world as it really is and shedding the illusion of a substantial self.

Buddhism

The main difference with Zen is in the method of teaching to obtain this enlightenment. Deep meditation is still required, but this is added to through the use of *Koans* (paradoxical anecdotes, stories, or riddles without solutions, used to demonstrate the inadequacy of logical reasoning and provoke enlightenment). Zen texts are, therefore, more implicit than explicit, prompting the novice to gain understanding through his own efforts. *The Oxford Companion to Philosophy* says that "one of the ideas in this teaching is to undercut any tendency to believe in, or take seriously, the literal truth of anything".

Famous examples of *koans* include: -

- "What is the sound of one hand clapping?"
- Baso said to a monk, "If I see you have a staff, I will give it to you. If I see you have no staff, I will take it away from you.
- If you meet the Buddha, kill the Buddha.

Or stories such as: -

Two monks were arguing about the temple flag waving in the wind.
One said, "The flag moves."
The other said, "The wind moves."
They argued back and forth but could not agree.
Hui-neng, the sixth patriarch, said: "Gentlemen! It is not the flag that moves. It is not the wind that moves. It is your mind that moves."

And...

Nan-in, a Japanese master, received a university professor who came to inquire about Zen.
Nan-in served tea. He poured his visitor's cup full, and then kept pouring.
The professor watched until he could restrain himself no longer.
"It's full," he said, "no more will go in."
"Like this cup," replied Nan-in, "you are full of your own opinions and speculations. How can I show you Zen unless you first empty your cup?"

And...

A man is being chased by a tiger and he comes to the top of a high cliff. He sees a vine hanging over and climes down using it. He is now suspended above a huge drop with a tiger waiting for him at the top of the cliff, and a mouse starts to chew through the vine. He sees a strawberry growing on the cliff face beside him. He reaches out, picks the luscious strawberry, and eats it.

An appeal of Buddhism is that it is a method of achieving individual understanding and peace of mind, while at the same time having a very humanistic outlook on the value of all life. Also, the Buddha claimed no divine authority in any form, he attributed all his realisations and achievements to human endeavour. His philosophy is entirely based on observation and reasoning.

Part Four

Philosophy Informed by Science

This section of the book looks at the relationship between philosophy and science. Both are concerned with knowledge of the natural world and our place within it, but how do they overlap and interact?

The point here is that philosophy can't ignore the findings of science. For example, given the scientific fact of evolution, we no longer need to invent divine intervention stories for our human origins. Also, with more knowledge on how brains function, any theory of how the mind works needs to take those facts on board.

That being said however, philosophy is still needed in order to interpret the findings of science, to systemise them and put them into a human perspective. Plus, there are areas of philosophy, like ethics, laws, and politics, where science might give some background facts but where the messiness of everyday life needs a humane approach to its problems.

50

Introduction to Philosophy Informed by Science

The essence of science: ask an impertinent question, and you are on the way to a pertinent answer.

Jacob Bronowski (*The Ascent of Man*)

Overview

While Eastern philosophy was centred around ethics, together with a personal understanding of our situation in the world, philosophy in the West placed epistemology (the theory of knowledge) at its heart. The reason for this is that unless we understand what we mean by knowledge, how it arises and what its limits are, how can we be sure that what we think we know is actually valid? Ethics remains a large part of Western philosophy, but it is just one branch of its wider scope, (refer back to chapter 2 for an outline of the broad range of subject matter covered by the term philosophy).

Wisdom in the East is to be found through the awakening of the individual – albeit with guidance from teachers and ancient texts. Knowledge in the West, however, is a collaborative enterprise, especially when it comes to the findings of science. Any theories and results presented by one person are checked and commented on by many other people until consensus is achieved, but with the remaining caveat that further research might require amendment. (Again, refer back to chapter 3 on epistemology, and in particular to the distinction between **deduction** and **induction**.) Also, it is worth repeating this quote, from chapter 1 of this book, by one of our current leading philosophers.

The reason we teach the history of philosophy is that it "is in large measure the history of very smart

> *people making very tempting mistakes, and if you don't know the history, you are doomed to making the same mistakes all over again".*
>
> **Daniel C. Dennett**

Natural Philosophy

Western philosophy starts (as far as written records go) in ancient Greece around two and a half thousand years ago, and at that time it was concerned with the attainment of all knowledge (a love of wisdom), there were no specialisations. This was called 'natural philosophy', which is the study of all nature and of the known physical universe.

As knowledge increased, some areas became more systematised, more elaborate, and more susceptible to logical analysis and experimental techniques. These split off to become disciplines in their own right. This was a gradual process however, and the early leading players still thought of themselves as philosophers. In fact, even Newton's great book, which really laid the foundations of the discipline of physics, was entitled **Mathematical Principles of Natural Philosophy**.

Mathematics was the first area to really become a separate field. Starting with Pythagoras, then Euclid with his axioms of geometry, followed by Aristotle who laid out the basis of logic, and then via many others over the years.

Astronomy probably split off next starting perhaps with Ptolemy, although he included astrology at the time. Then we get biology, physics, anthropology, palaeontology and all the other scientific disciplines.

In some ways it could be considered that it was the easy stuff which became sciences in their own right! Any area where it was possible to systematise the subject, where there could be an agreed theoretical basis and standardised experimental techniques, split off from natural philosophy and became a science.

Some areas only partly achieved this status. For instance, politics spawned sociology and economics, but it is difficult to be much more than systematically descriptive here, right and wrong answers being illusive in the messy field of human relations. Another example would be the philosophy of mind (see chapter 53), the reason here, however, is slightly different. There are fields of neurology, psychology, and psychoanalysis, but currently the science here is still in its infancy. Maybe in the (near) future there will be more knowledge and agreement.

Introduction to Philosophy Informed by Science

Other questions remain in philosophy, the harder stuff where we don't yet know what a systemised theory might look like. To become 'sciences' in their own right they would need agreed conceptual clarification to disentangle complex areas, an examination of alternative theories, standardised experimental approaches, and above all rational argument.

Having said the above, it might be thought that philosophy was reduced to those areas where we don't yet have answers, but it is much more than just the 'unknown'. Philosophy is the endeavour of understanding our place in the world, of thinking about our relation to other people and to society, how should we live and what constitutes meaning in our life. It is ethics, it is politics, it is aesthetics, and it is trying to make sense of the world and to put things into perspective.

Even in those areas that are recognised sciences, philosophy is still needed. Indeed, that is the subject of part four of this book. We need to accept what science tells us, but we then need to understand that in human terms. A simple example of that is with D.N.A. Now we can analyse our genetics it becomes obvious that all humanity is part of the same species (Homo sapiens), no more is it possible to think that some people are biologically inferior, no more can we tolerate slavery – we are informed by science, and we incorporate this into our philosophy.

A more complex example would be metaphysics. Science tells us information about the nature of things like time, space, matter etc. (which we have to take on board) but what does that mean in human terms, how should we make sense of these things? Philosophy is love of wisdom, we need the findings of science to correct any misconceptions we might fall for, but we also need to understand these findings with a human perspective.

51

Religion

As to religion, I hold it to be the indispensable duty of government to protect all conscientious professors thereof, and I know of no other business which government has to do therewith.

Thomas Paine (*Common Sense* 1776)

Overview

Initially, natural philosophy included gods and religions, but as philosophy became more structured, and knowledge became more evidence based, religion split off and became either the separate study of theology in general, or individual religions in particular. There is still a branch of philosophy that deals with the philosophy of religion, but this is more of a detached analysis of the phenomena of religion and includes subjects like the psychology of religion and comparative religious studies.

As noted, Western Philosophy places epistemology at its heart – how do we give credence to those things that we think we know? And it is here that, for a number of reasons, philosophy splits from religion.

Revealed knowledge

As we saw in chapter 3, epistemology (the theory of knowledge) identifies two categories of methods to attain knowledge – deduction and induction, with induction being split into three subcategories. Religion, however, introduces a third top level category, that of revealed knowledge. It provides no justification for knowledge of this type other than the fact that it feels right to the person receiving the revelation. A further complication here is that the knowledge in question then has to be passed to others, so you have all the issues of transmission to consider,

Religion

including the difficulties of defining terms, language translation, and length of time since the revelation, etc.

Abduction

Again, in chapter 3 we saw that, while inductive knowledge can't be considered to be 100% correct, it can get very close to that (e.g. if you drop something it will fall). Inductive knowledge is the basis of science, and the subcategory of abduction is used to decide on which theory best fits the rest of our knowledge. The tools it uses to do this are methods like evidence gathering and double-blind studies.

It is obvious that we don't know everything; many things are still unknown, like for instance the origin of the universe. Science is fairly sure there was a 'big bang' (i.e. a point origin) of some kind because evidence from a number of quite independent disciplines all point to this (astronomy, physics, mathematics etc.), but the reason for the big bang is currently unknown. There are several theories, but at the present time we have no way to choose between them.

Anyone can come up with a theory for the origin of the universe, indeed throughout history every civilisation has had its origin myths. Not least in western cultures is the notion that God created the universe and everything in it. The problem here is that the unknown is being explained with the inexplicable. To say 'God did it' is not an explanation, it is trying to establish a fact with no evidence.

But worse than that (in knowledge terms) it introduces a whole new set of issues in one sweep: the idea of a powerful entity, outside normal space and time, who can interact with the world somehow; the idea of a spirit world; the idea that some people can communicate with this entity and pass on things like its messages and its behavioural requirements to others. Not all conceptions of God include all the things listed here, but that is another problem, the lack of definition – which conception is correct?

Explaining the unknown with the inexplicable is really a nonstarter in terms of either science or epistemology. Science's answer to the unknown is to say 'agreed, we don't know, but how interesting, let's work on it together'.

Logic

In the past, while religion was still part of Natural Philosophy, many people tried to logically prove the existence of God, perhaps most famously St. Thomas Aquinas. In chapter 16 on St. Thomas Aquinas his five proofs were listed followed by the modern response to them. Here the point made is that trying to use logic to prove that God created the universe fails on three counts: -

1. It is an assumption that there must be a first cause to the series of causes and effects, but mathematics shows us that a series with no ends is possible.
2. If, however, there is a beginning, calling it God is an assumption with no evidence, there could be other explanations.
3. To use God to logically explain the necessity of a first cause only pushes the problem back one step because there would then be the problem of what God is and where He comes from.

For these reasons (and others, including scientific facts like evolution) most theologians these days don't try to prove God's existence, they use faith alone.

Faith

Indeed, modern theologians see the idea of relying on faith as one which makes their belief in God even stronger.

This, however, is one of the main reasons for the split between religion and Western Philosophy; faith, by definition, is 'belief in something without evidence'. As noted in chapter 3 on epistemology, people often use the words 'belief' and 'faith' as if they are interchangeable, but that is not the case. You can legitimately believe in something if you have evidence for it (e.g. that the world is round), but a belief in something without evidence is contrary to all that modern Western Philosophy stands for. The whole basis of Western Philosophy is the use of reason and rationality, which is why philosophy makes such a point of ensuring that it takes on board, and is informed by, science.

Religious Texts

One more difference between philosophy and religion is that religion usually bases its teachings around ancient texts, which remain fixed even if the interpretation changes slightly – think of the Bible and the Koran. Philosophy is not based on any texts, ancient or modern. It is simply honest rational inquiry to attain knowledge, it is love of wisdom, and it follows the evidence wherever that leads. There are, of course, areas of philosophy that are not definitive, people have different views, e.g. politics and ethics, but in all these cases people are using reason and rationality for their beliefs.

Note:

This is a short chapter, included just to give the reasons for the split between Western philosophy and religion.

52

The Philosophy of Science

Science is built up of facts, as a house is built of stones; but an accumulation of facts is no more a science than a heap of stones is a house.

Henri Poincare (French philosopher of science)
(From: *Science and Hypothesis* 1903)

Science is organised knowledge.

Herbert Spencer (English philosopher)
(From: *Education* 1861)

Overview

The philosophy of science concerns itself with two main areas, epistemology and metaphysics. With epistemology we want to understand both the methods science applies to achieve its findings, and the confidence we should attribute to its theories and results; this is really about justification and objectivity. While with metaphysics we want to understand how the findings of science affect our view of the world, how different individual results fit together into a coherent whole, and what meaning can be attributed to those areas where science provides puzzling and counter intuitive results. We start with some basic ideas on the methodology of science.

The Methodology of Science

The methodology of science is actually quite simple, it is a rigorous approach, and it applies to all branches of science.

1. Create an hypothesis that fits with all known facts (if it doesn't fit with the known facts it is not much good as an explanation).
2. Use that hypothesis to make predictions that can be tested for correctness (predictions that can't be tested for correctness are of no use for refining the hypothesis).
3. Test for the veracity of those predictions.
4. In the light of those test results either accept the hypothesis as a working model, reject the hypothesis as impossible, or go back to step 1 and amend it to cater for the new results.

It sounds easy, but as each branch of science becomes more complicated, then making tests and analysing results both become more difficult. That is why science becomes a collaborative enterprise with people working together and checking each other's results. When a scientist, or even a team of scientists, say they have found something new, they don't just say 'this is what we found', they say 'we think we have found this, but here is all our data, here are the techniques we used to collect the data, and here are the (often mathematical) analyses we used to interpret the data, please check our analysis for errors and collect your own data, to confirm the results'.

Scientific results are often first released to the public in respected scientific magazines. These magazines strive to maintain their reputation as serious publications, and so before publishing a scientific paper they send it to independent experts on the field in question for the paper to be peer reviewed.

Fact or Theory

In colloquial terms people often say things like 'that is just a theory' or 'there is a big difference between theory and practice'. Science, however, has a different, and much more rigorous, conception of the word theory. In science a theory is a hypothesis that fits all known facts and has not been shown to be false by any tests. Here are two examples: -

1. The theory of Evolution:

    When Darwin proposed the theory of evolution, he did so using his knowledge of facts from several different scientific disciplines: palaeontology, anatomy, physiology, embryology, and hereditary studies. In other words, his theory fitted all known facts at the time.

Any theory can be completely invalidated by a single new fact however small. For instance, if we found the fossil of say a bird in a stratum of rock that geology tells us was laid down prior to the evolution of birds then the theory would be falsified. But that has never happened, in fact the opposite has occurred.

A scientist named Neil Shubin used the theory to make a prediction. He knew from the fossil record that there were no land-living vertebrate animals 390 million years ago (they all lived in the sea at that time), but that there were such animals by 360 million years ago. However, we had no fossils of any transitional forms between sea living vertebrate animals with fins to land living vertebrate animals with limbs.

Shubin used information from geology textbooks to locate exposed rock strata of the correct age and type and predicted that if there were such transitional fossils then that would be the place to look. The nearest such stratum was in the Canadian Arctic and so he led several expeditions there over five years. In 2004 he finally found a fossil that was clearly an intermediate animal between sea living and land living, and he named it *Tiktaalik roseae*. This was a great example of using a theory to make a prediction and then confirming that prediction.

When Darwin proposed his theory, although it fitted all know facts at the time, he knew nothing about genetics. He knew about heredity, but did not know how that occurred, he assumed some sort of merging of traits from parents to offspring. Now, our new knowledge of genetics has not just added more evidence of evolution but has shown us the actual mechanism as to how it occurs. We can look at our own genome and actually see fossil genes inside it, genes that worked in our ancestor species but are now not needed. They are disabled due to damage or copying errors, but because they are no longer needed it doesn't matter, yet they are still there and still get passed on with the rest of the genome. One example is the genes needed for smell. These were important to our ancestor species, and they had thousands of such genes, but smell is not so important to humans so it doesn't matter if some of those genes don't work anymore, if they become disabled they just become part of our junk D.N.A., of which we have quite a lot.

Evolution is now so strong as a theory that it is rightly regarded as a scientific fact. Indeed, the latest example of evolution that we are all familiar with is the virus Covid-19, it is evolving new variants before our eyes.

The Philosophy of Science

2. The theory of Gravity:

We all know that when we drop something it drops, but it took Sir Isaac Newton to first put this into a mathematical law of nature. He did this by performing many experiments and measurements until he derived his law of universal gravity: -

- Every particle attracts every other particle in the universe with a force that is directly proportional to the product of their masses and inversely proportional to the square of the distance between their centres.

This law is easy to state in English, but behind it Newton put the maths of how to measure the forces and motions involved, and so it became possible to make accurate calculations as to how things moved in a gravitational field.

Newton's law of gravity works well at everyday distances and speeds. However, it was discovered that at very large distances and speeds there were slight discrepancies. It took Einstein to come up with a more accurate theory of gravity that was able to resolve these discrepancies; this was his General Theory of Relativity.

This does not mean Newton was wrong. Newton's theory continues to be used as an excellent approximation of the effects of gravity in most applications; Einstein just refined it to also work in extreme conditions. This is often how scientific theories develop, not by complete overthrow, but by successive refinement.

Thus, scientific theories become established as facts. Neither the theory of evolution nor the theory of General Relativity have ever been shown to be wrong, they fit all known facts, they can be used to make predictions, all of which have been proved correct. Are they complete? Probably not, they may well get refined further, General Relativity, for instance, still needs to be combined with quantum theory. They are both inductive theories (created using abduction – inference to best explanation) and as such can't be 100% correct, but that does not mean they must be 50% correct. These two theories are of the order of greater than 99% correct; you could bet your life on them.

Science and Epistemology

When you understand that science is based on induction, there is a tendency, in non-scientific thinking, to highlight the possibility that a given scientific theory is wrong. This could be called the 'media approach', because it often seems that whenever someone claims something, the media searches for someone else who holds the opposite view and gives them airtime, making a debate of the issue. Then as soon as you get a debate, the public assumes the issue is a 50/50 one and that people can choose for themselves which side is correct.

This happened, for instance, with climate change. Despite study after study reporting that it was both real and influenced by man, an inordinate amount of coverage was given to those that denied these facts. This is often made worse when invested interests are involved such as fossil fuel companies producing their own studies, rather like the cigarette companies did when they wanted to downplay the link between smoking and cancer.

The above shows the practical side of the problem with science based on induction, but there is an academic element to this too. Over the last hundred years or so a few philosophers have struggled with the problem of induction, (this was covered in chapter 45 'Other Ideas in Recent Western Philosophy') and so without wanting to repeat things here it is suggested that chapter 45 is reread in the light of this discussion. It might be an interesting exercise trying to rationalise induction, but the fact is we have no alternative; we have to accept that science, indeed knowledge, is based on probability, and that probabilities approaching 100% are good enough to attain the designation 'fact', not only in everyday life but in science too.

Another issue that is sometimes raised is that of a historical perspective, science has been wrong in the past so therefore we have reason to believe it might not be true now. As we saw with the theory of gravity, however, scientific theories are not usually wholly overthrown, they are more often refined and amended, and this is a well-accepted element of science. Indeed, such theories often come with their own assessment of the level of confidence in the data and the analysis.

We know, for instance, that gravity has not yet been reconciled with quantum theory, and that the 'standard model' of physics (while working really well) is not yet complete. But the point is they work: we can make vaccines; build power stations, cars, aeroplanes, and spaceships; and we trust our lives to these things.

What does it mean to be objective about things? One person's view is, by definition, subjective, but science has objectivity built into its methodology: - people working together, repeating each other's experiments, and agreeing on the analysis of their data. While it's difficult for one scientist, working away on their own, to be objective, how much harder is it for a lay person to form an objective opinion on a scientific matter? The only answer here is reading; reading all-round the subject from different sources and making a determination as to which sources should be trusted. It's not easy to understand our newly scientific world, but it is beholden on us to try because, as citizens, we will from time to time have to make choices (such as should we take the vaccine, should we vote for someone who does not believe in climate change or vote for someone who rejects evolution) and these choices matter.

The Metaphysics of Science

Overview

Science is predicated on the idea that there is an external reality, the nature of which it endeavours to uncover. In philosophical terms this is an empirical approach, as opposed to the rationalist or idealist who believes 'reality' is a mental phenomenon, or indeed the phenomenology approach which brackets external reality for future investigation and just concentrates on our mental intentional objects. One might remember Dan Dennett here, who tries to bridge the two camps with his 'Heterophenomenology', (see chapter 44).

Accepting that there is an external reality (the only alternative is some form of solipsism) the next question is can we gain knowledge of it? It seems that science is very good at investigating the world; we find that matter is made of elements (carbon, iron, oxygen, and the rest). But then we find that an atom of an element is made of protons, neutrons, and electrons, and then that protons are made of quarks. This has the appearance of being a never-ending series of Russian Dolls, each one being smaller and nesting inside the previous one.

Another problem with our concepts about atomic structure is that we can't see or touch these things, which is how we normally verify our everyday understanding. Such findings are often interpretations of the outputs from the machines we build to investigate reality. It appears that we are getting nearer the truth as to the makeup of the world in which we live but that we are not yet the whole way there. Maybe that is an unattainable goal. What does it mean 'getting the whole way there'? What does it mean to really know something? And then we are back to induction again.

As discussed above, science works, and it works well enough for us to rely on it. So, in the same way that we must accept that our knowledge is mainly based on induction and that induction is based on probability, it seems we also have to accept that we can approach closer and closer to the truth of our external reality but that perhaps we can never actually get there (whatever that means). [We will revisit this issue from a slightly different perspective in chapter 55 'Concepts and Understanding'.]

We want to know more about the world, we are curious animals, and we are discovering new things all the time. It is the job of philosophy to put that new knowledge into perspective, to show how it fits into the bigger picture, and to discuss its meaning – as well as discussing what we mean by 'meaning'. So next we will look at a few scientific ideas and discuss their meaning and significance.

Cause and effect

Cause and effect seems such a straightforward idea, it seems self-evident that if you kick a ball and the ball moves then it moved because you kicked it, your kick 'caused' the 'effect' of the ball moving. This is an empirical idea that we learn about the world as infants, and later as school children with formulas scientists have put together such as Newton's second law of motion, which states that 'the rate of change of momentum of a body over time is directly proportional to the force applied, and occurs in the same direction as the applied force' (or $F=MA$ in mathematical terms).

The philosopher David Hume, however, set the cat among the pigeons by questioning the existence of 'cause and effect'. This was discussed in chapter 24, but it is so important in the metaphysics of philosophy that the discussion is repeated here.

Hume says that if you repeatedly perceive one thing following another thing, then you conceive the idea that the first thing caused the second. But you have not actually perceived this causal relation, it is just a concept that you have built up in your mind. He says that the power by which one object produces an effect in another is not discoverable from the ideas of the two objects; therefore, we can only know cause and effect from experience, not from reasoning or reflection.

He maintains that when we say A causes B, we mean only that A and B are constantly observed to be conjoined, not that there is some necessary connection between them: - "We cannot penetrate into the reason of the conjunction." "Necessity," he says, "is something that exists in the mind, not in objects." And "all our reasonings concerning causes and effects are derived from nothing but custom."

He also extends these ideas to claim that past experience is not a rational justification that the future will be the same. The taste of an apple

The Philosophy of Science

yesterday is not a guarantee that it will taste the same today, it only increases the probability that it will.

When one billiard ball hits another and the second one moves, what was it that the first ball gave to the second to make it move? A scientist (like Newton) would say it imparted momentum, and he can even supply the mathematical laws whereby the effect on the second ball can be calculated. But how were these laws arrived at? Only through repeated experiments and measurements, which is just a more rigorous method of formulating the idea of 'cause and effect' than an infant learns through experience.

This is the same for all scientific laws. They only increase the probability of knowing how the universe works, albeit that probability often approaches 100%. [Again, this will be discussed further in chapter 55 'Concepts and Understanding'.]

Another way of formulating Hume's approach is given by the mathematician and philosopher F. P. Ramsey (1903 – 1930). He said that laws are a 'consequence of those propositions which we should take as axioms if we knew everything and organized it as simply as possible in a deductive system'. In other words, if we knew everything, induction would turn into deduction.

Many philosophers, from Kant onwards, have really disliked what they saw as Hume's scepticism, but none have been able to successfully replace it. As Socrates knew, everything should be doubted, and everything questioned; scepticism is the first step to wisdom.

Matter, Space and Time

Throughout the history of philosophy people have wanted to understand the makeup of the world and the things in it. The early Atomists in ancient Greece used logic to say that if you keep dividing a portion of a substance you will get down to the smallest possible bit of that substance that can't be further cut in half. So, for instance, a lump of iron is considered to be made up of atoms of iron.

As knowledge increased, and became more systematised in some fields, the science of physics developed. For Newton, space and time were backdrops within which matter moved according to discoverable laws. From a philosophical point of view, Newton assumed space to be a fixed grid within which bodies interacted, and he assumed time was a fixed background clock ticking away, the same everywhere and for everybody. This was the early empirical school of philosophy, but for some philosophers (the Rationalists and Idealists), matter, space and time were mental phenomena because they saw reason as the chief source and test of knowledge. Kant tried to bridge the two schools with his notion of "*a priori"* knowledge, where experience provides the start of an idea, but then, having discovered a general principle, the concept becomes an external fact or *"a priori"* knowledge. For many, however, this seemed an artificial distinction.

Back in the world of physics, Einstein (as we saw above) developed his Special and General Relativity, which extended Newton's ideas. While these had a number of counter intuitive implications they were still classed as classical physics. The biggest change here was that Newton's conception of space and time, as a background grid against which the universe played out, was replaced by the idea that space-time was a linked, four-dimensional entity, and that its structure can be locally distorted by any mass within it. Also, that mass can bend light passing near it because light follows the distortions of space-time caused by that mass.

Further still, it became impossible for two observers to agree what time an event occurred or even the correct sequence of events they both witnessed. This is because time runs at different speeds under different conditions such as high velocity, strong acceleration, and strong gravity. For instance, if you stayed on Earth and your twin brother accelerated away from Earth in a rocket ship, if he later came back the two of you would not be the same age, he would be younger than you.

These strange consequences of relativity have been proved true time and time again; even the GPS tracking satellites need to take relativistic time distortions into account when pinpointing your location on Earth on your smart phone.

The reason these things seem odd to us is because these effects only manifest themselves under conditions that don't usually occur on Earth (GPS aside). Evolution has designed us to be able to understand and deal with everyday conditions, and the concepts we use to understand the world have only developed through our experience of things occurring on this fairly benign planet. It is difficult to apply these ordinary concepts to the strange effects that physics tells us about, but at the same time we have to be guided by the finding of maths and physics.

Another strange result science tells us about is the origin of the universe in the big bang (although whether the universe had a start or whether it has existed forever is mind blowing either way, as is the related question why is there something rather than nothing?) The big bang is just a convenient name, it was actually not big and not noisy, just a point origin of very high energy and very low entropy. Science does not know all the details of the big bang, but it is a scientific fact that the universe started in a point origin of some kind, the evidence for that comes from several different, independent scientific disciplines: astronomy, particle physics, microwave radiation, and the mathematics of General Relativity.

The Philosophy of Science

In philosophical terms we need to accept the fact of the big bang as described by science, but we also need to understand the difference between a proven scientific fact, such as the existence of the big bang, and scientific speculation, such as the cause of the big bang. There are a number of competing scientific theories as to its cause, but as yet no way to distinguish between them, and the only way we, as non-scientific philosophers, can understand and make sense of these things is to keep reading around the subject from as many different sources as possible.

The Arrow of Time

One concept in metaphysics that usually does not worry us as non-scientists is the directionality of time, we were younger in the past and we get older as we move into the future. Scientists, however, want to know why this is so because many of the equations they use to understand the universe work just as well either way time moves.

The usual answer to this is to quote the second law of thermodynamics, which says the entropy of a closed system always increases, (entropy is a measure of disorder in a system). Think of a cup of black coffee and a jar of cream, while separated they are highly ordered – coffee in the cup and cream in the jug. Now pour some of the cream into the coffee. To start with you can see swirls of cream in the coffee, so it is less ordered than when separated but there is still some order there in the interesting patterns. Over time, however, there will be less and less order (or more disorder) until the coffee is the same colour throughout.

When the cream is first added and we get our interesting swirls, there are relatively few ways the molecules of cream can be arranged into swirls, but there are billions of other different ways those molecules could be arranged. Therefore, they are more likely to move towards these other ways when they move. You get the same effect with a heap of sand on a beach; there are only a few ways to make it into a sandcastle but billions of ways to not be a sandcastle. Left to itself the heap of sand will not form a sandcastle, but a sandcastle on a beach will not last long.

We can think of the universe that way. Starting with very low entropy and high energy we get interesting patterns developing, such as stars, planets, and people (which is the stage we are at now), but disorder (entropy) is increasing. In the far distant future, as the initial high energy is dissipated and the stars burn out, we get what scientists call the 'heat death' of the universe.

This turns the arrow of time problem for scientists into the question as to why did the universe start with such low entropy in the first place? Questions like this about the big bang, which scientists can't yet answer, might be answered by religion by saying that God started it all, but as well as not being based on evidence, this is no real answer, in fact it introduces a whole range of other questions about the nature of God. This tries to replace the unknown with the unknowable. The scientist is more honest by saying 'we don't know yet, but we are working on it'.

If one tries to introduce God as an explanation for the things that science can't yet explain, then every time scientists discover something new the areas left for God keep getting smaller, leaving God to be just a God of the gaps. This is another reason theologians base their belief in God on faith alone. That is a personal choice however, because (as noted before) faith is belief in something without evidence, and that also marks it as a separate way of thinking from Western Philosophy.

Determinism

This is linked with the idea of cause and effect. It says that any event that occurs is an effect of prior events occurring, so nothing happens that does not have a cause. It seems obvious, if we look backwards in time, to say that B only happened because A happened: - the ball moved because I kicked it; or the car skidded when I braked because it had been raining; or on a more natural level, the tsunami occurred because there was an undersea earthquake.

The problem with this analysis is that, if current events cause future ones, it seems to make the future an unavoidable consequence of the past. In strict terms, just as the past can't be changed, the future is inevitable. Even if you think you can sit down and make a logical rational decision to do something, your thinking process will only proceed in the way it does due to your prior experience and hence it is pre-determined.

A strict determinist will say that if we knew the position and velocity of every particle in the universe, we would be able to predict the future. That is obviously impossible, but the point is that every particle does have a current position and velocity, and they follow particular laws of movement and interaction, so even if we can't know how they will move, their journey is inevitable, the future is fixed. This is often known as the 'block' theory of time, made up of slices of 'now', with all time (past and future) already existing.

So, there is the **softer** theory, that past events and experiences in your life determine how you act and respond to things going forward, and the **stricter** theory that, from a particle perspective, the future already exists. On the softer side, it might seem possible to break the cycle of cause and effect by making a few decisions based on say the throw of a dice. For example, if I get an even number I will go to work today, if I get an odd number I will call in sick. On the strict side it will be claimed that even the roll of the dice is predetermined, although randomness might still contradict that due to the weirdness of quantum effects (see below).

The idea of determinism is a large element in the discussion about 'free will' and this will be discussed in more detail in chapter 57. A related argument is to do with how we use language to talk about the world, with different ways of talking, or different levels, depending on the idea that needs to be communicated (see chapter 56 on language).

Reductionism

A related idea to determinism is that of Reductionism. It is the nature of science that it breaks down the things it wants to investigate into small, manageable chunks. The problem many see with this approach is that it can miss any understanding at the macro level, i.e. is the whole greater than the sum of the parts? Also, that it diminishes an appreciation of the world: - If you look at a flower, does it help to know the details of the sap rising up the stem or would you rather read a poem about it?
The scientist's answer is of course 'why can't I do both?' Indeed, doing both adds to our appreciation of the world. In terms of a person, we need to study anatomy and physiology, if only to apply medical fixes when things go wrong, plus there are macro areas of study such as psychology, psychiatry, politics, and economics, but we also have Michelangelo and Shakespeare to give us insight into the human condition. All views are of value.

Quantum Reality

In many areas science endorses our intuitions about the world, but in some areas the knowledge it provides is very counter intuitive. Take evolution for instance; the fact that we share a common ancestor with both a house fly and a carrot is hard to take on board, but the evidence that all life on Earth is related is overwhelming. The implications of Relativity are also somewhat mind-blowing, but that too is still just classical physics and is extremely well evidenced and understood.

Quantum physics, on the other hand, is something that works, and is well evidenced, but is not well understood. The theories of quantum physics are all probability based, but having said that, the calculations physicists make and use are incredibly accurate to many decimal places. Einstein thought that probability was used because we did not understand the basic reality; he thought there must be some hidden variable not yet found. He famously expressed this by saying that 'God does not play dice with the universe', (not that he believed in God, he was just expressing his belief that the universe was deterministic at a basic level). Some other physicists, however, just subscribe to the "shut up and calculate" school of quantum physics, because it works.

One of the strange findings of quantum physics is the phenomenon of entanglement. This is where two particles are made to interact in such a way that the quantum state of one particle cannot thereafter be determined independently of the other, i.e. if you measure the spin of one particle to be clockwise then the other particle's spin will be counterclockwise. In order to make the measurement, however, the quantum 'wavefunction' of the system (the entangled particles) is forced to collapse, and this occurs and holds true however far apart the particles are when measured. In 1935, Einstein and others thought that such behaviour was impossible because it violated the local realism view of causality; he called it "spooky action at a distance" and argued that our formulation of quantum mechanics must therefore be incomplete.

In 1964, the physicist John Stewart Bell produced a paper showing that the 'hidden variables' theory favoured by Einstein could not explain the action at a distance because the variables would have to be non-local, with both halves of the pair of particles able to carry influences instantly between them no matter how far apart the two halves are separated. Experiments have since been performed with entangled particles so far apart that any influence would have to have travelled faster than the speed of light. So, quantum entanglement is a verified fact, it works, and it can even be exploited in areas like communication and computation. How it works, however, is still a mystery.

Another strange finding is to do with the nature of matter itself, we don't know if matter is made of particles or waves. The same is true of light, which is carried by (or made of) photons. The first measurement of this was performed on light by Thomas Young in 1801, long before the development of quantum physics. Here Young shone a light at a card with two slits in it, and behind the card was a screen to catch the pattern of light on the other side. This showed that light passing through a slit spread out on the other side like a wave, there was one wave for each slit and the two waves interfered with each other producing a distinctive banded pattern on the screen. From then on light was considered to be a wave.

Much later, when our experimental equipment became more accurate, we could fire individual photons at the two slits. If we put detectors behind the slits to see which slit the photon went through, we saw no interference pattern, giving us the conclusion that photons were particles, but if the detectors were removed the photons acted like waves again.

While that might just about be acceptable for light, the same thing happened when electrons were used, and then for atoms and even molecules. There was no doubt about it, even matter can sometimes be described in terms of particles and sometimes as waves, and here we again

The Philosophy of Science

get the idea of waveform collapse, together with the idea that an observer causes the collapse in some way when they perform a measurement. This view is often termed the 'Copenhagen Interpretation' of quantum mechanics and is mainly attributed to physicists Niels Bohr and Werner Heisenberg.

The physicist Erwin Schrodinger, however, agreeing with Einstein, tried to illustrate what he saw as the problems with the Copenhagen view. He devised a thought experiment with a cat in a box. The box also contained a flask of poison which could be released depending on a random subatomic event that may or may not occur. The Copenhagen Interpretation implies that after a while the cat is simultaneously alive and dead, but when one looks in the box one sees the cat in only one of the two states. This poses the question of when exactly quantum superposition ends and reality resolves into one state or another.

This superposition actually occurs, however, and can be used in, for example, quantum computing. Normal computers use two states – on or off – used as a one or a zero. Quantum computers use entangled particles that can be one, zero, or a superposition of one and zero. And such computers (although very difficult to build) have the potential to perform calculations that normal computers would take years to complete.

Summary

In this brief introduction to the philosophy of science we have seen both how science works to produce its findings and an overview of some of those findings. This was not an exhaustive review by any means, but it was a good pointer to the current state of scientific knowledge, together with an outline of the areas that work but that we don't yet know how or why. Science is an open-ended endeavour and operates as an open-minded questioning about how the universe works. Such an approach chimes well with the aims of philosophy.

Past philosophers have speculated about such things as matter, space, time, mind, and origins of both man and the universe, but now philosophy has to take on board what science says about these things while acknowledging both how science works and what its current limitations are. Leading the way in this respect are philosophers such as Daniel C. Dennett, so it might be worth re-reading the chapter on him, in particular the way he uses scientific findings in order to understand how the mind works and how consciousness emerges.

In terms of the current unknowns in science, in particular quantum science, there are many scientific hypotheses, including the ideas of 'many worlds', 'multiple universes', and 'hidden variables'. It is the job

An Introduction to Philosophy

of science to find ways to test those hypotheses to either refine them or rule them out. As mentioned, however, science is open-ended – will we ever completely understand how the universe works, and what do we mean by 'understand' in the first place? Over the next few chapters we will look at those questions, especially in chapter 55 'Concepts and Understanding'.

53

Philosophy of Mind

All the choir of heaven and furniture of earth – in a word, all those bodies which compose the mighty frame of the world – have not any substance without a mind.

George Berkeley
(From: - A Treatise Concerning the Principles of Human Knowledge)

Overview

Throughout the history of philosophy, both East and West, and indeed ever since we have had the leisure time to ponder the amazing fact of our existence, the human mind has been an awe-inspiring mystery to us. Where does it come from, how does it work, is it a physical phenomenon or a non-physical one? Many philosophers in the past (as we have seen in previous chapters) have attempted to answer these questions and have tried to fit those answers into their own particular comprehensive view of the world. Often their answers had something to do with the concepts of soul and spirit which were commonly held beliefs at the time that they were writing.

It is only in the past one to two hundred years that we have begun to gain some real scientific knowledge about the workings of the human mind. Darwin, for instance, showed us that we evolved from other animals, so in all probability our minds are just more complicated versions of animal minds. Freud gave us insights to the workings of the human mind (influences, motivations, subconscious desires, etc.) and areas like psychology and psychiatry were born. More recently, neurological studies have provided detailed knowledge of brain anatomy, and the chemistry of hormones and neurotransmitters.

How all this fits together to provide our human consciousness, is still a work in progress. Some current thinkers claim that such an understanding is beyond us (or even impossible) but many others think that that position is defeatist. The best of our current philosophers, however, (spearheaded by Daniel C. Dennett and others) are now giving us the most comprehensive answers we yet have by being incredibly well informed by the latest science.

Dualism

One of the most pervading, current, misconceptions in philosophy is that of dualism – the theory that mind and matter are two distinct things. Even Descartes, who attempted to create philosophy from first principles with his 'I think, therefore I am', made the assumption that dualism was correct. This, however, brought with it the pre-existing ideas of a soul or spirit of some kind inside us.

Believing such an idea is totally understandable, because, from an individual perspective, it does feel like there is a 'me' inside my body looking out at the world through the windows of my eyes. Note that even using the words "my body" and "my eyes" reinforces the view that there is a distinct 'owner' somewhere inside us. To some extent, that view might be a function of having to use both language and concepts to understand the world and to communicate with others, [see chapters 55 and 56 for more on this]. The philosopher Daniel Dennett, talking about this, says that the idea of a 'me', inside my body, is something that is generated by our mental "centre of narrative gravity", the 'self', he says, is a story about ourselves that is created by our mind.

The problem with the theory that 'mind and matter are two distinct things' is caused by the word 'things' in that sentence. As mentioned in chapter 19 on Descartes, the philosopher Gilbert Ryle identified this as a category error in his 1949 book ***The Concept of Mind***. The brain is a physical 'thing', we can see it, weigh it and dissect it, it is made of matter, but if we also call the mind a 'thing' it automatically becomes a non-physical thing (something not made of matter) and hence we have to reach for supernatural ideas such as soul or spirit to describe it. If, however, you change the category, and instead of calling the mind a 'thing' you call it a 'process', then you don't need the ideas of soul or spirit. The mind becomes the brain working, the processing of external and internal stimuli via electro-chemical pathways in real time.

An analogy that helps here is that of a computer. It is made of physical things, wires, chips, screens, keyboards etc. and when it's off it just sits there, but switch it on and give it inputs then processing happens, it can play chess or retrieve information for you based on search criteria. The analogy is not perfect, the two main missing elements are emotions and any evidence of understanding by the computer, but is this just because the brain is a number of levels more complex? For more on this see the 'Thinking Machines' section below.

To many people, it does seem a shame to have to lose the concept of 'soul', but we don't have to, we just need to repurpose it. Throughout the history of language words have constantly evolved and changed their meaning. All we need to do is get rid of any supernatural overtones to the concept and accept that its use is a more poetic one. We use it as a kind of shorthand for the totality of our emotional, moral, and psychological response to things, as in 'that story touched my soul' or when we refer to 'soul music'. Also, for the word spirit, a 'spiritual approach' is really a poetic description.

Life and Death

One of the other main reasons that the dualism of mind and matter is such a pervasive idea is the emotional difficulty in accepting death, either of one's self or of a friend or loved one. It is much more comforting to think that a person's spirit or soul is still around somewhere. Indeed, this is one of the things most religions promise, not only that the person still exists somewhere, but that the place they still exist in is a lovely, safe place, free of the suffering found in life. Then, added to this is, the hope that you will be joining them again when you pass away.

We are totally used to the idea that, when a loved one is not physically in our presence, they still exist somewhere, in another room, away at work, out shopping or playing golf. We learn this as babies when we start to recognise our mother's face, sometimes she is not there but then she comes back again, and we smile. So, it is entirely understandable that, when someone dies, we have the very strong impression that they are just somewhere else at the moment, and we will soon see them again.

If we logically think this through, we see the reality that living things die, even if we try to protect our children from such stark facts with nice stories. Science has never found any evidence of a soul or spirit. Indeed, the evidence is that our bodies and our brains work well just by using the known laws of nature; invoking a supernatural explanation is both unnecessary and brings with it a host of other unknowns.

Understanding the world

As the philosopher Daniel Dennett points out, invoking the idea of an aware spirit (or homunculus) inside our head, looking at all the incoming data from our senses as if it was watching a video screen, does not answer the question of how we understand the world. It just pushes the explanation a step further back because you would then have to explain how that homunculus processed the data.

There is no single place in the brain where understanding occurs; it is the whole brain working together that produces understanding. The brain is made of numerous, individual, specialised processing areas, as has been discovered, initially through testing patients with specific localised brain injury, and more recently using brain scanning techniques. Take vision for instance. The input from the eyes is split up and routed to a number of different areas that are specialised in identifying things like colour, edges, movement, texture, and relative size etc. with each area linked to each other and to other areas such as memory, rational processing, and emotional centres. This is parallel processing in real time, producing best guesses and discarding improbable ones with incredible rapidity, and constantly being updated with the never-ending flow of information. The brain can accurately be described as an incredibly efficient pattern recognition machine.

Going back for a minute to the idea of a free-floating, non-physical, spirit in our head watching the results of this brain processing, the question arises as to how it would gain its information after the death of the brain? It has no eyes to see with, no nervous system to feel a pinch on the arm with, no emotional system to react with. Such a concept goes back to a time before science, and it is kept alive only because the words 'spirit' and 'soul' still exist – now there is life after death!

Thinking Machines

There is, currently, a lot of hype about artificial intelligence, or A.I. as it's known, and perhaps rightly so in fields like chess, Go, language translation, speech recognition, computer vision, medical diagnosis, etc. But the big questions are: - 'can machines actually think?', 'can they 'understand' the world?', and 'can they ever become conscious?'

We are all familiar with the concept of robots, working in factories building cars for instance, and from science fiction books and films we are aware of the speculation as to the future of robots. Some of these speculations are benign – consider the android Data from Star Trek, the embodiment of an intelligent, helpful, conscious, robot. However, the dark side of intelligent robotics is also speculated on – think of the Daleks in Dr Who.

What sort of timescale are we talking about? Here are some facts. After the Second World War computers doubled their capacity every two years. In the 1980s this then speeded up to every 18 months, and since the

1990s the doubling in capacity increased to almost every 12 months. Only recently has a slight slowdown started but it's still increasing very fast. Given the continuing trend it will not be many years before the processing power of computers matches that of the human brain. Added to this are the new computing architectures of parallel processing and neural networks, both of which correspond to ways in which our brains work.

There is a lot of resistance to the idea of machine consciousness. We are used to the view that computers only do what we tell them, or programme them, to do; otherwise, they just sit there until we want to use them. We think of us humans as being something special, something more than 'just' a machine, but if we dismiss dualism then we really are meat machines, our brains being made of neurons and other cells existing in a wash of neurotransmitters, hormones, and numerous other chemicals.

If we are complex biological machines, designed by evolution to have consciousness as a very useful survival mechanism, then an example of machine consciousness already exists. Evolution took billions of years to produce consciousness with its hit and miss approach but look how much progress has been made in A.I. in less than 100 years through people working together. It would seem that computer A.I. consciousness of some kind is not only feasible but is actually not far off.

Consciousness

The idea that human consciousness is of a special order and that it is something that could never be fully understood, or even replicated artificially, is currently known as the 'hard problem' of consciousness. It's as if the idea of dualism still seems to exist in modern guise, perhaps without a supernatural element. Its proponents talk about things like 'qualia', by which they mean the subjective feeling of, for instance, seeing a red apple, such a feeling being unique to the person seeing it and hence being impossible to be fully understood by someone else. [Colour is certainly an interesting phenomenon, of which more will be said in the next chapter on perception.] The philosopher Daniel Dennett, however, believes the idea of qualia is ill conceived as a concept. He says that it has no real definition, different people use it in different ways, and while there might be a few interesting insights, the current philosophical writing about the idea is hopelessly entangled.

Returning to the idea that human consciousness is special, it should be remembered that consciousness comes in a spectrum of capabilities, for instance a dog is conscious, and certainly an ape is. It might seem that there exists a big difference between an ape's mind and a human one, but perhaps that gap only looks like a chasm because the intervening species of our ancestors, species like Australopithecus, Homo heidelbergensis, Homo erectus, Homo habilis, Neanderthal and many others, are no longer extant.

Dennett is representative of many modern philosophers who realise that we need to incorporate into philosophy the findings of science. He agrees that the mind is not an immaterial 'thing' but a process. In his book ***Consciousness Explained*** he clearly and accessibly incorporates current science into an explanation of how the mind works, and how consciousness is generated as an emergent phenomenon.

He fully recognises that we have a spiritual side, but he defines this as approaching the world's complexities with an attitude of humble, awestruck curiosity, trying to stay both centred and engaged, while letting go of the self.

He has adopted as his slogan **"Yes we have a soul; but it's made of lots of tiny robots."**

He writes:

> Tradition has it that we are responsible agents because we have in us immaterial, immortal clumps of Godstuff that inhabit and control our material bodies rather like spectral puppeteers. But this idea of immaterial souls, capable of defying the laws of physics, has outlived its credibility thanks to the advance of the natural sciences.
>
> What you are is an assemblage of roughly a hundred trillion cells, of thousands of different sorts. Each of your cells is a mindless mechanism, a largely autonomous micro-robot. It is no more conscious than a bacterium. Not a single one of the cells that compose you knows who you are, or cares. Each trillion-robot team is gathered together in a breathtakingly efficient regime that has no dictator but manages to keep itself organized to repel outsiders and serve as the headquarters of one conscious self, one mind. The differences among people are all due to the way their particular robot-team has been put together over a lifetime of growth and experience.
>
> Our brains have functional structures that give our brains powers, like for instance the ability to look ahead, and our capacity to reflect and to evaluate. It's this expandable capacity to represent reasons that we have, which gives us a soul. But what's it made of? It's made of neurons. It's made of lots of tiny robots. And with science we can actually explain the structure and operation of that kind of soul. Whereas an eternal, immortal, immaterial soul is just a metaphysical rug under which you sweep your embarrassment for not having any explanation.

So, yes we have a soul, but it's mechanical. It's still a soul; it still does the work that the soul was supposed to do. It is the seat of reason, and it is the seat of moral responsibility.

For more on these matters refer back to chapter 44 on Daniel Dennett and chapter 45 on Other Ideas in Recent Western Philosophy.

Behaviourism, Functionalism and heterophenomenology

One way to understanding consciousness and how the mind works has been to study behaviour, which is a psychological approach. The main proponent of this was B. F. Skinner with his stimulus-response theory of Behaviourism, but he was somewhat inconsistent in that sometimes he seemed to say only behaviour exists and to deny mental states exist, while at other times he referred to subjective inner states as existing but as being scientifically unknowable. This approach is also known as Analytic Behaviourism, the view that mental states are definable in behavioural terms, for instance, love could be defined by the way people act when they say they feel love.

The more recent approach is called Functionalism and is based on the theory of 'multiple instantiation' developed by Hilary Putnam and David Armstrong. In this view a mental state is understood by its functional role and in terms of its causal relationships, rather than by any supposed intrinsic features it might have. This describes mental states in terms of complex patterns linking perceptual inputs to behavioural outputs and to multiple other mental states.

There is a clear link with computing here with Turing's idea of a machine operating step by step on inputs using inner states to process the information resulting in changes to those states. Indeed, Putnam deliberately referred to a Turing machine when introducing Functionalism.

Another approach to the understanding of consciousness is outlined by philosopher Daniel Dennett. He coins the term heterophenomenology to combine the insights of first-person phenomenology with a scientific, third person, anthropological methodology. For more on this refer back to chapter 44 on Daniel Dennett.

Returning to the 'hard problem' of consciousness, Dennett thinks it is a defeatist attitude to *start* with a definition that says such an understanding is beyond reach. Like any problem, the more you break it down into its smaller constituents, the more progress you make. Science, over the last few decades, has made tremendous progress in understanding how the mind actually works, and modern philosophers, like Daniel Dennett, do their best work by being fully informed by science.

The next three chapters, on perception, concepts, and language, will continue to explore how the mind works and how it understands the world.

54

Perception

If the doors of perception were cleansed everything would appear to man as it is, infinite.

William Blake
(The marriage of Heaven and Hell, 1790-93)

Overview

The overwhelming feeling we all have is that what we see through our eyes is a true picture of how the world really is. And this feeling is the same concerning our other four senses, if we want to know something specific about the world then we touch it, smell it, taste it or listen carefully to it. Indeed, the information we acquire about the world via our senses must be pretty accurate or we would not survive in the world for very long.

However, as we saw in the previous chapter, there is not a central portion of the brain (or a spirit, or soul, or homunculus) viewing all the incoming data from our senses as if it was watching things on a video screen. It is the whole brain working together that understands the world via the use of a tremendous amount of pre-processing. The word 'perception' captures that notion to some extent, because 'to perceive' includes the idea of understanding the subject, but we can often be quite blasé in our use of the word 'perception', employing it as an alternative to the word 'see' for instance, which implies a more direct and less processed acquaintance with the subject.

In this chapter we will consider these matters through taking on board what science says about perception and about how the mind works, and we will find that, rather than us 'seeing' the world, what we actually 'see' is a construct of the brain. [Note the scare quote marks throughout!]

Illusions

We are all familiar with illusions, a drawing for instance that looked at one way seems to show one thing but looked at another way shows something else. Our brain is desperately looking for understanding, trying out different interpretations and rapidly suggesting alternatives, as it performs its specialised job of pattern recognition. Indeed, when we look at a picture, such as a landscape with well-drawn perspective, we can 'see' depth in it even though it is two dimensional.

Now try an experiment. Put two black dots on a piece of paper about an inch apart. Close your left eye and slowly bring the paper towards your right eye concentrating on the left-hand dot at the centre of your vision. When it gets to a particular distance the right-hand dot will disappear! All you will see is white paper where the dot should be. The reason for this is that the right-hand dot is being projected onto the back of your eye at a place where there are no receptor nerves, and that is because this is the place where all the eye's nerves converge into the optic nerve to pass through the back of your eye into the brain.

The interesting thing here is not so much that you don't see the dot but that you do see white paper, no hole, no blackness, but 'invented' white paper! The brain has created this as part of its visual model. Indeed, everything that you are 'seeing' is in fact a model of the world created by your brain, albeit a pretty good one or you would not survive.

The Picture we 'See'.

There is no 'picture' on a screen in your head; all there is are nerve cells, other cells, neurochemicals, and electrical signals. Likewise, there is no picture entering your eyes, all there is are photons of different wavelengths and intensities. Your brain creates the 'picture' of the world for you, in a similar way to a bat creating a picture of its world, good enough to fly through and catch prey on the wing, just by using sound.

We think we 'see' a complete picture of the world all the time our eyes are open, but in reality, we can only focus on a small area in front of us. Without our conscious awareness however, our eyes are constantly darting all round allowing the brain to construct our 'picture' of the world. A similar point here is that we have different receptor type nerves in the eye, colour receptors and black and white ones. The colour ones are only in a small, front facing area, but we think we see colour all round. Again, that is because... a) our eyes are constantly moving, and b) because it is the brain that creates the 'picture' we 'see'.

Talking about colour, it has been a long-standing debate in philosophy as to whether the colour of an object is a property of that object. Some philosophers talk about primary and secondary properties of objects. However, science tells us there is no such thing as colour in the world, all there is are photons of different wavelengths. Different objects reflect different wavelengths of light and we 'see' this as colour. But even then, it is more complex than that, because the colour we perceive an object to have can vary depending on what that object is next to, the intensity of the ambient lighting, and a host of other things. Looking for colour in an object would be as fruitless as looking for a musical note in a steel guitar string.

Colour is added to our picture of the world by our brain. Think of someone who is red/green colour blind, they don't know there is something missing from their picture of the world, they accept what their brain tells them as the right 'picture'. If you think they are missing something, well consider the fact that science tells us that birds and some insects can see more colours than us. We have receptors in our eyes for three different colours; birds and some insects have four or even five different colour receptors, so what is it that we are missing from our 'picture' of the world?

Model Building

The brain is a pattern recognition and model building device. At birth we understand nothing of the world. Gradually we begin to recognise things, such as mother's face, because they keep reappearing, patterns emerge and with them come predictions and expectations; mother gives comfort, food, touch etc. Gradually a mental 'model' of the mother is built. This is a work-in-progress, it is never finished, each new contact refines the model, and each refinement increases the accuracy of our predictions and expectations.

These predictions and expectations are an important aspect of our 'picture' of the world and forms a large part of our perception process. Perception is not a one-off snapshot; it is an on-going, real-time experience. Things are changing all the time, things move, you move, lighting changes, sounds occur and change, and all the time the brain is trying to make sense of it. Many things can be ignored because they are static, but part of the brain is always alert for a change in the background. The brain focuses on things deemed interesting and constantly tries out different interpretations based on expectations, in a search for understanding. Many interpretations are discarded, almost without thinking, because they don't comply with our modelling of the way we think the world works, but if our best prediction turns out wrong, then our models get updated. Studies on how babies learn about the world make great use of the fact that a baby will keep looking at something longer if that something does not fit with its expectations.

These ideas will be expanded upon in the next chapter on 'concepts and understanding', and in the following chapter on 'language'. For now, however, it is sufficient to take on board that perception involves a great deal of pre-processing, which includes: parallel processing in different brain areas, memory retrieval, expectation, and trial and error prediction. We interpret the photons which hit the nerve receptors of the eye, we add colour, we compensate for perspective, distance, and size, and we ignore things deemed unimportant. In short, the 'picture' we 'see' is something that is generated by the brain, and it is the brain as a whole that 'sees' and understands it, not any distinct portion of the brain.

Empiricism or Rationalism

As noted before in this book, historically there have been two main themes in the philosophy of our understanding of the world; Empiricism, which holds that knowledge is based on observation and experimentation; and Idealism (sometime known as Rationalism) which bases knowledge on reason, introspection, and intuition, saying that all we can rely on is the mind. This starts to change in the twentieth century, especially with the advent of science.

Bertrand Russell, in his excellent little book called '**The Problems of Philosophy**', starts with a chapter on 'Appearance and Reality', in which he discusses the appearance of a table in his room. He describes its shape, its colour, its texture, and the sound it makes if tapped. He points out that if several people are looking at it at the same time, and from different angles, they will perceive it differently. The problem for philosophers here, he says, is the relation between sense data and the physical object.

Russell's book (first published 1912) is a fascinating one, it gives a historical perspective on the philosophy of our knowledge of the world, and it also brings in the relationship between language structure and the reality described by that language. Although a little dated in terms of our current scientific knowledge of perception (for instance talking about 'sense data', which seems to ignore the processing attached to perception, as described above) it is still well worth a read as an introduction to these matters.

In 1945, the existentialist philosopher Maurice Merleau-Ponty published one of the landmark books of the 20th century called **Phenomenology Of Perception**. Here Merleau-Ponty brings a scientific perspective to his philosophy, making the primacy of perception central to his thinking. He argues against the subject-object dualism of Cartesian philosophy; it is the whole body that perceives the world, as opposed to consciousness being the source of knowledge. Indeed, the primacy of **embodiment** led him away from phenomenology towards what he was to call "indirect ontology" or the ontology of "the flesh of the world".

For him it is "being in the world" that gives us understanding of the world, and this includes being situated in the linguistic world just as much as being in the perceptual world. For more on Merleau-Ponty see chapter 42.

As so often happens, science begins to take over fields previously the purview of philosophy, knowledge based on observation and experimentation becomes more rigorous in its foundations. The findings of neurology and cognitive sciences cannot be ignored. Yes, there is an external reality out there, but it is the embodied mind that understands that reality, so not pure empiricism and not pure rationalism but somewhere in-between. It is the philosopher's job to take on board the findings of science and then interpret those findings. Modern philosophers are doing just that, and none better than Daniel Dennett with, for example, his book ***Consciousness Explained***, which looks at the findings from science on how the mind works and puts these together into a convincing narrative on consciousness. See chapter 44 for more on Dennett.

55

Concepts and Understanding

> ... *'Tis a thing impossible, to frame*
> *Conceptions equal to the soul's desires;*
>
> **Wordsworth** (from *The Excursion* book 4)

Overview

Philosophy's primary task is to understand the world. It is only after we understand how the world is and how the world works that we can then move on to ideas about how we should live our lives, how we should treat others, right and wrong, justice, politics, and the rest.

In chapter 3 we looked at epistemology (the theory of knowledge). There the topic was 'how do we give credence to our understanding of the world?' We saw that knowledge can be Deductive (100% correct, mainly maths and logic) or Inductive (less than 100% but can get very close to it). We also looked at how we attain inductive knowledge, with the example of Hume's billiard balls for an individual understanding at a subjective level, and more rigorously, via science, for a more objective perspective.

This chapter returns to Hume's subjective level and explores how we hold our understanding of the world via our mental concepts.

Introduction

We have to accept that a world external to our mind exists; otherwise we are just left with solipsism. Also, we should expect that our ideas about the physical aspects of that external world must be fairly accurate or we would not survive in it for long. But how do we come to know that external world and how do we give credence to our understanding of it?

Descartes started by saying that all he could know for certain was that he, as a thing that thinks, must exist or he wouldn't be thinking in the first place. But then he continued by assuming (without evidence) that God exists, and further continued by saying that his perceptions of the world must be right because God, being all goodness, would not trick him.

Edmund Husserl took a different approach. With his idea of phenomenology, he investigated only how the mind represented the external world internally and left the reality of the external world for others to investigate; he "bracketed" away external reality (for future work) and just concentrated on how objects are perceived.

It was Hume who first really tackled how we learn about the world and how we build mental concepts to understand it. In the previous chapter we touched on how babies learn and on how the brain works through pattern recognition and model building. In the next chapter we will look at language acquisition, and words as concepts, but here we will start with concepts themselves.

Hume

Let's remind ourselves of some of Hume's philosophy which we saw in chapter 24 on Hume.

Firstly, how do we acquire ideas, because as a baby we know nothing about the world? In the last chapter we saw that the brain is basically a pattern recognition device, for instance recognising the mother's face from repeated instances. As the baby grows it will be exposed to more and more things that repeat, and hence it will begin to anticipate and even mentally predict things.

Hume gave the example of seeing billiard balls colliding multiple times and gradually being able to predict the outcome of such a collision. He then extended this reasoning to acquiring the concept of cause and effect. He said that if you repeatedly perceive one thing following another thing, then you conceive the idea that the first thing caused the second, and so you gain the general concept of cause and effect. However, he is at great pains to point out that this is just a mental concept; we can only know cause and effect from experience, not from reasoning or reflection. Even a scientist, making accurate and repeated measurements, does not know what the first ball has given to the second one to make it move. The scientist will use terms like momentum, force, velocity etc, but these too are just concepts derived from repeated observation. Hume says that "all our reasoning's concerning causes and effects are derived from nothing but custom."

An Introduction to Philosophy

Understanding the World

We can extend these ideas to all our understanding of the world. Take, for instance, our ideas about matter. These have evolved throughout history, starting perhaps with the notion that everything is made from the four elements: air, fire, water, and stone. Then some ancient Greeks (the Atomists) argued that if you kept cutting something in half you would get down to the smallest element of that thing which could be divided no more, and this they called an atom of that particular substance. This was a good start (although it was a result arrived at rationally, not experimentally), and so the concept of matter being made of atoms was born.

With more experiments over time individual elements were refined and identified and the periodic table of elements was born. This grouped the elements by their chemical properties and by how they react and interact. As science progressed, we were able to use machines to look inside atoms and see that elements differed due to the number of protons and neutrons in their nucleus and the number of electrons orbiting the nucleus. These facts determined their place in the periodic table.

So, atoms are not solid, indivisible bits of matter, they had structure and were made of smaller things. Indeed, they were mostly empty space; if you increased the size of an atom to that of the Royal Albert Hall, the nucleus would be the size of a tennis ball in the centre and electrons would be like grains of sand flying round it. So we moved from the concept of an atom as a tiny solid chunk to a concept of an atom as being like a mini solar system.

Then, however, we find that protons and neutrons are not solid objects, they too are mostly empty space and have a structure made of different quark particles. Also, electrons only seem to exist in some sort of probability cloud or wave around the nucleus. What's more, strange things happen when we fire electrons at a board with two slits in it. If we measure which slit the electron goes through, we get an individual result, but if we don't measure then they go through both slits as if they are waves, as demonstrated by an interference pattern on a screen behind the slits. This implies that electrons can be conceived of as either waves or particles depending on how you measure it.

So, what's real about matter? We can't see atoms, all we have are our concepts about them, and those concepts both change over time and are nebulous; they are just our interpretations of the measurements made by our machines. We are striving to understand this strange quantum world using mental concepts our minds are familiar with from our macro world.

Concepts and Understanding

Similar problems exist with our ideas of space and time. We have built our subjective concepts of space and time from our everyday experience of the world we live in. We move around in a familiar three-dimensional space, we judge the distances between objects, we measure time by the sun in the sky. These concepts work for us, we can drive a car, we go to bed at night, space and time are real for us in the same way that matter is real when we kick a rock and feel pain.

One could almost, like Descartes, derive these things from first principles: I think therefore time must exist, and maybe even space? Then remember Kant (see chapter 27) who said that space and time are not substances in the external world, they are subjective, and are part of our *a priori* knowledge of the world. But it was Einstein who really showed how parochial our subjective concepts of space and time are. He demonstrated that space and time can be considered as a single fabric space/time, that space can be distorted by mass, and that time flows at different speeds depending on either acceleration or the presence of gravity. Indeed, two observers travelling at different speeds might not even be able to agree the order in which two events occurred. And there are other strange effects of relativity, such as mass increasing and length decreasing as an object approaches the speed of light.

Once again we are trying to understand the world using our familiar everyday subjective concepts. We really have no choice but to do this when, as noted, we can't see or touch these strange things. In terms of using science to understand the world, we have to trust it, just like we trust our sight to stop us bumping into things. Science gives us useful, repeatable results, like for instance medicine, or vaccines to fight infections that we can't see. In terms of useful extensions to our senses, science is second to none, but in terms of actually understanding the world we must accept that our understanding is only in terms of our mental concepts.

Here is a write-up from the back cover of a fascinating book called **'Inventing Reality, Physics as Language'** by astrophysicist Bruce Gregory: -

> Three umpires were discussing their roles in the game of baseball. The first umpire asserted, "I calls 'em the way I sees 'em." The next umpire, with even more confidence, and a more metaphysical turn of mind said, "I calls 'em the way they are!" But the third umpire, displaying a familiarity with twentieth century physics, concluded the discussion with, "They ain't nothin' until I calls 'em!" The players and fans have no doubt that the ball was either over the plate or it was not over the plate, but the umpire's call, and not any "fact of the matter," creates a

ball or a strike. Without the ball and the plate there would be no baseball, and without the world there would be no physics; but physicists, like umpires, "call the game" and in the process tell us how the world is "really" put together.

The American philosopher Richard Rorty says that "Interesting philosophy is rarely an examination of the pros and cons of a thesis. Usually it is, implicitly or explicitly, a contest between an entrenched vocabulary which has become a nuisance and a half-formed new vocabulary which vaguely promises great things." This does not happen overnight but is the gradual accumulation of new ways of looking at things, and the use of new scientific equipment. He paints a picture of "intellectual and moral progress as a history of increasingly useful metaphors rather than of increasing understanding of how things really are."

Rorty points out that Nietzsche went even further along these lines by suggesting we drop the notion of truth altogether. His definition of truth was as a "mobile army of metaphors", saying that representing reality by means of existing language should be abandoned. He saw self-knowledge as self creation, and this involved the process of inventing a new language and thinking up new metaphors.

Nietzsche was, of course, thinking as an individual, whereas science is a collaborative enterprise, people working together, repeating results, and checking analysis. It remains, however, that although there is a reality to the world, our understanding of it is only via our concepts and metaphors, and Rorty's view of entrenched vocabularies continually being superseded by new vocabularies and increasingly useful metaphors is pertinent. An example of this would be in our understanding of the mind. In earlier centuries it was almost magical, a non-physical thing, a spirit or soul. Now, with our better understanding of biology and neurology, plus with all our new computing metaphors, we see the mind differently, as a process, as software running on the hardware of the brain, as our 'centre of narrative gravity', etc.

Before moving on to the next chapter on language itself, as a transition to that chapter, we will take a short look at two more issues: - the concept of identity, and the problem of categories.

The Concept of Identity

What is it that makes you unique? What preserves your identity over the years as you change and get older? Are you the same person, the same individual as that child that you used to be? If so, what is it that keeps you

Concepts and Understanding

you, what attribute or quality is unchanging, meaning you are always you?

You grow, you take in food and make it part of your body, your mind develops as you learn new things, your personality develops, but it is never static, it keeps changing. Every atom of your body now is different from the atoms which made up your body say ten years ago.

It's a bit like a football team, e.g. Manchester United, every player, coach and manager changes but it is still called Manchester United. So, one might be tempted to say it is your name that makes you you, but even that can change by marriage or deed poll, and anyway two people could have the same name.

One way to think about yourself is how you sit in relation to society. Even though your body and personality keep changing, you have a father and a mother, grandparents etc, children possibly. You have a date of birth, a legal name, a bank account, and are probably on a voting register. Society knows you, although fraud can happen, and identities have been stolen.

Another way to conceive of an identity that keeps developing is to define the concept of a person not as three-dimensional object that exists at a particular location and time, but as four-dimensional object stretched across time from your birth till your death.

There is so much looseness to the concept of 'I', it's a tiny word which you use every day, and everybody understands you when you use it. However, as seen above, you change over time, but to say "I change" sounds like a contradiction!

Consider a pack of pencils, they are all the same weight, length, width, mass, and so on. However, they are distinct physical objects, they have some different properties, e.g. location in space. If you take one pencil out, perhaps it becomes your pencil, you sharpen it when the tip wears down, so it gets smaller and smaller, but it's still your pencil even though it keeps changing.

The concept of 'numerical identity' is a mathematical one, and it's not always easy to map a clean mathematical idea to a messy world where boundaries are fuzzy. Concepts and categories are things we use to make sense of the world, but do they exist in reality, or are they just mental constructs?

To continue with the pencil example, two pencils from the same batch are incredibly similar (in size, shape, composition, etc.) But they are not identical. You would, therefore, be inclined to say that only one pencil on its own is numerically identical to itself. But for that definition to hold over time you have to remember that this individual pencil also changes over time, it gets worn down. Therefore, to have any useful meaning, you must apply the concept of numerical identity to an object that can change over time but that can still be usefully considered as being the same object.

Returning to the concept of personal identity, David Hume suggested that we are all just bundles of perceptions, collections of experiences, and that there is no extra thing called "person" that exists above and beyond those bundles. Maybe that's a touch extreme; perhaps we just have to accept that the concept of person is a nebulous one, something more than the sum of the parts. You could try to define your personal identity as "A physical, growing body that develops and accumulates memories over its lifetime", but it's much easier to just say "I", and even if you haven't defined it, everyone will understand what you mean.

The problem of definite categories

The mind understands the world by categorising it. Take the example of naming a species. We are Homo sapiens, and we evolved in Africa from other species: Australopithecus, Homo habilis, Homo erectus, Neanderthal, etc, etc. These are names given to fossils of particular species living at a particular time. But that is just a convenience, there are no hard boundaries.

If you took your parents, and then their parents, and then their parents, and so on for a few million years, those ancestors of yours would probably be classified as one of the species mentioned above, yet there was no break in lineage. At any given time, all the interbreeding members alive at that time would be classified as a particular species, but when does one species start and another end?

It's a bit like saying to an aerospace engineer, I want you to take a spitfire and turn it into a jumbo jet by changing one bit at a time, with the added constraint that after each small change the thing must still fly: not just get up in the air but still fly like it was designed to fly really well. Any individual model in the middle of this process will not be a spitfire or a jumbo, but to usefully talk about it you would probably give it its own name.

There are no hard boundaries, just our categorising mind, or as Richard Dawkins memorably coined it: - "The tyranny of the discontinuous mind." This also reminds us of Plato's 'ideal forms', of which more in the next chapter.

A similar type of question is: 'when does a pile becomes a heap?' A pile of sand grains is smallish, and a heap is bigger, but if you keep adding one grain to a pile, at some point it will become a heap. This is an example of what some philosophers call an 'empty question'. Indeed, it may be that many philosophical problems from the past are just language

Concepts and Understanding

definition problems, or as Richard Rorty would say, 'a new set of metaphors might help'.

We love to name things, and rightly so, giving something a name makes it easy to remember (we don't have to re-analyse its evidence and its constituent parts every time), and it makes it easy to communicate ideas with others. The danger is, however, that a barrier is being put up between us and the world, the hidden assumption being "I know that, I don't need to think about it again."

This chapter points out that we understand the world, make decisions about it, and communicate with others, all via our mental concepts. This method of understanding and communication is a very powerful and incredibly useful tool; indeed we have no option, all we have are our senses and our pattern recognising brain. From the perspective of philosophy and epistemology however, it should be remembered that this understanding is Inductive; mental concepts built and refined from babyhood onwards. Even as our subjective learning becomes more 'objective', through contact and sharing with others, our mental concepts are still our own inductive constructions.

The next chapter on language will continue this line of argument by considering all words as mentally constructed inductive concepts.

56

Language and Meaning

> *Philosophy is a battle against the bewitchment of our intelligence by means of language.*
>
> **Ludwig Wittgenstein**

Note: -

The above proposition of Wittgenstein's is ambiguous, (read it again and see if you can see the two ways in which it could be taken). Does it mean that it is language itself that bewitches our intelligence; or does it mean that we can battle against our confusion by a more rigorous use of language?

Both meanings are possible, and both meanings are true, making it such a good quote! Words are slippery things, they often have multiple meanings and usages, and meanings change over the years, but language is all we have with which to do philosophy.

> *"Meaning is everywhere. There is always meaning. Or at least all things show a disturbing tendency to have meaning ascribed to them when intelligent creatures are present."*
>
> **Ian M. Banks**

Overview

In the previous chapter we looked at understanding the world via our concepts. We use ideas from our familiar, everyday experience to try and comprehend (what science tells us is) the strangeness of things like matter, space, and time. Such concepts are often macro ideas like cause and effect, wave / particle duality, space-time deformed by gravity etc. We have no option; we have to use our concepts to interpret what our scientific instruments tell us, because we can't directly experience these things via our senses.

In this chapter, however, we will apply the same type of reasoning to all language, not just macro concepts but individual words themselves, because fundamentally, each single word is a concept in its own right. We will also look at how words are used to convey meaning, and at what we mean by meaning in the first place.

Plato's Forms

In chapter 11 on Plato, we saw that one of the things that fascinated him was the general nouns we use for things, for example the noun 'dog'. We recognise a dog when we see one, but each dog is different. Two dogs of the same breed look similar, but they still have differences, but with two dogs of different breeds we still recognise each of them as a dog, even if we have never seen an example of one of the breeds before, we recognise something about them that puts them in the category of 'dog'.

Plato tried to solve this by postulating an ideal realm somewhere that held true 'forms' such as dog, cat, tree, man etc. and continued by saying any individual dog we see is only an imperfect shadow of the real 'form' dog from that ideal realm. He likened this to someone looking at a wall in a cave and seeing only a shadow of a 'real' dog cast by a fire behind him. Plato was looking for some kind of pure essence, which he assumed must exist, and which the physical world failed to live up to, and he applied the same type of reasoning to more complex concepts like 'Justice'.

Russell's Universals

Bertrand Russell too was fascinated by such abstract or general ideas, for which he used the term 'universals', although (unlike Plato) he did not claim they resided in some otherworldly realm. He acknowledged that general concepts like 'dog' were not physical things (as opposed to specific references like 'that dog'). He considered that they come from a mix of sense data, memory, and self-conscious introspection. His main interest was in how concepts relate to knowledge, and he said that we have to "guard against the supposition that whatever we can be acquainted with must be something particular and existent".

Russell also considered relational words as universals. Take the statement 'he is in his room'. He exists, his room exists, but does the word 'in' exist? Obviously not in the same way that 'he' and 'his room' both exist, yet it has meaning about the relationship between 'he' and 'his room'. Kant would say that it is the action of the mind that produces the relation 'in', but Russell wants to place relational knowledge in a world which is neither mental nor physical.

Hume said we build our concepts from examples. Take redness, for example, he says our concept of it is built from the many examples we have seen. Russell is closer to Plato here in that he thinks that having seen many examples we can extrapolate to some definitive, almost a-priori, knowledge of what general redness is, and without it being a physical or a mental thing, we have hit upon a logical truth.

Russell was, first and foremost, a mathematician and logician, and he spent years, trying to discover a logically ideal language that could be used to unambiguously talk about the world. It would, of course, use universals like relational words, and logical connectives such as "and" and "or". He thought that many of our concepts were meta-concepts and that they could be broken down into smaller, atomic like concepts, and thus developed his theory of **logical atomism**. This theory strongly influenced the early Wittgenstein, although later, Wittgenstein changed his ideas and began talking about describing the world using 'word games' (which is similar to Richard Rorty talking about new sets of metaphors constantly replacing older sets.)

Where Russell falls down is in proving that any given concept built by one brain is identical to a concept (referred to by the same name) built by another brain. Close, undoubtedly, but identical, virtually impossible. Any brain concept is built from examples presented, but also it does not stand in isolation in the brain, it is connected to a complex web of other, interrelated concepts and emotions, and as such is unique to that brain.

Is the concept 'red' in one brain the same as the concept 'red' in another? Is the perception of 'red' the same in one brain the same as the perception 'red' in another? (Remember from chapter 54 the word 'perception' implies a lot of pre-processing.) What about some sort of 'pure experience' of red in one brain and in another? Is there such a thing as 'pure experience' when awareness occurs after a lot of subconscious pre-processing? Does it matter? It must be close enough for two people to exchange meaningful information about an object that is red without either of them defining redness to the other, so even if one person's concept of redness is not identical to another's concept of redness, useful and meaningful information can be exchanged.

Language and Meaning

Words as Concepts

It might be assumed that redness is universal because the word exists: it is in our books; it is in our dictionaries, where it is actually defined. But any given word in a dictionary is only defined in terms of other words, ultimately dictionaries are self-referential. Even science can't help with the definition of redness. It can specify redness perception occurs when specific wavelengths of light enter the eye, but colour is an interpretation by the brain, there is no such thing as colour in the external world, just different wavelengths of electromagnetic radiation. As pointed out in chapter 54 on perception, looking for colour in an object would be as fruitless as looking for a musical note in a steel guitar string.

We learn our words at our mother's knee. She points to things or to pictures in a book and says 'dog', 'cat', 'red', 'fireman', etc. And our pattern recognising brain starts to build our concepts. It is worth reminding ourselves here of the intuition pump 'Daddy is a Doctor' given by the American philosopher Dan Dennett (mentioned in chapter 44).

> A five-year-old girl is asked what daddy does, and she replies that daddy is a doctor. Does she know what a doctor is? Perhaps she just thinks daddy helps people when they get sick. When she is eight, her concept of a doctor will have become more complex, and so on. But does the person asking the question know what a doctor is, as well as say a doctor himself or herself does? Does it matter however; meaning has been imparted.
>
> This story helps us to understand where meaning comes from, and that words are not definite things. Words (like doctor) are concepts, created by our brains and developed, modified, and refined over time from the experiences and information we are exposed to. Each one of us might have a slightly different concept of any given word, but we can still communicate with each other and impart useful meaning, even though the words we use are not definite.
>
> A second aspect that this particular intuition pump helps us to think about is the idea of belief. How much does the girl need to know in order to understand the proposition? If understanding comes in degrees, as this example shows, then belief, which depends on understanding, must also come in degrees. We could say that she **sort of** understands that her daddy is a doctor, which is not the same as saying that she has any reservations or doubts. This helps us to think more clearly about belief, meaning and mental concepts, all neatly

encapsulated, and made easy to remember, by the intuition pump 'Daddy is a Doctor'.

Every single word we learn is a concept built by our brains and interlinked with our other concepts. But as we have seen in the above example, concepts are not static in the brain, they are continually being added to, refined, and cross linked to further concepts and emotions. Words too are not a static part of our external environment, language evolves, new words are coined, and meanings change. Words are useful 'placeholders' for those things that we think we see. The important point here being 'useful', i.e. they can be used to convey meaning even without exact definition.

Quite a wide definition of the word 'concept' is being used here. Some definitions would restrict the word to only cover large ideas containing multiple elements under a short heading, some examples being: cause and effect; evolution; liberalism; God; citizen; the social contract; existentialism etc. Such a restricted view might see short individual words such as dog, road, in, and, tree etc. as fixed words existing in an external dictionary that we just have to learn.

The view taken here is that all words are concepts, built individually by each brain through experience (as in the 'daddy is a doctor' intuition pump), and that, although different brains seem to converge on logical and useful truths, a person's concepts are in a continual state of flux and refinement throughout their life as they experience more examples, and different usages made, of each word. Even a simple word like 'in', which we might learn as a child as, say, a ball being inside a box, gets refined when we learn different usages of it, such as being 'in trouble', or existing 'in perpetuity'. Our concepts of the words we learn are constantly being expanded with multiple links to other concepts. Also, they become uniquely coloured by any emotions linked to those learning experiences.

So individual words are concepts, but there is not always a one-to-one relationship with a word and a concept, some sophisticated concepts need multiple words to explain them, for instance the concept of 'cause and effect'. And many concepts need links with other concepts in order to work; we build webs of concepts to understand the world. Also, words have multiple meanings and which meaning or concept is intended often needs to be implied through the context in which it is used.

Non Linguistic Concepts

The question then arises as to whether we can have any non-linguistic concepts as well as our verbal ones. Well, that certainly occurs with babies

Language and Meaning

before they learn to speak. Think of building a tower of blocks in front of a pre-linguistic six-month-old baby. They soon learn that if they push it the tower will fall over; indeed, they even anticipate the adult's 'shocked' reaction and laugh at it. Here is a pre-linguistic learning of a concept of 'cause and effect'.

When studying babies of this age it is well known, and used in tests, that a baby will stare for longer at something that happens that it doesn't expect to happen. Researchers have made videos of shapes moving around, and if one shape bangs into another but the second one stays still (not moving in response to the collision) then six-month-old babies stare at this much longer. They had an early concept of cause and effect and were surprised when the second shape did not move following the collision.

Animals too build non-linguistic concepts of the world. Chimps or dogs for example have an understanding of cause and effect, if they see something happen, they will look round for the cause. And that's just one example of the many concepts they build about their world. Even animals with much smaller brains will have some sort of idea of their home (a safe place) and of how to navigate their environment to get there.

Adult humans also have sophisticated concepts about the world that are non-linguistic: think of catching a ball, playing tennis, playing snooker, riding a bike etc. It is incredibly hard to unravel the interaction of language acquisition and learning about the world, but science studies tell us that much of our everyday thinking about the world occurs at a pre-verbalisation stage and that the words we use are often a story we tell ourselves, as a rationalisation, after the act of thinking. Putting such things into words makes them more concrete to us and aids communication to others. Again, referencing the American philosopher Daniel Dennett (chapter 44), he refers to 'the illusion of self' as that which is generated by our 'centre of narrative gravity', i.e. the story we tell ourselves about the concept we have of our own self.

Meaning and Context

If all words are mental concepts in individual brains, and if the mental concept of a word in one brain is not identical to the mental concept tagged with the same word in another brain, it seems legitimate to ask how communication takes place and where does meaning come from?

Individual words by themselves are open to different interpretations. If one person says the word 'doctor', for instance, they could be referring to a medical doctor, a doctor of divinity, a doctor of science etc. All words have multiple meanings depending on their usage, and that is the key to meaning. Words are not used in isolation, they have other words around them in sentences, and more than that, there are other clues to someone's meaning, including: tone; body language; and the possibility of sarcasm, irony, and lying etc. The pattern recognising brain of the listener is constantly working to understand the speaker in real time as they utter each word, trying out multiple different interpretations of meaning, and discarding most of them, incredibly fast and virtually unnoticed.

Also supplying meaning to a communication between two people are all the previous discussions between those two people, and the shared environment they exist in e.g. talking about a film they have just watched, or an office meeting just attended.

American author Henry James (brother of philosopher William James) talks about the "solidity of specification" as a method of making his stories more real, i.e. putting in details of the place in which the scene is occurring in order that the reader can 'picture' it better in their mind. But this could be a two-edged sword. George Orwell, in his 1946 essay **Politics and the English Language,** talks about language designed "to give an appearance of solidity to pure wind". So where is this 'solidity'? It is only in the mind.

Meaning then, emerges from context. If someone says, 'the book you wanted is on the table by the window in the living room', the person being spoken to has received useful, and meaningful, information. Even though all fifteen words in the sentence might individually be ambiguous (and indeed undefined by the speaker) it is their combination, and the implied shared understanding of things like environment and motive, that delivers the meaning. The important point here is usefulness; if the second person can use the information, then meaning has been imparted.

To say, 'the book is on the table' is more straightforward than saying (for instance) 'the Prime Minister is too right wing for me'. But ultimately, each word is a concept built by the individual brain of the speaker from examples presented to it from babyhood onwards, and no two brains would have had exactly the same experiences. Some concepts, like right wing, are more complicated, but even a simple word like 'dog' can only be built as a concept in a brain from examples presented.

Note that because of the need for context in the conveyance of meaning, and that in many cases the context required has to be extensive in order to fully impart the meaning, we often find that poetry is the best tool for the job. Poetry usually approaches its subject obliquely, shedding new light from different perspectives. It incorporates emotion, and it often deliberately includes multiple interpretations. Done well, poetry can directly and poignantly convey meaning to the listener free of the multiple caveats and explanations of directed prose however well written.

Language and Meaning

> *On a poet's lips I slept*
> *Dreaming like a love-adept*
> *In the sound his breathing kept;*
> *Nor seeks nor finds he mortal blisses,*
> *But feeds on the aereal kisses*
> *Of shapes that haunt thought's wildernesses.*
>
> **Percy Bysshe Shelley** - (from *Prometheus Unbound*)

Here too is Virginia Woolf talking about words, meaning and great poetry.

> It is necessary to take that dangerous leap through the air without the support of words which Shakespeare also asks of us. For words, when opposed to such a blast of meaning, must give out, must be blown astray, and only by collecting in companies convey the meaning which each one separately is too weak to express. Connecting them in rapid flight of mind we know instantly and instinctively what they mean, but could not decant that meaning afresh into any other words. [...] The meaning is just on the far side of language.
>
> **Virginia Woolf** - (from *On not Knowing Greek*)

Language

Language is an incredibly useful tool in our lives, as is implied by the significantly large portion of our brains dedicated to its production and understanding. There is a theory that as the groups we lived in became larger in our evolutionary history, we each needed to be able to keep track of more individuals: who did what to whom; who owed what to whom; who to trust and who to be wary of etc. Larger brains by themselves would have helped in this, but the onset of language became incredibly useful, mainly because information about others could be shared - as opposed to just being based on one's own experience. In other words, the theory is that gossip was one of the drivers that fuelled the development of language.

Many of our enterprises have their own distinct subset of language, their own expressions and vocabulary. They often have their own restricted definitions of words that, in everyday use would mean something different. Think of professions like printing, fishing, medicine, philosophy, maths, politics, and physics for example. Once again context aids understanding, learn the vocabulary (the concepts) and communication on the subject becomes easier. This is partly what Wittgenstein meant by 'word games' – using the right language for the job of communication and understanding.

Another powerful element of language is the ability to talk about language itself. If we think of physics for example we can discuss (say) how to perform a particular experiment, but we can also move into metaphysics and talk about what the findings of that experiment means, not just in terms of physics but also in more philosophical terms about the nature of reality.

Something similar occurs with language. We can just use it to communicate with each other, or we can move to a kind of meta-language and talk about its structure (nouns, adjectives, grammar etc), or we can even move to a kind of meta-meta-language and talk in philosophical terms about concepts, meaning, information and understanding.

It is also important not to just use the right language subset for the listener, but to use the right level of language for the information being imparted. An example from computing will help here. Computers work with ones and zeros, represented by two different levels of electrical charge in the bits in their registers. These settings can be manipulated by programmers using a language called machine language, but that would be very long winded for more complex jobs, so programmers write in high level languages and then run their program through a compiler which changes it into machine code. If you want to discuss how to build a computer you will need to talk about the machine code, the bits and the registers, but if you want to talk about writing a chess program you will need to talk in the high-level language, and if you want to talk about chess strategy you will use ordinary language.

The chess program you are playing against ultimately works in ones and zeros, but talking about a move it has just made in terms of ones and zeros will get you nowhere. Note too that the neurons in our brain work on electricity flowing through different paths and connections in the presence of external and internal stimulation and various neurochemicals, but we would get nowhere talking about the move a chess grandmaster just made by talking about his neurons. We will meet this idea again in the next chapter on free will.

We all have to make decisions in our life and to do this we need an understanding of the world we live in. Language, along with maths, logic, and emotion, are the main tools we use in making those decisions. As we have seen above, however, even the great philosopher Bertrand Russell could not make language a precise logical enterprise. Language is messy and ambiguous, and sometimes, the more words you use, the more ambiguous it becomes. Also, decisions often have to take account of multiple variables and premises, which again makes the logic difficult. But having said all that, we humans are very good at making decisions based on limited and ambiguous data, and there is one area of maths and computing that sheds light on this ability: it's called 'fuzzy logic'.

In the classic logic of Aristotle there are only two values for any proposition, true or false. This has since been extended to 'many-value logic', in which there are more than two truth values per proposition. Fuzzy logic is a form of many-value logic that is employed to handle the concept of partial truth, where the truth of each of the multiple propositions may range in value somewhere between completely true and completely false. The term was introduced in 1965, but this type of logic has been studied since the 1920s. Fuzzy logic was developed from the observation that people make decisions based on imprecise and non-numerical information, and fuzzy models (or sets) are a mathematical means of representing the vagueness of information.

As well as its use in mathematics, fuzzy logic is often used in computing, and particularly in AI (artificial intelligence), but this type of variable value propositional calculus is, of course, what humans do all the time due to the imprecise and vague nature of language. We actually have no choice in the matter, language is the main tool we have (apart from maths and science) to make our decisions with, and those decisions must be based on our understanding of the world using the concepts our minds have built through our experience of the world. And even if some of those concepts are non-verbal ones, we still need to express our decisions in words, either explicitly to others, or as rationalisations to ourselves.

Idealism vs. Empiricism

This is a good place to take a step back and look at language and meaning from a historical and philosophical viewpoint, and this brings us back to some of the ideas we looked at when we considered individual philosophers, in particular the difference between Idealism and Empiricism.

Philosophers like Descartes and Kant were Idealists, they thought that the only thing that was 'real' were our thoughts, so ideas like 'tree' and 'dog' were just how we categorised things. This is a bit like Plato and his Forms, except that for Plato, the Forms (like dog) resided in some rarefied, almost spiritual place, and what we experience are just imperfect copies or shadows of the 'real' forms.

Other philosophers, like Lock, Hume, and Russell, were empiricists. They believed in a real external world which we try to understand. But they too realised that we create concepts to help us understand the world. Hume, for instance, says cause and effect is a concept that we create, from, for example, watching one billiard ball hitting another many times over, and then making a generalisation as to what might happen the next time. You don't actually see anything being passed from one ball to the next, all you actually see is just a succession of images, and from this we create the concept of cause and effect. And, in the same way, we create all our other concepts about the world, like for instance generalising the concept 'dog' from all the dogs we have seen.

Then the philosopher, Husserl, coined the term Phenomenology to just talk about our mental landscape; he "bracketed" any knowledge of a real external world, leaving it for future scientists/philosophers to deal with. This approach later morphed into Existentialism via the philosophers Sartre and Camus.

So, how do we understand the world? Are there such things as 'dogs' or 'persons', or are they just how we categorise the world? It often seems that the more you try to pin down a concept the harder it gets. Maybe we should just accept that we need different ways to talk about the same thing depending on the needs of the moment. All words are concepts that we have created to understand the world and to communicate with others. And communication is the real goal; as long as meaning (i.e. useful information) is exchanged, then job done. If someone shouts at you "look out there's a lion on the loose", you could both sit down and discuss if you both mean the same thing by 'lion' and 'on the loose', or you could just run: useful information imparted; job done.

Review

These last four chapters (Philosophy of Mind; Perception; Concepts and Understanding; Language and Meaning) have been an extended argument concerning the bedrock topic on which Western Philosophy is built, i.e. 'how do we understand the world and what constitutes knowledge?' Unless we understand epistemology (the theory of knowledge) it is difficult to talk meaningfully about other philosophical topics such as ethics, politics, and how best to live our lives.

Another important aspect of these last chapters is that the philosophy in them is one that is informed by science. That's not to say that science tells us everything, just that any philosophical theories cannot now ignore the findings of science. The above chapters include what science has discovered on the workings of the brain, on perception, and on how we learn about the world from babyhood onwards. One important point to emphasise here is that the scientific approach shows that there is no need for the old concept of dualism, there is no need to postulate a supernatural soul or spirit (for which there is no evidence). The human brain can understand the world by itself, just like a chimpanzee or a dog, but in our case it's somewhat more powerful.

So, in empirical terms, there is an external world out there, and science is the best tool we have to investigate it, but at the same time we have to realise that we only understand that world via the concepts we build with our pattern recognising brains. This should not be a surprise, because we are talking here about gaining knowledge by 'Induction', and as Hume showed, Induction can never be 100% certain. It can get extremely close to 100% however, and as we all live in the same world, one person's concepts will converge towards another's, even though they are built from the individual's own experiences. And if there are slight differences, it does not matter, it is usefulness and context that are the keys to communication; meaning has been imparted (or created) when the listener can successfully act in the world based on the speaker's words.

As well as poetry, another way to think about language and meaning is in terms of art, with words being like the brush strokes of an impressionist painting, coming together to create a picture which, although not as exact as a photograph, still depicts its subject in a way we can readily understand and empathise with because of our shared existence and experience in the same world.

Language is the art of manipulating high level, fuzzy, multi-meaning concepts; and that is what makes it so powerful. Even a six-year-old can have fun playing with different meanings of words, and a gifted political orator can make you believe almost anything!

As mentioned above, we think of words as concrete entities, their meanings defined in dictionaries for everyone to use, but this does not take into account how our brains build our concepts (remember the 'daddy is a doctor' intuition pump). Note also that Socrates seemed to know this over 2,400 years ago (refer back to chapter 10). Remember he wanted to know what things like 'justice' and 'virtue' were and he went round asking people, even the judges in the law courts. None of them could tell him, all they could do was to give him examples. Justice is a high-level concept, but exactly the same logic applies to words like 'dog' and 'tree'; indeed to all words.

If the idea that "words are not concrete entities" is still difficult to accept then consider this. We use words to describe and talk about the world, and to talk about things like relationships. It's a bit like using a map to navigate a landscape, but not only is it the case that 'the map is not the territory', it is also the case that the map you use is your map, created by your brain; it's a pretty good map or we wouldn't survive, but a map it is nevertheless.

57

Free Will

Freedom cannot exist without the concept of order.

Prince Metternich (Austrian Statesman 1773-1859)

Overview

The question "Do we have free will?" is a favourite for discussion among philosophers, and strong opinions are often held from both sides of the debate. The arguments from both sides will be presented and examined here, but as with most philosophical questions we also need to examine the question itself. We need to make sure that we are all talking about the same thing, and we need to examine different ways to think about the issue and about any subtleties involved. Some of that thinking will make use of the previous few chapters where discussion centred on how we understand the world via the concepts we build.

Introduction

The debate over free will has been going on for centuries.

Early on it was a religious question. It was claimed that God gave us free will so that we could choose between good and evil, and freely choose to worship him. However, there was a problem with this because it was also claimed that God (being omnipotent and knowing the future) already knew what choice each person would make. This seemed to say that our 'decisions' were pre-determined and therefore we had no real choice. This was, and perhaps still is, quite a problem for religion.

Another aspect (usually but not necessarily connected with some religions) is the idea of 'fate', i.e. we might think we are in control of what happens to us but outside forces actually rule our lives. This is perhaps best illustrated with a story from the film Lawrence of Arabia: -

Free Will

They are making a long crossing of a terrible stretch of desert. One of the Arabs is found to be missing, presumed dead. Lawrence refuses to give up, goes back into the desert and rescues him just in time. A few days later, this same Arab is found stealing from another Arab of a different tribe. To prevent a falling out between the two tribes, the only thing Lawrence can do is execute the man himself. Then, because the man is now dead anyway, despite being rescued from the desert, one of the Arab leaders comments "Ah, it was written".

Also connected with the idea of fate are other superstitions, like astrology. But then later, with the emergence of science, another perspective opened up, and the debate then became about whether you can have free will in a deterministic universe, i.e. if you know the position and velocity of every particle accurately, then (theoretically) you would be able to calculate what is going to happen in the future, and even if you can't do the calculations yourself, what's going to happen is still determined by the laws of physics. Hence you can't have free will in a deterministic universe.

However, this picture was further complicated with the arrival of quantum mechanics. This said that the universe did have truly random things in it, and that you couldn't know both position and velocity of any particle accurately. Some people think that this altered the debate, but others disagree.

Before continuing though, we should remember something from chapter 4 about what it is that philosophers actually do. Not only do they construct arguments, either in favour or against a given question, they also don't just take the question as given. Part of their job is to analyse the question itself in terms of what words are used; what are the meanings of the different words; could other words have made the question clearer; what hidden agendas are there in the question, is the question ambiguous; and so on.

There is often a tendency in philosophical debates to jump straight in with an answer, but that impulse should be resisted because in doing so we might miss some of the subtleties of the topic in question. We should always look at the question itself and at the language used, and we should look at the 'how', as well as the 'what'. So, debates are often started by analysing the question itself as well as the subject.

Analysing the Question: -

With that in mind, let's look a little closer at the question "Do we have free will?"

What do we mean by the word 'we'?

This makes the question general, but if I have free will then (solipsism aside) the rest of us do as well. So the question could also be 'Do I have free will?' What difference does this make? Well, it might depend on how we define 'I'.

- If 'I' equals my conscious self then what about all the other things my brain and body do subconsciously: instincts; emotions; hormones; reflexes; mental pre-processing of sensory data, breathing and other bodily functions, etc.
- Also, we have to put things into language in order to communicate (or even to reason internally) and that takes time, so when we decide something, we are often articulating an event or a mind state after the fact.
- Once again here science enters the debate. In 1983 neuroscientist Benjamin Libet tested people's decision making. He asked them to move a finger, at a time of their own choosing, while looking at a dot rotating on a clock-face. They had to note the position of the dot as soon as they became aware of their intention to act. At the same time, he used electrodes to monitor their brain activity. He found that there was a spike in the brain activity about 350 milliseconds before the subjects became consciously aware of their intention to move their finger. He interpreted this to mean that free will is an illusion because the decision to act is initiated subconsciously.
- Alternatively, however, you could say that the unconscious part of my brain is part of the whole 'me' and if there is a minor delay in a decision entering conscious awareness that need not mean the decision is not freely made by me as a whole. Once again, our conscious awareness is perhaps best thought of as a story told to ourselves after the fact.

What do we mean by the word 'free'?

- Is free choice meaningless if outside forces or other people control our lives e.g. someone being made redundant, or not doing something because it is against the law?
- If you are being coerced to do something, are you acting with free will?
- Do people use the word 'free' in different ways? We would need to ensure that any particular argument does not start out with one definition of 'free' and conclude using a different definition of it.

Does the question ask (or imply) whether or not we possess free will 'all the time'?

- What about when asleep?
- What about when intoxicated?
- Is there a difference between: -
    - Doing something automatic (like walking) or by habit (like brushing your teeth),
    - Doing something fast (on impulse or by instinct),
    - Or slow, considered, logical reflection (making a plan, considering alternate actions).

Perhaps the biggest unknown is what do we mean by our 'will'?

- We might say we have a 'will to survive', but is that a single thing or is it made up of a number of different 'drives'?
- Does our 'will' simply equate to our wants and desires?
- The philosopher Nietzsche (as we saw in chapter 35) admired strength of will above all things. "*I test the power of a will,*" he says, "*according to the amount of resistance it can offer and the amount of pain and torture it can endure and know how to turn to its own advantage.*"

Extra Note:

It is not the case here, but many debate topic questions start with the word 'why' (as in 'Why do we exist?' or 'Why is there evil in the world?' for example.)

An important point about the question 'why' is that it has two meanings; it can be asking 'how did something get the way it is?' or 'what is the reason behind something being this way?' In the words of philosopher Daniel Dennett, this is 'How come?' or 'What for?'

The 'how come?' question asks for some sort of logical, historical explanation as to why something is the way it is (e.g. think of using the theory of evolution as part of the explanation of why we exist). Whereas the 'what for?' question implies there is some design purpose to something being the way it is (e.g. think of talking about the 'social contract' when discussing why there are limits on liberty).

It is important to keep these two meanings separate when discussing a topic. By all means cover both aspects, but don't fall into the trap of starting with one meaning and ending with the other, and then thinking that you have logically proved something.

Historical Philosophical Perspective

Before moving on, let's look at what previous philosophers have said over the years: -

Plotinus:

> Given that the world inevitably has imperfections, Plotinus (like the Christians) had to account for sin. He says that sin is a consequence of free will, which he upholds against both the determinists and the astrologers.

St. Augustine:

> Believed in free will but said that Adam and Eve ate the apple because the devil had corrupted their free will with libido; before the fall they had had uncorrupted free will! Augustine saw free will (or perhaps more exactly free control of the will) as essential to Catholic theology, because otherwise an almighty God would not be justified in punishing ill-doers. He says it is true that God has foreknowledge of our sins, but we do not sin because of His foreknowledge.

St. Thomas Aquinas:

> Said that God has free will because He is able to do things, but Aquinas then (rather bravely) listed several things that God can't do.

Spinoza:

Spinoza completely rejected free will and chance in the world. For him, God understands everything and sees all time at once, so there is no evil. What seems like sin to us does not exist when viewed as part of the whole.

Leibniz:

Leibniz, remember, thought this the best of all possible worlds. He thought the world deterministic, but because it was so complex, the analysis required to deduce how someone will act is only possible for God. So, although human actions flow from prior causes that ultimately arise in God (and therefore are known as a metaphysical certainty to God) an individual's free will is exercised, he claims, within natural laws, where choices are merely contingently necessary, to be decided in the event by a "wonderful spontaneity" that provides individuals an escape from rigorous predestination.

It seems logically impossible for God to bestow free will and at the same time decree that there should be no sin. The world that resulted, however, does seem to contain an excess of good over evil (according to Leibniz) hence demonstrating it is the best possible world.

Hume:

Can I decide what I want and then decide to do it? Yes, I can. Whether or not what I decide is predictable doesn't bother me. I would be shocked if it wasn't because I would rather not be random. The only way I can be me is if I am determined.

Schopenhauer:

Man can indeed do what he wants, but he cannot want what he wants.

Freud:

Freud's groundbreaking view, that we have a subconscious, also influenced the debate. Expanding on this idea, he suggested that declarations of free will are in fact delusions; we are not entirely aware of what we think, and we often act for reasons that have little to do with our conscious thoughts.

An Introduction to Philosophy

G.E. Moore:

"I am free in performing an action if I could have done otherwise."

Charles Renouvier:

Free will is "the sustaining thought because I choose to when I might have other thoughts."

William James:

Consciousness cannot determine what ideas are presented to it, but, by effortful selective attention, it can decide which ideas will affect behaviour.

It might be profitable to re-read the above statements while keeping in mind the previous notes on 'analysing the question'. Are the above philosophers all talking about the same thing, what premises do they take for granted, and are they using their own definitions of words which often redefines the question and the debate?

We will look at the responses from currently existing philosophers within the context of the debate (outlined below) as it is usually framed today, and this of course includes a scientific perspective.

The Current Main Arguments Against Free Will

These split into two main groups, strict bottom-up versions based around particle physics, and softer top-down versions based around how we make decisions.

Bottom-up arguments

The main argument here is the Newtonian one mentioned above, i.e. if you know the position and velocity of every particle accurately, then (theoretically) you would be able to calculate what is going to happen in the future, and even if you can't do the calculations yourself, what's going to happen is still determined by the laws of physics. Hence the universe is deterministic. Every decision you make is determined by the existing state of the universe, all the particles in it and all their velocities, so what will happen is going to happen.

It might be thought that quantum mechanics, with its randomness, would change that from two perspectives. Firstly, radioactive decay seems random, for instance we don't know when the nucleus of a given atom of say radium-226 will decay to radon-222 through the emission of an alpha particle, but we do know its 'half-life' (i.e. the length of time it takes for a given quantity of the substance to reduce to half of its initial value), in this case it's 1.6 thousand years. Given that we know the half-lives of all the elements, and the fact that these half-lives are predictable, then the universe can still be considered deterministic. Also, although the actual instance of the decay of a single atom can't be predicted and is considered random, there is an assumption that there must be some mechanism at work, it's just that we don't know the details.

Secondly, quantum mechanics brings with it things like the fact that you can't know both the position and the velocity of particles. The more accurate you get with one of these measurements the less accurate you can be with the other. Also, for a given atom, we can't measure exactly where its electrons are, all we can do is calculate a kind of probability cloud for their orbit around the nucleus. Once again, however, this may well be down to our lack of knowledge about the fine detail of our universe.

These arguments are complex and incomplete, but the fact that we live in a deterministic universe is fairly obvious, even if we don't know the details. Indeed, it would have to be deterministic or we would not have evolved in it; for evolution to work, things like chemical and biological processes need to be dependable.

So, bottom-up arguments often reduce to one of logic: - the universe is deterministic (even if we don't know all details) and what will happen, must therefore, depend on its current state and previous history, in which case there is no choice – the future is determined by the past.

Top-down arguments

There are two main versions of top-down arguments against free will; one type could be labelled psychological arguments and the other neurological ones.

The psychological arguments start with the idea that every action has a cause, and that each cause itself has a prior cause, and so on. Why do we perform an action? It's due to the total history of our life so far, our genetic makeup and all the experiences we have had that make up our current mental state. (Remember from previous chapters, our concepts are dependent on our experiences.)

Therefore, what we decide to do in any given situation is totally dependent on our past. It might be thought that this only covers instinctive types of action, and that if you sat down and considered logically which action to take you could evade the past. But proponents say that the act of choosing to sit down and reason logically is itself generated by your past history, and even when you do reason in that way, the type of reasoning you do, and the things you include on your 'pros and cons' list, are all determined by your history and your makeup.

The neurological arguments go back to the experiments (mentioned above) by neuroscientist Benjamin Libet who discovered that a given decision made by a subject to move a finger can be detected (via instruments measuring brain activity) around 350 milliseconds before the subject becomes consciously aware of having made that decision and hence we have no conscious control over it.

To this can be added the Freudian psychological perspective that says we are driven by drives that we have no direct knowledge or control of. Such drives become buried or sublimated and often reappear in actions unconnected with the original drive. We project our own emotions and reasoning onto others, or we transfer our feelings about one person onto another person. In short, we often don't understand our own reasons and motives for our actions.

The American neuroscientist **Sam Harris** is an example of a current determinist of the top-down school. He argues that free will is an illusion because every action has a cause; he also says the origins of our thoughts are in our subconscious, so again we have no control over them. Harris does not (as others have) argue about determinism or quantum randomness, instead he takes the pragmatic view that decisions are made prior to them becoming conscious thoughts (backed by scientific experiments) and hence we have no control over them.

This might, however, be a difference of definition; Harris seems to be identifying the self as only our conscious awareness, whereas the self could be regarded as being wider than that. Just because something has not yet been articulated into words doesn't mean it's not a legitimate part of our decision-making process. Also, just because something is an urge doesn't mean we can't consider it rationally before acting.

Arguments For Free Will

It is widely accepted that we live in a deterministic universe, so arguments for us having free will contend that free will is actually compatible with living in such a universe, indeed free will, or even life itself, couldn't exist if the universe were not deterministic (as noted above). These arguments are called compatibilist arguments.

The simplest argument for free will claims that even though the universe can be considered mainly deterministic, chance enters via quantum mechanics randomness, and that this means the universe is not fully deterministic; therefore, future states of the universe cannot be completely predicted from past states. This removes the idea that the future is inevitable given the past. Even though it is acknowledged that the past has happened and can't be changed, different futures are still possible due to random events.

Another argument revolves around the idea that, if you decide to do something, could you have done otherwise? Having free will entails that you can freely choose to perform an action, or not perform it. There are proponents on both side of this argument, but it comes down to what we mean by 'freely choose'. Those arguing that we don't have free will would say the action you choose is completely determined by your past history, whereas those for free will would say that your choice is free if you are not being influenced or coerced by something or someone. In other words, they say we perform an action freely as long as we do so only in response to our own wants and desires.

This argument can get quite complex because it brings in another high-level concept, that of 'cause and effect', which, of course, has itself had philosophers arguing about it over the years (think of Hume, Kant and others, as noted in previous chapters). For instance, say you are at a dinner party, someone asks you to pass them the salt, and you do so. Are you forced by the situation, could you have said no? What is the cause of your action of passing the salt? Is it the request for the salt by the person asking for it that is the cause? Is it your desire to be friendly, or to fit in with the social norms, or to not start an argument that is the cause? Here again we see fuzzy, high-level concepts, having multiple usages and meanings.

Let's take a sidestep here and think again about particles. Think of a single hydrogen atom in (say) a protein in the cell wall of a neuron in a brain. That hydrogen atom could be replaced by a different hydrogen atom and the memories that that nerve cell is involved with would not change, because it is only the connections between nerve cells that hold those memories. So multiple different pasts could have given rise to the same present.

Here we have the idea of 'substrate independence' – it's the connections that are important for holding our memories and concepts, not the neurons themselves. This is a bit like a computer program that can run on different hardware and produce the same result. In the previous chapter we noted that we can use different levels of language to talk about a chess program; either machine code, bits and registers, or ordinary language chess strategy. Also, we noted that we would get nowhere talking about the move a chess grandmaster just made by talking about his neurons.

Ideas like 'cause and effect' and 'free will' are high level, multi meaning, nebulous concepts, built by our pattern recognising brain from our experiences, and stored in the connection pathway complexes of our neurons along with their associated neurochemicals and hormones. But talking about 'free will' in terms of our neurons would be unproductive. And even talk at the neurons level is a higher level than particle physics! We have to use the right level of meta-language to talk about high level fuzzy concepts like 'free will'.

This is why many current philosophers like to reframe the debate to one that talks about things like morality, self-control, responsibility, and society as a whole. If we redefine the debate like that, it highlights different, and perhaps more interesting, perspectives.

Patricia Churchland:

American philosopher Patricia Churchland, for instance, takes a pragmatic stance. She sees free will as a necessary social requirement; we need to be able to hold people responsible for their actions. Sometimes people genuinely can't help themselves if they commit a crime, but most of the time we do hold people responsible. She suggests moving the debate over free will away from metaphysics and towards the neurology of self-control, and the ways that this could be compromised. Unlike free will, self-control is a concept that can usefully be applied to other animals and hence brains in general. It is something that increases as the living being matures.

> *"It's metaphysical goofiness."* She says. *"The reason I just scratched my foot is because of that causal connection to the big bang? Get real."*
>
> *"But what is the 'self' of self-control? What am I?"* she asks. *"In essence, the self is a construction of the brain; a real, but brain-dependant organisational network for monitoring body states, setting priorities and, within the brain itself, creating the separation between inner world and outer world... Essentially,* [the self] *is a high-level tool... Is one cheapened by this neuroscientific knowledge? I think not... Each of us is a work of art, sculpted first by evolution, and second by experience of the world. With experience and reflection one's social perception matures, and so also does the level of autonomy. Aristotle called it wisdom."*

In her view you have to hold people responsible for their actions (apart from mitigating conditions such as mental illness). If you don't, society would just not work.

Daniel Dennett:

Another American philosopher, Dan Dennett, produces a rigorous analysis of the question (see chapter 44, but it's worth repeating here). He demonstrates that you can have free will even in a deterministic universe.

In his book '**Freedom Evolves**' he examines this problem of where freedom comes from if the world is fully deterministic. That is, if we imagine being able to know where every particle in the universe is and how it is moving then we would be able to work out what is going to happen in the future. In fact, from this point of view the future would be completely determined, hence we would not really be 'free' to act because everything we did would be pre-determined.

He points out two problems with this view. Firstly, there is a question as to the possibility of ever doing this because you would have to deal with things like chaos and the uncertainty principle in quantum mechanics (i.e. that it is impossible to determine both the exact position of a particle and its velocity at the same time). The second difficulty is that any model of the universe would itself be part of the universe and so would have to model itself, and to model itself modelling itself... ad infinitum.

So, although we can consider the universe to be deterministic, with effect following cause for instance, it is impossible to know what will happen in the future. Now obviously organisms in the world could not know what is going to happen but they will certainly survive better if they avoid predators and other dangerous situations. So they do best when they take in information about the world and make decisions based upon that information; run, fight, eat or mate. Simple instincts can do very well for many creatures. The biologist Stephen Jay Gould tells the story of when he was a youngster in the US navy, an older seaman gave him the following advice 'if it moves salute it, if it doesn't, paint it', a good way to keep your head down and survive without getting into trouble. Gould went on to show how simple, hard-wired instincts serve many animals very well, especially where the cost of running a large brain is prohibitive.

However, the more brain power you can bring to such decisions the more freedom you have to choose a good path. In other words, as per the title of Dennett's book, freedom evolves, even in a deterministic world. To Dennett, evolutionary theory, not physics, is the key to understanding freedom; it explains how we can be free when our parts aren't free.

Conclusion

Perhaps there is no answer to this question; it might be like trying to answer the question 'what happens when an unstoppable force meets an immoveable object?' Or perhaps it is just a problem of definitions; are we all talking about the same thing?

Apart from being an interesting question, this chapter has also been structured to demonstrate how philosophers go about analysing and discussing a problem: -

1. Firstly, the question itself should be analysed; what do the individual words mean, what do they mean together, are there any hidden agendas, if we rephrase the question does it make more sense, are we talking about the same thing, are we using the same definitions, and are we using language and meta-languages at the most appropriate level? Also important is the need to guard against starting with one meaning of a word and concluding with a different meaning.

2. Secondly, things can't be just made up; we need to take on board the findings of science. Not that science has all the answers (science still needs to be interpreted), just that we can no longer propose things that don't fit with science. In the above case science comes in a number of times, there is particle physics, quantum randomness, and (perhaps most relevant) how the brain creates and stores concepts (as described in previous chapters in this section).

3. Thirdly, it is important to read widely round the subject, read what other philosophers have said (both past and present), and then read any criticisms of those other philosophers, and any criticisms of those criticisms etc.

58

Ethics and Morality

Two things fill the mind with ever new and increasing wonder and awe, [...] the starry heaven above me and the moral law within me.

Immanuel Kant (Critique of Practical Reason)

Overview

After the bedrock of epistemology, ethics and morality constitute the landscape on which Western Philosophy builds its approach to life; how others should be treated, and how we should organise our societies to be just and fair.

This chapter will start with some definitions, then briefly consider religion's claim on these matters before moving on to look at what previous philosophers have said on the subject. Then, following the theme of part four of this book, we will see if science has anything at all to say about ethics and morality. We will also consider if there is any universal basis for morality, and we will finish with an overview of a number of different structures for ethical systems.

Definitions

It is worth repeating here the definitions we had from chapter seven. It is often the case that the two words 'ethics' and 'morality' are used in general conversation as if they were interchangeable. Although similar, they are two slightly different concepts: -

- Morality is to do with understanding the difference between right and wrong; it is more of an overriding guiding principle, often concerned with goodness or badness of character.

- Ethics, on the other hand, is to do with having specific sets of rules to help us implement our morality when we relate to other people.

Religion

Many people (indeed perhaps the majority of the world's population) turn to their religion as a guide to ethics and morality, to right and wrong, and to how one should live one's life. Sacred texts like the Bible and the Koran have specific instructions on these lines, and if the wording is ambiguous, there are priests, rabbis, and imams, etc. to interpret the meanings for you. Even the BBC, whenever a moral question turns up, will inevitably turn to a priest or bishop for comment.

These sacred texts do seem to contain many things that instinctively feel morally worthy, e.g. 'love thy neighbour', 'turn the other cheek', 'thou shalt not kill', etc. including numerous morality tales. Such things could perhaps be categorised as 'folk wisdom'. Unfortunately, however, they also contain many examples of people (especially women) being treated badly – certainly by today's standards. It must be remembered that these books were written thousands of years ago under different cultural traditions. There is also an element of each religion protecting itself against other religions and against the absence of religion; think of religious wars, the Inquisition, Catholic vs. Protestant, Shiite vs. Sunni, etc.

A good case could be made for the theory that individual religions evolve to persist and flourish in a kind of 'survival of the fittest' struggle, and for them building into their sacred texts instructions for spreading their particular religion at the expense of other religions. This view can also be seen in the way religion and politics support each other, for example – state occasions, weddings, funerals etc. They lend each other authority and hence legitimacy.

Western philosophy in general has an issue with basing morality on divine proclamation; remember the bedrock of its philosophy is epistemology (the theory of knowledge). Referring back to chapter three we see that knowledge is either deductive or inductive, no credence is given to 'revealed knowledge' because its veracity can't be established. It is something that can only be taken on faith (which, as noted earlier, is defined as 'belief without evidence').

Another issue is that sacred texts tend to become dogma that can't be questioned, whereas one of the main ideas in western philosophy is that everything should be questioned. Remember again that inductive knowledge can never be 100% certain, even though it can sometimes be close enough to 100% to be considered a scientific fact (because it's based on repeatable scientific evidence, for example evolution by natural selection). Hence (being recognised as inductive) any given scientific theory can't become dogma because it's always open to being questioned, and any new evidence could potentially change, improve, disprove, or supersede a current theory.

Before moving on to what philosophy has to say on ethics let's look at some of the above issues by taking an example from the Christian religion. It is often proclaimed that all we need to live a moral life is to follow the Ten Commandments. Even non-religious people might say something like that, probably because Christianity has been so successful at telling us that this is the case. However, many people who claim this are hard pushed to recite all ten. When asked they will often go straight to 'Thou shalt not kill' and perhaps then to 'Thou shalt not commit adultery' and 'Thou shalt not steal'. Try it yourself before looking at the list below.

The Ten Commandments

1. I am the Lord thy God, thou shall have no other gods before me
2. Thou shalt not make unto thee any graven image
3. Thou shalt not take the name of the Lord thy God in vain
4. Remember the Sabbath day, to keep it holy
5. Honour thy father and thy mother
6. Thou shalt not kill
7. Thou shalt not commit adultery
8. Thou shalt not steal
9. Thou shalt not bear false witness against thy neighbour
10. Thou shalt not covet thy neighbour's wife

This is meant to be a list of ethical rules to follow. Look closely however and we see the first four have nothing to do with ethics; they are all about religion protecting itself and trying to ensure it spreads to others and into the future. It's not until we get to number six that we are given a few 'shalt not's, perhaps something of a waste when you only have ten. [Maybe the reader could produce a better list of ten.]

To be fair, a close reading of the bible will supply a number of other ethical maxims to live by, as you might expect from a book purportedly aimed at moral guidance, but it is more often than not the Ten Commandments that are held up as all you need to live by.

From a philosophy perspective, however, another question arises. Ignoring for a minute the problem of how we know how God wants us to act, and (for the purpose of argument) assuming that God does exist, philosophy will want to ask, 'Is something right because God says it is right, or are there intrinsic rights and wrongs?'

One way to explore this would be to ask proponents of the Ten Commandments "what if there was another commandment on the list that says 'Thou shalt kill all first-born babies that are not male', would you follow it?" [Note, this is not an unknown practice in history. Also remember it is the job of philosophy to question things.]

The answer one might expect is "Oh, God would not make such a commandment". But this seems to show that rules for right and wrong acts are not ethical because they come from God, the person answering the question obviously has their own ideas of right and wrong. It also raises the question as to whether there is an intrinsic right and wrong whether God exists or not.

It often seems to be the case that religious people can't conceive of the idea of morality existing without God. Does that mean they think of atheists as immoral, or at best amoral? Thomas Jefferson (the third president of the United States) tried to construct an ethical code for living by cutting and pasting (literally with razor and glue) sections of the New Testament, omitting things like miracles, anything he deemed supernatural, and any passages portraying Jesus as divine. This has since become known as 'the Jefferson Bible'. And, all over the world, atheists bring up their children to have respect for others, a sense of fairness and an understanding of right and wrong.

Both the idea of intrinsic right and wrong, and the origin of people's own ideas of right and wrong, will be expanded on later in this chapter. In the meantime, however, if we are looking for something more comprehensive and much more nuanced than the Ten Commandments, it exists, it is the law. The law might not be perfect, and it is often only used when people can't agree by themselves, but it is a body of work that has been created and argued over by some of the best minds we have over hundreds of years of history.

One final note in this section on ethics and religion: - For people concerned about living a moral life but who can't take on board many of the faith-based ideas of religion, there are the less religious eastern philosophies [see part three of this book], but there is also the Humanist movement. This is a non-dogmatic, 'rational philosophy, informed by science, inspired by art, and motivated by compassion. It affirms the dignity of each human being and supports the maximization of individual liberty and opportunity consonant with social and planetary responsibility'. 'It considers human beings as the starting point for serious moral and philosophical enquiry'.

Previous philosophers

Of the many Western Philosophers covered in this book, only a few provided anything approaching a comprehensive system for ethical behaviour. Below is a short summary of the thinking of the more important philosophers in this field, but for more detail please turn to the individual chapter for each philosopher listed. Note however, that ethics and politics often intertwine, and so any philosophers missing from the list below, but who propose specific political systems, will often be doing so with a strong ethical approach in mind.

Aristotle

Aristotle's approach to ethics is an example of what today is called Virtue Ethics, the aim of which is to figure out how to achieve living a good life, because once you have become a good person, good actions will follow. For this, one needs three things: virtue, practical wisdom, and eudaimonia. Eudaimonia (a Greek concept) is often translated as happiness but that is inadequate, it is more to do with fulfilling one's unique function, and for humans this involves using reason (which is something unique to us). Hence doing philosophy is an important part of achieving a good life.

This is a somewhat different approach to ethics than normal. Instead of attempting to become the right kind of person by working out what actions to perform, you aim to become a good person first and then good actions will follow.

Epicurus

For Epicurus, the purpose of philosophy was to help people attain a happy, tranquil life characterized by ataraxia (peace and freedom from fear) and aponia (the absence of pain). He emphasized friendship as an important ingredient of happiness, and his school in many ways resembled a community of friends living together.

He has sometimes been misunderstood in that he was thought to advocate the pursuit of pleasure at all costs. Actually, his teachings were more about striving for an absence of pain and suffering, both physical and mental, and for a state of tranquillity that was free of the fear of death and the retribution of the gods. He argued that when we do not suffer pain, we are no longer in need of pleasure. Indeed, he explicitly warned against overindulgence because it often leads to pain.

Spinoza

Spinoza was very impressed by Euclid's geometry, and his great book 'Ethics' is laid out like that of a geometrical proof (although the book is actually about the nature of reality as much as it is about ethics). He is like Socrates, in saying that when you understand something perfectly then you will act correctly and wisely. His proofs are mainly to do with proving God's existence, and hence acting wisely because of your knowledge of God.

Having said that however, he had a dislike of all forms of religion which he regarded as superstitious and life-denying, and which view the present life as mere preparation for a life to come. Rather, he thought, our primary aim should be joyous living in the here and now.

Immanuel Kant

According to some philosophers, Hume for instance, morality is ultimately rooted in our sentiments, and reason has little, if anything, to do with right and wrong. Kant, by contrast, says that how we feel is morally irrelevant – what matters is that we do our moral duty, which reason alone can establish.

He says that what matters about an action, so far as its moral worth is concerned, is the 'intention' with which it is performed, the outcome is irrelevant. But what is the right intention? Kant says it is our moral duty to do the right thing; he calls it the '**Categorical Imperative**'. For him, moral principles have this categorical character. Our moral duty is: - 'don't steal', period. It's not: - 'don't steal if you don't want to get caught'.

How do we establish what our moral duty is? Kant says: -

> *"Act only according to a maxim by which you can at the same time will that it shall become a general law."*

Jeremy Bentham

Jeremy Bentham is best known as one of the founding fathers of an ethical system called ***Utilitarianism***. This is actually one form of a broader theory called **Consequentialism**, which says that the extent to which an action is morally right or wrong is determined by its consequences alone, nothing else matters. [Note that this is virtually the opposite of Kant's idea.]

Ethics and Morality

The question next becomes 'what consequence should we aim to achieve?' The answer according to utilitarianism is '**happiness**', Bentham argues that we should act to maximise pleasure and minimise pain. He says: -

> "...the greatest happiness of the greatest number is the foundation of morals and legislation."

He even developed a kind of calculus to try to ascertain the extent of someone's happiness by considering both the intensity and duration of their pleasure or pain.

Schopenhauer

He starts with a critique of Kant's ideas on morality. Kant, remember, said it was our moral duty to do the right thing; he called it the 'Categorical Imperative'. For Schopenhauer, the very idea of a categorical, as opposed to a hypothetical, imperative, is an absurdity. An imperative is normally an order of some kind, given by someone who can impose sanctions on those who do not conform to it. He believed that a 'categorical Imperative' only made sense to Kant because, unconsciously he took it as a command from God.

In contrast, moral goodness is identified by Schopenhauer with unselfish compassion for others. The good man is one who, not making the usual distinction between himself and others, is filled with universal compassion. Thus, he acts on the principle 'Injure no one; on the contrary, help everyone as much as you can.'

John Stuart Mill

Mill picks up *Utilitarianism* where Bentham left off, and his major contribution to it is an argument for the qualitative separation of pleasures. Bentham treated all forms of happiness as equal, whereas Mill argues that intellectual and moral pleasures (higher pleasures) are superior to more physical forms of pleasure (lower pleasures). He distinguishes between happiness and contentment, and claims that the former is of higher value than the latter.

Sometimes it is difficult to decide on what to do to obtain the 'greatest happiness' and utilitarianism is often split into either 'act' or 'rule' utilitarianism. An 'Act utilitarian' says each action should be judged solely on its ability to produce the greatest happiness, but 'Rule utilitarian' says we should follow those rules that will produce the greatest happiness.

Bentham is an 'Act utilitarian', but Mill believes we should be 'Rule utilitarians' except where we face a dilemma generated by two rules, for example the rule 'Do not steal' and the rule 'Do not allow people to starve'. If I can only feed a starving person by stealing food for them, I must break one of the two rules. Under these circumstances, says Mill, I must revert to being an 'Act utilitarian' and judge the case solely on what will produce the greatest happiness in that situation.

John Dewey

Moral and social problems, for Dewey, are concerned with the guidance of human action to the achievement of socially defined ends that are productive of a satisfying life for individuals within the social context. The central focus of his criticism of the tradition of ethical thought is its tendency to seek solutions to moral and social problems in dogmatic principles and simplistic criteria which in his view were incapable of dealing effectively with the changing requirements of human events. He located the motivation of the traditional dogmatic approaches in philosophy to the forlorn hope for security in an uncertain world. He maintains that Ideals and values must be evaluated with respect to their social consequences, either as inhibitors or as valuable instruments for social progress.

Dewey held that the education of children was key for them to be best prepared for the demands of responsible membership within a democratic community. Hence, he wrote much on education, structured as a process of self-directed learning, and guided by the cultural resources provided by teachers.

Jean-Paul Sartre

At root existentialism is a philosophy concerned with finding self, and the meaning of life, through free will, choice, and personal responsibility. In the view of the existentialist, the individual's starting point is characterized by what has been called **"the existential attitude"** or a sense of disorientation, confusion, or dread in the face of an apparently meaningless or absurd world.

The above definition would seem to make this a self-centred viewpoint and hence not much to do with ethics. However, this philosophy also includes the recognition that others are probably experiencing the same angst, and in Sartre's hands existentialism becomes an ethical theory. Indeed, Sartre once said that existentialism was just humanism by another name.

Ethics and Morality

Informed by Science?

It might be thought that science has nothing to say about ethics and morality: that such things are either instinctive feelings from the heart, or things learnt through an upbringing within a loving family or through the discipline of school life. [Just a pedantic note here... the heart is a pump for the blood, feelings and emotions are due to hormones and various other neurochemicals, mainly in the brain. That's not to say they are any the less for that of course; also, employing the word 'heart' for such things is a useful poetic metaphor.]

So, what part can Science bring to ethics and morality? Well first it must be admitted that family upbringing and schooling do play a huge part in training our pre-existing, instinctive, emotional potential, just like weightlifting trains pre-existing muscle potential. The question then becomes 'how should we best structure that training?' and it is here that science might have its say, see below for a list of examples. Note also that adults too can take these things on board to inform their ethics.

- **Evolution and genetics**: - This has shown us that we are all human; we can no longer think of other races as less than us, as savages or as slaves. In fact, there is no such thing as 'race' as a scientific definition; there is more genetic variation within a given country's population than on average between the populations of different countries. So ethically, we have no reason to discriminate against fellow humans from other countries, any differences are purely cultural or just skin deep. Genetically we are one family with identical mental capacity.
- **Global Warming**: - Science has more than confirmed that global warming has, in a large part, been caused by human activity. So, if we want to reduce our emissions, we have to do things differently and change our behaviour.
- **Environmental destruction**: - Like Global Warming, science can give us facts about the rate of environment destruction, things like endangered species, rainforest logging, plastic waste, pollution of rivers and oceans, air quality, etc.
- **Government policy**: - Science is all about counting things, so, given the right information, governments can act to help change people's behaviour. For instance, tax incentives for solar cells and home insulation, or laws on gun control. Governments can

instigate trial schemes and fund studies to see if they are successful.

- **Vaccinations**: - Science has not only given us vaccines, it also measures their success rate, and so informs people a) how safe they are, and b) that it should perhaps be our duty to take them in order to protect others by reducing the spread of the disease itself.
- **Smoking**: - Through gathering and analysing data from large epidemiological studies science has not only confirmed smoking is bad, but that passive smoking is too. This has had a large effect on people's behaviour and smoking is now largely viewed as antisocial.
- **Sexual behaviour in society after the pill**: - It cannot be doubted that since science has given us the pill, society's attitude to sexual matters has widely changed. There is a more liberal attitude in general and women in particular have more control over their bodies and their lives.
- **Animals have feelings too**: - Science tells us that intelligence, emotions and suffering are not just possessed by humans; these things exist on a spectrum throughout the animal kingdom. Indeed, there is a movement to grant rights to other great apes along the lines of 'the rights of man'.

The above list is by no means complete; the point to be made again is that we can't ignore science, indeed an argument could well be made that it is a moral duty to become scientifically literate in order to fully participate as citizens in our modern, complex societies.

Ethics and Logic?

The question arises, can we reason our way to ethical rules with logic?

Well, instinctively we feel that helping and cooperating with others (rather than being selfish) is a good way to behave, but can we logically show it to be beneficial?

Let's remember Thomas Hobbes and his idea of the 'social contract'. Hobbes' analysis was that there is a need for a social contract because, without it, people act in their own best interest, rather than in the interest of society in general, not realising that a stable, co-operating, and fair society would be in their best interest in the long run. A way to think about this is to look at the classic Prisoner's Dilemma problem.

Two suspects are caught by the police, but there is not enough evidence to convict them. If both prisoners remain silent, they will both be freed due to lack of evidence. If, however, one remains silent but the other confesses and testifies against his partner, he will be freed as a reward, but his partner will get 10 years. If both confess, then both will get the reduced sentence of two years.

The best solution is for both to remain silent, but that is taking a chance because if your partner confesses, he will go free and you will get 10 years. On the other hand, if you confess, you will only do two years at most and there is even a chance you will go free if your partner remains silent. Thinking then about your own best interest, you will probably confess.

Returning to Hobbes, he sees that cooperating with each other is clearly in everybody's interest, but because there is no mechanism in place to enforce this, individuals have a large incentive to break any agreement. Hobbes' solution was the social contract where you agree with others to give up some of your rights and then submit yourself to the protection of a sovereign power.

The problem with the Prisoner's Dilemma is that, as stated, it is a one-off dilemma. In reality, you will probably be dealing with the same person (and many other people) again and again on a day-to-day basis. It will be in your interest not to double cross them, or you will be shut out of future deals, indeed it will be in your interest to build up a reputation that you are a trustworthy person to do business with. Of course, you would still need the law of some kind, to deal with cheats, crimes of passion, or with any more complicated disputes.

Hobbes' view is that man is born selfish and needs society to civilise him. The opposite view would be the romanticism of Rousseau, where he talks about the 'noble savage' corrupted by civilisation. This touches on the nature/nurture debate with respect to our Human Nature. One naturally wants to say that our behaviour is generated by a mixture of the two; partly genetic and partly from our upbringing within our society. The problem of where things like kindness, co-operation and altruism come from (when these things seem to be against the interest of the individual) has long been debated by philosophers and scientists, more especially now since the discovery of genes and the role of genes as a contributing component of our behaviour.

An excellent (and very accessible) book that looks at all this in terms of where our co-operating behaviour comes from as a species is: - ***The Origins of Virtue*** by Matt Ridley. One of the things he describes is a number of computer-based tournaments where people were asked to submit programs to play a version of the prisoner's dilemma. The programs had different strategies and were pitted against all the other programs in a kind of society of different agents over extended time periods. In the long run, the strategy that did best was one which started with cooperation but retaliated against any defections (a sort of tit for tat) but also allowed the occasional defection so as not to get stuck in a loop (a forgiving tit for tat).

Evolution and Morality

Logic shows that cooperation is good for all involved, but it seems that it is already in our nature to help and care for each other... evolution got there first!

In 1976, the biologist Richard Dawkins wrote his groundbreaking book **The Selfish Gene**. This changed the way we look at evolution and genetics, it added a new perspective. Instead of thinking about evolution as being driven at a species level, or at an individual's level, the book pioneered looking at evolution from a gene's eye view.

Evolution is all about leaving more descendants. Genes sometimes mutate, either by bad copying or by damage. Most changes either harm the organism or are neutral, but the occasional change benefits the organism in such a way that it survives better and leaves more descendants, and hence more copies of that changed gene. Genes that cooperate to make a more successful organism in a sense could be said to be acting to help themselves spread, and so that is why Dawkins called his book The Selfish Gene, but he has since said he could have just as well called it The Cooperating Gene. He has been widely misunderstood as saying we are selfish because our genes make us so, but what he is actually saying is that our genes make us cooperate and make us care for each other.

Genes have first been selected to work together to make cells and bodies, and then if any genes arise that affect the behaviour those bodies have, that too will be available for evolution through natural selection to work on. If a gene arises that increases an individual's cooperating behaviour, that individual will survive better, leave more descendants, and more copies of that particular gene.

The question then becomes, how does a gene (or combination of genes) affect someone's behaviour? The answer is to do with feeling good. There isn't a gene that makes you logically work out that you must eat to survive, instead you get genes that make you feel hungry, and genes that make food taste good. There isn't a gene that makes you reason out that you should have children, but there are numerous genes that make sex feel good.

Cooperation feels good; it feels good to be included in a family or a group, it feels safe. From a genes' eye view, not only will cooperation benefit the individual (and hence that gene) but helping those near you will likely also help spread that gene because others near you (family) probably share the same gene variant.

In the section on logic above it was noted that we need to build up a reputation that we are a trustworthy person. How could genes help here? Well, as described in Matt Ridley's ***The Origins of Virtue***, we wear our heart on our sleeve; we show our emotions on our face, we blush red if we lie, along with many other involuntary signs. The very fact that we can't control these is evolution's way of demonstrating our trustworthiness.

Other organisms evolved different strategies to spread their genes into the next generations, but we evolved as part of a gregarious, group living species, and caring for others is literally written into our DNA. That gives us our starting position, but if we add in our large brains, our logic, and our new scientific knowledge, we can then use philosophy to try and formalise rules for ethical behaviour, for the structure of our societies, and for our law.

One drawback of caring for those near us, helping them, and the feel-good factor of being part of a group, is that it often creates a 'them and us' situation, an in-group, and an out-group. This easily spills over into fighting to protect your group and sometimes outright war. Once again science enters the picture showing us that we are all related, and then we need to use our large brains to work out how we can all live together in a way fair to all. [Some of that will be discussed in the next chapter on politics.]

Universal Right and Wrong?

When we looked at the religious argument for right and wrong earlier in this chapter, we considered the possibility of a new commandment that felt wrong (the expected response from religious people was that God would not make such a commandment). This threw up two possible reasons for it being considered wrong; either there is a universal right and wrong, or people have their own 'instinctive' ideas of right and wrong.

The quote marks above allowing a mixture of nature and nurture, as described in the previous section on evolution and morality: i.e. brain structures that provide the capacity for empathy, emotion, and rewards [Nature]; and the fact that we have to learn during our upbringing how to interact with others and participate in society [Nurture].

Indeed, other animals also have a concept of fairness. There was a case reported of two chimpanzees that had been taught to expect a reward for completing a certain task. One day, to see what would happen, the keeper had the first chimpanzee perform the task and gave it a reward, not a great reward but it was acceptable to the chimp (it might have been a carrot). Then, the keeper, while the first chimpanzee was watching, got the second chimpanzee to perform the same task, but rewarded the second chimpanzee with a much more valued prize (perhaps a favourite fruit). Well, the first chimp had a tantrum when he saw this, jumping around and screaming and throwing away his reward. He obviously knew he was not being treated fairly!

So, we all have an 'instinctive' feel for right and wrong, provided by genetics, upbringing, and then (as noted above) further informed by science. But the next question philosophy would naturally address is – could there be some kind of universal right and wrong, one that everybody would agree to if it was demonstrated to them?

Well, science shows us that the universe itself is a harsh place for life; mostly cold vacuum dotted with incredibly hot, radiation drenched stars. Life is only possible on the odd protected planet orbiting at the right distance from its sun for water to be liquid. Also, in the vast timescale of the universe we are here for only a fraction of a second relatively speaking (our star will one day run out of fuel and die). Life may well evolve around other stars, but that too will pass. Eventually all stars will expire in the far distant heat death of the universe.

The universe itself cares not for us; life is the only thing that is capable of caring. Life too is the only thing that is capable of suffering. In the same way that evolution gave us a reward system as an aid to survival and passing on our genes, it also gave us the capacity for suffering. This enables us to recognise things that would harm us so that we could take avoidance action and hence survive to spread our genes. Ethics is about how we treat others, so the argument goes that this only became relevant once suffering was available in the world.

David Hume argued that facts about the world can't tell us how we ought to behave. In the same vein, the philosopher G. E. Moore argued that goodness could not be equated with any property of human experience (e.g. happiness) because it would always be possible to question if that particular pleasure was actually good. This has become known as Moore's "open question argument".

Remember Jeremy Bentham's famous formulation of utilitarianism, which is also known as the "greatest-happiness principle". It holds that one must always act so as to produce the greatest aggregate happiness among all sentient beings, within reason. John Stuart Mill's major contribution to utilitarianism is his argument for the qualitative separation of pleasures.

More recently American Philosopher Sam Harris, with his book *The Moral Landscape*, has changed the argument slightly. Instead of trying to bring about the greatest happiness, which seems somewhat elusive, Harris says the goal should be acts which produce the least pain, and this he equates with the well-being of individuals.

In recent times, some thinking about morality has been that there is no such thing as an intrinsic right and wrong, i.e. that one has to understand the context, the background and the history of any actions and allow that different people can legitimately consider a given action as either right or wrong depending on their viewpoint. This is also known as cultural relativism.

Those who support cultural relativism claim that morality is different for different cultures, both for current cultures and historic ones. The argument is that an action in a different culture or time might need to be different depending on the cultural norms; maybe, for example, allowing a girl to get married at 12 is ok in different times, it is possible that she might accept it as the norm, and as such not suffer for it. But for Harris, the only way to decide is by basing it on maximising the well-being of the individual or the group. His position is that, if you allow cultural relativism, people can justify anything; say flying an aircraft into a building, shooting someone for drawing a cartoon, or the practice of F.G.M.

Harris sets out to convince us that right and wrong should be equated with 'well-being', whether taken individually or collectively, and as such could, in principle, be measured. He admits that you can't always perform the measurement but the fact that there must be such an answer (albeit possibly unknown) means that there is an intrinsic right and wrong and it's linked to suffering. In general, he lays out a rigorous case for this, backed up by numerous examples from scientific studies of both behaviour and brain neuroscience.

As an exercise, Harris's theory could be restated in the structure of a philosophical argument, with a logical conclusion based on two premises (refer to chapters 3 and 4 for details on the structure of philosophical arguments): -

Premise 1:

Right and wrong acts are acts that affect the **well-being** of conscious creatures.

[Note here that the claim is not that moral truths exist independently of the experiences of conscious beings; it just says that they are things that are only relevant to talk about in terms of their effect on conscious beings.]

Premise 2:

It is potentially possible to measure the **well-being** of conscious creatures.

[To take just one example from the book: - There was a recent neuroscientific study done on the difference in levels of the hormone oxytocin between children raised in normal homes and those that spent their first years in an orphanage. The orphanage children did not have normal levels under the same conditions, and such children also tend to have social and emotional difficulties in later life.]

[Note here the claim is not that we can measure everything, only that **well-being** is connected to facts about brain states and the environment. We can't know, for instance, how many people were bitten by a mosquito in the last sixty seconds, but there is a factual number, even if we can never know it.]

Conclusion: (based on the premises)

There is always a right action in any given situation, and it is connected to the **well-being** of either an individual or a group. We might not be able to determine what it is in every case, but logically it must exist. It might even involve some short-term suffering (like taking medicine) to obtain longer term gain.

Remember, with a philosophical argument, if you accept the premises as true, and you the think that conclusion is valid (i.e. it follows logically from the premises), then the argument is sound.

To summarise this section: - while the universe itself does not care for us, arguments can well be made that there are such things as intrinsic rights and wrongs. The problem, however, is that it is often impossible to determine exactly what action is right due to the complexities of the situation, even our 'instincts' (note the quote marks again), which are often good, are not infallible. And that is why philosophers have, over the ages, come up with many different systems and rules for living life in a moral way.

Ethical Systems

There seem to be three main current approaches to ethics: -

- **Deontology**
- **Consequentialism**
- **Virtue Ethics**

Having said that, all three contain quite a lot of overlap with each other, as you might expect, because they are all concerned with doing good in some way.

Deontology is an approach that emphasises duties or rules, saying 'if you follow this set of rules for your behaviour in respect of others, then you can't help but do the right thing'. Examples would be the Ten Commandments, or the rule 'Do unto others as you would be done by'.

A leading proponent of this approach was Kant with his ideas of duty expressed as 'categorical imperatives'. He says that in this moral system, for instance, it would not be right to help someone just because you felt sorry for them; you should help them simply because it is your moral duty to do so. He also says that what matters about an action, so far as its moral worth is concerned, is the 'intention' with which it is performed, the actual outcome is irrelevant.

The question here, of course, is how do you go about determining the rules. For Kant it was a rational exercise, documented in his book **Critique of Practical Reason.** For the Ten Commandments it is divine intervention. Other methods would include just using your experience of life to create your rules, or perhaps through debate with others (e.g. parliament creating laws).

Consequentialism differs from deontology in that it emphasizes the consequences of actions; it aims at maximising the well-being of others. The main historical proponents of this view are Jeremy Bentham and John Stuart Mill with their ethical idea of utilitarianism, which itself is sub-divided into act utilitarianism and rule utilitarianism. Rule utilitarianism brings in the addition of using rules for your actions (e.g. never steal), which hence incorporates something of deontology as opposed to simply judging each act solely on its foreseeable consequences. One criticism of rule utilitarianism is the claim that if two rules contradict each other (e.g.

don't steal a loaf of bread, and you must help a starving person), then rule utilitarianism just reverts to act utilitarianism.

A current proponent of Consequentialism is Sam Harris (mentioned above). And as noted, he brings a slightly different, and a more 'science informed', focus to the theory by aiming for a reduction of suffering (to promote well-being) instead of trying to increase happiness (which is both a nebulous concept at best and difficult to measure).

Virtue Ethics distinguishes itself from the previous two systems by simply placing virtue at the centre of its philosophy. Both Deontology and Consequentialism make room for virtues, defining them as traits possessed by those who 'do their duty' or perform acts that have 'good consequences'. Virtue Ethics, however, resists attempts to define virtues in terms of other more fundamental concepts; rather the virtues themselves (things like honesty, moral courage, compassion, fairness etc.) are taken as fundamental. It's really a theory based on the building of character in a person.

This approach can be traced back to Plato and Aristotle in the West and to Confucius in the East, although other philosophers since have produced their own version of it, notably perhaps Hume and Nietzsche.

A concept also central to Virtue Ethics is *phronesis* (a Greek word meaning moral or practical wisdom). This comes with experience of life; practical wisdom is to be wise about human beings and life in general. Another important Greek concept here is that of *eudaimonia*. This is often translated as happiness or flourishing or well-being, but any one of these would be incomplete, it is really about living well as a human being, but not in the sense of being overindulgent in any way. Again, it is about developing good character.

The Greek philosopher Epicurus was an early example of practicing *eudaimonia*, for him the purpose of philosophy was to help people attain a happy, tranquil life characterized by ataraxia (peace and freedom from fear) and aponia (the absence of pain). [Reread chapter 13 for more details.]

Many philosophers who promote Virtue Ethics have written extensively on the education of children to guide them in the development of virtues. To encourage this development, we need to be surrounded with others who are doing the same and exposed to appropriate teachings. But we also need practical wisdom, which is not yet fully formed in childhood, but develops with experience of life. For instance, a fireman who goes into a burning building to rescue someone is courageous, but if he does it already knowing it's a lost cause then he is foolhardy.

The Virtue Ethicist is not interested in such things as 'moral truths', rather their interest is in becoming a virtuous person. The idea of a 'moral exemplar' is of use here, i.e. a morally outstanding person who is admired.

We can discover what things constitute virtues by looking at how these moral exemplars conduct themselves.

Virtue Ethics has been criticised for not producing any codifiable principles for ethical action, but that rather misses the point. Virtue Ethics is concerned with the development of character, and once you have that you will naturally do the right thing.

Review

As noted above, we all have a good 'intuition' of right and wrong, derived from our upbringing and our genetic makeup as gregarious, group living animals. Also noted above, we see that science can add to this by giving us facts to enhance our ethical understanding such as: - we are all human, so other races (if indeed there is such a definition as 'race') are not mentally inferior; and smoking is harmful to others. The difficulty with deriving an ethical system for living is often the words themselves, remember Socrates could find no one who could define 'justice' for him, and similar problems exist for defining the virtues. Also, as soon as you come up with rules for right and wrong action, you will need rules for exceptions, and then rules for exceptions to those exceptions.

One might, for instance, want to put the idea of being free high on your ethical agenda, but as soon as you do a Socratic minded person will ask what you mean by freedom, and thereafter follows a protracted discussion! Indeed, the philosopher Jean-Paul Sartre wrote extensively on the concept of freedom, especially from an existentialist perspective, including his great fiction trilogy 'The Roads to Freedom'. He wanted to be free, but he could hardly decide what exactly he meant by that, in fact that turned out to be his point. In an uncertain world you can only strive for things that you can't fully conceptualise.

In previous chapters in this section of the book, we had extended discussions around concepts and their meanings. Language is brilliant for everyday conversation, meaning emerges when useful information is exchanged, but as soon as you use philosophy to try and pin down exact meanings, or create rules that are always true, it often seems that the more words you use, the further away you get from the everyday meaning of words.

Also remember the American philosopher Richard Rorty saying that "Interesting philosophy is rarely an examination of the pros and cons of a thesis. Usually it is, implicitly or explicitly, a contest between an entrenched vocabulary which has become a nuisance and a half-formed new vocabulary which vaguely promises great things."

Rorty goes on to say that moral principles "only have a point insofar as they incorporate tacit reference to a whole range of institutions, practices, and vocabularies of moral and political deliberation. They are reminders of, abbreviations for, such practices, not justifications for such practices. At best, they are pedagogical aids to the acquisition of such practices."

All this, of course, should not put us off from striving to study, understand, and attain, living an ethical life as far as is possible. The notes in this review section are just things to keep in mind, and pitfalls to be wary of, in that quest; and the ideas discussed throughout this chapter are provided as an introduction to the way philosophers have addressed this subject over the centuries.

59

Politics

History is past politics, and politics is present history.

E. A. Freeman (*Methods of Historical Study* 1886)

Democracy is the worst form of government other than all the other forms we know.

Winston Churchill

Overview

Ever since agriculture and trade expanded enough to produce the surplus to support large communities, some form of governance needed to appear. Initially feudal in structure, one of its main jobs was the defence of the community against outside aggressors. Since then, many systems of governance have been tried, and many philosophers throughout history have attempted to design the best possible system.

This chapter will look at the history and development of that political philosophy and then attempt to identify the main conceptual elements required for a good system of governance.

Early History

We tend to think of the rise of civilization as beginning with the Greeks, however, as mentioned in chapter nine, there had been other civilisations prior to the Greeks, for instance the Egyptians, the Babylonians, the Mycenaeans, the Ionians, and the Cretans among others, not to mention what was happening in China, India, and South America. But it was not until the rise of philosophy in Greece that we see serious consideration given as to what might constitute the best structure for government.

An Introduction to Philosophy

Such governments, however, were very different from today's states. Greece, for instance, comprised a large number of small, independent city states, each with its own government. Many of these were run by strong rulers with their own army, mainly for the protection of the state, but also to keep order and ensure the continuance of their rule.

We think of the Athens city state as the birthplace of democracy, but that was not always the case. Sometimes, during periods of wars or other unrest, it was ruled by strong leaders. When it was democratic however, it was by no means a full democracy, only some citizens could vote, and certainly not women or slaves.

Early governments also adopted the early religions, which had often started out as fertility cults combined with giving thanks to mother earth for good harvests. The state co-opted these to also give thanks for victory in war. Thereafter they became associated with morality, and hence lawmakers could claim that their codes of conduct were received from the gods. As noted in a previous section, government and religion lend each other authority, which is something still seen today with ceremonies like coronations, other state occasions, births, deaths, and marriages.

> "The various modes of worship, which prevailed in the Roman world, were all considered by the people, as equally true; by the philosopher, as equally false; and by the magistrate, as equally useful."
>
> **Edward Gibbon** -*The Decline and Fall of the Roman Empire*

Plato (For more depth and background see chapter 11)

In his main work, **The Republic**, Plato lays out his concept of utopia. His ideas in this area are very conservative, which is perhaps understandable as he was born into an aristocracy. He was used to the idea of owning slaves, and he was a young man when Athens was defeated, which he attributed to it being weakly ruled as a democracy. Plato proposes that societies should have a tripartite class structure: -

- **Productive** (The Workers) — the labourers, carpenters, plumbers, masons, merchants, farmers, ranchers, etc.
- **Protective** (The Warriors or Guardians) — those who are adventurous, strong, and brave, in the armed forces.

- **Governing** (The Rulers or Philosopher Kings) — those who are intelligent, rational, self-controlled, in love with wisdom, well suited to make decisions for the community.

He sees this as mostly hereditary but does concede that any child showing potential could be moved up to the next level, or in the opposite direction if necessary. The main problem he envisaged was how to make sure the warrior-guardians would carry out the intentions of the philosopher-rulers, and so he spends a lot of time detailing educational and religious proposals to ensure the structure of his utopia.

Quite a lot of The Republic is concerned with defining the idea of 'justice'. And Plato's conclusion is that it consists of everybody doing his own job, without interfering with the other classes.

Aristotle (For more depth and background see chapter 12)

His ideas in this area are, like Plato, largely governed by the city state model, which was the dominant political structure at that time. However, where Plato was more dogmatic, with his utopia ruled by philosopher/kings, Aristotle was more academic, laying out, discussing, and categorising several different possible forms of government.

He said three types of government were possible: – a **Royalty**, an **Aristocracy,** or a **Constitutional Government**. A government is good, he says, when it aims at the good of the whole community, and through discussing these three types he thinks that Royalty is better than Aristocracy and Aristocracy better than a Constitutional Government. However, when government becomes bad, Royalty turns into Tyranny, Aristocracy turns into Oligarchy and a Constitutional Government turns into a Democracy. Tyranny is then worse than Oligarchy and Oligarchy worse than Democracy.

In this way Aristotle arrives at a qualified defence of democracy. He also defends democracy with the thought that you get more wise thoughts from 100 people than from one, and any flaws will be identified and cancelled out. Rather than elections being held, citizens would be chosen for office by lot, and citizen, of course, did not include women or slaves. And, in talking about the law, he says that "Law is reason without passion".

Empires

The era of city states in Greece came to an end with Alexander the Great. From around 334 B.C. he conquered much of the Middle East, and defeated the Persian Empire, which at that time was the greatest the world had ever known.

The Roman Empire started to build from around 264 B.C. with the first of the Punic Wars. It took in much of the Mediterranean and then gradually spread through Spain, France and into England. This was a stable and peaceful empire for over two hundred years.

Empires in general are enabled by advances in technology and weaponry, allowing strong leaders to enlarge their territories and gather more riches, which they share with their close supporters, ensuring loyalty. As this wealth trickles down the country as a whole becomes richer, and this, combined with a firm control of propaganda ("our nation is the best", "God is on our side", etc.) becomes an almost unstoppable force.

The British Empire is a good example. Britain today is the fifth richest country in the world largely because the Industrial Revolution occurred there first, allowing it to dominate and exploit less technical countries, and capture slave labourers to use on their new plantations. It took Enlightenment thinking, and new-found freedoms of thought and expression in a parliamentary democracy, to end the slave trade. Other countries with totalitarian structures of government are, even today, expert at controlling the media and eliminating dissenting opposition voices, and are still able to try to expand their territories. But this is jumping ahead; let's return to the history and philosophy of political systems.

The Magna Carta Libertatum

Also just called Magna Carta (or Magna Charta). This was a royal charter of rights, signed by King John of England in 1215, in order to make peace with a grouping of rebel barons. It guaranteed the barons protection from illegal imprisonment, access to justice, and limitation on feudal payments to the crown. Over the next few years it went through several amendments, but then, in 1297, it was finally confirmed into the statute law of England, a concession made by King Edward 1 in return for the raising of new taxes.

The Magna Carta was, in effect, a legal restriction on the power of the sovereign to treat his subjects in any way he chose. It initially applied only to the barons, and they forced the king to sign it out of their own self-interest, they did not do it out of any concern for lower order subjects in the country. However, it was a start, and it subsequently became difficult to claim that any laws protecting the rights of one group of citizens did not also protect the rights of all citizens.

The political myth of the Magna Carta as a protection of personal liberties became iconic. It was influential in the formation of the United States Constitution and is still cited today as an important symbol of individual liberty, for example, in the 20th century, the English lawyer and judge Lord Denning described it as "the greatest constitutional document of all times – the foundation of the freedom of the individual against the arbitrary authority of the despot".

Thomas Hobbs (For more depth and background see chapter 18)

He was the first main philosopher of the more modern period to write extensively on government, its justification, and the place of the citizen within the country. He lays this out in his main work ***Leviathan*** which was written in 1651 during the English Civil War. It is mainly concerned with demonstrating the necessity of a strong central authority, to avoid the evil of discord and civil war. He says that the only way to avoid civil war is for every man to come to an agreement with every other man an abrogation of certain rights: -

> "as if every man should say to every man: *I authorise and give up my right of governing myself, to this man, or this assembly of men, on condition, that thou give up thy right to him, and authorise all his actions in like manner.* This done, the multitude so united in one person, is called a COMMONWEALTH."

Once formed, the sovereign power cannot be taken away from the sovereign (be that an individual monarch, or a parliamentary body), and no citizen can object or take action against the sovereign. Hobbes preferred the sovereign to be a monarch. He would accept a parliament alone, but he didn't like the idea of a power sharing arrangement between a monarch and a parliament.

Note that the agreement, or covenant as he calls it, is not between citizens and the ruling power, it is a covenant made by the citizens with each other to obey the government chosen by the majority. And this has become known as the **Social Contract**.

An Introduction to Philosophy

John Locke (For more depth and background see chapter 20)

Locke (1632 – 1704) is the foremost English philosopher in the early period of post Cartesian philosophy. He is significant in many areas of philosophy but in politics he virtually defined Liberalism, laying out the rights of the individual, the role of the state and a structure for government. His ***Two Treatises on Government*** was published in 1690 at the start of the period called The Age of Enlightenment.

Locke was entirely familiar with the writings of Thomas Hobbes who died when Locke was 38, and they both lived through some of the same political upheavals. Locke also wanted stability and saw the need for a social contract of some form, because he agreed with Hobbes that in a state of nature man is a free being with rights of his own. He differed from Hobbes, however, in the degree of power a government should have.

His justification of the social contract is strikingly close to Hobbes, but Locke insists that the sovereign power created needs to be one which can be checked by the common people. If they gave the sovereign absolute power, then they would "put themselves into a worse condition than the state of Nature". Locke insists, therefore, that all supreme power must itself govern "by declared and received laws, and not by extemporary dictates and undetermined resolutions". Sovereignty must reside with the people, and they alone can change its form, or appoint new governors.

In his first treatise he laid out arguments against any form of hereditary government. This seems self-evident to us today, but at the time it was considered somewhat revolutionary. The point here is a separation of economic power from political power. These days we think it natural that we should be able to leave our property and wealth to our children (i.e. we accept the hereditary principle as regards economic power) but we reject it when it comes to political power. In the past these two aspects of power were virtually identical.

In the second treatise Locke sets out what he conceives to be the true origin of government. It is here that he bases the need for government and a social contract around the need for the protection of lives and property of the citizens of the state.

The theory of checks and balances in government is one of the main ideas in Locke's writings; he saw it was important that the different areas of government can limit each other's powers. The two areas of government he considered were the executive and the legislative, which in his day were the king and parliament. In our day, in the U.K., the executive has come to mean the Prime Minister, the Cabinet, Government Departments and Civil Service, and the legislative is the two houses of parliament (which themselves keep a check on each other). Also added these days is the separation of the judicial functions from the executive and the legislative.

Jeremy Bentham (For more depth and background see chapter 28)

Bentham, with his theory of *Utilitarianism* (i.e. working towards the greatest happiness of the greatest number) represents the start of British radicalism and was one of the men who unintentionally paved the way for the doctrines of socialism. Adam Smith had discovered self-interest to be the mainstay of the economic life of man. Bentham expanded this notion of self-interest, firstly into a theory of jurisprudence, and thereafter into a more general political philosophy.

Bentham died on the day before the royal assent to the Reform Bill, the passing of which marked a triumph of his views, and of the British middle class, of which he was a member. His influence was very wide ranging. He provided the principle and draft legislation affecting laws, and the constitutions of the United States, Canada, and other countries on five continents, by which they included such phrases as "the pursuit of happiness". He also made a major contribution to International Law which provided the legal foundation for The League of Nations, the United Nations and the United Nations International Court at The Hague, offering the framework by which nations today can - indeed must - go to court not to war.

John Stuart Mill (For more depth and background see chapter 31)

Mill (seen as a successor to Bentham) contributed widely to social theory, political theory, and political economy, and has been called "the most influential English-speaking philosopher of the 19th century". His conception of liberty, laid out in his book *On Liberty* (1858) justified the freedom of the individual in opposition to unlimited state control.

In it he also includes an impassioned defence of free speech. Mill argues that free discourse is a necessary condition for intellectual and social progress. We can never be sure, he contends, that a silenced opinion does not contain some element of the truth. He also argues that allowing people to air false opinions is productive for two reasons. Firstly, individuals are more likely to abandon erroneous beliefs if they are engaged in an open exchange of ideas. And secondly, by forcing other individuals to re-examine and re-affirm their beliefs in the process of debate, these beliefs are kept from declining into mere dogma. It is not enough for Mill that one simply has an unexamined belief that happens to be true; one must understand why the belief in question is the true one.

Mill wrote both against slavery and for women's rights; and in his major work on political democracy, ***Considerations on Representative Government***, he defends two fundamental principles, extensive participation by citizens, and the enlightened competence of rulers.

Revolutions

Around the same time as Jeremy Bentham was writing there was the American Revolutionary War (1775 – 1783) also known as the American War of Independence, and inspired by that, the French Revolution (1789 – 1799). Both of these were driven by fundamental principles of liberal democracy with ideas like rights, freedom and equality front and centre.

The Irish-British statesman and philosopher Edmund Burke had been a supporter of American Independence, which was the legitimate creation of an independent country with its own constitution, but he was very worried by the French Revolution. He thought that the French people had thrown off "the yoke of laws and morals" and was alarmed at the generally favourable reaction of the English public to that revolution. He wrote a political pamphlet entitled ***Reflections on the Revolution in France*** in 1790 in which he gave an eloquent defence of British conservatism, favouring monarchy, aristocracy, property, and hereditary succession. It has been called 'a classical text in political theory', and it influenced conservative thinking right up to the 20th century.

However, many intellectuals of the time reacted strongly against Burke's pamphlet, including both Thomas Paine and Mary Wollstonecraft. Paine, an English-born American political activist and philosopher, had previously written ***Common Sense***, a hugely influential pamphlet supporting the American Revolution. Now he replied to Burke with another groundbreaking pamphlet entitled ***The Rights of Man*** (1791), in which he says that political revolution is permissible when a government does not safeguard the natural rights of its people.

The British writer and philosopher Mary Wollstonecraft also reacted strongly against Burke's pamphlet and wrote a pamphlet in response entitled ***A Vindication of the Rights of Men***. This was published in 1790, a good few months before Paine's pamphlet of similar name. She attacked not only the hereditary principle but also the rhetoric Burke used to defend it. This gained her fame, but she is more remembered for her 1792 book ***A Vindication of the Rights of Woman***, a strong feminist argument that women should not be considered property and that they should have the same rights and standards of education as men.

Another document about rights came out of the French Revolution; this was the ***Declaration of the Rights of Man and the Citizen*** (1789). It was originally drafted by Lafayette working together with his friend Thomas Jefferson, although much of the final draft was produced by Abbe Sieyes, a French clergyman and political writer who was the chief political theorist of the revolution.

The French Revolution, however, lost some of its lustre when different fractions struggled for power and the ultra-revolutionary Committee for Public Safety, headed by Maximilien Robespierre, came out on top, initiating a series of massacres and public executions. This became known as The Reign of Terror in which nearly 35,000 people were killed, including many who were members of the defeated Girondin revolutionary fraction. One of these was Marie-Jeanne Roland who, when she stood before the guillotine head bowed waiting for death, uttered the now famous words "O liberté, que de crimes on commet en ton nom" ['Oh freedom, what crimes are committed in your name'].

Back in America, both Thomas Paine's and Thomas Jefferson's ideas were very influential in the drafting of the **Bill of Rights**, which comprised the first ten amendments to the new American Constitution. The original draft of the constitution detailed the structure of government, with its separation of powers and checks and balances, based on things like the Magna Carta, and the writings of John Locke, but the Bill of Rights added to this: specific guarantees of personal freedoms and rights; clear limitations on the government's power; and declarations that powers not specifically granted to the federal government are reserved for the States or the people.

Communism

The rights of man (and woman), as argued for by Thomas Paine, Thomas Jefferson, Mary Wollstonecraft, and others, treated the subject of political theory from an individual perspective, they were aimed at things like freedom of thought and equality under the law. It was an intellectual and perhaps middle-class aspiration without any real economic consideration to the structure of society. The working classes, although now treated equal in law, still lived in poverty, owned no property and were exploited by the factory owners and landed gentry.

The philosopher, radical social theorist, and organiser of the working-class Karl Marx (1818 – 1883) changed that. He analysed the history of political systems as a progression; first there was the feudal society, then came the capitalist society, and that would eventually be replaced by a communist society. Each of these economic systems, he wrote, is shaped by the dominant productive forces of the day. Bertrand Russell says of him that "he is the last of the great system builders" in philosophy. (For more depth and background see chapter 33).

The goal of communism is a society where the socioeconomic order is centred around: common ownership of the means of production, distribution, and exchange; and the allocation of products to everyone in society according to the needs of each. It also involves the absence of social class, and in the ideal case, even the absence of money.

While this sound a very fair way to run society it has proved difficult to implement in practice, and usually takes a revolution to bring it about. The two main examples are Russia, with its revolution in 1917 during the First World War, and China, with it civil war of 1945 – 1949. In both cases a large working class and peasantry rebelled against a much smaller ruling class who held the concentration of wealth and land ownership.

One of the difficulties with communism is that to hold power requires a strong leader (initially Joseph Stalin in Russia and Chairman Mao in China) and such leaders maintain their power by eliminating all opposition voices. As such, the leaders are unopposed, unelected and remain in power a long time (Stalin for 30 years and Mao for 27 years) and essentially become dictators. Even today, while these two countries claim to have elections, the outcomes are in little doubt because opposition is quashed, and the state has full control of the media.

Another difficulty is that if nobody owns anything there is little incentive for entrepreneurs to set up businesses and make money. Indeed, if the state provides, then there is little incentive for anyone to work, this often leads to a society where people watch and report on each other for not pulling their weight. Both Russia and China have since relented in terms of private ownership and a capitalist economy is now encouraged, but only within a strict communist political structure.

Capitalism

Capitalism is often held up as the alternative to Communism but that, by itself, is too simplistic because Capitalism is just a term for an economic system based on the private ownership of both the means of production and the profits that it generates. That comparison ignores the political system within which the capitalist economy sits because, as we saw above, Communism can incorporate a capitalist element.

Since the Industrial Revolution many variations of Capitalism have been tried; free-market capitalism, anarcho-capitalism, state capitalism, and welfare capitalism to name but a few. This subject, however, is too vast to cover here; there are libraries of books on economics and many university courses on the subject. All we will mention here is a little about the philosophical and historical development of western political systems within which capitalist economies are embedded.

Philosophers like John Locke helped to give theoretical structure to government with separation of powers and checks and balances, but still at that time it was mainly the aristocracy and landowners who were in power. With the arrival of the Industrial Revolution new money entered the equation and with that a virtually unbridled expansion and exploitation of empire.

Towards the end of the 18th century philosophers like Paine and Wollstonecraft were arguing for more individual rights at the same time as the French Revolution by the working classes. The British government, worried about revolution at home, and prompted by philosophers Bentham and Mill, began to pass reform acts changing the electoral system to give the ordinary people fairer representation. Mill also, as noted above, championed the abolition of slavery.

With government having to become more responsive to the people, and enlightened industrialists providing better housing and medical care for their workers, it became obvious that capitalism worked better if it also included a safety net of some kind for those at the bottom. The first modern unemployment scheme was introduced in the United Kingdom with the National Insurance Act 1911, under the Liberal Party. This was improved in subsequent acts and other western countries brought in similar systems. Then in 1948 the newly elected Labour government created the National Health Service.

Western Capitalism has gone through a number of different stages depending on the political environment of the time. It does not seem to be heading in any one direction however; sometimes industries get nationalised, other times they get re-privatised, sometimes it goes through a 'greed is good' period, then, often following a crash of some kind, it goes back into a protectionist period.

Politics is not easy, and with the party system there are often swings from one ideology to the next and back again. As well as dealing with internal politics, a country must deal with other countries round the world each with their own agenda, and on top of that there are now large multinational corporations to deal with. It's not like science, a country can't experiment with capitalism one week and communism another week and then measure which system is best. Indeed, even if an economy does do well after a change in strategy, it does not logically mean it was because of that change, other external factors could well have caused the improvement and hence the economy may well have improved anyway without that strategy change.

Suffrage

Suffrage, or 'political franchise', is simply the right to vote. This is another right that evolved through history. In England, for example, in 1265 only a few percent of adult males could vote, and parliamentary elections occurred at irregular intervals. In 1432 Henry VI changed this to include male property owners if their property was worth more than a certain amount. A series of reform acts and representation acts gradually changed things and in 1918 all men over 21 and some women over 30 won the right to vote. In 1928 all women over 21 won the right to vote resulting in what's called universal suffrage, and in 1969 the voting age was lowered to 18. Other countries also went through a similar evolution of suffrage.

Some suffrage restrictions (different in different countries) still remain for things like voting age, prisoners, and people with mental health problems. There are also differences depending on being a permanent resident or being naturalized into that country.

More Rights

As well as two world wars, the Twentieth Century saw a gradual, hard won, increase of people's individual rights throughout Western societies. There often seems to be a tension between the rights people want or think they deserve and the interests of government, but sometimes the tension is actually between society and the wants of a minority within that society; and in these cases, it can be the government that leads the way.

Civil Rights in America is a case in point. The American Civil war may well have ended slavery in the 1860s but black people in society were still treated as second class citizens for many years afterwards. The civil rights movement from 1954 to 1968 was a series of nonviolent and civil disobedience campaigns that eventually secured new protections in federal law for all Americans. In 1954 the Supreme Court struck down many of the racial segregation and discrimination laws in the southern states as unconstitutional, and the Civil Rights Act of 1964 explicitly banned all discrimination based on race.

However, racism was still endemic in society with discrimination in jobs, housing, education, and politics, and the late 1960s saw the emergence of the Black Power movement, some sections of which engaged in more militant resistance. Change is slow and even today the fight for equality continues with campaigns like the Black Lives Matter movement.

Women's rights have long been fought for. Mary Wollstonecraft, for instance (as mentioned above), wrote *A **Vindication of the Rights of Woman*** in 1792 at a time when women had virtually no rights, and were regarded as the property of their husband. The suffragette movement of votes for women began in July 1848 during the first Women's Right Convention in New York. In 1949 the French female philosopher Simone de Beauvoir wrote her hugely influential book ***The Second Sex*** which, along with other books by and for women around that time, became the basis for the Feminist movement of the 1960s.

The struggle continues today. In several countries round the world women are still regarded as property, and denied basic rights such as an education, and even in western countries women still fight against things like sexual harassment and strict anti-abortion laws.

Homosexuality is another right being fought for around the world. It wasn't legalised in England and Wales until the Sexual Offences Act of 1967, and in many countries it is still illegal. Following on from gay rights, similar rights are also being fought for by the worldwide LGBT movement.

Many of these rights are to do with freedoms, the freedom of the individual to say whatever they want, to live how they want and to act how they want. Freedom is often held up as the defining element of Western society, free speech, freedom of information, and a free press are considered fundamental as both a right and for shining a light into the dark corners of society, exposing corruption and criminality. The basic idea is that, as long as nobody is harmed and national security is not compromised, then free speech is a right. Indeed, someone's right to say whatever they want would be defended wholeheartedly even if what they are saying is abhorrent; one argument for such a defence is that it gives the opportunity to rationally put the opposing viewpoint, rather than letting the sentiment remain covered up until it explodes in some kind of violent action. Rights and freedoms are quintessential to Western, rich, developed world countries, but tension between freedom and laws always exist; the discussion point is where to draw the line.

In practice, however, it becomes more complicated, for instance governments have passed laws against incitement to hatred, and against religious intolerance, and many countries around the world still have blasphemy laws on their statute. Also, a free press can often intrude into the private life of individuals, and if they get the story wrong, any apology can be small in comparison.

It was only recently that the UK law of Libel was updated via the **Defamation Act 2013**. Prior to this you could be taken to court for damaging someone's reputation through a written article and it didn't matter if the article was true or not, they only had to prove damage. The new act introduced a new statutory defence of truth, honest opinion, and "publication on a matter of public interest" or privileged publications (including peer reviewed scientific journals).

We started this section entitled 'more rights' by mentioning the two world wars, so it seems right to finish it by mentioning an international institution that helps to protect rights which grew out of the Second World War. The United Nations came into being in October 1945 with the specific aims of 'maintaining international peace and security', 'protecting human rights', and 'upholding international law'. It's not perfect and evaluations of its effectiveness have been mixed, countries each have their own agendas, but talking is much better than fighting and most conflicts eventually end in compromises of some sort. The UN also has an important peacekeeping role in post-conflict areas.

Another international organisation that protects human rights is the International Criminal Court in The Hague. This started operations in July 2002 upon entry into force of the Rome Statute, a multilateral treaty which serves as the court's charter. By March 2022 123 states had signed up as members, but that still left around 42 states not members. The court can only investigate and prosecute crimes committed in or by member states. Both the US and Russia were original members but have subsequently withdrawn.

Democracy and Sovereignty

Having looked at some of the history and evolution of politics and political philosophy, an important next step is to take a slightly closer look at the concepts of democracy and sovereignty. These two, emotionally laden, terms pepper the rhetoric of politicians, as well as forming the basis of many individual political discussions and arguments. As philosophers, however, we should always start with an examination of the terms we use before jumping into discussions and conclusions based on those terms.

To say that the United Kingdom (for example) is a democracy is a simplification. In a full democracy every eligible citizen would be asked to vote on every issue. A city state in ancient Greece might get closer to that but in a modern, large, industrial country that is obviously impracticable; beside the cost and the organization required, people just don't have the time, the interest, or the knowledge and expertise to vote on every issue.

The correct term for this system is a 'Representative Democracy'. Citizens can vote (once every few years) for a person who will represent their interests (both local and national) in a centralised national parliament. They also vote for similar representatives who sit in local council assemblies. For such representatives it becomes their full-time job, they learn about the structure of governance, and they can spend time learning about each issue they are asked to vote on. Also, they can be seconded onto various committees whose job it is to investigate particular issues more fully and report back to the full parliament. In short it is their professional job to represent their constituents who themselves have not got the time to become involved in the complexities of governance.

Different countries also have different ways of citizen's votes being counted. The U.K. and the U.S. for instance operate a 'first past the post' system, but some other countries use proportional representation (of which there are a number of different types).

A Representative Democracy is not a perfect system, but then (as Churchill indicated) other systems are probably worse. One problem with representative democracy is that the representatives themselves might be inclined to make decisions based not on the good of the country but on getting themselves re-elected. Other problems include the party system which makes representatives follow party lines; the polarisation of politics; the lobbying by large special interest groups; and (especially in the U.S.) the cost of running for office. Also, with the party system, the country might find making long term plans difficult if the party in power changes every few years.

Having identified some of the issues it is still difficult to envisage a better system. Representatives (senators, congressmen, members of parliament, etc.) are intelligent people who have chosen to serve their community. What better way is there of passing laws than getting together a few hundred of such people, and give them the time to properly investigate issues and to have serious discussions on them before deciding on the best course of action for the country?

In some cases, if a question is both large and contentious, an alternative, is to have a referendum (which sounds incredibly democratic), but such an act has its own problems. One issue is whether the public has all the facts about the question; many of them might keep themselves well informed, but many will not think through all the issues and will make a decision based on one aspect of the question at the expense of other considerations, and many will get persuaded by spin and rhetoric. A second issue is that if the vote is split close to 50/50, deciding the result by simple majority might swing one way one year and another way another year. If the question is important to the country and would represent something like a virtually permanent constitutional change, it might be prudent to design the referendum so that it requires a two thirds majority for it to pass.

Take, for instance, the United Kingdom's Brexit referendum of 2016. This was a huge change for the country, but it was passed by only 51.9%. After seeing the problems caused (Northern Island, traffic issues in Kent, red tape for businesses, etc.) might the result be slightly against Brexit if it was held again? A good case could probably be made that it should have needed a two thirds majority.

Also, at the time it was held, a large majority of MPs were against Brexit. These are the people whose job it was to understand the politics and economics involved. Did all the people who voted fully consider things like the Northern Island implications, the financial implications for the city, the trade tariffs, and the lack of trade arrangements with non-EU countries, etc? There was a lot of spin around at the time of the vote which reduced complex arguments to sound bites. If the UK had stayed in the EU, it would have been over with, but even six years afterwards the negotiations on leaving were nowhere near complete.

Closely related to democracy is the idea of sovereignty, but what do we mean by sovereignty and where does it come from? Initially it would have been feudal, a warlord ruling his particular area with force, both to fight off invaders but also to rule and tax his subjects. Over time, and through alliances and marriages, these areas became countries, but even then, the borders between the countries moved backwards and forwards. It might be easier to define a country if it is an island, although here too the borders can change over time. Think of the United Kingdom for instance, as well as England it currently includes Scotland, Wales, and Northern Island, and in times past it even included parts of northern France.

As noted above, Thomas Hobbs and John Locke first gave the concept of sovereignty a more philosophical underpinning using the idea of a 'social contract'. Remember this was not a contract between sovereign and their subjects, it was between the individual people themselves. It said, in effect, I will give up certain rights and freedoms to a sovereign as long as everyone else does the same, and then that sovereign can protect us and legitimately raise taxes to pay for that protection. Note that the sovereign power could be either a monarch or a parliament of some kind. All subsequent evolution of the scope of that sovereign power then became about exactly what rights and freedoms citizens should actually have while still retaining the protection of the sovereign.

So, sovereignty here is identified with the area the sovereign controls, which in effect is a country, but we have seen that the area constituting a country changes through things like wars, alliances, and marriages. In practice, the larger the area covered, the stronger the sovereignty becomes, but this is where the idea gets complicated and is often misunderstood. People often think that an alliance with another area makes the sovereignty smaller, as if sovereignty is a block of stone which gets bits knocked off it, but in fact it could be seen as sovereign power being expanded by the alliance.

Nationalism is an easy message to sell, it reaches into some of our deepest evolutionary psyche around protection of family and being part of a tribe, but what it ignores are the benefits of cooperation. As part of the nationalist message, you will hear things like 'we want our sovereignty back' and 'why should others have a say in running our lives?' Again, take the United Kingdom as an example, and you have leaving Europe with Brexit, and you have Scotland possibly breaking away. To emphasise by extremes perhaps Kent should be independent, or Canterbury become a city state! One way to give local people more control, and to remove unnecessary central control while retaining the benefits of alliance, is via things like devolution, county councils, and town councils.

Any time you join an alliance there are benefits of being part of a larger group, but to join a group you also have to abide by the rules of that group. Countries join many groups, some tighter but others more nebulous, for instance the European Union, NATO, the United Kingdom, the Commonwealth, the WHO, the IMF, the World Bank, the United Nations, the International Criminal Court in the Hague, etc. Every alliance you join makes you stronger.

The above section was mainly included to emphasise that the concepts of democracy and sovereignty are more complex than are commonly thought, but it was also included to demonstrate how a philosophical analysis might proceed when discussing a given question. If a discussion starts with such an analysis, then participants have more of a common ground and understanding when exploring the question.

What is needed for Good Governance?

The structure of good government is the big picture view, most of which was mentioned above: checks and balances; separation of powers; separation of church and state; limited terms; free and regular elections; and a constitution of some kind that can only be amended by a large (e.g. two thirds) majority.

After that, however, what are the responsibilities of an ideal government? The following is a possible list, the reader may want to add their own thoughts: -

1. The main responsibility would seem to be the care of its citizens. This falls into four main categories. Firstly, defence of the

country, which probably includes maintaining an army; entering defence alliances with other countries (e.g. via NATO or other); and perhaps intelligence gathering. Secondly, disaster preparedness and disaster relief. Thirdly, care for those at the bottom of society with housing, welfare, healthcare, and social care. And fourthly, a police force with powers to investigate and detain in line with the law.
2. Ensuring fairness and justice for its citizens, making sure the justice system is independent of government and that it applies equally to all regardless of status, wealth, gender, race, or religion. Also, that those at the bottom of society have equal access to the justice system.
3. Designing a tax system that is fair to all. It would probably be a tiered system of some kind where those with a larger income pay a higher percentage, but at the same time not so high that it stifles growth and investment. [Remember from chapter 45, the American philosopher John Rawls, who wrote extensively on fairness and justice in society. One of his ideas was something called "**the veil of ignorance**". In this you should design your tax system (and other elements of society) as if you had no knowledge ahead of time what position you would end up having in that society. The choice is made from behind a veil of ignorance, which prevents you from knowing things like your ethnicity, social status, gender, etc.]
4. Ensuring freedoms and rights of individual citizens as long as other citizens are not harmed by the action of others. This can be difficult, free speech is important, and people already have things like the laws of libel and slander to protect them, but do you pass extra laws against things like hate speech or religious intolerance? One reason for allowing unlimited free speech is that it brings prejudices and misunderstandings into the open where they can be examined and rationally argued against. The philosopher John Stuart Mill wrote a lot about liberty, and one of the points he made was that, while democracy is a good thing, we need to guard against the "threat of the tyranny of the majority".
5. Freedom of the press is also important; the alternative would be the state-controlled press and media which apply in some communist countries or dictatorships. Having said that, there are considerations of national security; in these cases, however, it would probably be argued out in the courts, which should of course be independent of government.

6. Different committees should be set up with powers to investigate and monitor things like government spending in a transparent way.
7. Good government should also base its policies on the best science available, and in some cases, it can even fund scientific studies and pilot studies to find the best approach to policy rather than relying simply on opinion. For instance, policies to reduce smoking, higher tax on leaded petrol, climate change policies, and food policies like the 2003 Danish ban on artificial trans-fat in food which has been estimated to have saved at least 1,200 there so far.

The above list is far from complete but is included to stimulate thought and discussion about the responsibilities of good government and how they might be achieved.

Politics Conclusion

This chapter is just an introduction to politics and political theory; whole libraries exist on this subject with books from every colour of the political spectrum but the main intention here is to provide a summary of the history of the philosophical underpinning to current western democracies.

Politics is a messy business: it's inexorably intertwined with economics; it's full of compromises; and it's often about just muddling through. Maybe all we can do is to try and learn some lessons from history and to constantly deal with the chaos the universe throws at us.

60

The Meaning of Life

[...], though without knowing how or why,
Made still a blund'ring kind of melody;
Spurred boldly on, and dashed through thick and thin,
Through sense and nonsense, never out nor in;
Free from all meaning, whether good or bad,
And in one word, heroically mad.

John Dryden – Absalom and Achitophel (1681)

Overview

This is often seen as the big question. When people think about philosophy, in a non-academic sense, it is usually in terms of things like: - looking for a reason why we are here; searching for spiritual solace; or trying to find the best way to live one's life. All of which deserve serious philosophical consideration. As noted before however, this book is an introduction to philosophy in the academic sense, and fundamental to that tradition, in Western philosophy, is epistemology (the theory of knowledge). Therefore, this chapter will consider the 'meaning of life' question in the light of that epistemology, including: - what do we know about the universe; how do we know those things; and what confidence can we attribute to that understanding.

As part of that approach, no matter how attractive other forms of philosophy are, if one really wants to understand the world and our place in it, the findings of science cannot be ignored. It is readily admitted that science does not, by any means, have all the answers, but the point is – the answers it does have really need to be incorporated into our understanding and analysis of any philosophical questions. For example, science might not have much to say in terms of our individual emotional perspective on life, but it can tell us (among many other things about the universe and the world we live in) that evolution is true, and that our emotional capacities as human beings are a product of that evolutionary process.

The Meaning of Life

[Note: - Any readers jumping straight to this chapter for answers to the meaning of life question are well advised to read previous chapters of this book, at the very least (and in order) all chapters in part 1 and all in part 4. This will enable a better understanding of the approach taken here.]

Why are we here?

When we ask a 'why' question there could [as noted in chapter 57] be two separate interpretations of that question, it could be asking 'how come' or it could be asking 'what for'. The 'how come' question asks how something got to be this way, what were the preceding steps, or the path taken. The 'what for' questions ask for the reasons something occurred, usually implying design reasons of some kind. As philosophers we need to be sure which version of the question is being asked, and which version we are actually answering. This needs to be made explicit; indeed, both versions of the question often need to be addressed in the answer, being careful of course to stipulate which answer goes with which version of the question.

Let's start with the 'how come' version of why we are here; how did we get here; how did the world get here; and how did the universe come into being? People are innately curious animals and are supreme story tellers, we have always speculated on our existence, and every culture has its own creation stories: giant eggs hatching; snakes swallowing their tail; a woman created from a man's rib; the world riding on the back of a giant turtle; etc. Even Plato, despite his other brilliant philosophy, said things like there is one soul for each star in heaven and that if a man lives well, he goes to death to live happily in his star, but if he lives badly, he will, in the next life, be a woman, and if she persists in evil doing, she will become a brute. Before we had science what else could people do but make things up?

With modern science we can go a long way to answering the 'how come' version of why we are here. Science tells us a logical, evidence based, story starting with a hot, dense, expanding plasma fractions of a second after the big bang, the evidence for a big bang of some kind being both overwhelming and satisfyingly supported from different branches of science (astronomy, particle physics and mathematics).

After the big bang, as the plasma expanded and cooled, atoms of hydrogen and helium formed, and then these were drawn together by gravity to make the first stars. These stars used fusion to burn their hydrogen fuel and make the heavier elements up to and including iron, and the largest of the stars exploded as supernova which, with the huge pressures involved, created all the other elements heavier than iron, and ejected these out into the galaxies. Other stars formed out of this gas and dust, and around them planets formed, some of which were rocky like our Earth.

So far it has all been physics, but then under the right conditions (like a rocky planet in a stable orbit around a star at the right distance) the basic elements can combine to make molecules and you start to get chemistry, then biochemistry, then biology and evolution. All logical small steps one after the other.

It is important to note here that this, evidence based, story does not claim that humans are inevitable. There is no planning involved, no guiding hand and certainly no 'destination' aimed for or implied. It seems incredibly likely that other planets in the universe will exist in stable enough conditions to reach biology and evolution, mainly because of the huge numbers involved; there are more stars in the universe than there are grains of sand on all the beaches on Earth! But evolution on other planets will not produce humans because their evolutionary history will be different. It may well be that such creatures, if intelligent and tool using, would have similarities because similar environments produce similar survival designs. Think of mammals like whales and dolphins looking superficially like fish even though their ancestors lived on land before returning to the water.

It is also important to note here that even on this planet humans were not inevitable. People often think of evolution as progress towards something, but it doesn't work like that. Evolution by natural selection has no goal it is aiming for, it knows nothing of the future, it is just selection of those elements of preexisting variation in a population that best survives and best passes on their genes in the current local environment. Sometimes more complex biology gets selected as being better able to survive and pass on their genes, so one might well expect some life forms to be complex, but at the same time simple strategies work well too; think of bacteria, they survive fine, indeed they will be here long after humans have gone.

So, no need for creation myths, and from previous chapters in this section no need for the dualism which postulates mind and body as two separate 'things', a physical body and non-physical mind. [Remember from chapter 53 – mind is not a thing, it is a process, it is the brain working; there is no need for a separate, non-physical, soul or spirit 'thing'. Those historic terms are perhaps best thought of today as poetic concepts – shorthand for our total emotional and psychological response to things.] Science, then, has addressed the 'how come' version of why we are here in all respects except one – what happened before the big bang?

The Meaning of Life

Here science holds up its hand and says, 'we don't know', but adds 'we are working on it'. Some people might say at this point 'well if you don't know, then my theory must be correct', be that God or whatever. But as philosophers we should point out that this would be bad logic; the fact that science doesn't know something does not make another particular viewpoint automatically correct. If that other viewpoint wants to be taken seriously it needs to provide its own evidence, otherwise it can't be considered knowledge or, indeed, philosophy.

There are several scientific theories relating to the 'prior to the big bang' question, but currently there is no way to verify any of them. For instance, the big bang could just be a bounce back from a previous 'big crunch', or it could be just one of a number of expanding bubble universes. Others say perhaps it makes no sense to talk about 'before' the big bang because time came into being as well as space in the big bang, so it would be a bit like asking what is north of the north pole, if you start by moving north and keep going in a straight line you will at some point find yourself moving south.

There seem to be two possibilities, either there was the start to the universe, or the universe has always existed – both possibilities are actually mind blowing! As is the question – "why is there something rather than nothing?" These will not be solved by sitting and thinking, only science has the potential to answer questions like how and why did the universe form, but it's entirely possible we can never find out. We think about the world using the concepts we derive from living in our familiar, three-dimensional, cause and effect, local environment, but science, with Relativity and Quantum Mechanics, evidences a world that is much stranger and more difficult to think about. So, any 'how come' answer to 'why we are here' needs both to incorporate the evidence-based discoveries of science, and find new concepts to deal with the weird quantum world we live in.

The 'what for' version of the question 'why are we here?' should also be considered in order that the philosophical analysis covers all meanings of the question. 'What for' questions usually look for design reasons, such as 'we are in the supermarket because we want to buy food', i.e. there is intelligence and planning implied with this answer.

The problem here is that most complex objects in our everyday experience are designed, everything from a tin opener to a shirt, to a watch, to a computer; we take it for granted that there is planning and intelligence behind complex things. When we think about ourselves, we see perhaps the most complex things in the universe, so it seems natural to presume a designer, indeed an intelligent designer. But science has given us the story that starts with particle physics and continues through chemistry, biochemistry, biology and evolution, all occurring naturally without a need for intelligent design or even a guiding hand; given the initial big bang, the rest just happens.

In terms of physics and chemistry etc. one may well accept that, but it often seems that evolution is where the mental block occurs. The biologist Richard Dawkins has given us a good intuition pump here with his analogy 'climbing mount improbable'. You are standing at the bottom of a massive vertical cliff and thinking 'how on earth am I going to get to the top?' What you don't realise is that, if you go round the back of the mountain, you will find an extremely long but very shallow slope that you can just take your time and walk up to the top climbing just a little with each step.

Evolution, he says, is like that; you look at the incredible complexity of a human being and think 'how on earth could such a complex, well-designed thing come into being without any intelligence behind the design?' The answer is that humans were not created in one go overnight, they have occurred following an incredibly long, one step at a time, process of evolution (like climbing mount improbable). It is the length of time involved that makes the difference, and which is perhaps hardest to comprehend, because we don't usually think in those terms. Our thinking about time is usually about minutes, hours, days, weeks and sometimes years; billions of years is incredibly hard to meaningfully get our minds around.

Having said that however, we actually are designed, but that designer is 'Natural Selection'. There are two important aspects to evolution, one is that the given organism needs to survive, and the second is that it needs to pass its genetic code on to its offspring. In any population of a species there is variation, even offspring don't look exactly like their parents, also copying errors can occur when passing on DNA. Most genetic changes by far are either bad for the individual or neutral, but just occasionally one might occur that increases the individual's survival prospects (running faster or whatever) or it helps the individual to leave more offspring. Contrary wise, any genetic changes that are bad for the individual often mean that individual dies before passing on those bad genes.

We are talking here not of good or bad in any moral sense, or even in any sense of heading towards a future goal, we are just talking about being good or bad with respect to surviving and leaving offspring in the current local environment the individual is in. So, in that sense, bad changes often get wiped out and good changes flourish.

It's a hard, 'survival of the fittest' view of nature, 'red in tooth and claw', (with 'fittest' meaning best adapted for that local environment), but that is the design process called 'Natural Selection', i.e. it is the local environment that does the selecting. [It should be noted here that the term 'local environment' includes a number of elements: the physical environment (desert, jungle, ocean etc.); any other species around (predators, competition, prey or beneficial); and then other individuals within the organism's own species.]

Science then, answers the 'what for' version of the question 'why are we here?' by saying that we are designed, but that there is no intelligence behind that design, not even a guiding hand of any kind. We are designed, but the designer is Natural Selection; we are designed solely for surviving and for passing on our genes. There are lots of ways to be good at that, and natural selection has tried many of them: every organism currently on Earth is good at that, a myriad of different strategies being employed. In our case though the strategies include (among many others) intelligence, curiosity, and an attraction to beauty, all of which, having developed to aid survival and procreation, can now also be used, almost as a byproduct, to give us our rich cultural life of arts and sciences.

Scepticism

At this point we should return to the bedrock of western philosophy, epistemology (the theory of knowledge), how can we give credence to the veracity of those things that we think we know? Remember back to chapter 3 on epistemology, knowledge is divided into two categories: - Deductive knowledge and Inductive knowledge. Deductive knowledge is obtained using maths and logic and, as such, can be 100% correct. Inductive knowledge, on the other hand, is everything else we think we know, but because it is obtained through a process of induction it can't be considered to be 100% correct – there is room for scepticism.

Our personal beliefs are built through induction, trial and error, and seeing what works, [refer back to chapters 55 and 56 on how beliefs are formed]. We throw a ball up and it comes down again, we talk to others and find they have similar experiences. Are we right? Is a belief wrong if it is just an approximation to the real world? When science gets involved, we can construct the theory of gravity to describe a body moving in curved space-time, a better approximation than our personal understanding of a ball falling. We know, however, that even Einstein's theory is incomplete, but it has still passed every measurement test so far conducted.

Scepticism often gets a bad name: e.g. the person who can't be convinced by any argument; a doubting Thomas; even someone who is out to criticise everything without putting forward any ideas themselves. In epistemology however, scepticism finds its true place: an acknowledgment that something taken as being correct might someday be replaced by a more accurate idea. In layman's terms, we take things with a pinch of salt; from experience we trust some sources more than others when they tell us things. With science the criteria for acceptance is much higher, while at the same time acknowledging that a questioning scepticism is a vital part of the scientific process. Indeed, it is integral to the process; a scientist says here is my data, this is my analysis, please check it all for any errors.

Life is complex and messy, one has no option but to ascribe a probability to events; for example, is the accused guilty? The jury decides, but sometimes miscarriages of justice occur. Science is much stricter and needs very large positive probabilities before accepting something as fact, but even then, it accepts the possibility of a better theory appearing. Note that often in science a given theory is not proved wrong, just incomplete, as in Newton's theory of gravity being improved by Einstein's, and Einstein's being known as still incomplete. Other times however, theories are proved wrong, an example being the 'steady state' theory of the universe losing out to the 'big bang' theory.

Scepticism then is a vital element of our world view, both at a personal level, and within science. It should be seen as a celebration of our acceptance that our knowledge of the world is Inductive in nature. It is an acknowledgement of how our brain works, and it is also responsible for the success of the scientific method. Everything should be questioned, 'de omnibus disputandum' (everything should be doubted). But given this built-in questioning, if science says something is a fact (e.g. its probability of being correct is over 99.9%), as for example evolution, then that should undoubtedly be incorporated into our philosophical thinking.

Meaning

In chapter 56 we considered meaning in relation to language and concepts. The analysis showed that words and concepts are not concrete entities and can't be tied down 100%, but that in spite of this, meaning arises when the listener can successfully act in the world based on the speaker's words, i.e. usefulness of information is the key to meaning. The implication for this chapter is that meaning only occurs after evolution produces organisms that can usefully process information.

The universe is a harsh place for life (empty space, cold, full of radiation, etc.) but we know that evolution by natural selection can produce life – given a protected environment that is stable for the required billions of years. As mentioned above, science shows that, given the big bang, there is a logical progression through physics, chemistry, biochemistry, biology, and evolution, all possible without any intelligence or guiding hand, and hence without any intent or meaning.

Yet there is meaning, there is meaning when we communicate, there is meaning when we think, and there is meaning when we value things. One could postulate all sorts of reasons why the universe is here in the first place, but you would of course be doing so without evidence. Given the big bang however, we don't need to invoke meaning in the universe until organisms arise that can usefully process information. Meaning then becomes something personal to thinking, feeling individuals.

Evolution designed us as thinking, caring, gregarious, and emotional animals. We care deeply about things that are important to us – our families, our friends, and our ideals. These might well be different for different people, but as we learn and talk to others, so the things we care about may well evolve. Ultimately then, the meaning of life question has nothing to do with things like 'before the big bang'. There is no 'intrinsic' meaning to the universe, the meaning of life is a personal question that each one of us has to consider: individually we need to work out what things we each care about – and then it is those things that give meaning to our lives.

Conclusion

The aim of this book is to provide a clear but comprehensive introduction to a subject that is often viewed as complicated and perhaps even elitist. Part one laid out a straightforward structured approach to Western Philosophy and introduced the type of language philosophers use (learn the language and you have an easier introduction to the concepts involved). Part two gave a history of Western Philosophy showing how philosophical ideas developed and changed over time, and how later thinkers were influenced by earlier ones. Part three provided a short introduction to Eastern Philosophy, both as a contrast and as being fascinating in its own right. Part four looked at how modern philosophy is strongly influenced by science (not that science has all the answers, it's just that the answers it does have can't be ignored). This part also provided an extensive discussion, over several chapters, on the nature of concepts, language, and meaning, as we struggle towards some sort of clearer understanding of this amazing universe we inhabit.

By nature we are curious animals, it is embedded in our psyche both to explore the world we live in and to explore ideas; we are nothing if not storytellers, and philosophy is perhaps the ultimate story. The tools storytellers use are words, concepts and ideas, and philosophers employ these to try to understand the world, understand reality. Words, however, can only create a map of reality, we can be more and more accurate (especially when we cooperate and exchange ideas with others), but it's still just a map made from words and concepts in our heads, and a map is not the territory.

The journey to such an understanding though is both fascinating and rewarding. Philosophers often ask, 'what is real?' Well relationships are real, and it is these that bring a lot of the meaning to our lives, but another avenue to the meaning of life is via the gift of our curiosity, so we will finish therefore as we started by quoting Socrates: - "The unexamined life is not worth living".

Acknowledgements

My editorial role within this book falls into two main areas. Firstly, to summarize the history of Western philosophy from ancient Greece to the current day showing the development of its main philosophic ideas and themes, together with a counterbalancing introduction to Eastern philosophy. And secondly, to provide an outline conceptual framework for thinking about, and practicing, philosophy, giving particular attention in part four to the two-way interaction between philosophy and science.

The field of philosophy is huge and in compiling this introduction I have only scratched the surface. As well as original texts from individual philosophers, there exists innumerable other commentaries, criticisms, summaries, interpretations, and criticisms of criticisms. The ones I have relied on most are referenced both within the text and in the bibliography, but any errors within the book are mine alone. I am also grateful for the work of those who put together philosophy web sites and other sites containing original texts.

Once again, my role has been in the selection of what to include, and in the ordering of it within an overriding framework drawing on my lifelong interest in both philosophy and science.

Finally, I would like to thank my good friend Nina Chislett for her invaluable help in proof-reading the manuscript and for our many discussions which helped clarifying my thinking.

Stephen Welch

Bibliography

Ayer, A.J. 1946. *Language, Truth and Logic*. Pelican Books.

Bakewell, Sarah, 2017. *At The Existentialist Cafe*. Vintage, Penguin.

Baggini, Julian, 2018. *How the World Thinks*. Granta Publications.

Baggini, Julian, and Fosl, Peter S. 2010. *The Philosopher's Toolkit*. Wiley-Blackwell.

Barnes, Jonathan, 1982. *Aristotle*. Oxford University Press.

Carroll, Sean B. 2009. *The Making of the Fittest*. Quercus.

Coyne, Jerry A. 2009. *Why Evolution is True*. Oxford University Press.

Chavez-Arvizo, Enrique, (Editor) 1997. *Descartes Key Philosophical Writings*. Wordsworth Classics.

Damasio, Antonio, 2003. *Looking for Spinoza*. Harvest.

Dennett, Daniel C. 1991. *Consciousness Explained*. Penguin Books Ltd.
    1996. *Darwin's Dangerous Idea*. Penguin Books.
    2003. *Freedom Evolves*. Penguin Books Ltd.
    2006. *Breaking the Spell: Religion as a Natural Phenomenon*. Penguin Books.
    2013. *Intuition Pumps and other Tools for Thinking*. Penguin Books Ltd.
    2017. *From Bacteria to Bach and Back*. Allen Lane, Penguin Books.

Richard Dawkins, 1989. *The Selfish Gene*. Oxford University Press.
    1996. Climbing Mount Improbable. Norton.

Gettier, Edmund, 1963. *Is Justified True Belief Knowledge*. A paper in the journal *Analysis*, published by Oxford University Press.

Grayling, A.C. 2008. *Scepticism and the Possibility of Knowledge*. Continuum UK.

Bibliography

Harris, Sam, 2010. *The Moral Landscape*. Transworld Publishers.

Hawking, Stephen, 1989. *A Brief History of Time*. Bantam.

Heidegger, Martin, 1988. *The Basic Problems of Phenomenology*. Indiana University Press.

Hobbes, Thomas, 1981. *Leviathan*. Penguin English Library.

Honderich, Ted, (Editor) 1995. *The Oxford Companion to Philosophy*. Oxford University Press.

Hume, David, 1969. *A Treatise on Human Nature*. Penguin Books
2007. *An Enquiry Concerning Human Understanding*. Oxford World's Classics.

James, William, 1990. *A Pluralistic Universe*. Free Ebook, download from Project Gutenberg.

Krauss, Lawrence M. 2012. *A Universe from Nothing*. Free Press.

Lao Tzu, 1973. *Tao Te Ching*, (Translation by Gia-Fu Feng and Jane English) Wildwood House Ltd.

Lock, John, 1969. *An Essay Concerning Human Understanding*. Fontana/Collins.

Lucretius, 2007. *The Nature of Things*. Penguin Classics.

McGreal, Ian P. (Editor) 1995. *Great Thinkers of the Eastern World*. Harper Collins Publishers.

Merleau-Ponty, Maurice, 2014. *Phenomenology of Perception*. Routledge.

Paine, Thomas, 2004. *Common Sense*. Penguin Books.

Paul, Leslie, 1952. *The English Philosophers*. Faber and Faber.

Plato. *The Republic*. Penguin Classics, 3rd edition (31 May 2007).

Poirier, Agnes, 2018. *Left Bank*. Bloomsbury Publishing.

Reps, Paul, 1971. *Zen Flesh, Zen Bones*. Penguin Books.

Ridley, Matt, 1997. *The Origins of Virtue*. Penguin Books.

Rorty, Richard, 1989. *Contingency, irony, and solidarity*. Cambridge University Press.

Rousseau, Jean-Jacques, 2004. *The Social Contract*. Penguin Books.

Russell, Bertrand, 1905. *On Denoting*. An essay in the journal *Mind*, published by Oxford University Press.
    1948. *A History of Western Philosophy*. George Allen and Unwin Ltd.
    1967. *The Problems of Philosophy*. Oxford University Press.
    2004. *In Praise of Idleness*. (A reprint of his 1935 book) Routledge Classics.

Ryle, Gilbert, 1949. *The Concept of Mind*. Penguin Books.

Sartre, Jean Paul, 2003. *Being and Nothingness*. Routledge Classics.

Schick, Theodore and Vaughn, Lewis, 2007. *How to Think about Weird Things*. McGraw-Hill.

Shubin, Neil, 2009. *Your Inner Fish*. Penguin.

Stanford Encyclopedia of Philosophy (SEP). An on-line encyclopedia with peer-reviewed original papers in philosophy.

Taylor, A.E. 1943. *Aristotle*. Thomas Nelson and Sons Ltd.

Todd, Janet, 2000. *Mary Wollstonecraft a revolutionary life*. The Orion Publishing Group.

Ward, Andrew, 2012. *Starting with Kant*. Continuum International Publishing Group.

Watson, Peter, 2014. *The Age of Nothing*. The Orion Publishing Group.

Wilson, A.N. 2000. *God's Funeral*. Abacus.

Wittgenstein, Ludwig, 1971. *Tractatus Logico-Philosophicus*. Routledge and Kegan Paul Ltd.
    1969. *The Blue and Brown Books*. Blackwell.

Woolf, Virginia, 1948. *The Common Reader*. Harcourt, Brace and Company.

Index

Abduction, 13-16, 30-31, 34, 40, 357, 363
Absolute, 37, 84, 116, 129, 157, 157, 192, 194-195, 199, 215, 299, 446
Absurd, 113, 158, 205, 221, 287, 291, 295, 427-428
Ad Hominem, 27
Aesthetics, 4, 74, 121, 178, 254, 355
Artificial Intelligence, 325-326, 378, 405
America, 50, 59, 88, 126, 134, 152-153, 168, 176, 185, 190, 231-232, 237, 254-255, 261, 277, 309-310, 320-326, 329, 331, 392, 399, 401-402, 416, 418-419, 434, 439, 441, 448-449, 452, 458
American Pragmatism, xi, 49, 168, 231, 233-234, 236-238, 254-256, 258, 261, 286, 323-324
Analogy, 13, 16, 30, 69-70, 84, 198, 201, 203, 236, 376, 463
Analyse, x, 23, 30, 36-37, 248, 253, 268, 273, 275-276, 278, 311, 322, 355, 361, 395, 409-410, 420, 449
Analytic, xi, 38, 49, 114, 121, 140-150, 164, 219, 261-262, 264, 266, 269, 277, 289, 283-285, 289, 295, 297-298, 303-304, 321-322, 324, 381
Analytical Philosophy, xi, 49, 277
Anaxagorsa, 50
Antinomies, 180-181
A posterior, xi, 36
A priori, xi, 36, 179-180, 183, 248, 281. 297, 301, 303, 322, 367-368, 391

Aquinas, St Thomas, 44, 48, 65, 97-104, 106-107, 148, 173, 218, 253, 358, 412
Ambrose, St, 89-90
Antithesis, 180,193-195, 215, 227
Argument, ix, xiv, 5, 8, 12-14, 16, 18-21, 25-32, 35-36, 40, 60, 64, 73, 78-79, 83, 86, 93, 99-104, 107, 124, 130, 133, 138, 146-149, 155, 157, 163, 172-173, 175, 180-182, 188, 193-194, 211-212, 214, 236, 274, 292-293, 411, 321, 323, 325-326, 355, 371, 395, 406, 408-409, 411, 414-417, 423, 427, 430, 433-436, 446, 448, 453-454, 456, 465
Aristocracy, 61, 68, 173, 190, 197, 262, 442-443, 448, 451
Aristotle, xiii, 7-9, 12, 44, 48, 51-53, 55-56, 60, 67-75, 77, 80, 82-83, 86, 97-101, 103-108, 113, 119, 122, 133, 194-195, 208, 210, 251, 354, 405, 418, 425, 438, 443, 470, 472
Armstrong, David, 381
Astronomy, 52, 90, 122, 178, 207, 247, 354, 357, 368, 461
Atheism, 117, 120, 141-142, 163-164, 262, 302, 309
Atheist, 141, 153, 160, 200, 206, 221, 230, 262-263, 309, 424
Athens, 56-58, 61-62, 67-68, 76, 442
Atom (ism) (ist), xi, 18, 42, 50, 52-55, 77, 86, 105, 108, 146, 157, 194, 249, 259, 266-267, 273-274, 296, 365, 367, 372-373, 390, 393, 398, 415, 417, 461

Index

Attribute, xii, 10, 12, 22, 38, 54, 69-70, 123-124, 132, 138, 145, 155, 163, 226, 250-251, 261, 320, 360, 393, 442, 460
Augustine, St, 44, 48, 65, 89-95, 97, 103, 105, 198, 412
Axiom, xi, 31-32, 35-36, 42, 52, 138-139, 163, 265, 354, 367
Ayer. A. J. 49, 164, 284, 301-308, 470
Babylonians, 50, 441
Bacon, Francis, 48, 105-113, 128, 164
Beauvoir, Simone de, 286-287, 291, 293-295, 300, 453
Behaviourism, 296, 307, 381
Belief, 6-7, 12, 14, 16, 22, 25, 34, 38, 50-52, 58, 61, 64, 78, 80, 83-84, 86, 133, 163, 166, 168, 172, 178, 190, 194, 199, 211-212, 216, 218-219, 230, 234-238, 242, 249-250, 252, 254, 258, 261, 265, 267, 291, 295, 304, 307, 315-317, 323-324, 344, 358-359, 370-371, 375, 399, 422, 447-448, 465, 470
Bell, Stewart, 372
Bentham, Jeremy, xiv, 44, 48, 81, 104, 117, 185-191, 207-209, 212, 214, 226, 426-427, 434, 437, 447-448, 451
Berkeley, George, 8-9, 48, 119, 134, 151-159, 161, 164, 166-167, 169, 303, 312, 325, 375
Bible, 11, 89, 137, 175, 240, 358, 422-424
Big Bang, 102, 357, 368-369, 418, 461-464, 466-467
Bill of Rights, 130, 134, 331, 449
Biology, 42, 44, 50, 55, 67, 309, 311, 354, 392, 462-463, 467
Brentano, Franz, 247, 249, 288, 294, 311
Bohr, Neils, 373
Buddha, 201, 205, 235, 331-333, 344-350
Burket, Walter, 51

Calculus, 126, 144, 149, 157, 188, 190, 247, 405, 427
Cambridge Platonists, 88, 277
Camus, Albert, 286-287, 290-291, 293, 295, 406
Capitalism, 450-451
Capitalist, 226, 228, 449-451
Cartesian, 119, 121-122, 125, 127, 137, 227, 296, 313-314, 387, 446
Categorical Imperative, xiv, 182-183, 205, 426-427, 437
Category, 9, 12, 32-33, 36, 74, 109, 126, 161, 238, 322, 356-357, 376, 397
Catholic, 89-90, 95, 97-99, 101, 104-106, 119-120, 128, 136, 141, 167, 171, 198, 271, 278, 412, 422
Causal (ity), 21, 70, 102, 162, 164, 166, 202, 211, 296-297, 301, 366, 372, 381, 418
Causation, 14, 25, 101, 203
Cause, xi, xiii, 12, 54, 70, 90, 101-102, 124, 162, 168, 177, 195, 202-204, 315, 332, 346-348, 358, 366, 367, 370, 389, 396, 400-401, 406, 415, 417, 419, 463
Cave, 54, 110, 397
Checks and balances, 45, 130, 134, 446, 449, 451, 457
China, 50, 329, 331, 335-336, 339-340, 342, 345, 348, 441, 450
Chinese, 325-326, 332, 335, 337, 339-340, 348
Chinese Room, 325-326
Christian, 52, 57, 63, 65, 72, 77, 81-82, 86-95, 98-99, 104, 106-108, 117, 125, 135-136, 195, 204, 206, 213, 215-218, 223, 228, 242-245, 248, 263, 343-344, 412, 423
Churchland, Patricia, 418

Citizen, 45, 56, 58, 62, 68, 113, 115-117, 128-130, 134, 169-170, 173, 175, 197-198, 213, 365, 400, 430, 442-443, 445-446, 448-449, 452, 454-458

Climate change, 164, 202, 293, 303, 309, 387

Cognitive, 164, 202, 293, 303, 309, 387

Compatibilist, 164, 416

Communism, 294, 299, 449-451

Communist, 174, 199, 225-226, 228, 299, 340, 449, 450, 458

Concept(s), x, xiii, 4, 7, 12, 16, 25, 30-32, 36, 38, 43-44, 53, 61, 64, 67-70, 83, 93, 103, 105-106, 114-115, 125, 135, 137, 141-142, 162, 168, 173, 178, 180-181, 183, 192-194, 196, 202, 207, 215, 217, 220-222, 238, 246-251, 253, 259, 272, 276, 278, 288, 294, 296, 311, 315-316, 318, 320-322, 324, 331-336, 340, 343, 346-347, 355, 357, 361, 365-366, 368-369, 382, 388-402, 404-408, 415, 417-418, 420-421, 425, 433, 437-439, 441-442, 447, 454, 456-457, 462-463, 466-469, 472

Conclusion, xii, xiii, 6, 8, 13-15, 18-21, 26-27, 30-31, 54, 58, 62, 65, 73, 99, 104, 108, 110, 131, 145, 149, 161-162, 164, 180, 203, 221, 252, 263, 306, 346, 372, 419, 435-436, 443, 454, 459, 467

Confirmation Bias, 25

Confucian (ism), 331-332, 335, 339-343, 348

Confucius, 311, 335, 339-343, 438

Conscious (nes), xii, 3, 10, 23, 55, 65, 71, 80, 95, 141, 161, 192, 195, 203, 205, 215, 219, 226, 228, 233, 235, 237-239, 247-252, 259-260, 280-282, 288, 290-291, 293-297, 300, 310-314, 317-318, 325-326, 345, 373, 375, 378-381, 384, 387, 397-398, 410, 413-414, 416, 427, 435-436, 470

Consequentialism, 188, 256, 426, 437-438

Consistency, 31, 206, 270

Constitution, 68, 72, 97, 129, 131, 134, 167, 180, 183, 191, 251, 443, 445, 447-449, 452, 455, 457

Contradiction, 35, 59, 100, 146, 154-155, 180, 257, 393

Cosmological, 101, 147, 173, 181

Cosmology, 55, 62, 82, 102, 105

Correlation, 14, 25

Cretans, 50, 441

Darwin, Charles, 103, 256, 263, 315, 361-362, 470

Dawkins, Richard, 34, 309, 316-317, 384, 432, 464, 470

Deduction, 14, 16, 30, 36, 77, 179, 210, 353, 356, 367

Deductive knowledge, 8, 13, 29, 41, 36, 40, 73, 106, 111, 138, 160, 322, 367, 388, 422, 465

Definition(s), ix-x, 5-8, 12, 21, 26, 32, 37, 40, 42, 44-45, 57, 59-60, 74, 83, 138-139, 256, 265, 286, 290, 304-305, 318, 321-322, 332, 357-358, 364, 379, 381, 392-393, 395, 399-400, 403, 411, 414, 416, 420-421, 428-429, 439

Democracy, 44-45, 56, 58, 61-62, 68, 171, 173, 190-191, 196, 199, 213, 254, 264, 299, 319, 441-444, 448, 454-458

Democritus, 50, 52-55, 76-77, 108

Dennett, Daniel C. ix, 33, 35, 43, 49, 277, 309-318, 320, 326, 354, 365, 373, 376-377, 379-382, 387, 399, 401, 412, 419, 470

Deontology, 104, 437-438

Descartes, Rene, 8, 33, 36, 48, 60, 91, 106, 113, 119-127, 133-138, 144-146, 149, 152, 155, 157

Determinism, 164, 189, 370-371, 416
Deterministic, 3, 148, 189, 203, 314-315, 371, 409, 413-417, 419
Dewey, Dr. John, 49, 206, 231-232, 237, 254-261, 264, 428
Dialectic, 57, 105, 181, 194-196, 198-199, 224-227, 229, 298-299
Dogma (tic), 38, 68, 104-105, 110, 163, 177, 211, 236, 259-260, 263, 269, 321, 343, 345, 422-424, 428, 443, 447
Dominic, St. 97
Dominicans, 97-98
Dualism, 33, 63, 90, 92, 124-126, 137, 192, 233, 268, 290, 296, 313-314, 318, 320, 326, 376-377, 379, 387, 407, 426
Dualistic, xi, 254
Duty, xiv, 104, 116, 182-183, 197, 205, 218, 224, 237, 331, 356, 426-427, 430, 437-438
Effect(s), xi, 12, 15, 36, 72, 74, 90, 102, 108, 132, 162, 177-180, 187, 189, 191, 234, 236, 244, 259, 261, 315, 317, 325, 332, 346-348, 358, 363, 366-371, 389, 391, 396, 400-401, 406, 417, 419, 430, 435, 456, 463
Egyptians, 50, 441
Einstein, Albert, 10, 53, 157, 165, 264, 363, 368, 371-373, 391, 465-466
Empedocles, 50
Empiricism, xii, 8-9, 38, 60, 67, 108, 125, 127, 133-134, 144, 164, 177, 183, 231, 233-234, 253, 256, 258, 269, 297, 301, 303, 305, 321, 386-387, 405
Empiricist, 36, 42, 48, 60, 75, 105, 119, 138, 151, 153, 158, 164, 167, 179, 185, 227, 256, 290, 297, 305, 312, 321, 405
Engels, Friedrich, 198, 223, 225-226

Enlightenment, x, 9, 67, 86, 125, 135, 159, 192, 224, 333, 339, 342, 347-349, 444, 446
Enneads, 82-83, 85
Entanglement, 372
Entropy, 368-369
Enumerative Induction, 13, 16, 30
Epicurus, 48, 76-81, 190, 425, 438
Epistemology, xi, 4-16, 22, 40-41, 60, 64-65, 77, 119, 126, 134, 152, 159, 166, 206, 219, 231, 253-254, 261-262, 265-267, 272, 276, 281, 303, 306-307, 321-324, 353, 356-358, 360, 364, 388, 395, 406, 421, 422, 460, 465
Essence, 70, 84, 86-87, 99, 138, 144-147, 196, 250, 257, 289, 353, 397, 418
Ethics, x, 3-4, 41, 43, 50, 55, 57, 65, 70-73, 75, 100, 104-105, 112, 117, 136-138, 141, 144, 166, 205, 215, 219, 254, 259, 261-262, 264, 266, 269-270, 275-276, 286, 315, 322, 326, 334-335, 342, 348, 351-353, 355, 359, 406, 421-440
Euclid, 9, 31-32, 52, 113, 138, 202, 207, 263, 354, 426
Eudaimonia, 71, 425, 438
Evidence, ix, 6-7, 9-12, 14, 16, 18, 22, 24-25, 40, 54, 68, 77, 102, 111, 131, 136, 161, 181, 210, 236, 242, 267, 306-307, 311-312, 333, 346, 356-358, 362, 368, 370-371, 376-377, 388, 395, 407, 422-423, 430, 461-463, 467
Evolution, 12, 24, 34-35, 103, 190, 206, 223, 254-255, 309, 313, 315, 317, 319-321, 351, 358, 361-363, 365, 368, 371, 379, 400, 403, 412, 415, 418-419, 423, 429, 432-434, 452, 454, 456-457, 460, 462-464, 466-467, 470

Existentialism, xii, 49, 215, 219, 221-222, 245, 278, 284, 286-288, 290-292, 295-296, 300, 312, 386, 400, 406, 428, 439, 470

Fact, xii-xiv, 6, 11, 13, 22, 26, 28, 36, 65, 91, 106-109, 111, 157, 164, 201, 220-221, 237, 243, 256-257, 260-261, 266-267, 273-275, 282, 303-306, 315, 321, 330, 334, 351, 357-358, 360-364, 368-369, 371-372, 375, 377-378, 384-386, 390, 410, 415, 423, 429, 433-436, 439, 455, 463, 466

Faith, 4, 12, 16, 87, 95, 98-99, 104, 114, 116, 171-172, 218-219, 221, 240, 242, 272, 289-291, 296, 311, 358, 370, 422, 424

Fallacies, x, 25-29, 31, 40, 214, 237, 245, 315, 326

Fate, 78, 220, 283, 408-409

Felicific calculus, 188

Flaw, 7, 20, 26-27, 31, 68, 265, 291, 443

Forms, (Plato), 38, 43, 61, 63-65, 105, 108, 394, 397, 405

Fossil, 362, 364, 394

Francis, St. 97

Franciscans, 97, 248

Freedom, 61, 76, 79, 120, 129, 134, 137-138, 164, 182, 189, 192, 196-197, 205, 207, 228, 270, 287-291, 295, 298-299. 301, 310, 314-315, 324, 331, 333, 347, 408, 419, 425, 438-439, 444-445, 447-449, 453, 456, 458, 470

Free will, 3, 23, 77, 87, 90, 93-95, 100, 140, 146, 148, 164, 166, 236, 291, 295, 314, 371, 404, 408-419, 428

Frege, Gottlob, 262, 265, 272

Freud, Sigmund, 141, 232, 245, 291-292, 375, 413, 416

Functionalism, 326, 381

Fuzzy logic, 405

Game. 11, 23, 271, 275-176, 324, 391-392, 398, 404

Geist, 194, 227

Genetics, 317, 355, 362, 429, 432, 434

Geometry, 9, 31-32, 36, 52, 55, 112-113, 115, 119, 121, 123, 138, 149, 163, 202, 266, 353, 426

Gettier, Edmund, 7, 470

Gibbon, Edward, 442

Gnostic, 85-86, 90

God, 8, 51, 63-64, 69-71, 78-79, 84, 90-95, 99-103, 108, 114, 116-117, 123-125, 133, 137-142, 145, 147-148, 151-153, 156, 161, 163, 167, 172, 181-182, 187, 190, 203, 205, 216, 218-219, 221, 236-239, 242-245, 249, 271, 303-304, 315, 345, 357-358, 369-371, 388-389, 408, 412-413, 423-424, 426-427, 433, 444, 463, 472

Gods, 75, 77-79, 93-94, 109, 173, 321, 330, 346, 356, 423, 425, 442

Godstuff, 380

Godel, Kurt, 253, 270

Gould, Stephen Jay, 315, 419

Government, x, 4, 44-45, 56, 58, 68, 93, 97, 115-116, 118, 127-131, 134, 137, 171, 173-174, 183, 186-187, 189, 196-197, 199, 209-211, 213, 224-225, 262, 264, 339, 341, 356, 429, 441-446, 448-449, 451-453, 457-459

Gravity, 10, 196, 314, 363-364, 368, 376, 391-392, 396, 401, 461, 465-466

Greece, x, 44, 50, 67, 78, 81, 129, 331, 345, 367, 441-442, 444, 454, 469

Greek, ix, 6, 35, 42, 44, 47-48, 50-55, 57, 62-63, 67-68, 73, 76-77, 79-80, 82, 84, 87-88, 91, 93-94, 98, 105, 108, 127, 173, 185, 196, 207-208, 221, 240, 242,

244, 283, 302, 312, 390, 403, 425, 438, 441
Gregory, Bruce, 391
Hard problem (the), 318, 325-326, 379, 381
Harmony, 52, 100, 146-147, 189, 204, 332, 335-336, 338-339
Harris, Sam, 309, 416, 434, 437, 471
Hegel, Georg, 40, 48, 63, 134, 164, 181, 184, 192-202, 215-216, 218-220, 223-229, 255-256
Heidegger, Martin, 49, 253, 278-288, 290, 293-296, 471
Heisenberg, Werner, 373
Heraclitus, 50, 61
Heterophenomenology, 312-313, 318, 365, 381
Hobbes, Thomas, 48, 106, 112-120, 124, 128-129, 137, 163-164, 170, 173, 185, 259, 430-431, 445-446, 471
Homunculus, 377-378, 383
Humanism, 80, 220, 269, 291, 310, 339, 340, 346, 350, 424, 428
Hume, David, xiv, 6, 8-12, 36, 48-49, 60, 63, 81, 102, 119, 125, 134, 138, 157, 159-168, 171, 177-179, 182, 185, 189, 210-211, 269, 301, 303, 305, 312, 366-367, 388-389, 405-407, 413, 417, 426, 434, 438, 471
Husserl, Edmund, 32, 49, 95, 247-253, 278-280, 283, 286-288, 290, 293-296, 311-312, 389, 406
Hypothesis, 15, 31, 54, 58-59, 107, 111, 238, 254, 258, 304-305, 360-361, 373-374
Idealism, xii, 125, 169, 177, 185, 192, 194, 200-201, 206, 221, 234, 238, 252-253, 255, 258, 260, 262, 268, 272, 297, 386, 405
Idealist, 36, 40, 42, 48, 88, 151, 156, 192, 200, 227, 247, 268, 290, 307, 365, 367, 405

Identity, 35, 38, 51, 84, 141, 146, 150, 171, 196, 220, 392-394
Idols, 109-110
Illusion, 9. 14, 25-26, 53, 61, 123, 157, 164, 194, 196, 204, 216, 228, 290, 296, 348, 384, 401, 410, 416
Immortality, 52, 58, 61, 71, 84, 86, 99, 182
India, 50, 142, 200, 204, 209, 237, 239, 329-332, 344-346, 441
Indiscernible, 146
Induction. 13-14, 16, 22, 30, 36, 73, 108, 165, 168, 179, 210-211, 322, 354, 356, 364-367, 407, 465
Inductive knowledge, 9-10, 12-13, 16, 36, 40, 54, 106, 108, 111, 160, 179, 301, 306-307, 322, 357, 363, 388, 395, 422-423, 465-466
Inquisition, 97, 135, 422
Intentional stance, 34, 249
Intentionality, 247-249, 253, 280, 288-290, 294, 296, 310-312
Intuition, xii, 24, 33, 36, 83, 180, 251-252, 297, 371, 386, 439
Intuition Pump, 33-34, 316, 318, 399-400, 407, 464, 470
Ionians, 50, 441
James, William, 49, 164, 206, 220, 231-237, 255-256, 258, 402, 414, 471
Jefferson, Thomas, 81, 110, 134, 175, 424, 449,
Jerome, St. 89
Johnson, David K. 7
Justice, 6-7, 44, 57-58, 62, 65, 71, 80, 86, 115, 129, 157, 182, 205, 219, 263, 299, 322-324, 339, 342, 388, 397, 407, 439, 443-444, 458, 466
Justified, xiii, 4, 7, 16, 40, 64, 95, 102, 165, 186, 207, 236, 267, 324, 412, 447, 470

Kant, Immanuel, xiv, 36, 38, 48, 74, 91, 102, 104, 119, 134, 157, 164, 177-183, 185, 188, 190, 192-194, 200-203, 205, 218-220, 224, 252, 278, 290, 297, 322, 367, 391, 398, 405, 417, 421, 426-427, 437, 472

Karma, 332, 346-348

Kierkegaard, Soren, 48, 95, 165, 215-222, 282

Knowledge, ix, xi-xiii, 3-10, 12, 15-16, 32, 36, 38-41, 50-61, 54, 57-58, 60, 63-65, 67, 73-75, 77-78, 82, 89, 92, 94-95, 98-99, 102, 105-107, 112, 114-116, 119-125, 127, 131-134, 137-138, 140-141, 143-144, 151-155, 157, 159-161, 163-164, 166-167, 178-179, 192, 195, 202-206, 216, 219-220, 227, 242-243, 245, 247, 250, 254-259, 266-267, 273, 276-277, 281, 288, 293, 295-298. 301, 303, 305-307, 312, 319-320, 322-324, 333, 345, 351, 353-354, 356-358, 360-362, 364-368, 371, 373, 375, 386-388, 391-392, 397-398, 406-407, 412, 415-418, 422, 426, 433, 454, 458, 460, 463, 465-466, 470

Koran, 358, 422

Kuhn, Thomas, 320-321, 324

Language, ix, xi, 4, 22-23, 30, 32, 37-38, 41-43, 45, 50, 65, 69, 78, 90, 102, 105, 110, 143, 149-150, 158, 168, 189, 208, 237, 240, 257, 262, 265-267, 271, 273-278, 283-285, 292, 297-299, 301-304, 307, 317, 320, 322-325, 333-334, 337-338, 340, 342, 348, 357, 371, 376-378, 382, 386, 389, 391-392, 394-407, 409-410, 417-418, 420, 439, 466-467, 470

Lao Tzu, 235, 329, 331, 335, 471

Law, 4, 10, 23, 34-35, 50, 52-53, 55, 58-59, 62, 77, 80, 93, 106-109, 111, 115, 117, 119, 122. 125, 129-130, 135, 137, 144, 146, 148, 157, 163, 181-182, 186, 189-191, 197, 202, 211, 213, 223-224, 226, 229, 248, 323, 326, 331, 334, 341-342, 352, 363, 366-367, 369-370, 377, 380, 407, 411, 413-414, 421, 424, 426, 429, 431, 433, 437, 442-449, 452-455. 458

Leibniz, Gottfried, 48, 119, 126, 134, 138, 143-150, 157, 177, 179, 264, 343, 413

Leucippus, 50, 52-53

Liberal, 90, 127, 136-137, 199, 207, 214, 224-225, 245, 262, 299, 319, 322, 400, 430, 446, 448, 451

Liberties, 129-130, 445

Liberty, 115, 129, 163, 173-174, 190, 200, 207, 209, 211, 322, 324, 412, 424, 445, 447, 458

Libet, Benjamin, 313-314, 410, 416

Locke, John, 8-9, 33, 36, 48, 80, 111. 119-120, 127-134, 128, 144, 151-153, 155, 159, 164, 166-167, 173, 175, 179, 185, 189, 210, 256, 296, 301, 312, 446, 449, 451, 456

Logic, ix, xi, xiii, 3-4, 7-9, 13, 16, 18-26, 28-30, 35, 37, 39-40, 42, 50-52, 54, 64-65, 73-75, 77, 83-84, 87, 105, 108-109, 111, 115, 117, 134, 145-146, 148-151, 155-157, 160, 164-165, 172, 177-179, 193-198, 208-211, 221-222, 227, 237, 242, 247-251, 254, 256-259, 262-263, 265-268, 270-277, 283-284, 286, 301-305, 307-308, 311, 321-322, 329, 349, 354, 357-358, 367, 370, 377, 388, 398, 400, 404-405, 407, 411-413, 415-416, 430, 432-433, 435-436, 451, 461-463, 465-466, 470

Logical atomism, 267, 398

Index

Logical Positivism, 164, 284, 301-303, 307-308
Lucretius, 77-78, 81, 471
Magic, 11, 28, 201, 329
Magna Carta, 97, 331, 444-445, 449
Manichaean, 90, 92
Marx, Karl, 48, 81, 142, 198, 220, 223-230, 287, 291-292, 294, 299, 449
Material, 33, 38, 53-55, 58, 63, 70, 77, 83, 86, 92, 106, 108-109, 113-114, 117, 125, 131-132, 141-142, 146, 153, 155-157, 167, 191, 198, 223, 226-227, 229, 233-234, 238, 268, 318-319, 326, 380
Mathematics, xi, 3-4, 9, 51-52, 55, 61, 65, 70, 83-84, 105, 113, 115, 119-121, 157, 160, 179, 206, 208, 247-248, 262-263, 265-266, 270-273, 286, 303, 354, 357-358, 368, 405, 461
Matter, xii, 3, 8, 42, 51, 53-54, 69-70, 77, 86, 90-91, 100, 124-125, 137, 145-146, 151-152, 154-155, 196, 222, 234, 269-270, 355, 365, 367, 372-373, 376-377, 390-391, 396
Meaning, ix-x, 3, 18, 21, 32, 37-38, 41-43, 45, 59, 233, 242, 245, 251-252, 257, 259, 271, 273-276, 280-282, 291, 293, 295, 298, 301, 303, 316, 321-322, 324, 337-338, 366, 377, 396-407, 409, 411-412, 417, 420, 428, 439, 460-468
Meme, 34-35, 316-317
Mereology, 249,
Merleau-Ponty, M. 49, 286, 293-300, 386-387, 471
Metaphysics, xi-xii, 3, 41, 65, 69, 82, 84, 88, 101, 105, 121, 137, 149, 161, 177-178, 180, 190, 195, 197, 201, 205, 231, 254, 258, 262, 265-266, 283-284, 290, 292, 355, 360, 365-366, 369, 404, 418

Mill, John Stuart, 44, 48, 187, 207-214, 226, 262-263, 269, 427-428, 434, 437, 447-448, 451, 458
Mind, ix, xi-xiv, 3, 8, 24-25, 32-33, 35-36, 42, 60, 65, 70-71, 75, 78, 84-85, 91-92, 94, 102-103, 105-107, 109, 114, 117, 119, 121, 123-126, 131-133, 137-140, 145-147, 153-157, 161-162, 166, 168, 178-180, 182-183, 192-194, 202-203, 227, 232-234, 238, 248-249, 252, 254, 256, 259, 264, 269-272, 277, 281, 288, 293, 295, 297, 306, 308-311, 313-314, 317-320, 323, 325-326, 346-351, 354, 356, 373, 375-383, 386-390, 392-394, 398, 402-403, 405-406, 410, 421, 462, 472
Miracle, 11, 114, 163, 424
Monad, 51, 144-147, 150
Monism, 234, 268
Moore, G. E. 262-263, 414, 434
Morality, x, xiv, 3, 37, 45, 57, 63, 90, 103, 163, 178, 182-183, 190, 205, 215, 219, 241-242, 244-245, 264, 275, 315, 330, 341, 347, 418, 421-440, 442
Mycenaean, 50, 441
Mystery, 28, 137, 172, 337, 372, 375
Nagel, Thomas, 318, 326
Natural Philosophy, 111, 115, 121, 354, 356-357
Natural selection, 12, 34-35, 103, 255, 423, 432, 462, 464-466
Neo-Platonism, 48, 81-85, 87-88, 95, 98, 105
Newton, Isaac, 10, 50, 52, 111, 126-127, 132, 134, 142, 144, 149, 157, 186, 354, 363, 366-368, 414, 466
Nicomachean, 67, 71, 73
Nietzsche, Friedrich, 49, 72, 95, 206, 239-246, 286, 289, 411, 438

Nirvana, 204-205, 239, 344, 347-348
Nominal, 108, 113-114, 173
Noumenal, 201-202
Nous, 84-88,
Nozick, Robert, 324-325
Nurture, 44, 431, 433
Objective, 4, 10, 16, 36-37, 163, 195, 217, 219, 227, 234-235, 242-243, 245, 248, 252, 313, 318, 320, 325, 360, 364-365, 388, 395
Occam's Razor, 34
Oligarchy, 68, 191, 443
Ontological, 99, 124, 138, 147, 172-173, 181, 251-252, 258, 325
Ontology, xii, 253, 284, 289, 293, 295, 287
Orwell, George, 314, 402
Paine, Thomas, 81, 134, 356, 448-449, 451, 471
Paradigm, 320-321, 332
Parmenides, 50, 52-53, 61, 63, 65
Peirce, C. S. 168, 232, 234-235, 237, 255
Perceive, 36, 41, 63, 65, 69, 86, 130-131, 138, 151, 153-158, 162, 168, 179, 203, 220-221, 250-251, 257, 291, 293, 306, 334, 343, 366, 383, 385-387, 389
Perception, 4, 6, 41-42, 54, 63, 67, 123-124, 147, 151, 153-158, 160-162, 166-168, 179, 195, 202, 219, 222, 227, 282, 293-294, 296-298, 319, 338, 379, 382-387, 389, 394, 398-399, 406, 418, 471
Peripatetic, 67
Phenomena, 53, 110, 115, 156, 164, 201-204, 210, 239, 249-250, 288, 290, 295, 298, 303, 311-313, 325, 347, 356, 367
Phenomenology, xii, 95, 193, 247-248, 250-251, 253, 261, 279-281, 285-291, 293-296, 298-300, 311-313, 318, 365, 381, 386-387, 389, 406, 471
Philology, 240-242
Phronesis, 438,
Physics, 112-113, 115, 119, 121-122, 177, 207, 247, 266, 286, 315, 354, 357, 364, 367-368, 371-372, 380, 391-392, 404, 409, 414, 418-420, 461-464, 466
Plato, 7, 38, 43-44, 48, 51-53, 55-57, 60-65, 67-69, 72-77, 81-88, 90-92, 94-95, 98-100, 105, 108, 113, 122, 132, 172, 207, 283, 332, 394, 397-398, 405, 438, 442-443, 461, 471
Plotinus, 48, 65, 80-88, 105, 148, 194, 412
Poetry, 74, 162, 176, 208-209, 275, 283-284, 337, 339, 402-403, 407
Politics, 4, 37, 41, 55, 61-62, 65, 68-69, 72, 105, 113, 127, 134, 136, 144, 163, 169, 175, 183, 213, 223-225, 229, 254, 262, 268-270, 293, 299, 307, 323, 329, 351, 354-355, 359, 371, 388, 402, 404, 406, 422, 425, 433, 441-459
Pope, 89, 97, 100, 110, 152-153, 238
Popper, Karl, 165, 199, 319-320
Porphyry, 82-83, 87-88
Positivism, 164-165, 284, 301-303, 307-308
Pragmatism, 49, 168, 231, 233-234, 237, 254-256, 258, 261, 286, 323-324
Premise, xii-xiii, 8, 13, 18-22, 26-27, 30-31, 73-74, 291, 325, 405, 414, 435-436
Prisoner's Dilemma, 430-431
Probability, 10-13, 22, 30, 133, 162-163, 179, 237, 305, 319-320, 364, 366-367, 371, 375, 390, 415, 466

Proof, 8, 99, 101, 124, 137-139, 147, 156, 172, 180-181, 210, 218, 269, 278, 358, 426
Proposition, xi-xii, 8, 28, 35, 108, 113, 133, 139, 146, 179, 210, 248, 252, 256, 258, 266-267, 271, 274-276, 281, 284, 303-305, 316, 367, 396, 399, 405
Protagoras, 50
Protestant, 117, 127, 152, 169, 171-172, 192, 422
Psychology, 42, 75, 95, 109, 164, 189, 192, 201, 206, 215, 231-232, 235, 237-238, 247-249, 255, 258, 262, 279, 286, 292-294, 296, 298, 300, 312, 318, 354, 356, 371, 375, 377, 381, 415-416, 462
Putnam, Hilary, 261, 381
Pythagoras, 50-52, 61, 63, 75, 84, 332, 354
Qualia, 318, 379
Quality, 54, 74, 123, 132, 147, 155, 158, 167, 180, 195, 201, 233, 290-291, 297, 318, 393
Quantum, 10, 53, 315, 363-364, 371-373, 390, 409, 414-416, 419-420, 463
Quark, 365, 390
Quine, Willard, 38, 261, 310, 321-322, 324
Ramsey, F. P. 367
Rational, ix-x, xiv, 21, 24-40, 58, 62, 70-73, 81, 83, 100, 104, 125, 133, 138, 140-141, 162, 168, 183, 186, 190, 197, 199, 218, 223, 239, 259, 323, 333, 355, 358, 366, 370, 378, 390, 416, 424, 437, 443, 453, 458
Rationalism, xii, 60, 77, 119, 134, 183, 215, 223, 256, 297, 307, 319, 343, 386-387
Rationalist, 36, 42, 48, 60, 63, 75, 105-106, 135, 138, 143, 151, 164, 178-179, 186, 220, 256, 290, 297, 339, 367
Rawls, John, 322-324, 458

Reason, ix-xiv, 4, 6, 9-12, 14-15, 18, 24, 30-31, 36, 38, 40, 51-54, 62-65, 69-71, 79, 83, 85-86, 88-90, 94, 99-100, 102, 104, 106, 108, 110-111, 114, 117, 119, 124-125, 129-131, 133, 140, 143, 146-149, 151, 159, 162, 164-165, 167, 172-173, 178-183, 187, 190-191, 193, 196, 198, 201-202, 210-212, 218, 220-221, 231, 242, 259, 266, 269, 282, 297, 302, 304, 310, 315, 322, 330, 347, 349-350, 353-354, 356-359, 364, 366-368, 370, 377-381, 384, 386, 389, 397, 410, 412-413, 416, 418, 421, 425-426, 429-430, 432-434, 437, 443, 447, 458, 460-461, 463, 467
Reductionism, 187, 247, 276, 306, 321, 326, 371, 437
Refutation, 20, 31
Reid, Thomas, 48-49, 166-168
Relative, xiii-xiv, 37, 156-158, 369, 378, 434
Relativism, 184, 320, 435
Relativity, 10, 91, 165, 363, 368-369, 371, 391, 463
Religion, 12, 34, 37, 44, 50-51, 55, 72, 78-80, 87, 90, 94, 104-105, 108-109, 115-117, 133, 136, 141-142, 160, 163, 171-172, 175, 177, 181, 186, 190, 192, 206, 215, 217-218, 220, 224, 228, 231, 234-235, 237-238, 240, 243-244, 262, 275-276, 310-311, 315, 330, 332-336, 339, 343-345, 348, 356-359, 369, 377, 408, 421-424, 426, 442, 458, 470
Renaissance, 54-55, 67, 74, 88
Renouvier, Charles, 414
Representation, 168, 201, 203, 206, 209, 239-240, 256, 272, 306, 323, 337, 339, 451-452, 455

Republic, 60-62, 64, 113, 119, 183, 225, 247, 254, 336, 442-443, 471
Rescript, 97
Revealed knowledge, 12, 356, 422
Revolution, 128, 130, 134, 157, 168, 175, 177-178, 185-186, 190, 193, 201, 225, 229, 264, 299, 320-321, 340, 444, 446, 448-451, 472
Ridley, Matt, 431, 433, 472
Rights, 62, 116, 127-130, 134, 137, 169, 174, 190, 211, 213, 287, 291, 324, 331, 341, 424, 430-431, 436, 444-446, 448-449, 451-454, 456, 458, 475
Roman, 67, 77, 80, 82, 89, 94, 167, 196, 244, 278, 442, 444
Romantic, 48-49, 97, 153, 169-171, 175, 177, 223, 226, 287, 340, 431
Rorty, Richard, 261, 285, 323-324, 392, 395, 398, 439, 472
Rousseau, Jean Jacques, 48, 92, 165, 169-177, 185, 193, 197, 199, 431, 472
Rule, 43-44, 58, 62, 68, 110, 121, 129, 172, 175, 179, 212-213, 219, 236, 265, 275-277, 298, 303, 338-339, 341-342, 374, 408, 422-424, 427-428, 430, 433, 436-437, 439, 442-443, 448, 456-457
Russell, Bertrand, 9, 22, 35, 38, 43, 47, 49, 52-55, 58-59, 63-64, 67-70, 72-74, 78, 80, 82-89, 91-92, 95, 104, 106, 108-111, 116-117, 120, 122, 125, 130-131, 135, 139-140, 145, 149, 158-159, 161, 172-173, 175, 183, 187, 189-191, 193, 195, 197-198, 201, 203, 206, 211, 214, 222-223, 227, 229, 232, 234, 237-239, 245, 257, 260-273, 284, 301, 303-304, 307, 322, 386, 397-398, 404-405, 450, 472
Ryle, Gilbert, 32-33, 125, 238, 302, 310, 376, 472
Sartre, Jean-Paul, 49, 215, 221, 253, 284, 286-296, 406, 428, 439, 472
Sceptic, 3, 7, 9-10, 12, 40, 59, 92, 114, 117, 123-124, 133, 153, 159, 162-163, 167, 178, 195, 202, 211, 237-238, 251, 269, 296, 306, 324, 367, 465-466, 470
Schick, Theodore, 15, 472
Schiller, F. C. S. 175, 231
Scholastic, 34, 87, 97, 107-108, 113, 119, 122, 124-125, 127, 149, 208, 227
Schopenhauer, Arthur, 48, 95, 157, 164, 168, 200-206, 239-240, 272, 413, 427
Schrodinger, Erwin, 373
Science, x, 4, 10, 12-16, 20, 22, 26, 29, 33, 35, 37, 42-44, 49-51, 53-54, 57, 59, 65, 67, 75, 77, 88, 90, 105-112, 114-115, 119-121, 127-128, 134, 137, 146, 153, 157, 164, 170, 177, 185-186, 193-194, 198, 200, 206-211, 217, 219, 223, 226, 229, 231-232, 234-235, 237-239, 241-242, 247, 251-253, 255, 258, 260, 269-270, 275-276, 283, 286, 293-294, 296-300, 305-313, 316-325, 329, 333
Science, (philosophy informed by) 351-469
Searle, John, 318, 325-326
Selfish gene, 34, 432, 470
Semantics, 37
Sensation(s), 77, 79, 80, 132-133, 153, 155-156, 162, 167-168, 179, 202-203, 226-227, 267, 277, 296-297, 318
Set Theory, 265-266
Shakespeare, 3, 18, 24, 371, 403
Shubin, Neil, 362, 472
Skinner, B. F. 381

Slippery slope, 26
Social Contract, 4, 45, 80, 112, 116, 128-130, 137, 163, 170-171, 173-175, 259, 322, 331, 400, 412, 430, 431, 445-446, 456, 472
Socialism, 185, 191, 214, 223, 225, 230, 262, 264, 269, 279, 447
Socrates, v, xiii, 6-9, 43-44, 48, 52-53, 56-61, 65, 68, 73, 105, 139, 175, 212, 251, 331, 367, 407, 426, 439, 468
Society, 4, 24, 41, 44-45, 62, 80, 94, 111, 116-117, 127-129, 144, 163, 166, 170-171, 173-174, 211, 214, 216-218, 224, 227-229, 232, 241-244, 259-260, 264, 302, 310, 319, 322-325, 330, 332, 339, 341-342, 348, 355, 393, 418, 430-431, 433, 449-450, 452-453, 458
Sociology, 230, 286, 292, 354
Solipsism, 156, 203, 365, 388, 410
Soundness, 19, 31
Soul, 51-53, 55, 58, 61-64, 69-71, 77, 83-87, 91-93, 98-100, 121, 125, 137, 145, 147, 161, 172, 194, 201, 232-233, 240, 304, 313, 375-378, 380-381, 383, 388, 392, 407, 461-462
Sovereign, 116-117, 128-129, 137, 174, 188, 197, 431, 444-446, 454, 456-457
Space, 10, 37, 42, 53, 64, 77, 92, 105, 124, 157, 163, 178-180, 183, 193, 201-203, 222, 239, 270, 274, 338, 355, 357, 367-368, 373, 390-391, 393, 396, 463, 465-466
Spinoza, Benedictus, 48, 119, 120, 134-142, 144-146, 149, 194, 203, 412-413, 426, 470
Spirit, x, 62, 65, 78, 84-86, 90, 108, 117, 141, 155-156, 161, 167, 192, 194-197, 201, 206, 218, 227-228, 237, 252, 318, 333,
339, 344, 357, 375-378, 380, 383, 392, 405, 407, 460, 462
State, (country), 44, 50, 57-58, 62, 68-69, 74, 81, 89, 95, 97, 103, 105, 110, 117-118, 127, 130, 137, 163, 169, 173-175, 183, 191, 197-199, 207, 213, 218, 231, 245, 264, 287, 323-324, 331, 335, 422, 424, 442-447, 449-450, 452, 454, 457-458
Stein, Edith, 253
Stoic, 72, 86, 140, 167
Strawman, 27
Subconscious, 10, 314, 375, 398, 410, 413, 416
Subjective, xiv, 4, 36-37, 54, 91, 155, 179, 183, 193, 195-197, 215, 217, 219, 235, 257-258, 290, 298, 312-313, 325, 364, 379, 381, 388, 391, 395
Sufficient, 37, 76, 110, 146-148, 201-202, 266, 325, 386
Suffrage, 452-453
Superposition, 373
Syllogism, 8-9, 73-74, 105, 110, 282
Symbolic, 27, 148, 249, 257, 265
Syntax, 37
Synthetic, 36, 38, 297, 301, 321-322, 324
Taoism, 331-332, 335-339, 348
Teleological, 54, 102
Ten Commandments, 44, 315, 423-424, 437
Theodicy, 144, 147-150
Theology, 87, 95, 101, 108, 112, 136, 161, 172-173, 181, 216, 224, 236, 240, 278, 292, 330, 356, 412
Theory, xii, 3, 5-6, 8, 12, 34, 40, 44, 51-52, 54, 60-61, 63-65, 73, 79, 83, 91, 95, 105, 107-112, 115, 117, 119, 121, 127, 130-131, 134, 136-138, 151-152, 159-160, 164-166, 169, 172-173, 185, 188, 206-207, 209, 211, 227, 231, 233, 248-249, 261,

Theory (continued), 265-269, 277, 282, 289-292, 296, 298, 300, 303, 313, 315, 319, 321-322, 324, 326, 332, 351, 353, 355-357, 361-364, 370, 372, 376, 381, 388-389, 403, 406, 412, 419, 422-423, 426, 428, 435, 437-438, 446-449, 459-460, 463, 465-466

Thermodynamics, 369

Time, (the concept of), 3, 10, 37, 53, 63-64, 74, 91-92, 95, 99-100, 105, 116, 140, 142, 157, 179-181, 183, 193, 196, 201, 203, 222, 239, 253, 278-280, 282-284, 287, 289, 295, 314, 355, 357, 367-370, 373, 376, 378, 384-385, 391, 393, 396, 402, 410, 413, 463-465, 471

Tokens, 38

Tools, x, 22, 29-40, 281, 316-317, 321, 357, 395, 402-405, 407, 418, 462, 467, 470

Transcendental, 51, 88, 103, 200-201, 247, 252-253

Transmigration, 51-52

Truth, xiii-xiv, 11, 18, 22, 27, 35, 54, 56, 58, 65, 72, 86, 92, 98-99, 103, 105, 113, 121, 123, 139, 144, 146-147, 183, 195, 197, 211, 216, 218-220, 227-228, 233-237, 240, 255, 257, 261, 265, 267, 269, 273, 278, 281-284, 289, 299, 301-305, 307, 320, 324, 337, 345-347, 349, 365-366, 392, 398, 400, 405, 435, 438, 447, 454, 470

Turing, Alan, 150, 273, 325, 381

Types, 13, 21, 24, 36, 38, 68, 70-71, 73, 114, 124, 137, 160, 265, 290, 306, 415, 443, 455

Universal, 12, 43, 52, 64-65, 69, 77, 95, 99-100, 105, 108, 113-114, 132, 149-150, 175, 184, 189, 196-197, 205, 229, 243, 248, 251, 305, 331, 363, 397-399, 421, 427, 433-434

Universe, 52, 55, 77-78, 84, 99, 135, 142, 146-147, 152-153, 158, 181, 193, 198, 203, 211, 219, 239, 310, 314-315, 331-332, 335-336, 354, 357-358, 363, 367-371, 373-374, 409, 414-417, 419, 434, 436, 459-463, 466-467, 471

Upanishads, 330

Utilitarian(ism), 44, 104, 117, 164, 185, 187-188, 190, 207, 210, 212, 214, 269, 306, 322, 426-428, 434, 437, 447

Validity, 19, 31, 256, 263, 266, 305

Vaughn, Lewis, 15, 472

Veil of ignorance, 323, 458

Virtue, 4, 43, 57-58, 71-72, 75, 83, 88, 94, 104, 146, 153, 175, 182, 189, 203-204, 244, 291, 295, 315, 321, 340-342, 348, 407, 425, 427, 431, 433, 437-439, 472

Virtue Ethics, 71, 75, 104, 342, 348, 425, 437-438

Voltaire, 110, 134, 145, 148-149, 170, 172, 175, 200, 224, 343

Vulgate, 89

Watson, Peter, 65, 235, 243, 245, 475

Whitehead, Alfred North, 263, 265, 270, 273

Will (the or a), 94, 114, 174, 205, 220, 233, 239, 241, 244, 411-412

Wittgenstein, Ludwig, 22-23, 32, 49, 110, 142, 158, 206, 220, 262, 267, 271-277, 302-303, 322, 324, 396, 398, 404, 473

Wollstonecraft, Mary, 448-449, 451, 453, 472

Xenophon, 56, 207

Young, Thomas, 372

Zen, 333, 343-345, 348-349, 472

www.ingramcontent.com/pod-product-compliance
Lightning Source LLC
Chambersburg PA
CBHW050146130526
44591CB00033B/700